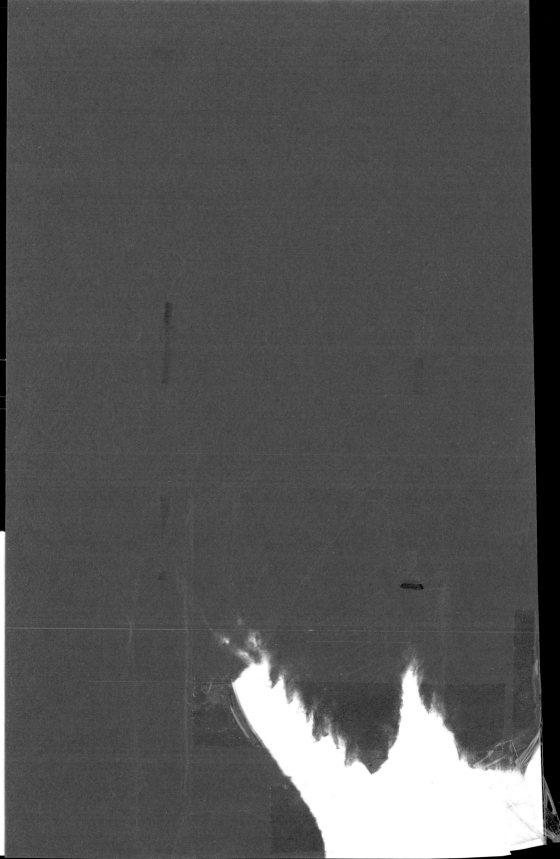

A reader who finds either an error or additional information regarding any family or individual in this volume down to the birth of sixth generation children, but not beyond, is urgently requested to send such material, with documentation, to:

FIVE GENERATIONS PROJECT, P.O. BOX 3297, PLYMOUTH, MA 02361

TABLE OF CONTENTS

ROBERT S. WAKEFIELD

Robert S. Wakefield was one of the most respected genealogists in the country. Born in San Mateo, California, he was employed for many years by the Southern Pacific Transportation Company. He is descended from both Stephen Hopkins and John Howland, and in 1973 joined the California Society of Mayflower Descendants. He held the prestigious title of Fellow of the American Society of Genealogists. Many of his articles have appeared in leading genealogical publications. Mr. Wakefield had been an active member of the Five Generations Project of the General Society of Mayflower Descendants since 1976, when he undertook preparation of the Richard More manuscript for publication in Mayflower Families Two. In 1977 he began work on the Peter Brown Family manuscript, co-authored the Edward Winslow family in Mayflower Families Five, and contributed substantially to many more Project families since that time. He had been a member of the Five Generations Project Committee for twelve years. He was a very important member of both the Project and the General Society of Mayflower Descendants. After years of dedicated service to the Mayflower Society and the Five Generations Project, Robert S. Wakefield passed away on 1 June 2002 in Redwood City, California.

PETER BROWN

Governor Bradford's account of the Mayflower passengers written early in 1651 lists Peter Browne as a passenger on the MAYFLOWER and states "Peter Browne married twice. By his first wife he had two children who are living and both of them married; and the one of them hath two children. By his second wife he had two more. He died about sixteen years since."

At Cape Cod on 11 November 1620 Peter Brown was one of the 41 signers of the "Mayflower Compact."

In the "1623 Division of Land" Peter Brown received one acre of land indicating he had not married by that date, but he must have married widow Martha Ford shortly after that date. The widow Ford received 4 acres in that division.

In the "1627 Division of Cattle" Peeter Browne, Martha Browne and Mary Browne received shares. John Ford and Martha Ford (Martha's children) also received shares in the same lot.

He was one of the Purchasers who assumed Plymouth Colony's debt to the Merchant Adventurers in 1628.

Some time bet. 1628 and 1630 Peter's wife Martha died and he married Mary who has not been identified.

Peter Browne is in the 1633 list of Freemen of the Colony and on 25 March 1633 he was taxed.

Peter Brown died shortly bef. 28 Oct. 1633 when his inventory was taken, probably from the epidemic that occurred that year.

Nothing is known of Peter Brown's background. He has not been found in any Leyden record, so he must have joined the Pilgrims in England.

1

The claim that Peter Brown of Windsor CT is his son is very doubtful. Peter Brown's land was divided in thirds bet. his three daughters. If Peter Brown's son was alive in 1647 (when he was barely a teen), he surely would have received a share.

References: MD 1:15(Bradford), 77-9(Compact), 79-82(inv.), 152(div. of cattle), 228-9(div. of land). PLYMOUTH COLONY RECS 1:10(taxed); 12:4-5(1623 div.), 11(1627 div.). NGSQ 67:253-4(Peter Brown of Windsor CT). GREAT MIGRATION BEGINS 1:259-61.

PETER BROWN

FIRST GENERATION

1 PETER[1] BROWN b. prob. England bef. 1600; d. Plymouth
bet. 25 March 1633 (when he was taxed) and 28 Oct. 1633 (date of
inventory).

He m. (1) Plymouth ca. 1624 MARTHA (_____) FORD, b.
prob. England; d. Plymouth bet. 1628 and 1630. She m. (1) _____
Ford with whom she came to Plymouth on the ship FORTUNE, by
whom she had John, Martha and an unnamed son.

He m. (2) Plymouth ca. 1630 MARY _____ who was living
27 March 1634 when she was taxed. She d. prob. bef. 27 Oct. 1647
as there is no mention of widow's dower in a deed of that date.

"Peeter Browne", Martha Browne and Mary Browne were
listed in the 1627 division of cattle.

On 28 Oct. 1633 Mary Browne, widow of Peter Browne late
of New Plymouth dec., presented an inventory of his estate. On
11 Nov. 1633 the court ordered money set aside for Peter's daus.
[by his first wife] Mary Browne and Priscilla Browne, with the
rest of his estate allowed to the widow to bring up her two
children by Peter.

Children (BROWN) b. Plymouth to Peter and Martha:

2 i   MARY[2] b. ca. 1626
3 ii   PRISCILLA b. ca. 1629

Children (BROWN) b. prob. Plymouth to Peter and Mary:

4 iii   REBECCA b. ca. 1631
   iv   child b. bef. settlement of the estate in 1633 but
         dead by 1647, as it does not share in the div. of
         Duxbury property.

References: MD 5:29-37(set. Peter's est.; deeds). TAG 42:35-42;
            56:32(Ford article). PLYMOUTH COLONY RECS
1:10 (Peter Brown taxed 25 March 1633), 17-9(set. est. Peter

Brown), 28(widow Browne taxed); 12:4(one share in 1623 div. to Peter Brown), 5(1623 div. 4 shares to widow Ford), 11(1627 div. of cattle). MQ 53:10-3.

NOTE: The Mary Browne who m. Thomas Willet 6 July 1636 is the dau. of Peter Brown's brother John who lived in Duxbury.

SECOND GENERATION

2   MARY[2] BROWN (Peter[1]) b. Plymouth ca. 1626; d. aft. Nov.
1689 when she gave consent to sale of land bet. sons John and
"Elkiah."

She m. Plymouth ca. 1646 EPHRAIM TINKHAM, b. prob.
England; d. bet. 17 Jan. 1683/4 (date of will) and 20 May 1685
(date of inventory).

In 1633 Mary Browne, dau. of Peter, was placed with Mr.
John Doane for nine years. Mary's term with John Doane ended
10 Oct. 1644. "Memorand, the tenth of October 1644; that wheras
Mr. John Doane had some tyme since fifteen pounds, the childs
porcon of Mary Browne, whom he was to keep and bring up untill
shee should accomplish the age of seventeen years, and should
have the use of the said pcon untill then--now, the said terme
being expired, the said John Doane hath delivered, with the
consent of the said Mary Browne, and by order of the court, unto
John Browne of Duxborrow, two cowes at 13 pounds and fourty
shillings in swyne and wheate, and is by the Court discharged of
the said 15 pounds; and the said John Browne is to keep the said
two cowes and their encrease for their milk, with the rest of the
stock as aforesaid, untill said Mary shal be marryed or thought fit
to marry, whereunto the said Mary hath consented."

On 23 July 1634 Timothy Hatherly "hath turned over his
servant, Ephraim Tinkcom, to dwell with John Winsloe, of New
Plymouth, for the whole terme of years expressed in a certayne
pare of indentures."

On 2 Aug. 1642 Ephraim Tinckhame was granted 25 acres of
land for his service by indenture and on 27 Sept. 1642 Ephraim
Tinckhame was granted ten acres of upland.

Ephraim Tinkham was a resident of Plymouth in the 1643
list of men able to bear arms.

On 27 Oct. 1647 Ephraim Tinkeham and Mary his wife sold
to Henry Sampson "all that third part of that lott which was
formerly the land of Peter Brown deceased."

On 1 May 1655 Ephraim Tinkham and Arther Hathaway
desired liberty of the Court to go up with their families to live on
the lands of John Barnes, at Lakenham [in Plymouth].

Ephraim Tinkham and John Smith Jr. are listed as the

owners of lot 5 on Puncateesett Necke [now in Rhode Island] on 22 March 1663.

On 5 June 1666 the court granted 12 acres to Sergent Ephraim Tinkham. Ephraim Tinkham was a frequent member of juries over a long period of time. He was one of the Selectmen for Plymouth, 1 June 1675.

The will of Ephraim Tincom Senir of Plymouth dated 17 Jan. 1683/4, proved 5 June 1685, names wife Mary; eldest son Ephraim; sons Ebenezer, Peter, Elkiah, John & Isaac; dau. Mary Tomson. The inventory of his estate was taken 20 May 1685.

   Children (TINKHAM) b. Plymouth:

	i	child[3] b. ca. 1647; living 1651 if Bradford is correct that they had 2 ch. by March 1650/1
5	ii	EPHRAIM b. 5 Aug. 1649
6	iii	EBENEZER b. 30 Sept. 1651
7	iv	PETER b. 25 Dec. 1653
8	v	HELKIAH b. 8 Feb. 1655
	vi	JOHN b. 7 June 1658; d.y.
9	vii	MARY b. 5 Aug. 1661
10	viii	JOHN b. 15 Nov. 1663
11	ix	ISAAC b. 11 April 1666

References: TAG 42:35-42.   MD 4:122(Ephraim's will). PLYMOUTH COLONY RECS 1:18(Mary placed), 31(E.T. indenture); 2:43(25 acre grant), 48(10 acre grant), 76(Mary's term ended); 3:77(Lakenham land); 4:130(12 acre grant); 5:164(selectman); 8:7(b. Ephraim), 12(b. Ebenezer), 15(b. Peter), 16(b. Helkiah), 17(b. John), 26(b. Mary, 2nd John), 31(b. Isaac), 189 (atba); 12:146(1647 deed). PLYMOUTH TOWN RECS 1:62(Puncaeesett land). PLYMOUTH VR pp. 657(b. Ephraim), 659(b. Ebenezer), 660(b. Peter), 661(b. Helkiah), 662(b. John), 665(b. Mary, John, Isaac). Plymouth Colony PR 4:2:110-1(Ephraim Tinkham).

3 PRISCILLA[2] BROWN (Peter[1]) b. Plymouth ca. 1629; d. aft. 17 Feb. 1697/8 (date of her husband's will).

   She m. Sandwich 21 March 1649 WILLIAM ALLEN, b. England ca. 1627; d. Sandwich 1 Oct. 1705 (as stated in inv. of his est.); son of George and Catherine (Starkes?) Allen.

In 1633 Priscilla Browne, dau. of Peter, was placed with William Gilson for 12 years.

On 28 Oct. 1645 the Court ended her term with William Gilson. "Priscilla Browne, dau. of Peter Browne, dec., having accomplished the terme shee was to dwell with Wm. Gilson of Scituate, who was to pay her 15 pounds in the end of her terme, now the said Priscilla came into the Court, and hath chosen John Browne, her unckle, to be her guardian, and to have the placeing and disposeing of her untill the Court shall judge her meete to be at her owne disposeing; and likewise to take her porcon, viz, fifteen pounds and to improve it by putting it into a breeding stock, and keepe them, and give her half the increase, or els to use it as his owne, and to pay her the said fifteen pounds when the court shall judg it meete for her to have it as her owne disposing."

On 15 April 1668 William Allen sold to Henry Tucker, one third of a share which was granted "unto Peter Browne deceased as a Purchaser or old comer."

The will of William Allen of Sandwich dated 17 Feb. 1697/8, sworn 26 Oct. 1705, names nephew Daniel Allen of Sandwich son of his brother George Allen dec.; wife Priscilla; mentions "my friends called Quakers."

No known children.

References: MD 5:36-7(1668 LR); 32:26-7(will). PLYMOUTH COLONY RECS 1:19(Priscilla placed); 2:89(1645 Ct. Rec.); 8:9(m.). Barnstable Co. PR 2:210(Wm. Allen). SOME DESCENDANTS OF RALPH-GEORGE-RALPH-SAMUEL ALLEN, Hugh Sweet Austin & Carlton Winters, 1968 p. II.

4   REBECCA[2] BROWN (Peter[1]) b. Plymouth ca. 1631; d. aft. 9 March 1698/9 when she is named in her husband's will.

She m. ca. 1654 WILLIAM SNOW, b. England ca. 1617; d. Bridgewater 31 Jan. 1708 as mentioned in the inventory of his estate.

William Snow is apparently the William Snow, ae 18, who arrived on the SUSAN AND ELLEN in 1635.

On 31 Aug. 1638 Mr. Richard Derby transferred his servant William Snow to Edward Dotey with William to serve 7 years longer. In the 1643 list of men able to bear arms he was a resident of Plymouth. In 1657 William Snow was a Freeman in Bridgewater.

In a deed dated 25 March 1667/8 [sic] William Snow of Bridgewater, husbandman, sold to Ephraim Tinkham of New Plymouth, 1/3 part of a whole share of upland and meadow in Dartmouth which was granted by the court unto Peter Browne, a purchaser or old comer.

On 7 Nov. 1679 William Snow of Bridgewater sold to John Brown all his one third of 25 acres of land, formerly of Peter Brown of Duxbury, wife Rebecca consented.

The will of William Snow Senr. of Bridgewater, dated 9 March 1698/9, proved 4 March 1708, mentions wife (unnamed); sons Joseph and Benjamin; son William to maintain parents for life; daus. Mary, Lydia, Hannah and Rebecca.

Children (SNOW) b. prob. Bridgewater:

i   MARY[3] living 9 March 1698/9 when named in her father's will*

ii   LYDIA living 9 March 1698/9

12 iii WILLIAM b. ca. 1662 (bef. 1664 if age 21 or over in 1685 Titicut div.)

13 iv JOSEPH b. bef. 1664 (same as above)

14 v   HANNAH b. ca. 1664 (based on age at death)

15 vi BENJAMIN b. ca. 1669

16 vii REBECCA b. ca. 1671 (based on age at death)

viii JAMES d. 1690 on The Canadian Expedition. Inv. taken 14 May 1690 with brother Benjamin Snow admin. of estate 4 June 1691.

References: MD 8:101(William will). GEN ADVERTISER 2:62(adm. James). PLYMOUTH COLONY RECS 1:94(servant); 8:185 (1657 Freeman), 188(1643 atba). TAG 42:35-42. Plymouth Co. LR 3:111(to Ephraim Tinkham); 5:197(to John Browne). BANKS PLANTERS p. 132(Susan & Ellen). NGSQ 67:253. Plymouth Co. PR 2:175-7(William Snow).

*No proof found she m. John Rickard as suggested in FAMILIES OF THE PILGRIMS (see MQ 49:122).

THIRD GENERATION

5 EPHRAIM TINKHAM[3] (Mary[2] Brown, Peter[1]) b. Plymouth
5 Aug. 1649; d. Middleboro 13 Oct. 1714 in 66th yr.
   He m. prob. Plymouth, shortly after 9 June 1676 when Esther
signed for her share of her brother's estate, ESTHER WRIGHT,
b. Plymouth 1649; d. Middleboro 28 May 1717 in 68th yr.; dau. of
Richard and Hester (Cooke) Wright, a granddau. of Pilgrim
Francis Cooke. The will of Richard Wright of Plimouth dated 8
June 1691 names children Adam, Esther and Mary (no surnames).
   Ephraim Tinkham was a constable in Middleboro in 1681.
   On 13 July 1691 Ephraim Tinkham and wife Esther sold to
Adam Wright land left to them by their father Richard Wright.
   The will of Ephraim Tinckom of Middleboro dated 17 Sept.
1714, proved 3 March 1714/5, names wife Esther; two daus.
Martha Soul and Mary Tinckom; eldest son John Tinckom; sons
Isaac and Samuell Tinckom; and (unnamed) children of dec. son
Ephraim.
   On 1 March 1731/2 Isaac Tinkham, Samuel Tinkham, John
Soule and wife Martha, Henry Wood and wife Mary, all of
Middleboro, sold to John Tinkham their rights to a 100 acre lot
where their father Ephraim Tinkham dwelt and was given by him
to son Ephraim Tinkham late of Middleboro dec.
   No Plymouth Co. PR for Esther Tinkham.

   Children (TINKHAM) b. prob. Middleboro:

17   i   MARTHA[4] b. ca. 1678
18   ii   JOHN b. 22 Aug. 1680
19   iii EPHRAIM b. 7 Oct. 1682
20   iv   ISAAC b. "last June" 1685
21   v   SAMUEL b. 19 March 1687
22   vi   MARY bp. Plymouth 1691

References: MD 1:221-3(b. ch.); 4:165-7(Richard Wright will);
            5:31-2(deed Ephraim/"Easter"); 15:101(d. Ephraim,
Esther); 17:162-3(will Ephraim); 24:83-6(ch. of Richard & Hester
Wright). PLYMOUTH CH RECS 1:271(bp. Mary). MIDDLEBORO
DEATHS p. 201(d. Ephraim, Esther). PLYMOUTH COLONY

RECS 6:60(const.), 86(Proposed freeman); 8:8(b. "Hester" Wright). Plymouth Co. LR 7:65(Ephraim Tinkham); 26:194 (Isaac Tinkham, etc.). MIDDLEBORO VR 1:2(b. John, Ephraim), 3(b. Isaac), 4(b. Sam.). Plymouth Co. PR 1:165(Richard Wright); 3:358-9(Ephraim Tinkham).

6   EBENEZER TINKHAM[3] (Mary[2] Brown, Peter[1]) b. Plymouth 30 Sept. 1651; d. Middleboro 8 April 1718 "morning" ae 67.
He m. bef. 7 July 1676 ELIZABETH BURROWES, b. Marshfield 5 March 1654; d. Middleboro 8 April 1718 "evening" ae 64; dau. of Jeremiah and _____ (Hewes) Burrowes. When the estate of John Burrowes late of Marshfield dec. was divided on 7 July 1676, one portion went to his sister Elizabeth Tinkham.
The record of Ebenezer Tinkham's death calls him Deacon. He was one of the original members of the First Church of Middleboro and one of its first deacons.
The will of Ebenezer Tinkham Sr. of Middleboro, yeoman, dated 3 April 1718, sworn 28 April 1718, names sons Ebenezer and Shuball; dau. Joanna Macomber; wife Elizabeth; son Jeremiah Tinkham's children: Jeremiah, Ebenezer & Joanna and their mother Joanna Tinkham; and granddau. Elizabeth Tinkham.

Children (TINKHAM) first 3 b. Middleboro, rest bp. Plymouth:

23   i   EBENEZER[4] b. 23 March 1679
24   ii   JEREMIAH b. 7 Aug. 1681
     iii   PETER b. 20 April 1683; d. Middleboro 10 July 1713. No PR.
25   iv   JOANNA bp. 1685
      v   ELIZABETH bp. 1688; d. Middleboro 27 March 1715
     vi   PRISCILLA bp. 1690; d. Middleboro 16 April 1715
26 vii   SHUBALL bp. 1692

References: MD 1:221(b. Ebenezer, Jeremiah, Peter); 2:4(m. Burrowes/Hewes), 6(b. Eliz.); 4:73(d. Eben.), 74 (d. Eliz. wife/dau.; Priscilla); 15:100-01(d. Ebenezer, Eliz.); 17:164-5(Eben. will), 186-7(J. Burrowes est). PLYMOUTH CH RECS 1:257(bp. Joanna), 262(bp. Eliz.), 268(bp. Priscilla), 274(bp.

Shubael). MIDDLEBORO DEATHS p. 201. MIDDLEBORO BY
WESTON p. 55. MARSHFIELD VR p. 4(b. Eliz. Burrowes).
MIDDLEBORO VR 1:2(b. 1st 3 ch.), 28(d. Eben., Eliz., dau. Eliz.,
Prisc.). Plymouth Co. PR 4:78(Ebenezer Tinkham).

7   PETER TINKHAM[3] (Mary[2] Brown, Peter[1]) b. Plymouth 25
Dec. 1653; d. Middleboro 30 Dec. 1709 ae 56.
     He m.* ca. 1690 MERCY MENDALL, b. Marshfield 3 Aug.
1666; d. after 10 May 1711; dau. of John Mendall. The will of
John Mendall of Marshfield dated 10 May 1711 names dau. Mercy
Tinckum.**
     A list of the proprietors in 1690 of the Twenty-six Men's
Purchase in Middleboro shows Peter Tinkham holding Peter
Brown's share.
     On 10 March 1709/10 Mercy Tincum widow of Peter Tincum
late of Middleboro was granted administration on his estate.
Settlement of the estate dated 22 Sept. 1710, names eldest son
Samuell, son Seth, eldest dau. Marcy and youngest dau. Joanna.
On 19 Sept. 1717 Samuel Tinkham, son of Peter late of Middleboro
dec., being over 14 but under 21, chose John Bennet Jr. of
Middleboro his guardian.

     Children (TINKHAM) b. prob. Middleboro:

     27   i   MERCY[4] b. ca. 1692 (based on age at d.)
     28   ii   JOANNA b. ca. 1695 (based on age at d.)
     29   iii   SAMUEL b. bet. 1696 and 1698
     30   iv   SETH b. Middleboro 15 May 1704

References: MARSHFIELD VR p. 15(b. Mercy Mendall).
     MIDDLEBORO VR 1:41(b. Seth). MD 7:242(b. Seth);
15:102 (d. Peter). PN&Q 2:55(John Mendell will). MIDDLEBORO
BY WESTON pp. 593-4. Plymouth Co. PR 2:115; 3:56-7(Peter
Tinkham); #20902(Samuel Tinkham gdn.). MIDDLEBORO
DEATHS p. 201 (d. Peter).

*No evidence found to show that Peter m. Mercy Hoar as claimed
in Tinkham Ms. p. 74, but we only know that Mercy Mendall was
his wife when he d. A RECORD OF DESCENDANTS OF
HEZEKIAH HOAR OF TAUNTON, MA by Norton T. Hoar, 1907,

p. 7 says Mercy[2] (Hezekiah[1]) Hoar, b. 31 Jan. 1654; m. John Spur 26 Dec. 1676. She d. bef. 1692.

**There are no John Mendall deeds naming a wife in Ply. Col. or Plymouth Co.

8   HELKIAH TINKHAM[3] (Mary[2] Brown, Peter[1]) b. Plymouth 8 Feb. 1655; d. bet. 1724 (church member) and 25 Sept. 1731 (will sworn).

He m. ca. 1684 RUTH _____*, who d. after 2 April 1737 (deed).

In 1692 Hilkiah Tinkham and wife Ruth were admitted to the Plymouth Church and on 27 March 1692 children Hilkiah, Mary, John and Jacob were baptized.   Both Helkiah and Ruth were in the 1724 list of members.

Helkiah Tinkham Sr. of Plymouth, yeoman, sold to son-in-law Ebenezer Courtis of Plymouth part of homestead with wife Ruth giving up dower on 3 Nov. 1715; acknowledged same day.

The will of Helkiah Tinkcome of Plymouth dated 14 Dec. 1716, proved 29 Sept. 1731, names wife Ruth; sons Helkiah, John, Jacob and Caleb; daus. Mary Courtis; Ruth Tinkcome; sons Ebenezer and Peter; son-in-law Ebenezer Courtis. A codicil of 20 May 1718 mentions that dau. Mary Courtis is dead and her share is to go to her children Jacob, Caleb, Mary and Sarah.

On 10 April 1734 William Griffeth of Plymouth, hatter, and wife Sarah received their share due the Curtis children from Ruth Tinkcom of Plymouth, widow.

On 2 April 1737 Peter Tinkham and Ebenezer Tinkham, sons of Helkiah Tinkham of Plymouth, dec., divided land given them in their father's will. The deed mentions that their mother Ruth was to have the premises for life.

Children (TINKHAM) b. Plymouth:

31   i   HELKIAH[4] b. 15 Aug. 1685
32   ii   MARY b. 13 Aug. 1687
33   iii   JOHN b. 27 March 1689
34   iv   JACOB b. 15 June 1691
35   v   CALEB b. 12 Oct. 1693

    vi   SARAH   b. 30 Jan. 1696; d. Plymouth 22 Feb.
             1714/5
36 vii   EBENEZER b. 3 May 1698
37 viii RUTH b. 13 Feb. 1701
38 ix   PETER b. 1 April 1706

References: MD 4:110-1(b. ch; d. Sarah); 12:145-8(Helkiah will, receipts); 16:84(d. Sarah). Plymouth Co. LR 11:36(Helkiah Tinkham Sr.); 31:44(Peter and Ebenezer Tinkham). PLYMOUTH CH RECS 1:227(1724 members), 274(bp. 4 ch.), 275(bp. Helkiah, Ruth). PLYMOUTH VR p. 33(b. ch.; d. Sarah). Plymouth Co. PR 6:81(Helkiah Tinkham).

*No evidence found that Helkiah's wife was a desc. of Pilgrim Francis Cooke or even born a Cooke (as in "FAMILIES OF THE PILGRIMS" by Hubert K. Shaw). The deeds for Helkiah Tinkham and the Cooke Family do not shed any light on Ruth's parentage. TORREY'S MARRIAGES does not call her Cooke. See MD 36:189.

9 MARY TINKHAM[3] (Mary[2] Brown, Peter[1]) b. Plymouth 5 Aug. 1661; d. Middleboro 1731 ae 67 [sic] "widow of John."
     She m. ca. 1680 JOHN TOMSON, b. Plymouth 24 Nov. 1649; d. Middleboro 25 Nov. 1725 in 77th yr.; son of John and Mary (Cooke) Tomson; grandson of Pilgrim Francis Cooke.
     The will of John Tomson of Middleboro dated 19 Oct. 1724, sworn 23 Dec. 1725, names eldest son John; sons Ephraim and Jacob; wife Mary; daus. Mary, Martha and Sarah Tomson; sons Shubaal, Thomas, Peter, Ebenezer, and Frances; "my eleven children."

     Children (TOMSON) b. Middleboro:

    i   MARY[4] b. 2 May 1681; d. Halifax 30 May 1742 in 62nd yr.; unm. as "Mrs. Mary Tomson." On 3 Dec. 1745 Jacob Tomson was appointed to admin. the est. of Mary Tomson late of Halifax, spinster.
39 ii   JOHN b. 9 Aug. 1682
40 iii EPHRAIM b. 16 Oct. 1683
41 iv   SHUBEAL b. 11 April 1686
42 v   THOMAS b. 29 July 1688

vi   MARTHA b. 4 Jan. 1689/90; d. Halifax bet. 1 July
       1760 and 16 May 1770. The will of Martha
       Tomson of Halifax dated 1 July 1760, presented 16
       May 1770, names sister Sarah Tomson; Peter Jr.,
       Francis, Nathan & James sons of her brother
       Thomas Tomson, dec.; and children of brother
       Jacob dec.

vii   SARAH b. 3 March 1691/2; d. Halifax bet. 1 July
       1760 and 7 Jan. 1771. The will of Sarah Tomson of
       Halifax dated 1 July 1760, presented 7 Jan. 1771,
       names sister Martha Tomson; Peter Jr., Francis,
       Nathan and James, sons of her brother Thomas
       dec.; & children of her brother Jacob dec.

viii   PETER b. 11 May 1694; d. Middleboro bet. 19 Oct.
       1724 and 23 June 1726 when his brothers John &
       Ephraim Tomson were appointed admin. of his
       estate. Settlement of the estate of Peter and
       Ebenezer Tomson "that deceased without issue,"
       dated 18 June 1728, names: eldest brother John
       Tomson, brothers Ephraim, Shubael, Thomas,
       Francis & Jacob Tomson; sisters Mary, Martha and
       Sarah Tomson.

ix   ISAAC b. 10 March 1696/7; d. without issue bef.
       19 Oct. 1724

x   EBENEZER b. 19 June 1699; d. Middleboro bet. 19
       Oct. 1724 & 22 March 1726/7, without issue, when
       his brother John Tomson was appointed to
       administer his estate.

xi   FRANCIS (son) b. 27 Jan. 1700/1; d. Halifax 24
       July 1734 without issue. On 7 Oct. 1734 John
       Tomson of Halifax was named administrator on
       the estate of Francis Tomson. A division of 11
       Feb. 1734 names brothers and sisters Mary, Martha,
       Sarah, Ephraim, Jacob, John, and Thomas Tomson;
       nephews John and Thomas Tomson (sons of
       brother Shubael Tomson dec.)

43 xii JACOB b. 24 June 1703

References: MD 1:221(b. Mary, John, Ephraim); 2:41(b. Shubael
           thru Francis), 104(b. Jacob); 10:103(d. dau. Mary);

14:219(d. John, Mary); 20:159-3(John Tomson will); 30:49-52. PLYMOUTH COLONY RECS 8:8(b. John). THOMSON (JOHN) DESC pp. 29, 30, 32-3. MIDDLEBORO DEATHS p. 194. Plymouth Co. PR 5:266-9(John Tomson); #20549(Francis Tomson); #20608(Mary Tomson); #20624(Peter Tomson); #20536(Ebenezer Tomson); 7:47 (Peter & Ebenezer Tomson); 20:360(Martha Tomson), 456(Sarah Tomson). MIDDLEBORO VR 1:2(b. Mary, John), 3(b. Ephraim), 5(b. Shubeal thru Francis), 7(b. Jacob). HALIFAX VR p. 1(d. Francis). PLYMOUTH VR p. 657(b. John).

10   JOHN TINKHAM³ (Mary² Brown, Peter¹) b. Plymouth 15 Nov. 1663; d. Dartmouth bef. 15 Jan. 1739/40 when administrator of his estate was appointed.

He m. bef. 1720 SARAH _____ who d. prob. Dartmouth after 10 April 1759 when she acknowledged a deed.

On 7 March 1714/5 Ebenezer Tinkham and John Thomson, both of Middleborough, sold to their brother John Tinkum of Dartmouth one whole share of both upland and meadow in Dartmouth. The 7 March 1714/5 deed clearly proves John was alive on that date.

On 15 Jan. 1739 John Tinkcom of Dartmouth was appointed administrator on the estate of his father John Tinkham late of Dartmouth, yeoman, dec. and on 18 March 1739 Hezekiah and Martha Tinkcom, children of John Tinkham last of Dartmouth dec., both over 14 years, chose Henry Sampson of Dartmouth, yeoman, their guardian. On the same day Peter Tinkcom also over 14, another son of John of Dartmouth chose [his brother-in-law] Joseph Taber as guardian. Inventory of the estate included a homestead of about 258 acres on the east side of the Acushnet River in what would eventually become New Bedford and then Fairhaven. On 20 April 1741 the estate was divided among eldest son John, sons Peter and Hezekiah, dau. Mary Taber and dau. Martha Tinkcom. (This is in the probate file but not copied into the Probate Record Book.)

On 15 Oct. 1757 Sarah Tinkham of Dartmouth, county of Bristol, widow and relict of John Tinkham late of Dartmouth, sued her dau. Martha Ellis and her husband Joseph Ellis of Dartmouth, cordwainer, for payment due on the estate.

On 9 May 1758 Sarah Tinkcom, mother of Martha Ellis, quitclaimed her rights to land, ack. 10 April 1759.

Children (TINKHAM) b. prob. Dartmouth:

44	i	JOHN[4] b. bef. 1720
45	ii	MARY b. bef. 1721
46	iii	MARTHA b. Dartmouth 19 May 1722
47	iv	PETER b. 8 Feb. 1723/4
48	v	HEZEKIAH b. 10 Nov. 1725

References: VR DARTMOUTH 1:277(b. 3 ch.). Bristol Co. PR 9:364-6(Tinkham gdn.). Bristol Co. LR 9:65 (Ebenezer Tinkham, etc.); 41:210 1/2(John & Sarah Tinkham); 53:383(Sarah Tinkham). Suffolk Co. Court Rec. #78878(Sarah Tinkham).

NOTE: While it is unusual, but not unknown, for a man of this age to start raising a family, a thorough search of Bristol Co. deeds leads to the conclusion that this is the case. There are many John Tinkham deeds and none call him Sr. or Jr., leading to the conclusion that there was only one John Tinkham. The 7 March 1714/5 deed clearly proves John was alive on that date.

The 1921 Tinkham ms. by Horace W. Tinkham says he m. 1st HANNAH and that she d. Dartmouth 6 Oct. 1694. It also lists a son SETH who d. 1725. No documentation has been found to support these statements.

NOTE: On 28 April 1719 a writ was written for the arrest of John Tinkham "of Newport on Rhode Island, Distiller, now resident in Boston in County of Suffolk" (Suffolk Superior Court File #13116). Nothing has been found to link this man with the descendants of Peter Brown.

11   ISAAC TINKHAM[3] (Mary[2] Brown, Peter[1]) b. Plymouth 11 April 1666; d. prob. Plympton bet. 1 Oct. 1730 & 5 April 1732.

He m. Plymouth 17 Nov. 1692 SARAH KING, d. aft. 9 Dec. 1734, who has not been identified.

Sarah Tinkham wife of Isaac Tinkham was listed in the 10 March 1703 and 1724 list of Plymouth Church members.

The will of Isaac Tinkham of Plymouth, yeoman, dated 25 Feb. 1708/9, proved 5 April 1732, grants to "wife Sarah Tinkham the use & improvement of ye one halfe of all my lands and meadows." The will does not dispose of the other half of his lands.

On 1 Oct. 1730, ack. same day, Isaac Tinkham, yeoman, and Helkiah Tinkham Jr., seafaring ·man, both of Plimton sold to Elisha Whitten of Plimton land in Plimton.

On 9 Dec. 1734 Sarah Tinkham, late of Plymouth, now of Kingston, signed quitclaim of land in Plymouth left to her by her late husband Isaac Tinkham to Hilkiah Tinkham of Plymouth, fisherman.

No known children.

References: MD 13:206(m.); 17:166(will). Plymouth Co. PR 6:160 (Isaac Tinkham). Plymouth Co. LR 25:221(Isaac Tinkham); 29:91 (Sarah Tinkham). PLYMOUTH CH RECS 1:192, 227(Sarah member).

NOTE: The "Sarah Tinkham nurse" in the 1742 list of church members is probably the widow (PLYMOUTH CH RECS 2:527).

12 WILLIAM SNOW[3] (Rebecca[2] Brown, Peter[1])   b. prob. Bridgewater ca. 1662; d. prob. there bef. 7 Nov. 1726.

He m. Bridgewater "last of Dec." 1686 NAOMI WHITMAN, b. prob. Bridgewater ca. 1664; d. aft. 12 Jan. 1711; dau. of Thomas and Abigail (Byram) Whitman. The will of Thomas Whitman of Bridgewater dated 12 Jan. 1711 names dau. Naomy Snow.

James Snow of Bridgewater was appointed administrator of the estate of his father William Snow late of Bridgewater on 7 Nov. 1726. Division of the estate on 22 Nov. 1726 names sons James, William, Eleazer, and John Snow; daus. Bethiah wife of Elisha Howard and Susanna wife of Israel Alger, both of Bridgewater.

On 17 May 1728 James Snow and John Snow divided land in Bridgewater given them by their father William Snow.

Children (SNOW) b. Bridgewater:

49 i   BETHIA[4] b. 28 Sept. 1688
50 ii   JAMES b. 14 Oct. 1691
51 iii SUSANNA b. 27 Sept. 1694
52 iv   WILLIAM b. 14 Aug. 1697

53   v   ELEAZER b. 14 July 1701
54   vi   JOHN b. 14 Aug. 1704

References: MD 2:242(m.); 15:47(b. ch.); 22:47-8(Wm. Snow estate).
VR BRIDGEWATER 1:300-4(b. ch.); 2:350 (m.).
BRIDGEWATER BY MITCHELL p. 315. BRIDGEWATER
EPITAPHS p. 19. Plymouth Co. PR #12096(Joseph King);
#18729(Wm. Snow); #22802(Thomas Whitman). Plymouth Co. LR
38:119(Wm. Snow). Plymouth Co. PR 6:160(Isaac Tinkham).

13   JOSEPH   SNOW[3]   (Rebecca[2]   Brown,   Peter[1])   b.   prob.
Bridgewater   bef. 1664;   d.   there   18 Dec.   1753 "husband   of
Hopestill."

He m. ca. 1689 HOPESTILL ALDEN, who d. after 18 Dec.
1753; dau. of Joseph and Mary (Simmons) Alden, granddau. of
Pilgrim John Alden. The will of Joseph Alden of Bridgewater
dated 14 Dec. 1696 does not mention any daus.

On 25 Jan. 1689/90 Thomas Hayward of Bridgewater deeded
land in Bridgewater to "my kinsman Joseph Snow."

On 16 June 1718 Joseph Snow of Bridgewater gave son
Joseph Snow of Bridgewater 50 acres in Bridgewater.

Joseph Snow Sr. of Bridgewater sold to John Field of
Bridgewater a lot in Flaggy Meadow and 3 acres, 16 Dec. 1724,
ack. 10 May 1725.

Joseph Snow of Bridgewater sold to Daniel Alden of
Bridgewater land near Buckhill Plain in Bridgewater 16 June
1729, ack. 22 Sept. 1735.

See the deed under their son Joseph Snow for the best proof
(besides her first name) that Hopestill was a dau. of Joseph Alden.

There is also the letter dated 14 April 1801 from John[4] Alden
(John[3], Joseph[2], John[1]) that states his grandfather had two daus.
"married into the family of Snow of Bridgewater."

There are no probate records for Joseph or Hopestill Snow
in Plymouth Co.

Children (SNOW) b. Bridgewater:

55   i   JOSEPH[4] b. 7 Sept. 1690
56   ii   MARY b. 1 Nov. 1691
57   iii   JAMES b. 16 Aug. 1693

58 iv   REBECKAH b. 25 June 1696
59 v   ISAAC b. 22 July 1700
60 vi   JONATHAN (twin) b. 27 Sept. 1703
61 vii   DAVID (twin) b. 27 Sept. 1703

References: MD 6:71-4(Joseph Alden will); 110-4(Gen. letter of
         John[4] Alden); 14:208(b. ch.), 209(d. Joseph). VR
BRIDGEWATER 1:301-3(b. ch.); 2:559(d. Joseph). Plymouth Co.
LR 18:38(Thomas Hayward); 18:38(to son Joseph Snow); 21:70;
34:105(Joseph Snow). MF 16:1:102-3.

NOTE: It is not clear how Thomas Hayward was kinsman to
Joseph Snow. His wife was Sarah Ames and he left no children.

14 HANNAH SNOW[3] (Rebecca[2] Brown, Peter[1]) b. prob.
Bridgewater ca. 1664; d. prob. Yarmouth 29 March 1723 in 59th yr.
     She m. (1) Plymouth 7 Nov. 1683 GILES RICKARD, b.
Plymouth 1659; d. there 29 Jan. 1709/10; son of Giles and Hannah
(Dunham) Rickard.
     She m. (2) Plymouth 9 March 1713/4 JOSEPH HOWES, b. ca.
1660; d. prob. Yarmouth 24 Dec. 1743 in 84th yr.; son of Joseph
and Elizabeth (Mayo) Howes. He m. (1) Yarmouth 28 Nov. 1689
Mary Vincent by whom he had Mary, Thankful, Elizabeth,
Joseph, Isaac, Judah, and Philip.
     The will of Giles Rickard of Plymouth dated 13 Dec. 1709,
proved 10 March 1709/10, names adopted child Desire Doten;
kinsman Samuel Rickard, son of his brother Henry; kinsman John
Rickard, son of his brother John; Giles, eldest son of his brother
Josiah; Samuel, son of his brother Samuel; Sarah, dau. of his
brother Eliezor; John Whiting, son of his sister Abigail; Elezor
Faunce, son of his sister Judith; Mercy Eaton, dau. of his sister
Hannah; wife Hannah.
     No Barnstable Co. PR for Joseph or Hannah Howes.
     Apparently no children.

References: MD 13:204(1st m.); 14:37(2nd m.). NEHGR 100:321 (d.
         Hannah, Joseph). PLYMOUTH CH RECS 1:209(d.
Giles). GENEALOGY OF THE HOWES FAMILY IN AMERICA,
Joshua Crowell Howes, Yarmouthport MA, 1892 pp 10, 12.
Plymouth Co. PR #16896(Giles Rickard). YARMOUTH VR

1:128(Joseph's 1st m.).

15 BENJAMIN SNOW[3] (Rebecca[2] Brown, Peter[1])   b. prob.
Bridgewater ca. 1669 (even this date makes him 2 yrs. younger
than second wife Sarah); d. there 28 May 1743.
     He m. (1) Bridgewater 12 Dec. 1693 ELIZABETH ALDEN,
b. ca. 1673; d. Bridgewater 8 May 1705; dau. of Joseph and Mary
(Simmons) Alden, a descendant of Pilgrim John Alden. The will
of Joseph Alden of Bridgewater dated 14 Dec. 1696 does not
mention any of his daus., but a letter from John[4] Alden (John[3],
Joseph[2], John[1]) states that his grandfather had two daus. "married
into the family of Snow of Bridgewater."
     He m. (2) Bridgewater 25 Oct. 1705 SARAH (ALLEN) CARY,
b. Bridgewater 14 April 1667; living there 12 Sept. 1738; dau. of
Samuel and Sarah (Partridge) Allen. The will of Samuel Allen of
Bridgewater dated 29 June 1703 names dau. Sarah Cary. She m.
(1) prob. Bridgewater ca. 1687 Jonathan Cary by whom she had
Recompense, John, and Jonathan.
     Benjamin Snow of Bridgewater was a representative to the
General Court of Massachusetts in 1721.
     The will of Benjamin Snow of Bridgewater, husbandman,
dated 12 Sept. 1738, proved 6 June 1743, names youngest son
Ebenezer; sons Benjamin and Solomon; wife Sarah; daus. Rebecca
Campbell and Elizabeth Carver; and grandson Seth Pratt, son of
his dau. Sarah dec.

     Children (SNOW) 5 by first wife, 1 by second, b.
Bridgewater:

     62   i   REBEKAH[4] b. 7 Nov. 1694
     63   ii   BENJAMIN b. 23 June 1696
     64   iii   SOLOMON b. 6 April 1698
     65   iv   EBENEZER b. 29 March 1701
     66   v   ELIZABETH b. 5 May 1705
     67   vi   SARAH b. 20 Aug. 1706

References: MD 6:71(Joseph Alden will), 110-4(Gen. letter from
           John Alden);   14:203(b. ch.; d. 1st wife);
22:99-100(Benj. Snow will). VR BRIDGEWATER 1:30(b. Sarah),
300-4(b. ch.); 2:347(both m.), 558(d. Benjamin, Elizabeth).

BRIDGEWATER BY MITCHELL pp. 35, 92. GEN ADVERTISER 1:2(1st m.). CARY (JOHN) p. 65. Plymouth Co. PR 2:73(Samuel Allen); 9:83(Benj. Snow). TORREY'S MARRIAGES p. 134. MF 16:1:103-4.

16 REBECCA SNOW[3] (Rebecca[2] Brown, Peter[1]) b. prob. Bridgewater ca. 1671; d. Plympton 4 April 1740 ae ca. 69.
      She m. Plymouth 31 Dec. 1689 SAMUEL RICKARD, b. Plymouth 14 Jan. 1662; d. Plympton 7 Sept. 1727 ae ca. 63; son of Giles and Hannah (Dunham) Rickard.
      On 19 Jan. 1719 Samuel Rickard Sr. of Plimpton gave to son Samuel of Plimton land in Plimton "where I now dwell," and on that same day gave to son Eleazer, a minor, the rest of his lands reserving a life interest for himself and his wife.
      On 17 May 1739 Joseph Byram and his wife Hannah; Arthur Harris and his wife Mehitable; both of Bridgewater sold to Samuel Rickard and Eleazer Rickard of Plympton, yeoman, all their rights to the estate of their father Samuel Rickard.
      No Plymouth Co. PR for Samuel or Rebecca Rickard.

      Children (RICKARD) first 7 b. Plymouth, last 2 b. Plympton:

	i	REBECKAH[4] b. 9 Feb. 1690/1; bp. 1692; n.f.r.
68	ii	HANNAH b. 25 Sept. 1693
69	iii	SAMUEL b. 21 May 1696
	iv	BETHYAH b. 15 Oct. 1698*
	v	HENRY b. 4 Feb. 1700*
	vi	MARY b. 8 April 1702; n.f.r.
	vii	ELKANAH b. 7 June 1704*
70	viii	MEHETEBELL b. 1 April 1707
71	ix	ELEAZER b. 8 March 1709/10

References: MD 1:177(d. Samuel, Rebecca), 211(b. Rebeckah, Hannah); 3:15(b. Bethyah, Henry, Mary, Elkanah), 94; 11:116(g.s. Samuel, Rebecca); 13:205(m.). VR PLYMPTON pp. 162(b. Eleazer), 165(b. Mehetebell), 507(d. Rebecca, Samuel). Plymouth Co. LR 14:230 (Samuel Rickard). PLYMOUTH COLONY RECS 8:13(m. Giles-Hannah), 23(b. Samuel). Plymouth Co. PR 8:17(Joseph Byram, etc.). PLYMOUTH CH RECS 1:274(bp. Rebecca), 280(bp. Hannah). PLYMOUTH VR pp. 12(b. 1st 2 ch.),

30(b. Bethyah, Henry, Mary, Elkanah), 86(m.), 663(b. Samuel).

*Samuel Rickard and his brother Henry both had children named Bethiah, Henry and Elkanah. The settlement of the estate of Henry Rickard dated 6 Dec. 1728 names eldest son Henry Rickard; son Elkanah Rickard; grandson Elkanah Fuller only child of James Fuller and Judah Fuller his wife who was dau. of the dec.; widow Marcy Rickard; dau. Bethiah Chandler wife of John Chandler Jr. of Duxborough; and dau. Mercy Weston the wife of Jonathan Weston of Duxborough (Plymouth Co. PR 5:491-2). This proves it was Henry's dau. Bethiah who married John Chandler. Plymouth Co. LR 26:69-70 proves that it was Henry's son Henry who married Alice Oldham. Henry's son Elkanah signed his name on deeds, while there is another Elkanah who signed deeds by a mark, he does not seem to be the son of Samuel because, like Bethia and Henry, he did not participate in the quitclaim.

FOURTH GENERATION

17   MARTHA TINKHAM[4] (Ephraim[3], Mary[2] Brown, Peter[1]) b.
prob. Middleboro ca. 1678; d. Middleboro 16 Feb. 1758 in 80th yr.
She m. Middleboro 8 Dec. 1701 JOHN SOULE, b. Duxbury ca.
1675; d. Middleboro 19 May 1743 in 69th yr.; son of John and
Rebecca (Simmons) Soule, a descendant of Pilgrim George Soule.
  The will of John Soule Senr of Middleboro dated 1 March
1743, proved 6 June 1743, names his wife Martha; sons John and
James; daus. Martha Thomson, Sarah Snow, Ester Soule, Mary
Samson, Rebecca, and Rachel Soul.
  The will of widow Martha Soule Senr of Middleborough
dated 19 Nov. 1751, proved 2 May 1758, names son John Soul's
heirs; son James Soul; heirs of dau. Sarah Snow dec.; daus. Martha
Thompson, Ester Soul, Mary Samson, Rebecca Soul, and Rachel
Vaughan.

  Children (SOULE) b. Middleboro:

  72   i   MARTHA[5] b. 11 April 1702
  73   ii   SARAH b. 8 Oct. 1703
  74   iii   JOHN b. 13 April 1705
       iv   ESTHER b. 16 April 1707; d. Middleboro 15 May
             1793 in 87th yr. The will of Esther Soul of
             Middleboro, spinster, dated 16 Oct. 1792, proved 11
             June 1793, names niece Esther Bryant, wife of
             Isaac Bryant; nephews Nathan Tomson and John
             Soule; other heirs-at-law.
  75   v   MARY b. 14 March 1709
  76   vi   JAMES b. 15 April 1711
       vii   REBECCA b. 1 Oct. 1713; d. Middleboro 24 Jan.
             1759 in 46th yr. The will of Rebecca Soule of
             Middleboro dated 23 Sept. 1758, proved 26 April
             1759, names sisters Esther Soul, Martha Tomson,
             Mary Samson, & Rachel Vaughan; brother James
             Soul; children of dec. sister Sarah Snow; cousin
             John Soule.
       viii NATHAN b. 1 Oct. 1717; d. 8 Feb. 1731/2 in 15th
             yr.

77 ix   RACHEL b. 16 Nov. 1719

References: MD 1:220(m.); 2:105(b. Martha, Sarah, John, Esther),
       Esther), 107(b. Mary), 201(b. James, Nathan); 3:84
(b. Rebecca), 233(b. Rachel); 14:133-4(deaths); 19:136-41 (wills).
MIDDLEBORO DEATHS p. 168. Plymouth Co. PR #18813(John
Soule); #18836(Martha Soule); 15:280(Rebeckah Soul); 33:374-5
(Esther Soule). MF 3:17-8. MIDDLEBORO VR 1:1(m.), 8(b. 1st 4
ch.), 10(b. Mary), 13(b. James, Nathan), 15(b. Rebecca), 19 (b.
Rachel), 58(d. Nathan), 66(d. John).

NOTE: No record found for a son William (twin of Nathan) as
claimed in MF 3:18.

18 JOHN TINKHAM[4] (Ephraim[3] Mary[2] Brown, Peter[1]) b.
Middleboro 22 Aug. 1680; d. there 14 April 1766 in 86th yr.
    He m. Middleboro 11 Dec. 1716 HANNAH HOWLAND, b.
Middleboro 6 Oct. 1694; d. there 25 March 1792 in 98th yr.; dau.
of Isaac and Elizabeth (Vaughn) Howland, granddau. of Pilgrim
John Howland. The will of Isaac Howland Sr. of Middleboro
dated 6 Feb. 1718 names dau. Hannah Tinkham. On 11 May 1724
John Tinkham and wife Hannah and others, all of Middleboro,
and daus. of Isaac Howland late of Middleboro dec., sold land
except what was given to their mother Elizabeth Howland.
    The will of John Tinkham of Middleboro dated 13 Feb. 1766,
presented 23 May 1766, names wife Hannah; sons John, Abisha,
and Amos; daus. Esther Vaughn, Hannah Weston, Susannah Cobb,
Mary Weston, and Zilpah Miller; and brother [in-law] Seth
Howland dec.; sons John and Amos executors.
    Susanna Cobb, widow of James, late of Middleboro dec. and
Mary Weston, wife of Edmund Weston, both of Middleboro, sold
to John Miller rights of their father John Tinkham of Middleboro
dec., signed and ack. 3 May 1787.

    Children (TINKHAM) b. Middleboro:

    i   CORNELIUS[5] b. 31 Aug. 1717; d. Middleboro 16
          April 1739 in 22nd yr. No PR.
78 ii   JOHN b. 8 May 1719
79 iii   ESTHER b. 26 April 1721

80   iv   HANNAH   b. 10 April 1723
81   v   SUSANNAH   b. 19 March 1724/5
82   vi   ABISHAI   b. 23 May 1727
83   vii AMOS   b. 10 July 1729
84 viii   MARY   b. 17 Jan. 1731/2
     ix   SETH   b. 27 Aug. 1734 "shot accidentally; marked
          his powderhorn Lake George NY 11 July 1758. He
          was a sergeant." No PR.
85   x   ZILPAH   b. 25 July 1737

References: MD 1:224(b. Hannah); 3:86(b. Cornelius), 233(b. John),
           234(b. Esther); 4:69(b. Hannah), 70(m.);
6:147-2(Isaac Howland will), 228(b. Susanna), 229(b. Abisha);
7:242(b. Amos); 8:249(b. Zilpah); 9:48(b. Mary); 12:232(b. Seth);
15:100(d. Cornelius), 101(d. Hannah), 102(d. John).
MIDDLEBORO DEATHS pp. 201(d. John, Hannah), 206(d. Seth).
Plymouth Co. PR 4:408-9(Isaac Howland); 19:370(John Tinkham).
Plymouth Co. LR 23:44(John Tinkham); 66:254(Susanna Cobb etc.).
MIDDLEBORO VR 1:4(b. Hannah), 17(b. Cornelius), 18(b. John),
20(b. Esther), 23(b. Hannah), 24(m.), 36(b. Susanna), 38(b. Abishai),
41(b. Amos), 45(b. Zilpah), 48(b. Mary), 54(b. Seth).

19   EPHRAIM TINKHAM[4] (Ephraim[3], Mary[2] Brown, Peter[1]) b.
Middleboro 7 Oct. 1682; d. there 11 July 1713 in 31st yr.
     He m. Middleboro 24 June 1708 MARTHA COBB, b.
Middleboro 23 March 1691/2; d. there 8 Aug. 1775 in 85th yr.; dau.
of John and Rachel (Soule) Cobb, a descendant of Pilgrim George
Soule. She m. (2) prob. Middleboro ca. 1716 Aaron Simmons by
whom she had David, Aaron, Patience, and Martha. The will of
John Cobb Sr. of Middleboro dated 29 May 1727 names wife
Rachel and dau. Martha Simmons.
     On 18 Sept. 1713 Martha Tincom, widow of Ephraim late of
Middlebury, was appointed administratrix of his estate. The
settlement in March 1714 mentions two small children. On 2 Feb.
1727 Ephraim and Moses Tinkham chose Mr. James Soul of
Middleboro as their guardian.

     Children (TINKHAM) b. Middleboro:

     i   MOSES[5] b. 16 Aug. 1709; d. Middleboro 27 April

1730 in 21st yr.
ii EPHRAIM b. 13 Feb. 1711/12; d. Plympton 13 May
1730 in 19th yr.

References: MD 2:42(b. Martha Cobb), 157(m.), 202(b. Tinkham
ch.); 3:233(Simmons ch.); 5:40(Simmons ch.);
11:165(d. ch. Ephraim); 12:130(Simmons ch.); 17:163-4(his estate).
MIDDLEBORO DEATHS pp. 162(d. Martha), 201(d. Ephraim Sr.),
203(d. Moses). COBB FAM p. 48. Plymouth Co. PR 3:240
(Ephraim Tinkham); #4546 (John Cobb). MF 3:46. VR
PLYMPTON p. 528(d. son Ephraim). MIDDLEBORO BY
WESTON pp. 650, 653. MIDDLEBORO VR 1:5(b. Martha), 10(m.),
13(b. ch.).

20 ISAAC TINKHAM[4] (Ephraim[3], Mary[2] Brown, Peter[1]) b.
Middleboro "last June" 1685; d. Halifax 7 April 1750 in 65th yr.

He m. Middleboro 12 Dec. 1717 ABIJAH WOOD, b.
Middleboro 20 Feb. 1688/9; d. Halifax 25 Dec. 1777 in 88th yr.;
dau. of Abiel and Abiah (Bowen) Wood. The will of Abiel Wood
of Middleborough dated 18 Dec. 1719 mentions dau. Abijah only
by her first name.

Isaac Tinkham was one of those dismissed in 1734 from
Middleboro First Church to form a church in the newly
incorporated town of Halifax. In 1735 he was chosen as one of
their deacons.

On 1 June 1750 Abijah Tincom Sr., widow, signed receipt for
her share of the estate of Isaac Tinkham. On 21 June 1750 Noah
Tinkcom, Nathan Tinkham and Abijah Tinkham of Halifax,
children of Isaac Tinkham, signed receipt for their share of the
estate.

On 31 Dec. 1750 Isaac Tinkham, Noah Tinkham, Nathan
Tinkham and Abijah Tinkham, all of Halifax, sold land of "our
deceased father Deacon Isaac Tinkham late of Halifax deceased
intestate," except for their mother's life interest.

No Plymouth Co. PR for Abijah Tinkham.

Children (TINKHAM) b. Middleboro:

i EPHRAIM[5] b. 8 Nov. 1718; d. Halifax or
Middleboro 10 Jan. 1734/5 in 17th yr.

86	ii	ISAAC b. 21 April 1720
87	iii	NOAH b. 25 July 1722
88	iv	NATHAN b. 18 April 1725
89	v	ABIJAH b. 21 March 1727/8
	vi	MOSES b. 3 Feb. 1730/1; d. Halifax 15 April 1750 in 20th yr.

References: MD 2:106(b. Abijah Wood); 3:30(d. Ephraim), 32(d. Deacon Isaac, Moses), 233(b. Ephraim), 235 (b. Isaac); 4:68(b. Noah), 70(m.); 6:228(b. Nathan); 12:230(b. Abijah, Moses); 14:10(d. Isaac - yr. wrong, Abijah, Moses), 221(d. Ephraim); 26:181(chosen Dea.). MIDDLEBORO DEATHS p. 203(d. Ephraim). MIDDLEBORO BY WESTON pp. 462, 652. Plymouth Co. PR 15:212, 213(Abiel Wood); #20864(Isaac Tinkham). Plymouth Co. LR 41:103(Isaac Tinkham et al.). Middleboro Mortality Records pp. 75(d. Abijah), 76(d. Isaac). MIDDLEBORO VR 1:9(b. Abijah), 18(b. Ephraim), 20(b. Isaac), 23(b. Noah), 25(m.), 37(b. Nathan), 52(b. Abijah, Moses).

21 SAMUEL TINKHAM[4] (Ephraim[3], Mary[2] Brown, Peter[1]) b. Middleboro 19 March 1687; d. there 16 March 1775 "aged 87 years to a day [sic]."

He m. (1) Middleboro 20 Feb. 1717/8 PATIENCE COBB, b. Middleboro 23 Sept. 1693; d. there 4 Nov. 1727 in 35th yr.; dau. of John and Rachel (Soule) Cobb, a descendant of Pilgrim George Soule. The will of John Cobb Sr. of Middleboro dated 29 May 1727 names wife Rachel and dau. Patience Tinkham.

He m. (2) Middleboro 22 March 1730/1 MELATIAH EDDY, b. ca. 1704; d. Middleboro 8 Oct. 1798 in 94th yr.; dau. of Samuel and Malatiah (Pratt) Eddy.

The will of Samuel Tinkham of Middleboro dated 3 Nov. 1773, proved 6 May 1776, names wife Maltiah; grandsons Ephraim and Samuel Tinkham and their (unnamed) sister; daus. Patience and Lois Tinkham; son Silas Tinkham; and heirs of Ephraim Tinkham dec.

No Plymouth Co. LR for Silas Tinkham with Patience, Lois, Fear, Martha, Samuel, or Sarah.

Children (TINKHAM) by second wife, b. Middleboro:

90	i	EPHRAIM[5] b. 30 April 1733

           ii   PATIENCE b. 9 Jan. 1734/5; unm. 3 Nov. 1773. No
                 PR.
           iii   SAMUEL   b. 16 April 1737; prob. d. bef. 3 Nov.
                 1773. Apparently the Samuel, s. of Samuel who d.
                 Middleboro 1747.
     91   iv   SILAS b. 25 April 1739
           v   FEAR b. 14 March 1740/1; prob. d. bef. 3 Nov.
                 1773; (not in father's will)
           vi   MARTHA b. 27 March 1743; prob. d. bef. 3 Nov.
                 1773; (not in father's will)
           vii   LOIS b. 2 Oct. 1745; unm. 3 Nov. 1773. No PR.
           viii SARAH b. 18 June 1748; prob. d. bef. 3 Nov. 1773;
                 (not in father's will)

References: MD 2:42(b. wife Patience); 4:70(1st m.); 5:38(d.
             Patience); 8:249(b. Sam.); 9:46(2nd m.); 12:131 (b.
Ephraim), 233(b. Patience); 14:221(d. Samuel, Melatiah, Patience),
245(b. Silas); 15:120(b. Fear), 220(b. Martha); 16:107(b. Lois);
18:151(b. Sarah); 24:35(John Cobb will).   COBB FAM p. 48.
Plymouth Co. PR 24:107(Sam. Tinkham); #4546(John Cobb).
EDDY FAM p. 60. MIDDLEBORO DEATHS pp. 203(d's. Sam.; 2
wives), 207(d. Samuel).   MF 3:47.   MIDDLEBORO VR 1:5 (b.
Patience Cobb), 25(1st m.), 30(d. Patience), 46(b. Samuel), 47(2nd
m.), 51(b. Ephraim), 56(b. Patience), 66(b. Silas), 68(b. Fear), 75(b.
Martha), 87(b. Lois), 111(b. Sarah).

22 MARY TINKHAM[4] (Ephraim[3], Mary[2] Brown, Peter[1]) bp.
Plymouth 1691; living 10 May 1751.
      She m. Middleboro 24 Dec. 1717 HENRY WOOD, b.
Middleboro ca. 1677; d. there bet. 10 May 1751 and 4 May 1752;
son of Samuel and Rebecca (Tupper) Wood.
      On 31 Aug. 1730 Henry Wood and wife Mary and other heirs
of [their brother] Ephraim Tinkham late of Middleboro dec., were
quitclaimed land by Aaron Simmons and wife Martha [Ephraim's
widow].
      The will of Henry Wood of Middleboro dated 10 May 1751,
exhibited 4 May 1752, names wife Mary and children Henry
Wood, Moses Wood, Joanna Wood, and Susanna Wood.
      No Plymouth Co. PR for Mary Wood.

Children (WOOD) b. Middleboro:

    i   SAMUEL[5] b. 27 Sept. 1718; d. bef. 10 May 1751; (not in father's will)

    ii   ESTHER b. 31 Jan. 1720/1; d. Middleboro 9 May 1721 ae 3m 9d

    iii   JOANNA b. 30 March 1722; d. Middleboro 7 April 1797 ae 75; unm. No PR.

92 iv   SUSANNA b. 24 April 1724

93 v   HENRY b. 27 Feb. 1726/7

94 vi   MOSES b. 3 Feb. 1730/1

References: MD 3:233(b. Samuel); 4:70(m.), 74(d. Esther); 6:179(b. Esther, Joanna); 8:29(b. Susanna, Henry, Moses); 48:19-20(Wood fam.). MIDDLEBORO DEATHS p. 235(d. Esther, Joanna). Plymouth Co. PR 13:5(Henry Wood). Plymouth Co. LR 28:151(Aaron Simmons). MIDDLEBORO VR 1:18(Samuel), 25(m.), 28(d. Esther), 33(b. Esther, Joanna), 43(b. Susanna, Henry, Moses).

23 EBENEZER TINKHAM[4] (Ebenezer[3], Mary[2] Brown, Peter[1]) b. Middleboro 23 March 1679; d. there 31 Aug. 1726 ae 49.

He m. (1) Middleboro 28 Oct. 1703 PATIENCE PRATT, b. ca. 1682; d. Middleboro 29 March 1718 in 37th yr.

He m. (2) Scituate 9 July 1719 HANNAH (HATCH) TURNER, b. Scituate 15 Feb. 1681/2; d. Middleboro 13 April 1771 in 91st yr.; dau. of Samuel and Mary (Doty) Hatch; a descendant of Pilgrim Edward Doty. The will of Samuel Hatch Sr. of Bridgewater, yeoman, aged, dated 13 June 1728 named his dau. Hannah Tincom. She m. (1) ca. 1705 Japhet Turner by whom she had Hannah, Japhet, Israel, and Elizabeth. She m. (3) Middleboro 23 Dec. 1729 Capt. Ichabod Tupper.

Shuball Tinkham of Middleboro was appointed administrator of the estate of his brother Ebenezer Tinkham of Middleboro dec. on 7 Nov. 1726. On 22 March 1726/7 Ephraim Wood of Middleboro gave bond as guardian of Ebenezer's children: Peter under 21, and Priscilla and Patience both under 14.

The will of Hannah Tupper of Middleboro, widow, dated 26 Aug. 1766, proved 11 Oct. 1771, names her Turner children and many grandchildren.

Children (TINKHAM) by first wife, b. Middleboro:

95 i   ELIZABETH[5] b. 13 Oct. 1704
96 ii   MARY b. 30 Jan. 1705/6
97 iii PETER b. 5 Sept. 1709
    iv   JABEZ b. 29 Dec. 1711; prob. d. bef. his father
98 v   PATIENCE bp. 11 April 1714
99 vi   PRISCILLA bp. 22 April 1716

References: MD 2:43(1st m.), 202(b. Elizabeth, Mary, Peter, Jabez); 4:74; 15:102(d. Patience), 103(d. Hannah Tupper); 21:97-101(will, Hannah's 3 m's.); 41:189-91(probate papers). MIDDLEBORO DEATHS p. 201(d. Eben., Patience). VR SCITUATE 1:173(b. Hannah); 2:293(2nd m.). Middleboro First Ch. Bp. p. 2(bp. Patience, Priscilla). Plymouth Co. PR #9591(Samuel Hatch); 5:158(Ebenezer Tinkham); 21:78(Hannah Tupper); #20898(gdns.). MIDDLEBORO VR 1:7(1st m.), 13(b. 1st 4 ch.), 28(d. Patience).

24 JEREMIAH TINKHAM[4] (Ebenezer[3], Mary[2] Brown, Peter[1]) b. Middleboro 7 Aug. 1681; d. there 5 April 1715 in 34th yr.
     He m. ca. 1709 JOANNA PARLOW, d. bet. 26 July 1727 and 9 Sept. 1734; dau. of Thomas and Elizabeth (Liscomb) Parlow. She m. (2) Middleboro 23 Dec. 1720 Robert MacFun by whom she had at least 4 children: Agnes, Elizabeth, Patience and Robert.
     On 17 July 1718 Joanna Tinkham, widow, was appointed administratrix of the estate of Jeremiah Tinkham of Middleboro. The settlement of the estate on 24 June 1720 mentions the widow and three small children viz Joana, Jeremiah, and Ebenezer.
     On 25 Jan. 1720 John Tinkcum was appointed guardian to Joanna, Ebenezer, and Jeremiah, all under 14.
     In a settlement of the real estate of Thomas Parlow late of Middleboro dec., dated 26 July 1727, dau. Joanna Mackfun wife of Robert was named. On 9 Sept. 1734 Robert MacFun of Middleboro quitclaimed 1/9 of the estate of father-in-law Thomas Parler late of Middleboro dec., which was set off to his wife Joanna MacFun, late of Middleboro dec.
     No Plymouth Co. PR for Joanna Tinkham.

Children (TINKHAM) b. Middleboro:

  i JOANNA[5] b. 8 Dec. 1711; d. Middleboro 1763 in 53rd yr.; unm. On 31 Oct. 1734 Joanna Tinkham of Middleboro sold to Jeremiah Tinkham of Middleboro her third of lands which were given to her in partnership with her brother Jeremiah Tinkham by will of her grandfather Ebenezer Tinkham late of Middleboro dec. Joanna left no Plymouth Co. PR.

100 ii JEREMIAH b. 20 Feb. 1712/3
101 iii EBENEZER b. 16 Dec. 1714

References: MD 3:84(b. Joanna, Jeremiah), 86(b. Eben.); 4:72 (her
    2nd m.); 6:180, 227, 229(b. MacFun ch.).
MIDDLEBORO DEATHS pp. 201(d. Jeremiah), 206(d. dau. Joanna) . Plymouth Co. PR 4:139, 146, 217(Jeremiah Tinkham); #20868 (gdns.). Plymouth Co. LR 15:108(Robert & Joanna Mackfun); 29:54(Robert MacFun), 177(Joanna Tinkham). MIDDLEBORO VR 1:15(b. Joanna, Jeremiah), 17(b. Ebenezer), 26(her 2nd m.), 28(d. Jeremiah), 33(b. 2 McFun ch.), 35(b. Patience McFun), 37(b. Robert McFun).

25 JOANNA TINKHAM[4] (Ebenezer[3], Mary[2] Brown, Peter[1]) bp. Plymouth 1685; d. Marshfield 29 April 1766 in 81st yr.
  She m. Middleboro 14 June 1709 THOMAS MACOMBER, b. Marshfield 2 July 1684; d. there 5 Oct. 1771 in 88th yr.; son of Thomas and Sarah (Crooker) Macomber.
  Thomas Macomber was chosen Deacon of First Church of Marshfield 21 May 1741.
  The will of Thomas Macomber of Marshfield dated 19 Aug. 1767, presented 17 Oct. 1771, names daus. Elizabeth Winslow, Sarah Barker, and Joanna Macomber; grandsons Thomas and Onesimus Macomber, sons of Onesimus dec.; grandsons William and Thomas, sons of Thomas dec.

  Children (MACOMBER) b. Marshfield:

102 i THOMAS[5] b. 28 April 1710
  ii URSULA b. 10 Dec. 1711; d. Marshfield 10 Nov. 1748 in 37th yr. No PR.
103 iii SARAH b. 27 Oct. 1713

104 iv ELIZABETH b. 22 Feb. 1715
105 v ONESIMUS b. 18 June 1720
vi JOANNA b. 20 April 1722; d. Marshfield 2 March 1791 in 69th yr. No PR.

References: MD 2:158(m.); 19:16-21(Thomas Macomber will etc.); 31:161-3(bp. ch.); 32:17(chosen Deacon). MARSHFIELD VR pp. 8(par. Thomas), 13(b. Thomas Sr.), 33(b. Onesimus, Joanna), 38(b. Eliz., Thomas), 45(b. Ursula, Sarah), 405(d's. both Joanna's, Thomas, Ursula). MIDDLEBORO VR 1:10 (m.). Plymouth Co. PR 21:46-8(Thomas Macomber).

26 SHUBALL TINKHAM⁴ (Ebenezer³, Mary² Brown, Peter¹) bp. Plymouth 1692; d. Middleboro 29 March 1739 in 47th yr.

He m. Marshfield 17 Dec. 1718 PRISCILLA CHILDS, b. Marshfield 5 Nov. 1693; d. Middleboro 11 July 1739 in 45th yr.; dau. of Joseph and Elizabeth (Seabury) Childs. The will of Joseph Childs of Marshfield dated 6 March 1717/18 does not name his daus.

In March 1734 Shubael Tinkham and others petitioned the court to build a slitting-mill on the Nemasket River.

The will of Shuball Tinkham of Middleboro, yeoman, dated 26 March 1739, proved 15 May 1739, names wife Priscilla exec.; sons Joseph, Ebenezer, and Peres Tinkham; and daus. Elizabeth Donham, Sarah Tinkham, and Priscilla Tinkham.

At the April 1740 Suffolk Co. Court Joseph, Ebenezer, and Perez Tinkham of Middleboro, minors, by John Tinkham their guardian, petitioned for partition of their father Shubael Tinkham's estate now that their mother is dead.

Children (TINKHAM) b. Middleboro:

106 i ELIZABETH⁵ b. 1 Oct. 1719
107 ii JOSEPH b. 16 Dec. 1721
108 iii SARAH b. 23 Feb. 1723/4
109 iv PRISCILLA b. 10 June 1726
110 v EBENEZER b. 2 Jan. 1728/9
vi PEREZ b. 4 Aug. 1736; d. Middleboro 25 Nov. 1760 in 25th yr. The will of Perez Tinkham of Middleboro, laborer, dated 17 Nov. 1760, presented

1 Dec. 1760, names brother Capt. Joseph Tinkham; sisters Elizabeth Donham, Sarah Blackman, and Priscilla Cushman; cousins John Cobb & Martha Cobb, ch. of his sister Priscilla.

References: MD 5:40(b. Elizabeth, Joseph); 6:180(b. Sarah), 229(b. Priscilla); 7:242(b. Eben.); 8:248(b. Perez); 15:102(d. Perez, Priscilla), 103(d. Shuball). MARSHFIELD VR pp. 24(b. Priscilla Childs), 35, 40(m.). MIDDLEBORO BY WESTON p. 359. Plymouth Co. PR #3879(Joseph Childs); 8:35 (Shuball Tinkham); 16:29 (Perez Tinkham). TORREY'S MARRIAGES p. 150(ident. Eliz. Seabury). MIDDLEBORO VR 1:32(b. Eliz., Jos.), 33(b. Sarah), 37(b. Priscilla), 41(b. Ebenezer), 45(b. Perez). Suffolk Co Court Recs #51367(petition).

27   MERCY TINKHAM[4] (Peter[3], Mary[2] Brown, Peter[1]) b. prob. Middleboro ca. 1692; d. there 17 April 1723 age 31.

She m. Middleboro 27 Dec. 1716 JAMES RAYMOND (or RAYMENT), b. Beverly 1 June 1689; d. prob. Pomfret CT after 19 Jan. 1771 (ack. deed); son of John and Martha (Woodin) Raymond. He m. (2) Plympton 30 Jan. 1723/4 Elizabeth Fuller, a descendant of Pilgrims John Billington, Francis Eaton, and Samuel Fuller by whom he had Patience, Elizabeth, Martha, Rachel, Bathsheba, James, Amaziah, Joshua, and Ithamar.

On 15 Sept. 1721 James Rayment and wife Mercy both of Middleboro signed and acknowledged a deed to land originally belonging to their grandfather Ephraim Tinkham.

On 17 March 1753 James Raymond of Middleboro bought 129 acres in Pomfret CT. On 30 Aug. 1753, James Raymond and wife Elizabeth were admitted to the Abington Congregational Church in Pomfret CT from the Middleboro First Church.

On 25 May 1770, ack. 19 Jan. 1771, James Raymond of Thompson, yeoman, sold land to William Plank.

Neither James nor Mercy Raymond left probate records.

Children (RAYMOND) b. Middleboro:

111   i   PETER[5] b. 27 March 1718
      ii   MERCY b. 3 April 1720; n.f.r.

References: MD 3:234(b. ch.); 4:70(1st m.); 14:84(d. wife Mercy).
Plymouth Co. LR 15:227(James Rayment). VR
PLYMPTON p. 367(2nd m.). MIDDLEBORO BY WESTON p. 652.
MF 10:17-8; 21:58-9. MIDDLEBORO VR 1:19(b. ch.). Pomfret CT
LR 4:395; 5:205(James Raymond). CSL Ch. Recs. for Pomfret CT.
VR BEVERLY 1:275(b. James).

28   JOANNA TINKHAM[4] (Peter[3], Mary[2] Brown, Peter[1]) b. prob.
Middleboro ca. 1695; d. there 28 June 1738 in 42nd or 43rd yr.
She m. Middleboro 16 April 1716 JOSEPH BATES, b. prob.
Weymouth ca. 1692; d. Middleboro 31 Aug. 1778 ae 86 yrs.; son of
Edward and Elizabeth (_____) Bates. He m. (2) int. Barnstable
16 April 1743 Mary Blossom by whom he had Mary, Hannah and
Mehitable.
On 9 April 1729 Joseph Bates and wife Joanna of Middleboro
sold to Isaac Tinkham land which did formerly belong to their
grandfather Ephraim Tinkham dec.
On 9 June 1757 Joseph Bates Jr. and Elizabeth Bates, John
Jackson and wife Joanna, Hezekiah Purrington and wife Mercy,
Ebenezer Cox and wife Priscilla, all of Middleboro, sold to Joseph
Besse of Wareham land in Middleboro of their grandfather Peter
Tinkham dec. The deed was acknowledged on 23 July 1768 by
Joseph Bates, John Jackson, Mercy Purrington, Ebenezer Cox, and
Priscilla Cox. On the second Tuesday of April 1769 the witnesses
to the deed swore they had seen Elizabeth Bates, Joanna Jackson,
and Hezekiah Purrington "all since deceased" sign.
The will of Joseph Bates of Middleboro dated 27 July 1773,
sworn 5 Oct. 1778, names sons Joseph and Thomas; dau. Mehitable
Bates unm.; six daus. or heirs of dec. daus.: Joanna Jackson, heirs
of Marcy Purrington, Priscilla Cox, Mary Smith, Hannah Smith,
and Mehitable Bates.

Children (BATES) b. Middleboro:

112   i   JOANNA[5] b. 28 May 1718
113   ii   MERCY b. 8 Aug. 1719
114   iii JOSEPH b. 18 March 1721/2
       iv   ELIZABETH b. 12 Jan. 1722/3; d. bet. 9 June
            1757 and April 1769. No PR.
115   v   THOMAS b. 9 Nov. 1724

116 vi   PRISCILLA b. 6 Jan. 1726/7

References: MD 2:158(first m.); 4:68(b. Joseph, Mercy, Joanna);
            6:227(b. Eliz., Thomas); 7:241(b. Priscilla); 12:68(d.
Joanna), 69(d. Joseph); 15:24(d. Joanna); 33:166(2nd m.).
MIDDLEBORO DEATHS p. 13(d. Joseph, Joanna). WEYMOUTH
BY CHAMBERLAIN 3:23(Joseph's par.). MIDDLEBORO BY
WESTON pp. 652, 664. Plymouth Co. LR 25:220; 54:226(Joseph
Bates). Plymouth Co. PR #1554(Joseph Bates). MIDDLEBORO
VR 1:11(m.), 22(b. 1st 3 ch.), 35(b. Eliz., Thomas), 39(b. Priscilla),
67(d. Joanna), 76(b. Mary), 90(b. Hannah).

29   SAMUEL TINKHAM[4] (Peter[3], Mary[2] Brown, Peter[1]) b. prob.
Middleboro bet. 1696 and 1698; d. there bef. 21 May 1747.
       He m. Middleboro 1 Dec. 1719 MARY STAPLES, d. bet. 9
Sept. 1748 and 8 May 1749; prob. the one b. Braintree 26 March
1700 to Benjamin and Mary (Cox) Staples.
       On 29 Sept. 1725 Samuel Tinkham Junr of Middleborough
sold to Shubael Tinkham and Joseph Bate both of Middleboro
land in Plympton which belonged to his father Peter Tinkham
and uncle Ebenezer Tinkham.
       On 21 May 1747 Peter Tinkham of Middleboro, yeoman, was
appointed to administer the estate of Samuel Tinkham Jr. late of
Middleboro dec. and on 9 Sept. 1748 or thereabouts, part of the
estate was set off to his widow Mary Tinkham. On 8 May 1749
Peter Tinkham, husbandman, of Middleboro posted bond as
administrator of the estate of Mary Tinkham late of Middleboro
widow dec. On 14 May 1750 Samuel's estate was divided among
dau. Deborah Tinkham, eldest son Peter, dau. Keziah Tinkham,
son Gideon, daus. Joanna Tinkham and Mercy Donham, and son
Samuel.
       On 9 May 1757 Samuel Tinkham Jr., Gideon Tinkham,
Deborah Tinkham, Jonathan Reed and wife Joanna, all of
Middleboro, Joseph Besse and wife Mercy of Wareham, and
Keziah Tinkham of Bridgewater sold to Ebenezer Tinkham of
Middleboro land in the 12 Mens Purchase bounded by land of
brother Peter Tinkham dec.

       Children (TINKHAM) b. Middleboro:

117	i	MARTHA[5] b. 23 Aug. 1720
118	ii	PETER b. 16 May 1722
119	iii	SAMUEL b. 13 March 1723/4
120	iv	MERCY b. 24 Aug. 1726
121	v	DEBORAH b. 7 Sept. 1728
122	vi	GIDEON b. 24 April 1731
123	vii	JOANNA b. 15 May 1734
124	viii	KEZIA b. 15 Aug. 1738
	ix	LYDIA b. 10 May 1741; d. Middleboro 24 Dec. 1747 in 7th yr.

References: NEHGR 116:20(b., par. Mary). MD 4:69(b. Martha, Peter), 71(m.); 6:229(b. Samuel, Mercy); 9:49(b. Deborah, Gideon); 12:233(b. Joanna); 14:244(b. Kezia); 15:217(b. Lydia); 18:80(d. Lydia). Plymouth Co. PR 10:430, 434; 11:96, 406, 407(Samuel Tinkham); #20887(Mary Tinkham). Plymouth Co. LR 20:56(Samuel Tinkham); 47:51(Samuel Tinkham Jr. etc.). MIDDLEBORO DEATHS p. 207(d. Lydia). BRAINTREE RECS p. 678(b. Mary). MIDDLEBORO VR 1:23(b. Martha, Peter), 25(m.), 37(b. Sam., Mercy), 50(b. Deborah, Gideon), 55(b. Joanna), 64 (b. Kezia), 71(b. Lydia).

30 SETH TINKHAM[4] (Peter[3], Mary[2] Brown, Peter[1]) b. Middleboro 15 May 1704; d. there 9 Feb. 1750/1 in 47th yr. (VR says 9 Feb. 1751).

He m. ca. 1724 MARY _____, b. ca. 1700; d. Middleboro 16 June 1745 in 45th yr.

Seth Tinkham was a yeoman, gravestone maker and town clerk. On 9 March 1750 John Tomson of Middleboro, yeoman, posted bond to administer the estate of Seth Tinkham of Middleboro, yeoman. On 13 March 1750 Mercy Tinkham and Seth Tinkham, both over 14, chose Joseph Tinkham of Middleboro, husbandman, as guardian, and he was appointed guardian for Elizabeth and Joanna Tinkham.

Children (TINKHAM) b. Middleboro:

| 125 | i | BATHSHEBA[5] b. 10 July 1726 |
| | ii | EBENEZER b. 21 March 1727/8; d. Middleboro 16 May 1729 in 2nd yr. |

	iii	son stillborn 26 Jan. 1729/30
	iv	dau. stillborn 12 Feb. 1730/31
126	v	MERCY b. 25 July 1732
127	vi	SETH b. 13 Nov. 1734
	vii	ELIZABETH b. 11 May 1737; d. Middleboro 3 Feb. 1777 in 41st yr.; unm. No PR.
	viii	dau. stillborn 10 June 1739
	ix	JOANNA b. 1 Jan. 1740/1; d. Middleboro 24 Feb. 1813 age 73 yrs.; unm. No PR.

References: MD 5:38(d. Ebenezer); 6:228(b. Bathsheba); 7:241 (b. Eben.); 8:249(b. Eliz.); 9:49(b. Mercy); 12:233(b. Seth); 13:5(d. 2 stillb. ch.); 15:24(d. stillb. 1739), 100(d. Eben.), 102(d. Mary), 103(d. Seth), 120(b. Joanna); 18:81(d. Seth). MIDDLEBORO DEATHS pp. 201(d. Seth, Mary), 204(d. Eliz., Joanna), 207(d. 3 still b. ch.). MASKS OF ORTHODOXY, Peter Benes 1977 p. 103. Plymouth Co. PR #20909 (Seth Tinkham); #20910(Tinkham gdn.). MIDDLEBORO VR 1:29(d. Ebenezer), 37(b. Bathsheba), 39(b. Ebenezer), 46(b. Eliz.), 49(b. Mercy), 55(b. Seth), 58(2 stillborn ch.), 67(last stillborn ch.), 68(b. Joanna).

NOTE: The deeds for Seth Tinkham do not provide any clue to Mary's maiden name.

31 HELKIAH TINKHAM[4] (Helkiah[3], Mary[2] Brown, Peter[1]) b. Plymouth 15 Aug. 1685; d. there bef. 17 Dec. 1746.

He m. Marblehead 15 Dec. 1709 ELIZABETH HEISTER (or HEYTER) bp. Marblehead 17 July 1692 "dau. of Hannah Heyter"; d. Plymouth bef. 15 Nov. 1763, prob. the widow Elizabeth Tinkham who d. Plymouth 27 May 1762.

On 17 Dec. 1746 administration on the estate of Hilkiah Tinkham of Plimouth, mariner, was granted to Elizabeth Tinkham of Plimouth widow. On 12 Nov. 1747 she posted bond as guardian of Ruth and Lydia, minor daus. of Helkiah, and of Ebenezer Tinkham, son of Helkiah.

Isaac Tinkham of Plymouth, fisherman, signed and acknowledged a deed on 25 April 1748 in which he mortgaged to Samuel Nelson of Plymouth a dwelling house and land in Plymouth, the whole of the real estate that Helkiah Tinkham late of Plymouth dec. died seized of except the widow's dower, said

Samuel and Isaac having 9 bonds to Hannah Tinkham, Elizabeth
Saunders, Sarah Tinkham, Benjamin Eaton, and wife Mary,
Zedekiah Tinkham, Martha Tinkham, Ruth Tinkham, Lydia
Tinkham, and Ebenezer Tinkham.

On 29 April 1748 Elizabeth Tinkcom of Plymouth, widow of
Helkiah late of Plymouth, sold land to Fear Cobb.

On 15 Nov. 1763 Zedekiah Tinkham of Plymouth, mariner,
was appointed administrator of the estate of Elizabeth Tinkham.

There are no Plymouth Co. PR's for Hannah, Sarah, Ruth or
Ebenezer Tinkham.

Children (TINKHAM) b. Plymouth:

	i	HANNAH[5] b. "last day" Oct. 1710; bp. Marblehead 8 July 1711; living unm. 25 April 1748.
128	ii	ELIZABETH b. 5 July 1713
129	iii	ISAAC b. 27 Dec. 1715
	iv	SARAH b. 5 Aug. 1718; living unm. 25 April 1748
130	v	ZEDEKIAH b. 11 July 1721
	vi	JOHN b. 29 Sept. 1723; d. Plymouth 13 Oct. 1723
131	vii	MARY b. 14 Sept. 1724
132	viii	MARTHA b. 29 Dec. 1726
133	ix	RUTH (twin) b. 9 July 1729; living unm. 25 April 1748
	x	LYDIA (twin) b. 9 July 1729; d. Plymouth 22 Oct. 1732
	xi	EBENEZER b. 26 June 1732; living 25 April 1748
134	xii	LYDIA b. 10 March 1734/5

References: MD 5:99, 100(b. ch; d. John, Lydia).   VR
            MARBLEHEAD 1:254(bp. Elizabeth), 511(bp.
Hannah); 2:427(m.). Plymouth Co. PR #20836(Hilkiah Tinkham);
17:117, #20838(Elizabeth Tinkham). Plymouth Co. LR
39:118(Isaac Tinkham). PLYMOUTH CH RECS 1:392(d. Eliz.),
430(bp. 1732 ch. Isaac thru Eben. exc. 2 who d.). PLYMOUTH VR
p. 41(b. ch.; d. John, Lydia).

NOTE: TORREY'S MARRIAGES does not identify the husband
of Hannah Heister.

32   MARY TINKHAM[4] (Helkiah[3], Mary[2] Brown, Peter[1])   b. Plymouth 13 August 1687; d. there 17 March 1717/8 in 31st yr.

She m. Plymouth 19 Jan. 1709/10 EBENEZER CURTIS, b. Plymouth ca. 1685; living 4 May 1744 (when dismissed to Third Church Plymouth); son of Francis and Hannah (Smith) Curtis. He m. (2) Plymouth 7 Oct. 1718 Martha Doty, a descendant of Pilgrims Francis Cooke and Edward Doty, by whom he had Eunice, Martha, Seth, and Ebenezer.

On 16 Feb. 1733 Jacob Curtis, chairmaker, and Nathaniel Churchell, cordwainer, and wife Mary, all of Plymouth, gave their receipt to Ruth Tinkcom of Plymouth, widow of Helkiah, for their share (of their grandfather's estate).

At the May 1742 Plymouth County Court Isaac Robinson sued Ebenezer Curtis of Plymouth, chairmaker, for debt.

Children (CURTIS) b. Plymouth:

135   i   JACOB[5] b. 11 Oct. 1710
      ii   CALEB b. 15 Aug. 1712; d. Plymouth 19 Nov. 1729; in 18th yr.
136   iii   MARY b. 21 Dec. 1714
137   iv   SARAH b. 19 Aug. 1717

References: MD 7:208(b. 4 ch. by ea. wife; d. Caleb); 12:145-8(Helkiah Tinkham will, receipt); 14:36(m.), 38(2nd m.).   (PLYMOUTH) ANC LANDMARKS 2:76. (PLYMOUTH) BURIAL HILL pp. 10(d. Mary), 15(d. Caleb). PLYMOUTH TOWN RECS 3:425 (1743 members 3rd Ply. Ch include Eben Curtis, Jacob Curtis). PLYMOUTH CO CT RECS 6:333. PLYMOUTH CH RECS 1:296(Ebenezer dismissed to Third Church). PLYMOUTH VR pp. 45(b. ch.; b. ch. by Martha; d. Caleb), 89(m.), 91(his 2nd m.). Plymouth Co. PR 6:81(Helkiah Tinkham).

NOTE: The EBENEZER CURTIS who d. Hanover 6 March 1753 with wife Elizabeth does not appear to be the same man.

33   JOHN TINKHAM[4] (Helkiah[3], Mary[2] Brown, Peter[1])   b. Plymouth 27 March 1689; d. Kingston 12 May 1730.

He m. Plymouth 30 Dec. 1714 ANN GRAY, b. Plymouth 5

Aug. 1691; d. Kingston 6 Sept. 1730 ae 39y 1m; dau. of John and
Joanna (Morton) Gray, a descendant of Pilgrim James Chilton.
The will of John Gray of Kingston dated 23 Sept. 1728 names
son-in-law John Tincom and dau. Anne Tincom.

On 31 July 1730 Mr. Samuel Gray of Kingston was appointed
administrator of the estate of John Tinkham of Kingston.

Guardians were appointed for the children of John
Tinkham, late of Plymouth dec., as follows: On 1 Jan. 1730/1
Samuel Gray of Kingston for Joseph, Edward, Ephraim, John and
Ann Tinkham, all under 14; on 15 Feb. 1738 Ebenezer Fuller for
Joseph and Anna Tinkham; and on 24 Nov. 1738 Ebenezer Cobb
of Kingston for Ephraim, Edward, and John Tinkham.

Children (TINKHAM) first two b. Plymouth; rest Kingston:

	i	MARY[5] b. 25 June 1718; d. Kingston 25 July 1730 ae 12y 1m
138	ii	EDWARD b. 2 Feb. 1719/20
139	iii	JOHN b. 1721 (based on age at d.)
140	iv	EPHRAIM b. 25 March 1724
141	v	ANN b. 6 Aug. 1726
142	vi	JOSEPH b. 14 May 1728

References: MD 7:221-2(d. wife Anne, Mary); 13:33(b. Mary,
        Edward); 14:37(m.); 21:62-4(John Gray will). VR
KINGSTON pp. 145(b. last 3 ch.), 386(d. John, Ann). Plymouth
Co. PR 5:745, #20876(John Tinkham). MF 15:117-8. PLYMOUTH
VR pp. 5(b. Ann), 60(b. 1st 2 ch.), 90(m.).

34 JACOB TINKHAM[4] (Helkiah[3], Mary[2] Brown, Peter[1]) b.
Plymouth 15 June 1691; d. Mendon 18 July 1733.

He m. (1) Plymouth 16 Nov. 1721 HANNAH COBB, b.
Plymouth 27 Feb. 1699; d. there bet. 28 Feb. 1724 and 18 Nov.
1725; dau. of Ebenezer and Mercy (Holmes) Cobb. Distribution of
the estate of Ebenezer Cobb of Plymouth on 6 Aug. 1753 names
"Jacob Tinkham only child of Hannah Tinkham, one of the
daughters of said deceased."

He m. (2) Plymouth 18 Nov. 1725 JUDETH HUNT of
Plymouth; d. prob. Amenia, Dutchess Co. NY bef. 19 April 1800
when Jacob Benson made his will. She m. (2) Smithfield RI 8 Nov.

1736 Jacob Benson by whom she had Jacob, Joseph, William, John, Samuel, and prob. some daus.

On 15 Sept. 1730 Jacob Tinkcom of Plymouth, cordwainer, signed and acknowledged a deed to Joshua Holmes of Plymouth of "the house lot and house wherein I now dwell."

Widow Judith Tincomb was appointed administratrix of the estate of her husband Jacob Tincomb late of Mendon dec. on 14 Aug. 1733. Guardians were appointed for the children of Jacob Tinkham late of Mendon husbandman as follows; Judith Tincomb widow and Samuel Thompson husbandman both of Mendon for Hannah Tincomb aged about 4 years and Lydia Tincomb aged about 2 years on 14 Aug. 1734; and the next day for Jacob Tincomb aged about 10 years; Consider Howland posted bond in Plymouth as guardian for Jacob Tincomb on 2 June 1740.

On 12 Oct. 1753 Jacob Tinkham signed a receipt for his share of his grandfather Ebenezer Cobb's estate.

No Worcester Co. PR for Hannah or Lydia Tinkham or Jacob or Judith Benson.

Children (TINKHAM) b. Plymouth to Jacob and Hannah:

   i   MARCY[5] b. 27 Sept. 1722; d. 20 April 1724
143 ii   JACOB b. 28 Feb. 1723/4

Children (TINKHAM) b. Plymouth and Mendon to Jacob and Judith:

  iii   HANNAH bp. 24 May 1730; living 14 Aug. 1734
   iv   LYDIA b. ca. 1732; bp. Uxbridge 2 Sept. 1733; living 14 Aug. 1734

References: MD 13:115(b.&d. Marcy; b. Jacob); 14:39(1st m.), 71(2nd m.); 18:124(2nd m. int.), 143(int. 1st m.); 39:32-3(prob. rec.). PLYMOUTH CH RECS 1:238(Judeth joins church), 240(bp. Hannah). COBB FAM pp. 49, 55, 59. Plymouth Co. LR 26:139(Jacob Tinkham). Plymouth Co. PR #20865(Jacob Tinkham); #4498, 13:91(Ebenezer Cobb). Worcester Co. PR #59351 -#59354(Tinkham gdns.). JACOB BENSON, PIONEER AND HIS DESCENDANTS, Arthur T. Benson, Poughkeepsie NY 1915, pp. 15-7. RI VR Smithfield 3:6:18(2nd m. Judith). PLYMOUTH VR

pp. 15(b. Hannah), 68(b. 1st 2 ch.), 92(1st m.), 94(2nd m.). VR
UXBRIDGE p. 168(bp. Lydia).

NOTE: No m. of daus. Hannah or Lydia at Grafton, Hopkinton,
Sutton, Milford, or Douglas.

35   CALEB TINKHAM[4] (Helkiah[3], Mary[2] Brown, Peter[1])   b.
Plymouth 12 Oct. 1693; d. there bef. 14 May 1748.
    He m. Plymouth 20 Oct. 1724 MERCY HOLMES, b. Plymouth
26 Dec. 1701; d. there bet. 2 June 1762 and 29 Oct. 1765; dau. of
Nathaniel and Eleanor (Baker) Holmes. The will of Nathaniel
Holmes dated 1734 (no day or month) names wife Eleanor and
dau. Mercy Tinkham. On 14 May 1748 Mercy Tinkham, widow,
Patience Holmes and Meletiah Holmes, all of Plymouth, sold land
in Plymouth with Eleanor Holmes quitclaiming.   On 2 June 1762
Eleanor Holmes, widow of Nathaniel of Plympton; and Mercy
Tinkham, widow of Caleb; and others, children and heirs of
Nathaniel Holmes dec., all of Plymouth, sold land.
    On 26 Oct. 1765 Joseph Rider of Plymouth was appointed to
administer the estate of Caleb Tinkham of Plymouth. Division of
the real estate of Caleb Tinkham late of Plymouth was made 29
Oct. 1765 among his five children: Mercy Tinkham, Patience
Tinkham, Fear Waterman, representatives of Sarah Smith, and
Nelle Bryant.
    Helkiah Tinkham, mariner, and wife Mercy, Patience
Tinkham, spinster, Samuel Bryant, husbandman, and wife Eleanor
all of Plymouth children and grandchildren of Nathaniel Holmes,
son of John Holmes, sold land 17 Dec. 1792; ack. by Samuel and
Eleanor 14 March 1793 and by Patience 22 July 1793.
    No Plymouth Co. PR for Mercy Tinkham.

    Children (TINKHAM) b. Plymouth:

    144   i   MARCY[5] b. 8 May 1726
           ii   PATIENCE b. 16 July 1729; living unm. 27 Dec.
                 1799 when she deeded land to her nieces. No PR.
    145   iii   FEAR b. 5 Nov. 1731
    146   iv   SARAH b. 28 Dec. 1733
           v   NATHANIEL b. 12 Aug. 1736; d. bef. 29 Oct. 1765.
                 No Plymouth Co. PR or LR for Nathaniel.

    vi   CALEB b. 20 March 1738; d. bef. 29 Oct. 1765*.
          No PR.
147 vii   ELEANOR (or NELLIE) b. ca. 1740

References: MD 2:165(b. Mercy Holmes); 14:70(m.); 15:113-4(b.
        first 6 ch.). Plymouth Co. PR 10:84, 336-8 (Nath.
Holmes); 17:152; 19:300, 301(Caleb Tinkham). Plymouth Co. LR
39:132(widow Mercy Tinkham, etc.); 47:224(widow Mercy
Tinkham, etc.); 73:239(Helkiah Tinkham, etc.); 88:125 (Patience
Tinkham). PLYMOUTH VR pp.21(b. Mercy), 93(m.), 121(b. 1st 6
ch.).

*It is unlikely that the Caleb Tinkham who m. Middleboro 1764
Deborah Babbitt is the son of Caleb and Mercy (Holmes)
Tinkham, because he did not share in the 1765 division of his
father's estate. There is no deed from Caleb to son Caleb. The
Mayflower Society has accepted members on this purported line
bet. 1921 and 1981 (see #38).

36   EBENEZER TINKHAM[4] (Helkiah[3], Mary[2] Brown, Peter[1])
b. Plymouth 3 May 1698; living 24 Dec. 1764 when he was warned
from Plymouth.
     He m. (1) Plymton 20 July 1732 MARY BONNEY, b.
Plympton 9 May 1704; d. Plymouth 1736; dau. of William and
Mehitable (King) Bonney. On 19 Sept. 1748, division of the real
estate of William Boney late of Plimton dec., gave one-third to
Sarah Tinkham granddau. of dec. who was representative to Mary
Tinkham, except for dower to widow Mehitable Boney.
     He m. (2) Plymouth 9 Nov. 1736 JANE PRATT, prob. the one
b. Plympton 20 March 1710/11 to Eleazer and Hannah (Kennedy)
Pratt; d. Plymouth 22 Feb. 1788 "near 80."
     On 21 Nov. 1747 William Boney of Plimton, husbandman,
gave his bond as guardian to Sarah Tinkham minor dau. of
Ebenezer Tinkham, with Ebenezer himself, seafaring man, signing
as surety. Two days later Sarah named "my uncle Wm. Bonney of
Plimton" to handle her part of the inheritance from "my
grandfather Wm. Bonney late of Plimton deceased."
     On 3 Oct. 1763 constables were to warn out Jane, wife of
Ebenezer Tinkham of Liverpool NS and her three daus. who came
to Plymouth in Sept. and on 24 Dec. 1764 Ebenezer Tinkham, who

came into Plymouth from Nova Scotia Nov. last was warned out.

According to the Plymouth Church records in 1770, Jane Tinkham was a member of the Middleboro Church, and therefore must be the Jane Pratt who joined the Middleboro Church 17 March 1734.

There are no Plymouth Co. probates for Ebenezer or Jane Tinkham. No James or Sarah Tinkham Plymouth Co. LR 1760-1781.

Children (TINKHAM) b. Plymouth, two by first wife, rest by Jane:

147A   i   SARAH[5] b. 22 Nov. 1733; living 19 Sept. 1744(div. of est. of grandfather William Bonney).
        ii   EBENEZER b. 20 Feb. 1735/6; d.y.
        iii MARY b. 7 Oct. 1737; d. Plymouth 18 April 1739 [sic]
148   iv   MARY b. 9 April 1739 [sic]
        v   EBENEZER b. 14 April 1741
        vi   JAMES b. 19 Jan. 1743/4
149 vii   PHEBE b. 12 July 1746
150 viii   SUSANNAH b. 15 Sept. 1748
151   ix   PRISCILLA b. 26 July 1755

References: MD 14:157(2nd m.); 15:113(b. ch.; d. Mary); 18:123(1st m. int.). VR PLYMPTON pp. 27(b. Mary), 157(b. Jane), 412(1st m.). PLYMOUTH CH RECS 1:335-6(1770 rec. Her conduct so contrary to Gospel they want her to withdraw from Ordinance), 416(d. Jane), 441(bp. both daus. Mary). MIDDLEBORO BY WESTON pp. 655-6. Plymouth Co. PR #20906(Sarah Tinkham). PLYMOUTH CO CT RECS 3:118, 207. PLYMOUTH VR pp. 99(2nd m.), 120(b. ch.; d. dau. Mary).

37   RUTH TINKHAM[4] (Helkiah[3], Mary[2] Brown, Peter[1])   b. Plymouth 13 Feb. 1701; d. Middleboro 7 Oct. 1726 in 25th yr.

She m. int. Plymouth 28 July 1722* EBENEZER COBB, b. Plymouth 22 March 1694; d. Middleboro 8 Dec. 1801, "ae 107y 8m 6d"; son of Ebenezer and Marcy (Holmes) Cobb. He m. (2) Plymouth 14 Dec. 1727 Lydia Stephens by whom he had Ruth, Lydia, John, Mercy, Sarah, William, Meletiah, Seth, and Hannah.

He m. (3) Marshfield 14 Dec. 1747 Joanna Williamson.

In Dec. 1743 Ebenezer Cobb, minor son of Ebenezer Cobb of Kingston sued, by his father, Peter Tinkham (Plymouth Marriner) over partition of 7 acres and a dwelling house in Plymouth, part of the real estate that was lately Helkiah Tinkham's late of Plymouth who was grandfather to the said minor.

The will of Ebenezer Cobb of Kingston, dated 4 Sept. 1793, proved 17 Dec. 1801, names "the children of my late son Ebenezer."

Children (COBB):

152   i   EBENEZER[5] b. Plymouth 4 March 1723/4
      ii   RUTH b. Middleboro 23 Sept. 1726; n.f.r. Prob. d.y. as 1st child by 2nd m. also named Ruth.

References: MD 2:19(b. Ebenezer Sr); 5:37(d. Ruth); 6:229(b. dau. Ruth); 7:25(d. Ebenezer); 13:116(b. Ruth, Lydia by 2nd wife); 14:39(1st m.), 72; 18:144(1st m. int.). COBB FAM 1:85-9. Plymouth Co. PR #4500(Ebenezer Cobb). VR KINGSTON p. 193(3rd m.). PLYMOUTH CO CT RECS 6:386. MARSHFIELD VR p. 161(3rd m.). MIDDLEBORO DEATHS pp. 39(d. Ruth), 40(d. Ebenezer). MIDDLEBORO VR 1:29(d. Ruth), 37(b. dau. Ruth). PLYMOUTH VR pp. 15(b. Ebenezer), 69(b. son Ebenezer), 91(m.), 95(his 2nd m.), 178(int.).

*The mar. record says they m. 8 1722, with the month omitted.

38   PETER TINKHAM[4] (Helkiah[3], Mary[2] Brown, Peter[1]) b. Plymouth 1 April 1706; perhaps he d. Middleboro Nov. 1783.

He m. Kingston 6 Jan. 1736 MARY BENNETT, b. Middleboro 5 Nov. 1708; living there 19 March 1765; dau. of Joseph and Joanna (Perry) Bennett. On 26 July 1737 the estate of Joseph Bennet late of Middleboro dec. was set off to the widow Joanna and children including dau. Mary Tinkcum wife of Peter of Plymouth, who was to have a share in the 16 Shilling Purchase.

In 1742, day and month not given, Peter Tinkham of Plymouth and wife Mary and others sold land in Middleboro reserving to their mother Joanna Bennett her rights, acknowledging the deed 12 Sept. 1745. On 24 Jan. 1750, acknowledged same day, Peter Tinkham of Plymouth, seafaring man, sold land in Plymouth with wife Mary releasing her dower. On 19 March 1765 Peter Tinkham of Middleboro, mariner, signed and acknowledged a deed to Caleb Tinkham of land in the 16 Shilling Purchase, with wife Mary giving up her dower.

No Plymouth Co. LR for Jacob or Arthur Tinkham, nor PR for Peter Tinkham.

Children (TINKHAM) b. Plymouth:

	i	JACOB[5] b. 29 May 1738; prob. d.y.
153	ii	CALEB b. ca. 1739 (based on age at d.)
	iii	ARTHUR b. 7 June 1742; prob. d.y.
	iv	HILKIAH b. ca. 1750; d. Middleboro 25 Dec. 1773 ae 23 yrs. No PR.

References: MD 2:203(b. Mary); 12:224(b. Jacob, Arthur). VR KINGSTON p. 291(m). NEHGR 115:95. Plymouth Co. PR #1826 (Joseph Bennet). MIDDLEBORO DEATHS p. 204(d. Hilkiah). Plymouth Co. LR 37:173; 41:44; 57:44(Peter Tinkham). MIDDLEBORO VR 1:14(b. Mary). PLYMOUTH VR p. 56(b. Jacob, Arthur). Middleboro Morgality Recs. p. 78(d. Peter).

NOTE: Caleb is probably a son of Peter. While the deed does not call him son, it is apparently a father selling land to a son. Caleb named his first child Arthur, which could be for his brother. These are the only cases of this name in the early Tinkham generations. See the comments under #35.

39   JOHN TOMSON[4] (Mary[3] Tinkham, Mary[2] Brown, Peter[1]) b. Middleboro 9 Aug. 1682; d. Halifax bet. 11 May 1757 and 5 July 1757.

He m. Middleboro 24 Oct. 1723 ELIZABETH THOMAS, b. Middleboro 19 Nov. 1690; d. Aug. 1776; dau. of Jeremiah and Lydia (Howland) Thomas, a descendant of Pilgrim John Howland. The will of Jeremiah Thomas of Middleboro dated 29 Sept. 1735 names wife Mary (2nd wife); dau. Elizabeth Tomson and other children.

The will of John Thomson of Halifax dated 11 May 1757, proved 5 July 1757, mentions wife Elizabeth; son John; daus.

Lydia Tomson and Elizabeth Fuller.
No Plymouth Co. PR for Elizabeth Tomson.

Children (TOMSON) b. Plympton:

154   i   JOHN⁵ b. 18 Feb. 1724/5
155   ii   ELIZABETH b. 7 Aug. 1726
156 iii   LYDIA b. 13 Aug. 1730

References: MD 2:107(b. Eliz. Thomas); 4:72(m.). VR PLYMPTON
          p. 215(b. ch.). THOMAS GEN p. 8(d. & anc.
Elizabeth).   Plymouth   Co.   PR   7:267(Jeremiah   Thomas);
14:312(John   Tomson).   MIDDLEBORO   VR   1:10(b.   Eliz.).
MIDDLEBORO BY WESTON p. 652(d. Elizabeth).

40 EPHRAIM TOMSON⁴ (Mary Tinkham³, Mary² Brown,
Peter¹) b. Middleboro 16 Oct. 1683; d. Halifax 13 Nov. 1744 in
62nd yr.
     He m. Middleboro 6 Nov. 1734 JOANNA THOMAS, b.
Middleboro 28 Feb. 1707/8; d. Ashford CT 9 March 1795 in 89th
yr.; dau. of Jonathan and Mary (Steward) Thomas. She m. (2)
Halifax 23 Oct. 1745 Joseph Works of Ashford CT.
     On 6 Dec. 1744 Benjamin Weston of Plimpton posted bond as
administrator of the estate of Ephraim Tomson, late of Halifax
dec. Settlement of Ephraim's estate on 15 May 1746 mentions an
agreement by Joseph Works and wife Joanna with Ephraim's
surviving brothers and sisters and the legal representatives of
Shubal Tomson dec. (who was also their brother): John Tomson Sr.;
Thomas Tomson of Halifax; John Tomson of Middleboro and
Thomas Tomson of Bridgewater, sons of Shubal; Martha Tomson;
Sarah Tomson; Francis Tomson, dec.; Jacob Tomson.

Children (TOMSON) b. Halifax:

     i   dau.⁵ d. 5 Dec. 1735
    ii   JOANNA b. 23 July 1738; d. Halifax 17 Dec. 1744
          in 7th yr.
   iii   EPHRAIM b. 8 April 1742; d. in April 1742 ae 21
          days

iv   EPHRAIM b. 8 May 1744; d. 25 May 1744 ae 14
      days

References: MD 2:43(her par. m.), 202(b. Joanna Thomas); 3:30(d.
Ephraim Tomson Sr., ch. Joanna, 2nd ch. Ephraim);
10:103(d. dau., 1st Ephraim); 13:251(1st m.); 14:6 (d. Ephraim Sr.,
2nd Ephraim ch.), 7(d. ch. Joanna); 27:33 (Joanna, wife of
Ephraim Tomson adm. Halifax Church 29 Aug. 1742). HALIFAX
VR pp. 1(d. Ephraim & 3 ch.), 33(2nd m.), 42(b. ch.). Ashford CT
VR 4:74(d. Joanna). Plymouth Co. PR #20546, 10:160(Ephraim
Tomson). THOMAS GEN p. 10. MIDDLEBORO VR 1:14 (b.
Joanna), 61(m.).

41 SHUBAEL TOMSON[4] (Mary Tinkham[3], Mary[2] Brown,
Peter[1]) b. Middleboro 11 April 1686; d. there 7 July 1733 in 48th
yr.
      He m. Middleboro 10 Dec. 1713 SUSANNA PARLOUR (or
PARLOW) b. ca. 1688; d. Middleboro 9 June 1734 in 47th yr.; dau.
of Thomas and Elizabeth (Liscomb) Parlour. Division of Eliza
Lewis's dower from the estate of her first husband Thomas
Parlow Sr., late of Middleboro, made among his children 8 July
1746 mentions legal representatives of Susanna Thomson dec.
      Settlement of the estate of Shubal Tomson late of
Middleboro dec., on 18 March 1733/4, names widow Susanna; dau.
Mary Tomson; sons Thomas, John and Shubael, and eldest son
Isaac Tomson.
      On 23 Dec. 1734 the estate of Susanna Tomson of
Middleborough, widow of Shubael Tomson, was divided among
the 3 surviving children.

      Children (TOMSON) b. Middleboro:

      i   ISAAC[5] b. 24 Sept. 1714; d. Middleboro 30 April
            1740 in 26th yr. Order to divide the estate of Isaac
            Tomson was signed 2 June 1740, half to go to John
            Tomson & half to Thomas Tomson "brethren of sd.
            deceased."
      ii   SHUBAEL b. 27 March 1716; d. Middleboro 18
            June 1734 in 19th yr.
157 iii   JOHN b. 11 June 1717

    iv   MARY b. 24 Sept. 1719; d. Middleboro 23 June
          1734 in 15th yr.
158 v   THOMAS b. 28 July 1721

References: MD 2:158(m.); 3:86(b. 1st 3 ch.); 6:227(b. last 2 ch.);
            13:5(d. Susanna, ch. Shubael, Mary, John); 14:218(d.
Isaac), 220(d. Shubael, ch. Shubael, Susanna). Plymouth Co. PR
10:322(Eliza Lewis); #20642(Shubael Tomson); #20644(Susanna
Tomson); 8:191-2, 318(Isaac Tomson). TORREY'S MARRIAGES
p. 560. MIDDLEBORO VR 1:11(m.), 17(b. 1st 3 ch.), 35(b. Mary,
Thomas), 58(d. Shubael, Susanna, son Shubael, Mary).

42   THOMAS TOMSON[4] (Mary Tinkham[3], Mary[2] Brown, Peter[1])
b. Middleboro 29 July 1688; d. prob. Halifax bet. 7 July 1759 and
7 April 1760.
     He m. Middleboro 25 April 1732 MARTHA SOULE, b.
Middleboro 11 April 1702; d. there 18 March 1772 in 70th yr.; dau.
of John and Martha (Tinkham) Soule, a descendant of Pilgrims
Peter Brown, Francis Cooke and George Soule. The will of John
Soule dated 1 March 1743 names wife Martha and dau. Martha
Thomson (see #72).
     The will of Thomas Thompson of Halifax, dated 7 July 1759,
proved 7 April 1760, names wife Martha; sons Peter, Nathan,
Francis, and James.

     Children (TOMSON) first b. Middleboro, rest Halifax:

159   i   PETER[5] b. 8 Oct. 1733
160   ii   FRANCIS b. 15 March 1734/5
161   iii   NATHAN b. 10 Dec. 1736
162   iv   JAMES b. 11 Nov. 1739
      v   THOMAS b. 1 June 1743; d. Halifax 16 Sept. 1747

References: MD 2:105(b. Martha); 3:31(d. Thomas Jr.); 12:66 (d.
            Martha), 230(b. Peter); 13:249(m.). HALIFAX VR
pp. 2(d. son Thomas), 46(b. last 4 ch.). MIDDLEBORO DEATHS
p. 195(d. Martha). Plymouth Co. PR 15:479(Thomas Tomson);
#18813(John Soule). MF 3:55. MIDDLEBORO VR 1:8(b. Martha),
52(b. Peter), 60(m.).

43   JACOB TOMSON[4] (Mary Tinkham[3], Mary[2] Brown, Peter[1]) b.
Middleboro 24 June 1703; d. Halifax 17 Feb. 1750/1 in 48th yr.

He m. Bridgewater 4 Sept. 1735 MARY HOWARD (or
HAYWARD), b. Bridgewater 24 July 1718; d. Halifax 18 March
1769 in 44th yr. [sic]*; dau. of Joseph and Sarah (Crossman)
Hayward.

The will of Jacob Tomson of Halifax dated 5 Jan. 1750,
proved 1 April 1751, gave his homestead to sons Jacob and
Ebenezer; wife Mary to have use until son Jacob arrives at age of
21; sons Nathaniel, Ephraim and Daniel were given other land.
On 15 Oct. 1762 the court ordered the division of the cedar swamp
that had been set off to Jacob, Ebenezer, and Nathaniel, the three
sons of Jacob Tomson of Halifax dec., with Nathaniel's share
going to his heirs.

On 15 Oct. 1762 Ebenezer Tomson of Halifax was appointed
guardian of Ephraim and Daniel Tomson, sons of Jacob Tomson
of Halifax. No Plymouth Co. PR for Mary Tomson.

Children (TOMSON) b. Halifax:

163	i	JACOB[5] b. 9 July 1736
164	ii	EBENEZER b. 14 Oct. 1737
	iii	NATHANIEL b. 23 July 1740; d. bef. 6 April 1761. On 6 April 1761 Jacob Tomson of Halifax was appointed administrator of the estate of Nathaniel Tomson. The estate of Nathaniel Tomson of Halifax, husbandman, was divided 16 Oct. 1762 with equal shares to [his bros.] Jacob, Ebenezer, Ephraim, and Daniel Tomson.
	iv	MARY b. 7 Sept. 1743; d. Halifax 21 Aug. 1747
	v	MARTHA b. 1 Jan. 1745/6; d. Halifax 7 Sept. 1747
165	vi	EPHRAIM b. 1 Aug. 1748
166	vii	DANIEL b. 24 Oct. 1750

References: MD 14:7(d. Jacob), 8(b. Mary, Martha; d. Martha, 2
Marys). VR BRIDGEWATER 1:151(b. Mary); 2:368
(m.). HALIFAX VR pp. 2 (d. dau. Mary; Martha), 3(d. Jacob),
43(b. 1st 4 ch.), 51(b. last 3 ch.). Plymouth Co. PR 12:296-9;
16:415(Jacob Tompson); 16:416; 17:17(Nath. Tomson); 18:106,
109(gdn.).

*The gravestone apparently should read 18 March 1761. She apparently d. bef. her son Nathaniel.

44 JOHN TINKHAM[4] (John[3], Mary[2] Brown, Peter[1]) b. prob. Dartmouth bef. 1720; d. bef. 3 May 1785, apparently in that part of Dartmouth which was incorporated as New Bedford two years after his death.

He m. Dartmouth 13 May 1741 MARY ALLEN, b. Dartmouth 9 July 1718; d. bet. 4 Oct. 1785 and 6 May 1794; dau. of William Allen. The will of William Allen of Dartmouth, yeoman, dated 6 Dec. 1752 names wife Elizabeth and dau. Mary Tinkham.

On 3 May 1785 dower was ordered set off to "the widow" from the estate of John Tincom, late of Dartmouth dec. intestate. On 4 Oct. 1785 John Tinkham and Ephraim Tripp, administrators of the estate, swore to the inventory. Division of the part of the estate of John Tincom, late of New Bedford, dec., which had been set off to the widow Mary Tincom, who is dec., was ordered 6 May 1794 among: Mary Tripp; Marmeduke Tinckham; Huldah Tinckham; Hannah Mirick, in right of her dec. mother; Almy Tripp; Susanna Tinckam; eldest son John Tinckham; Hannah Paul; Samuel and William Waggoners in the right of their dec. mother; and the heirs of Abigail Tinckham.

An indenture of 22 April 1786 bet. John Tinkcom; Ephraim Tripp, cooper, in right of wife Ame; Thomas Tripp, cooper, in right of wife Mary; Deborah Waggoner, widow; Huldah Tinkcom, seamster; Susanna Tinkcom, seamster; Marmaduke Tinkcom, mariner; Abigail Tinkcom seamster, all of Dartmouth; and Barbra Mirick, widow, and Joseph Paul, yeoman, in right of wife Hannah of Berkley heirs of father John Tinkcom of Dartmouth agreed to divide the land into 10 shares.

Children (TINKHAM) b. Dartmouth:

	i	ELIZABETH[5] b. 17 July 1741; d. bef. 22 April 1786; unm. (not in indenture)
167	ii	JOHN b. 10 May 1743
168	iii	AMY (or ALMY) b. 15 Sept. 1745
169	iv	MARY b. 4 Sept. 1747
170	v	BARBARA b. 14 July 1749
171	vi	DEBORAH b. 22 May 1751

vii   ABIGAIL d. unm. bef. 1 Oct. 1799 when the real
       estate of Abigail Tinkham, late of New Bedford,
       spinster, dec. intestate, was divided among oldest
       brother John Tinkham; sister Susanna Tinkham;
       Samuel & William Waggoners, sons and only heirs
       of a dec. sister; brother Marmaduke Tinkham;
       sisters Ame Tripp wife of Ephraim and Hannah
       Paul wife of Joseph of Berkley; sister Huldah
       Townsend wife of Gilbert of Berkley; Mary Tripp
       wife of Thomas; Hannah Tripp wife of John and
       only heir of sister Barbary Mirick.

172 viii   HANNAH b. 3 Dec. 1754
173 ix   MARMADUKE
174 x   HULDAH b. ca. 1758 (based on age at d.)
175 xi   SUSANNA

References: VR DARTMOUTH 1:23(b. Mary), 276-7(b. 7 ch.).
           Bristol Co. PR 17:126(Wm. Allen); 28:476;
29:36(John Tinkham); 35:20(Mary Tinkham); 36:431(Abigail
Tinkham). Bristol Co. LR 74:264(indenture). Tinkham ms. p.
88(m.).

45   MARY TINKHAM[4], John[3], Mary[2] Brown, Peter[1]) b. prob.
Dartmouth bef. 1721; d. after 23 May 1785.

       She m. Dartmouth 15 Sept. 1739 JOSEPH TABER, b.
Dartmouth 15 Feb. 1710; d. bet. 25 Jan. 1772 and 29 June 1772; son
of Joseph and Elizabeth (Spooner) Taber, a descendant of Pilgrim
Francis Cooke.

       The will of Joseph Taber of Dartmouth, yeoman, dated 25
Jan. 1772, presented 29 June 1772, names wife Mary; son William
to be executor and to have the farm; his mother-in-law
[step-mother] Lydia Taber; daus. Elizabeth Taber and Jemima
Taber, unm.; and daus. Rubee Brightman and Hannah Eldridge.

       The will of Mary Taber, widow of Joseph Taber of
Dartmouth, dated 23 5th month 1785, names daus. Elizabeth Hart,
Jemima Taber, Rube Brightman, and Hanna Eldredge; son William
Taber; and son-in-law Edward Eldredge.

       Children (TABER) b. Dartmouth:

176	i	WILLIAM[5] b. 24 Feb. 1741
177	ii	ELIZABETH b. 5 Feb. 1743
178	iii	RUBE (dau.) b. 22 March 1745/6
179	iv	HANNAH b. 30 Aug. 1750
180	v	JEMIMA b. 17 Dec. 1753

References: VR DARTMOUTH 1:268-72(b. Joseph; b. ch.); 2:487 (m.). TABER DESC p. 12. SPOONER DESC p. 40. Bristol Co. PR 22:220(Joseph Taber). MF 12:537. MD 43:173-4 (Mary's will).

46 MARTHA TINKHAM[4] (John[3], Mary[2] Brown, Peter[1]) b. Dartmouth 19 May 1722; d. after 18 Oct. 1798 (deed).

She m. Dartmouth 21 Feb. 1742/3 JOSEPH ELLIS of Harwich, b. ca. 1709; d. bet. 29 June 1792 and 1 Aug. 1795; son of John and Martha (Severence) Ellis.

On 25 June 1744 Joseph Ellis of Harwich and wife Martha sold land in Dartmouth "that fell to said Martha from her father John Tinkum, late of Dartmouth, deceased." Joseph Ellis and wife and three children were warned out of Dartmouth in June 1754. On 9 May 1758 Joseph Ellis of Dartmouth, cordwainer, and wife Martha sold land in Dartmouth "with consent of Sarah Tinkom, mother of Martha Ellis." All acknowledged their signatures 10 April 1759. Seth, Luke, John, and Elijah Ellis, all of New Bedford, sons of Joseph Ellis, "having purchased of our father his homestead farm where he now liveth" divided the land on 15 April 1788, the division being "consented to by the said Joseph the father." Seth Ellis of New Bedford sold land there on 26 Feb. 1790 with Joseph Ellis of New Bedford "father of Seth" and his wife Martha giving up their rights, and all acknowledged the deed 10 April 1790.

On 29 June 1792 Joseph Ellis and son Seth Ellis sold to Samuel Sprague, Seth's part of the division of the family land. Martha signed by a mark. On 1 Aug. 1795 Martha Ellis quitclaimed land in New Bedford to Edward West. Seth and John Ellis were witnesses. On 18 Oct. 1798 Elijah Ellis sold land in New Bedford to Samuel Sprague. Martha Ellis, and Rebekah Ellis also signed the deed.

No Bristol Co. PR for Joseph or Martha Ellis.

Children (ELLIS): (Three children b. bef. the 1754 warning.)

      i   SETH[5] b. ca. 1745; living New Bedford 1810 (census); d. bef. 1 May 1812, apparently unm. The inventory of the estate of Seth Ellis was dated 1 May 1812. On 10 Dec. 1812 Manasa Kempton, administrator of the estate of Seth Ellis, sold his land to Thankful Ellis spinster of New Haven.

      ii   JOHN b. bef. 1755; prob. d. unm. On 3 Aug. 1802, ack. same day, John Ellis of New Bedford, laborer, sold to Thankful Ellis of New Bedford, spinster, his share of his father's homestead.

181 iii ELIJAH b. aft. 1755

182 iv LUKE b. aft. 1755

183 v   THANKFUL b. ca. 1763 (based on age at death)*

References: VR DARTMOUTH 2:179(m.). HARWICH VR p. 79(int.). NEHGR 120:104-6; 121:41-42. Bristol Co. LR 53:383 (Joseph Ellis); 62:263(Jos. Ellis); 68:416(Luke Ellis); 69:136(Seth Ellis); 71:508(Joseph Ellis); 74:174(Martha Ellis); 77:261(Elijah Ellis); 78:309(Seth, Luke, John, Elijah Ellis); 81:309(John Ellis). DAR PATRIOT INDEX p. 219. Bristol Co. Ct. Recs. Ct. of Sess. 1746-1777 p. 101. Bristol Co. PR 47:231; 116:511 (Seth Ellis).

*Her death certificate says she is dau. of Joseph Ellis.

47 PETER TINKHAM[4] (John[3], Mary[2] Brown, Peter[1]) b. Dartmouth 8 Feb. 1723/4; living Rochester 31 Dec. 1772 (deed).

    He m. Rochester 12 June 1746 EUNICE CLARK, who was living in Rochester 31 Dec. 1768 (deed).

    On 27 May 1754 Peter Tinkcom of Dartmouth, yeoman, sold land at Dartmouth that fell to him by lineal descent from his father John Tinkham, with wife Eunice giving up her dower. Peter acknowledged his signature 5 July 1754. On 1 Sept. 1746 Peter Tinkcom of Dartmouth sold the easterly part of his homestead in Dartmouth, bounded by land set off to Hezekiah and Martha Tinkham, acknowledging the deed at Bristol Co. on 8 Feb. 1755.

    On 18 Dec. 1767 Peter Tinkham of Rochester and wife

Eunice sold land in Rochester to Nathaniel Hammond. On 31 Dec.
1768 Peter Tinkham of Rochester, yeoman, sold land in Rochester
to Walter Cornell; signed by Peter and Eunice, but only ack. 1 Dec.
1769 by Peter.

On 31 Dec. 1772 Peter Tinkham of Rochester, yeoman, sold
land in Rochester to sons Charles and Ephraim Tinkham of
Rochester.

Peter Tinkham is probably the one who was 2-0-1 in the
1790 census of Rochester.

No Plymouth or Bristol Co. PR for Peter or Eunice Tinkham.

Children (TINKHAM) first four b. Dartmouth, last 3 b.
Rochester:

184	i	CHARLES[5] b. 16 June 1747
	ii	CLARK b. 7 Feb. 1748/9. Did he m. Boston 1 Dec. 1796 SARAH CHURCH and perhaps Charleston SC 16 April 1805 SUSAN FOFFLER?*
185	iii	EPHRAIM b. 27 Jan. 1750/1
186	iv	SARAH b. 14 Dec. 1753
	v	ELIZABETH b. ca. 1755; living New Bedford 31 May 1839 in 84th yr. when she swore to pension of brother Ephraim. Apparently the "Betsey" who d. New Bedford 12 Jan. 1847 ae 91.
187	vi	HEZEKIAH b. 8 Oct. 1759
188	vii	EUNICE
189	viii	REUBEN b. 6 May 1768

References: VR DARTMOUTH 1:276(b. 1st 3 ch.), 277(b. Sarah).
VR NEW BEDFORD 3:171(d. Eliz.). VR
ROCHESTER 1:293(b. Hezekiah), 294(b. Reuben); 2:304(m.).
Bristol Co. LR 47:567; 48:454(Peter Tinkham). Revolutionary War
Pension #W14024(Ephraim Tinkham). Plymouth Co. LR 54:10;
55:68; 56:257(Peter Tinkham). BOSTON VR 30:155 (m. Clark
Tinkham).

NOTE: CLARK GEN BY RADASCH p. 17 says Eunice dau. of
Andrew & Elizabeth m. 1755 Samuel Foster, so this is apparently
another Eunice.

NOTE: No proof found for daus. Abigail and Mary as stated in Tinkham ms. p. 97.

*There are no Bristol, Plymouth or Suffolk Co. PRs or LRs to prove this possibility. Both marriages are Baptist marriages. He was a sea captain. A Captain Clark Tinkham was bur. 27 March 1827 in Mazyckborough SC and the death of Clark Tinkham of Charleston SC was reported in the 11 April 1827 issue of the Columbian Centinel indicating a N.E. connection. If it is the same man, the SC census records indicate a number of children.

48   HEZEKIAH TINKHAM[4] (John[3], Mary[2] Brown, Peter[1]) b. Dartmouth 10 Nov. 1725; d. Smithfield RI 1809.

He m. int. Rehoboth 28 Dec. 1745 GRIZZELL WEST, b. Rehoboth 9 Oct. 1729; d. ca. 1810; dau. of John and Abigail (Wheeler) (Martin) West. No Bristol Co. PR for John West.

Hezekiah Tinkham was of Swansea 23 March 1746 when he bought a farm in Scituate RI. On 20 Sept. 1752 Hezekiah was of Glocester RI when he sold seven acres in Scituate with Grizzell signing off her rights. Hezekiah was a blacksmith.

Hezekiah Tinkham of Swanzey, laborer, sold his lot of salt marsh meadow in Dartmouth to Wm. Wood on 4 April 1747, signed by Hezekiah and the mark of Sarah Tinkham 21 March 1752. He ack. at Providence 11 Aug. 1752 with Grizzell releasing her dower at Providence.

Hezekiah Tinkham of Swanzey, husbandman, sold to Jabez Jenne of Dartmouth 14 acres of Dartmouth bounded by land of brother Peter Tinkham, as per division of estate of John Tinkham, father of said Hezekiah, dated 5 Dec. 1746; ack. 21 March 1752 at Providence.

Hezekiah Tinkcom 2m over 16, 4m under 16, 3 females over 16, 1 under 16 in 1774 census of Glocester RI.

In the 1782 census of Glocester Hezekiah Tincom "and John" had 4 males under 16; 2 females 16-22; 1 male 22-50; 1 female 22-50 and 1 male over 50.

Hezekiah Tinkham was 4-0-1 in the 1790 census of Glocester RI.

On 7 June 1796 Hezekiah Tinkom deeded land to Simon Smith with wife Grizle giving up dower.

Glocester town council records lists payments to Nehemiah

Tinkham, son of Hezekiah, for the support of his parents. The payments ended in 1810.

Children (TINKHAM) first b. Swansea, rest b. prob. Scituate RI or Glocester RI:

190 i ELIZABETH[5] b. 11 May 1746 (apparently from g.s.)
191 ii JOANNA b. ca. 1750 (based on age at death); she filed a deposition in 1836 for her sister Renew (Tinkham) Smith.
192 iii RENEW b. ca. 1751
193 iv JOHN
194 v SARAH b. ca. 1755
vi PETER b. 1757; d. 17 Nov. 1776 in Rev. Army
vii GRIZZELL
195 viii NEHEMIAH b. 1766
196 ix DANIEL b. Glocester RI 30 April 1767
197 x SAMUEL b. 1769 (based on age at death)
198 xi PHILIP

References: REHOBOTH VR pp. 381(m. her par.), 505(int.), 767 (b. Grizzell). Scituate RI LE 3:426; 4:283 (Hezekiah Tinkham). Tinkham MS p. 90. Bristol Co. LR 39:408; 48:456(Hezekiah Tinkham). Glocester RI LE 5:78(Hezekiah Tinkham). NEHGR 128:56(1782 census).

NOTE: Children are from Tinkham MS. The late Charles W. Farnham FASG investigated this family and concluded the children are valid.

49 BETHIA SNOW[4] (William[3], Rebecca[2] Brown, Peter[1]) b. Bridgewater 28 Sept. 1688; d. bef. 31 July 1747 (3rd m.).
    She m. Bridgewater 1 Feb. 1720/1 ELISHA HAYWARD, b. Bridgewater prob. in 1670's; d. there bet. 28 Sept. and 7 Nov. 1748; son of Nathaniel and Hannah (Willis) Hayward. He m. (1) Bridgewater 20 Jan. 1708/9 Experience Harvey by whom he had Elisha, Experience, Hannah, Tabatha and Abner. He m. (3) Bridgewater 31 July 1747 Abigail (Hathaway) Eddy, widow of Benjamin Eddy.

On 23 July 1734 Elisha Hayward of Bridgewater sold to Nathaniel Hayward of Bridgewater land of father Nathaniel Hayward.

The will of Elisha Hayward of Bridgewater dated 28 Sept. 1748, exhibited 7 Nov. 1748, states wife Abigail to have "household stuff and goods that was her own before marriage...excepting what was my second wifes." Also named are son Elisha; youngest son Ezra; son Abner; daus. Experience, wife of Benjamin Cortis; Hannah wife of Joseph Snow; Tabitha wife of Jacob Hayward, Jr.; Bethia wife of Thomas Willis; Naomy wife of Joseph Alger Jr.

On 27 March 1758 Elisha Hayward, yeoman, of Halifax; widow Experience Curtis of Halifax; Ezra Hayward, yeoman, Jacob Hayward, yeoman, and wife Tabitha, Joseph Alger, yeoman, and wife Naomi, all of Bridgewater; and Thomas Willis, yeoman, and wife Bethiah, of Taunton, sold land that Elisha Hayward gave to his dau. Hannah in his will to Samuel Dunbar.

Children (HAYWARD) b. Bridgewater:

199	i	BETHIAH[5] b. 7 April 1722
200	ii	NAOMI b. 25 March 1726
201	iii	EZRA b. 16 Nov. 1729

References: VR BRIDGEWATER 1:144(b. Bethiah), 147(b. Ezra), 152(b. Naomi); 2:166(m.), 170(his 1st & 3rd m.). BRIDGEWATER BY MITCHELL pp. 181, 183, 315. Plymouth Co. LR 33:183(Elisha Hayward); 45:29(Elisha Hayward, etc.). Plymouth Co. PR 12:40 (Elisha Hayward).

50 JAMES SNOW[4] (William[3], Rebecca[2] Brown, Peter[1]) b. Bridgewater 14 Oct. 1691; d. there 28 Aug. 1749 in 58th yr.

He m. Plympton 4 Nov. 1719 MEHITABLE KING, who d. bef. 5 Nov. 1747; dau. of Joseph and Elizabeth (Bryant) King. The will of Joseph King of Plympton signed 2 Sept. 1730 names daus. Mehitable Snow and Mercy Snow, and son-in-law James Snow.

Eleazer Snow and wife Mercy, both of Bridgewater, yeoman, sold to William Snow of Bridgewater 1/4 part of housing and lands in Halifax given to Mahitable Snow, wife of James Snow, by her father Joseph King, signed 5 Nov. 1747, ack. 8 Aug. 1749

by both.
      No Plymouth Co. PR for James Snow.
      Apparently no children.

References: VR EAST BRIDGEWATER p. 217(d. James). VR
         PLYMPTON p. 394(m.). Plymouth Co. PR
#12096(Joseph King). Plymouth Co. LR 40:97(Eleazer Snow).
TAG 30:12(King).

51 SUSANNA SNOW[4] (William[3], Rebecca[2] Brown, Peter[1]) b.
Bridgewater 27 Sept. 1694; d. bet. 1729 and 24 June 1731.
      She m. Bridgewater 25 Dec. 1717, ISRAEL ALGER, b.
Bridgewater 9 Sept. 1689; d. there 13 Nov. 1762; son of Israel and
Patience (Hayward) Alger. He m. (1) prob. Bridgewater ca. 1712
Alice Hayward who d. Bridgewater 30 Jan. 1715/6, by whom he
had dau. Patience "upon occasion was called Alice." He m. (3)
Bridgewater 24 June 1731 Rachel Wade, dau. of Thomas and
Elizabeth (Curtis) Wade.
      The settlement of the estate of William Snow on 22 Nov. 1726
names Susannah ye wife of Israel Alger.
      Israel Alger of Bridgewater, yeoman, sold to son Daniel of
Bridgewater land in Bridgewater and Easton where his son Israel
late of Bridgewater dec. dwelt - about 73 acres with dwelling
house and barn signed 17 Sept. 1755, ack. 21 March 1757. On the
same date he sold land in Bridgewater to son James Alger.
      No Plymouth Co. PR for Israel Alger.

      Children (ALGER) b. Bridgewater:

      202   i   ISRAEL[5] b. ca. 1725; bp. 24 Sept. 1727
      203   ii   DANIEL bp. W. Bridgewater 24 Sept. 1727
      204   iii   JAMES bp. W. Bridgewater 23 March 1728/9

References: MD 16:98(3rd m.), 185(m.); 22:48(William Snow estate).
            VR BRIDGEWATER 1:23(b. Israel); 2:23(m.; his 3rd
m.), 427(d. Israel). VR WEST BRIDGEWATER p. 12(bp. Daniel),
13(bp. Israel, James). BRIDGEWATER BY MITCHELL pp. 89,
315, 335. Plymouth Co. LR 47:90, 130(Israel Alger).

52   WILLIAM SNOW[4] (William[3], Rebecca[2] Brown, Peter[1]) b.
Bridgewater 14 Aug. 1697, apparently d. after 31 March 1774, as
his wife's death is recorded as "wife of."
      He m. Bridgewater 8 Nov. 1722 MARY WASHBURN, b.
Bridgewater 28 Oct. 1694; d. there 31 March 1774 in 79th yr.; dau.
of James and Mary (Bowden) Washburn, a descendant of Pilgrim
Francis Cooke. The will of James Washburn of Bridgewater,
yeoman, dated 14 Jan. 1747 names dau. Mary, wife of William
Snow.
      No Plymouth Co. PR for Wm. Snow.

      Children (SNOW) b. Bridgewater:

      205   i   WILLIAM[5] b. 10 Aug. 1723
      206   ii   SETH b. 7 Aug. 1725
      207   iii   JAMES b. 4 April 1729
      208   iv   MARY b. 12 Aug. 1731
            v   SUSANNA b. 2 March 1735/6
            vi   child d. 19 Nov. 1744

References: MD 16:52, 53(James Washburn will), 188(m.). VR
            BRIDGEWATER 1:301-4(b. ch.), 333(b. Mary);
2:350(m.), 559(d. William, Mary, child). BRIDGEWATER BY
MITCHELL p. 315. BRIDGEWATER EPITAPHS p. 121.
Plymouth Co. PR 11:236(James Washburn). MF 12:278-9.

53   ELEAZER SNOW[4] (William[3], Rebecca[2] Brown, Peter[1]) b.
Bridgewater 14 July 1701; d. there 18 Feb. 1796 ae 95.
      He m. Bridgewater 11 July 1728 MERCY KING, b. 16 Feb.
1707 (under Snow in Bwtr. VR); d. Bridgewater 29 March 1789;
dau. of Joseph and Elizabeth (Bryant) King. The will of Joseph
King of Plympton dated 2 Sept. 1730 names dau. Mercy Snow.
      Eleazer Snow, yeoman, and wife Mercy, both of Bridgewater,
sold to William Snow of Bridgewater 1/4 part of housing and
lands in Halifax given to Mehitable Snow wife of James Snow by
her father Joseph King, late of Halifax dec. and since the death
of their sister Mehitable did by heirship belong to them, signed 5
Nov. 1747, ack. 8 Aug. 1749 by both.
      Eleazer Snow of Bridgewater sold to son Eleazer Snow Jr. of
Bridgewater 50 acres there 1 July 1759.

No other Plymouth Co. LR from Eleazer or Mercy Snow to children.
No Plymouth Co. PR for Eleazer Snow.

Children (SNOW) b. Bridgewater:

209   i   BETTY[5] b. 9 March 1729
210   ii   REUBEN b. 16 April 1731
211   iii   ELEAZAR b. 30 Oct. 1734
212   iv   MERCY b. 22 March 1737
213   v   DANIEL b. 30 April 1742

References: MD 14:35(Mercy par.); 16:45(m.). VR BRIDGEWATER 1:300-3(b. ch.; b. wife Mercy); 2:558(d. Eleazer), 559(d. Mercy). BRIDGEWATER BY MITCHELL p. 315. Plymouth Co. LR 40:97; 54:128(Eleazer Snow). Plymouth Co. PR #12096(Joseph King). TAG 30:12(King). VR WEST BRIDGEWATER p. 170(m.).

54 JOHN SNOW[4] (William[3], Rebecca[2] Brown, Peter[1]) b. Bridgewater 14 Aug. 1704; d. there bef. 4 Sept. 1786.
He m. (1) Bridgewater 11 July 1731 HANNAH HAYWARD, b. Bridgewater 2 July 1711; d. there 1 Aug. 1756 ae 45; dau. of Elisha and Experience (Harvey) Hayward. The will of Elisha Haward of Bridgewater dated 28 Sept. 1748 names wife Abigail and dau. Hannah wife of John Snow.
He m. (2) Bridgewater 30 Nov. 1756 HANNAH (HARLOW) WILLIS, b. Plymouth 20 Nov. 1721; living 3 June 1769; dau. of William and Joanna (Jackson) Harlow, a descendant of Pilgrims Isaac Allerton and Richard Warren. She m. (1) Bridgewater 11 Aug. 1741 Stoughton Willis by whom she had Jonathan, Azariah, Stoughton, Hannah and Abigail.
On 3 June 1769 John Snow and wife Hanna and the other children of William Harlow signed a quitclaim deed to William Harlow.
The will of John Snow of Bridgewater, yeoman, dated 9 Sept. 1766, presented 4 Sept. 1786, names wife Hannah executrix; dau. Sarah Snow under 18, son John Snow Jr. On 7 May 1794 Daniel Tomson of Bridgewater on behalf of wife Sarah, dau. of John Snow of Bridgewater dec., petitioned to be appointed

administrator on the estate. John Snow of Bridgewater was cited to appear at court to show cause why Daniel Tomson of Bridgewater should not be granted admin. of the estate of John Snow.

Children (SNOW) by 2nd wife, b. Bridgewater:

214   i   SARAH[5] b. 23 March 1758
215   ii   JOHN b. 4 Jan. 1762

References: VR BRIDGEWATER 1:147(b. 1st wife Hannah), 302(b. son John), 303(b. Sarah). BRIDGEWATER BY MITCHELL pp. 182, 315. GEN ADVERTISER 1:39(1st m.). Plymouth Co. PR #18688(John Snow); 12:40(Elisha Hayward). HARLOW GEN pp. 160-2. MD 12:12(b. Hannah Harlow). TAG 24:189(quit claim). Plymouth Co. LR 71:234(quit claim).

55 JOSEPH SNOW[4] (Joseph[3], Rebecca[2] Brown, Peter[1]) b. Bridgewater 7 Sept. 1690; d. Providence RI 24 July 1773 in 84th yr.

He m. (1) prob. Bridgewater ca. 1714 ELIZABETH FIELD, b. Bridgewater 4 Aug. 1698; d. Providence RI 15 April 1768 ae 69y 8m 19d; dau. of Capt. John and Elizabeth (Ames) Field. The will of John Field of Providence dated 26 June 1757 names dau. Elizabeth Snow and others.

He m. (2) Providence RI after 1768 MARCY (SMITH) (BURLINGAME) MC CLELLAN, b. Providence RI ca. 1696; d. there 10 Nov. 1782 in 87th yr.; dau. of John and _____ (_____) Smith. She m. (1) _____ Burlingame. She m. (2) after 1724 Humphrey McClellan by whom she had Mercy, Sarah, and Prudence. The will of John Smith dated 10 Feb. 1724 names dau. Mercy Burlingame.

Joseph Snow Jr. of Bridgewater sold to Capt. John Field 2/3 purchase right in the 7 great shares in Bridgewater and 1/3 of the 32nd lot on the Buckhill Plain which fell to Joseph Alden dec. and 9 acres in Snells Meadow part of lot of Joseph Edson dec.; signed 28 May 1726, ack. 20 March 1726(/27).

Joseph Snow of Easton, yeoman, sold to Jacob Allin land in Bridgewater 21 April 1728, ack. 4 July 1734.

Joseph Snow was a Selectman of Easton in 1729 and moved to Providence RI bef. 16 March 1737/8 when as Deacon Joseph

Snow of Providence, yeoman, he sold land in Bridgewater to Caleb Phillips. On 14 Oct. 1743 he was elected to the office of ruling elder of the Beneficient Congregational Church.

The will of Joseph Snow of Providence, Esq. dated 12 Jan. 1765, sworn 7 Aug. 1773, names wife Elizabeth; "Grandchildren whom my oldest daughter Elizabeth Deen, late of Providence, deceased left: Sibble Deen and Elizabeth Deen"; 3 sons Joseph, Daniel and James Snow, executors and to have land in this government and in Mass. Bay.

On 1 April 1774 Joseph Snow, Daniel Snow, and James Snow all of Providence, yeomen, sold to Daniel Snow, gentleman of Bridgewater, all their purchase rights in Taunton No. Purchase which descended to them from their father Joseph Snow of Providence, dec.

On 5 July 1774 Joseph Snow, clerk, and wife Rebecca; Daniel Snow, gent., and wife Sarah; James Snow, housewright, and wife Hannah, all of Providence, sold the homestead of Joseph Snow dec. to Silas Talbot of Providence, reserving the dower right of his widow.

Children (SNOW) first 6 b. Bridgewater, rest b. Easton except John prob. b. Providence RI:

216	i	JOSEPH[5] b. 26 March 1715
	ii	JOHN b. 19 April 1717; d. 3 Dec. 1738 ae 21y 7m 14d
217	iii	ELIZABETH b. 4 May 1719
218	iv	SUSANNA b. 12 Dec. 1722
	v	SARAH b. 3 Feb. 1725; d. Providence RI 8 Jan. 1745 ae 22y 11m 4d
219	vi	DANIEL bp. W. Bridgewater 12 Nov. 1727
220	vii	JAMES b. 30 Dec. 1730
	viii	MARY b. 20 April 1733; d. Providence RI 12 Feb. 1751 ae 18y 9m 12d
	ix	LYDIA b. 8 Feb. 1735; d. 10 Dec. 1738 ae 2y 10m 2d
	x	JOHN b. 1739; d. 10 July 1739 ae 2m 17d

References: VR BRIDGEWATER 1:110(b. wife Eliz.), 301-4(b. ch.).
VR WEST BRIDGEWATER p. 99(bp. Daniel).

EASTON HIST p. 642(selectman). Benns Grave Records 4:82(d. Joseph, Eliz., ch.). Providence RI Will Book 6:71-2(Joseph Snow). RHODE ISLAND HISTORY 21:18-19 (Mercy Smith). Plymouth Co. LR 21:199; 33:187; 34:105(Joseph Snow); 36:11. RI VR 14:291(d. Joseph, Mercy). Providence RI Wills 3:301(John Smith); 5:156(John Field). Bristol Co. LR 56:241(1774 deed). Providence RI LE 20:404(Joseph Snow, etc.). MD 42:151-4(deeds, etc.).

56 MARY SNOW[4] (Joseph[3], Rebecca[2] Brown, Peter[1]) b. Bridgewater 1 Nov. 1691.
      She m. Bridgewater 17 Jan. 1718 JOSEPH LATHROP, b. Bridgewater 5 June 1693; d. aft. 11 April 1724 (father's will); son of Samuel and Sarah (Downer) Lathrop.
      No issue according to Lathrop Gen (p. 327) and Mitchell (p. 233).
      No Plymouth or Barnstable Co. PR for Joseph or Mary Lathrop.

References: VR BRIDGEWATER 1:202(b. Joseph);2:230(m.). MD
                  16:185(m.).   LO-LATHROP GEN pp. 323, 327.
BRIDGEWATER BY MITCHELL p. 233.

57 JAMES SNOW[4] (Joseph[3], Rebecca[2] Brown, Peter[1]) b. Bridgewater 16 Aug. 1693; d. there bet. 19 March 1760 (date of will) and 12 May 1760 (date presented).
      He m. (1) prob. Bridgewater bef. 22 April 1719 RUTH SHAW, b. Bridgewater 25 Jan. 1698; d. prob. Bridgewater bet. 31 March 1736 (b. John) and 3rd Tues. Dec. 1739 (deed); dau. of Joseph and Judith (Whitmarsh) Shaw. The division of the estate of Joseph Shaw of Bridgewater, weaver, dated 22 April 1719 names dau. Ruth Snow and others.
      He m. (2) Weymouth 6 Aug. 1741 HANNAH HOVEY, b. Weymouth 4 Feb. 1703, living 19 March 1760 (will of James); dau. of Deacon Ebenezer and Joanna (Benson) Hovey. The will of Ebenezer Hovey of Weymouth, yeoman, dated 9 July 1744 names dau. Hannah Snow and others.
      James Snow and wife Ruth of Bridgewater sold land to Jonathan Snow of Bridgewater where Joseph Shaw dec. formerly lived, signed 28 Dec. 1732; ack. 3 July 1740. On 3d Tues. Dec.

1739 witnesses testified they saw James and Ruth now dec. sign.

On 13 July 1752 James Snow of Bridgewater deeded land to son Nathan Snow of Abington, blacksmith.

The will of James Snow of Bridgewater, husbandman, dated 19 March 1760, presented 12 May 1760, names wife Hannah; children Ruth Boney, Mary Foster, Nathan Snow, Abigail Egerton, Susanna Edson, John Snow, and Sarah Harris; son Nathan exec.

No Plymouth Co. PR for Hannah Snow.

Children (SNOW) b. Bridgewater, all by first wife except last by Hannah:

221	i	RUTH[5] b. 12 May 1720
	ii	ABIJAH b. 12 Feb. 1721/2; not in father's will
222	iii	MARY b. 28 Feb. 1724
223	iv	NATHAN b. 9 July 1725
224	v	ABIGAIL b. 27 May 1727
225	vi	SUSANNA b. 15 Feb. 1729
	vii	JEDEDIAH b. 15 March 1731; not in father's will
226	viii	SARAH b. 6 April 1732
	ix	JAMES b. Aug. 1734; d.y.
227	x	JOHN b. 31 March 1736
	xi	JAMES b. 28 May 1742; not in father's will

References: MD 5:249(b. Ruth); 15:87(b. 1st 2 ch.). VR BRIDGEWATER 1:289(b. Ruth), 300-4(b. ch.). VR WEYMOUTH 1:140(b. Hannah); 2:175(2nd m.). WEYMOUTH BY CHAMBERLAIN 3:298; 4:613-4. Plymouth Co. LR 33:159(James, Ruth Snow); 43:80(James Snow). Plymouth Co. PR #18684(James Snow). Suffolk Co. PR 21:374-5(Joseph Shaw); 51:311(Ebenezer Hovey).

58 REBECKAH SNOW[4] (Joseph[3], Rebecca[2] Brown, Peter[1]) b. Bridgewater 25 June 1696; d. there bet. 29 July 1734 and 5 May 1743.

She m. Bridgewater 20 Dec. 1722 THOMAS WADE, b. Scituate ca. 1680; d. Bridgewater 22 Jan. 1789; son of Thomas and Hannah (Ensign) Wade. He m. (2) Bridgewater 5 May 1743 Elizabeth Hanmer. He m. (3) Bridgewater 20 Jan. 1752 Abigail Ames who d. Bridgewater 27 Sept. 1789 in 85th yr.

No Plymouth Co. PR for Thomas Wade nor any Plymouth Co. LR to children.

Children (WADE) b. Bridgewater:

228   i   HOPESTILL[5] b. 13 July 1725
      ii   MARY b. 25 Nov. 1727; n.f.r.
229 iii   KEZIAH b. 18 Oct. 1729
230   iv   DAVID b. 14 March 1732
231   v   REBECCA b. 29 July 1734

References: MD 16:43(b. ch.), 187(m.). VR BRIDGEWATER 1:322
            (b. ch.); 2:379(all 3 m.), 568(d. Thomas, Abigail).
BRIDGEWATER BY MITCHELL pp. 315, 335.

59 ISAAC SNOW[4] (Joseph[3], Rebecca[2] Brown, Peter[1]) b. Bridgewater 22 July 1700; d. there 10 July 1737.

   He m. Bridgewater 19 Nov. 1722 HANNAH SHAW, b. Bridgewater 31 July 1704; d. there 30 March 1762; dau. of Joseph and Judith (Whitmarsh) Shaw. She m. (2) Bridgewater 16 March 1742 John Whitman by whom she had Daniel and Ezra.

   No Plymouth Co. PR for Isaac Snow or Hannah Whitman nor any Plymouth Co. LR to children.

Children (SNOW) b. Bridgewater:

232   i   HANNAH[5] b. 14 Nov. 1723
233   ii   ISAAC b. 16 Feb. 1726
234 iii   MARTHA b. 15 Nov. 1728
235   iv   PETER b. 25 July 1731
      v   JOSEPH b. 23 May 1734
236   vi   JUDITH b. 7 Dec. 1736

References: MD 16:187(m.). VR BRIDGEWATER 1:288(b.
            Hannah), 301-3(b. ch.); 2:348(m.), 400(her 2nd m.),
559(d. Isaac), 578(d. Hannah). BRIDGEWATER BY MITCHELL
pp. 315-6.

60 JONATHAN SNOW[4] (Joseph[3], Rebecca[2] Brown, Peter[1]) b. Bridgewater 27 Sept. 1703; d. Middleboro 17 Jan. 1783 in 81st yr.

He m. (1) Middleboro 18 Dec. 1728 SARAH SOULE, b. Middleboro 8 Oct. 1703; d. there 12 April 1743 ae 39y 8m 4d; dau. of John and Martha (Tinkham) Soule, a descendant of Pilgrims Francis Cooke, Peter Brown, and George Soule. The will of John Soul Sr. of Middleboro dated 1 March 1743 names wife Martha, dau. Sarah Snow and other children. The will of Martha Soul Sr. of Middleboro dated 19 Nov. 1751 mentions among others "heirs of daughter Sarah Snow deceased." (See #17 & 73)

He m. (2) Middleboro 22 Jan. 1746 RUTH BENNET, b. Middleboro 24 Aug. 1714; d. there 30 April 1783 in 69th yr.; dau. of Samuel and Ruth (Perry) Bennet. The will of Samuel Bennett of Middleboro dated 1 Aug. 1757 names wife Jemima and dau. Ruth Snow. Receipt of Jonathan and Ruth Snow for their share of the estate of Samuel Bennett, late of Middleboro, is dated 25 July 1774.

No Plymouth Co. PR for Jonathan Snow nor any Plymouth Co. LR to children.

Children (SNOW) b. Bridgewater, all exc. Ruth by 1st wife:

237	i	SAMUEL[5] b. 20 Sept. 1729
238	ii	JESSE b. 8 Feb. 1730/1
239	iii	SARAH b. 3 Dec. 1732
240	iv	REBECCA b. 16 Oct. 1734
241	v	JONATHAN b. 10 March 1735/6
	vi	MOSES b. 27 Sept. 1737
	vii	AARON bp. East Bridgewater 28 Sept. 1740. He must be the Aaron, son of Jonathan & Sarah who d. Middleboro 4 Jan. 1741 in 12th yr. [sic.]. (Prob. should be 12th month.)
242	viii	RUTH b. ca. 1747

References: VR BRIDGEWATER 1:302-3(b. 1st 6 ch.). VR EAST BRIDGEWATER p. 125(bp. Aaron). MD 2:105(b. Sarah); 5:40(1st m.); 7:240(b. Ruth); 15:196-7(b. first 7 ch.); 18:79. MF 3:56. MIDDLEBORO DEATHS pp. 166-7(deaths). MIDDLEBORO BY WESTON pp. 656, 659. Plymouth Co. PR 9:82(John Soule); 14:452 (Samuel Bennett); 15:29(Martha Soule); 21:362(Samuel Bennett). MIDDLEBORO VR 1:8(b. Sarah), 32(1st m.), 39(b. Ruth), 105(2nd m.).

61   DAVID SNOW[4] (Joseph[3], Rebecca[2] Brown, Peter[1]) b.
Bridgewater 27 Sept. 1703; living 13 Oct. 1770 (deed).
     He m. Bridgewater 11 March 1730/1 JOANNA HAYWARD,
b. Bridgewater 15 Aug. 1704; d. East Bridgewater 23 Nov. 1794 ae
90; dau. of Joseph and Mehitabel (Dunham) Hayward. The will
of Joseph Hayward of Bridgewater dated 6 July 1751 names wife
Mehitable and dau. Joanna Snow.
     On 2 Jan. 1768 David Snow and Joanna Snow sold a lot that
had belonged to their father Joseph Hayward to Joseph Snow of
Bridgewater, yeoman.
     On 4 Feb. 1768 David Snow of Bridgewater, husbandman,
gave land to son Joseph Snow of Bridgewater.   On 8 Dec. 1768
David Snow and Joanna Snow of Bridgewater gave land in
Bridgewater to dau. Joanna Edson, wife of Nathaniel Edson of
Bridgewater.   On 13 Oct. 1770 David Snow and Joanna Snow of
Bridgewater gave land to dau. Lydia Whitman, wife of John
Whitman 3rd of Bridgewater.
     No Plymouth Co. PR for David Snow or Joanna Snow.

     Children (SNOW) b. Bridgewater:

	i	DAVID[5] b. 12 Dec. 1732; d. Bridgewater 25 May 1753. No Plymouth Co. PR.
243	ii	JOSEPH b. 27 June 1734
244	iii	JOANNA b. 27 Nov. 1735
	iv	MEHITABEL b. 18 Sept. 1737; d. Bridgewater 23 March 1766. No Plymouth Co. PR.
245	v	LYDIA b. 16 Feb. 1740
246	vi	RHODA b. 7 Oct. 1742

References: MD 16:98(m.). VR BRIDGEWATER 1:149(b. Joanna),
              301-3(b. ch.); 2:347(m.), 558(d. son David), 559(d.
Mehitabel).   VR EAST BRIDGEWATER p. 391(d. Joanna).
BRIDGEWATER BY MITCHELL pp. 315-6. Plymouth Co. PR
14:498 (Joseph Hayward).   Plymouth Co. LR 55:9(gift to Joseph),
193 (to Lydia); 73:3(to Joanna); 75:43(sale to Joseph).

NOTE: There is a David Snow who d. Bridgewater bef. 7 Oct. 1773
(BOSTON NEWS OBITS 3:391).

62   REBEKAH SNOW[4] (Benjamin[3], Rebecca[2] Brown, Peter[1]) b. Bridgewater 7 Nov. 1694; d. there 4 Sept. 1763 in 69th yr., "wife of Mr. Ebenezer."

   She m. bef. 1732 EBENEZER CAMPBELL, b. Taunton 30 Nov. 1697; d. after 15 May 1764; son of Ebenezer and Hannah (Pratt) Campbell. He m. (2) Bridgewater 15 May 1764 Hannah (_____) Pratt.

   Ebenezer Campbell of Bridgewater, weaver, was sued in 1731.

   Rebeckah Campbell was admitted to the Bridgewater church from Taunton in 1732.

   Neither Rebecca nor Ebenezer Campbell left probate records in Plymouth or Bristol Cos. Also no Plymouth Co. LR for Ebenezer Campbell.

   Apparently Ebenezer and Rebecca Campbell were childless.

References: VR BRIDGEWATER   2:71(his   2nd   m.),   443(d. Rebekah).   VR TAUNTON   1:77(b. Ebenezer). BRIDGEWATER   EPITAPHS   p.   89(d.   Rebecca;   adm.   ch.). PLYMOUTH CO CT RECS 5:394.

63   BENJAMIN SNOW[4] (Benjamin[3], Rebecca[2] Brown, Peter[1]) b. Bridgewater 23 June 1696; d. there 29 Oct. 1760 in 65th yr.

   He m. Bridgewater 7 March 1721/2 JEMIMA SNELL, b. Bridgewater 3 May 1704; d. there 6 Feb. 1784; dau. of Amos and Mary (Packard) Snell.

   Elijah Snow of Bridgewater, yeoman, was appointed administrator of the estate of Benjamin Snow late of Bridgewater 6 April 1761.

   On 8 July 1769 Jemima Snow of Bridgewater, widow, sold to Elijah Snow of Bridgewater, cordwainer, 3 acres in Bridgewater "which fell to me in division of my father Amos Snell."

   In July 1761 ten men were found guilty of being voluntarily disguised and disfigured did unlawfully, riotously and routously assemble and gather together to disturb the peace and did beset the dwelling house of Elijah Snow of Bridgewater, yeoman, in which house then were his mother Jemima Snow and Lucy Snow of Bridgewater, spinster.

   Children (SNOW) b. Bridgewater:

    247   i   JEMIMA[5] b. 5 Jan. 1723
    248   ii   BENJAMIN b. 25 Aug. 1724
    249   iii   DANIEL b. 26 July 1726
    250   iv   ELIJAH b. 6 Nov. 1728
           v   ELIZABETH b. 2 April 1730
           vi   CHARITY b. 20 Oct. 1733; d. 30 Oct. or 1 Nov.
                 1733
    251   vii   LUCY b. 27 May 1735
           viii AMOS b. 13 March 1738; d. 18 Jan. 1738/9
           ix   JOSEPH b. 27 March 1740; d. 26 Aug. 1740
           x   SETH b. 5 April 1743; d. 17 Aug. 1743
           xi   JOSEPH b. 5 Oct. 1746; d. 23 Oct. 1746

References: MD 16:187(m.).   VR BRIDGEWATER 1:296(b.
             Jemima), 300-4(b. ch.); 2:347(m.), 558-9(deaths).
BRIDGEWATER BY MITCHELL pp. 315-6. Plymouth Co. PR
#18662(Benjamin Snow). Plymouth Co. LR 55:115(Jemima Snow).
PLYMOUTH CO CT RECS 3:156.

64   SOLOMON SNOW[4] (Benjamin[3], Rebecca[2] Brown, Peter[1]) b.
Bridgewater 6 April 1698; d. there bef. 26 Jan. 1741.
     He m. Bridgewater 8 April 1724 BATHSHEBA MAHURIN,
b. prob. Taunton ca. 1698; almost surely the "widow Snow" who d.
Bridgewater 5 Jan. 1748; dau. of Hugh and Mary (_____)
Mahurin.
     On 18 May 1737 Solomon Snow of Bridgewater sold to Seth
Staples land in Bridgewater including land of father Benjamin
Snow; wife Bathsheba released her dower.
     Bathsheba Snow of Bridgewater widow posted bond 26 Jan.
1741 as administratrix of the estate of her husband Solomon
Snow, late of Bridgewater dec. Sureties were Jonathan Cary,
gent., and John Fobes, husbandman, both of Bridgewater.
Undated account of Jonathan Cary of Bridgewater administrator
of estate of Solomon Snow dec. mentions payment to Benjamin
Mehurin; necessities set off to widow.
     The inventory of the estate of Solomon Snow was made 24
March 1741; Barsheba Snow administratrix made oath to it 20
May 1742.
     No Plymouth Co. PR for Bathsheba Snow.

Children (SNOW) b. Bridgewater:

252   i   LEMUEL[5] b. 1729
253   ii   BATHSHEBA b. ca. 1732
      iii child d. Bridgewater 4 June 1739

References: MD 16:45(m.). VR BRIDGEWATER 2:350(m.), 559(d. Bathsheba, child). NEHGR 136:17-20(b. Bathsheba). Plymouth Co. PR #18723; 8:495-6 (Solomon Snow). Plymouth Co. LR 31:177(Solomon Snow).

65   EBENEZER SNOW[4] (Benjamin[3], Rebecca[2] Brown, Peter[1]) b. Bridgewater 29 March 1701; d. Raynham 30 Nov. 1786 ae 85.
     He m. (1) prob. Bridgewater ca. 1728 SARAH PRATT, b. prob. Bridgewater; d. there 23 June 1737; dau. of Joseph and Sarah (Benson) Pratt. The will of Joseph Pratt of Bridgewater dated 13 March 1755 mentions grandchildren, children of dau. Sarah dec.; Ebenezer, Nathaniel and Caleb Snow.
     He m. (2) Bridgewater 14 Dec. 1737 SARAH (HOOPER) LEACH, b. Bridgewater 9 Oct. 1705; d. Raynham 25 Dec. 1761; dau. of John and Sarah (Harden) Hooper. She m. (1) Bridgewater 5 May 1725 Stephen Leach by whom she had Anne, Sarah and Stephen.
     He m. (3) Raynham 14 Nov. 1762 LYDIA (DEANE) WILBORE, b. Taunton 11 Dec. 1704; d. Raynham 6 Nov. 1786; dau. of Benjamin and Sarah (Williams) Deane. She m. (1) Dighton 4 Dec. 1729 Ebenezer Wilbore.
     On 29 March 1748 Ebenezer and Sarah Snow of Bridgewater sold to Nehemiah Packard several tracts in Bridgewater including his homestead.
     On 10 April 1778, ack. 30 June 1778, Ebenezer Snow of Raynham and wife Lydia sold to Benjamin Willis a tract in South Bridgewater that he bought from Willis in 1740.
     Ebenezer Snow of Raynham, yeoman, sold to Solomon Snow of Raynham gent. "all my lands and buildings" on 10 Nov. 1783.
     No Bristol or Plymouth Co. PR for Ebenezer Snow.

     Children (SNOW) all b. prob. Bridgewater, 4 by first wife, rest by second:

254	i	EBENEZER[5] b. 16 Nov. 1729
255	ii	NATHANIEL b. 6 June 1731
	iii	SARAH b. 27 July 1733; prob. d.y.; (not named in 13 March 1755 will of grandfather Joseph Pratt)
256	iv	CALEB b. 8 June 1736
	v	FRANCIS b. 26 March 1740; he is prob. the "Fras" Snow that Rev. Isaac Backus recorded as d. at Westfield returning from camp 14 Dec. 1760.
257	vi	SOLOMON b. 13 Dec. 1741 [sic]
257A	vii	REBECCA b. 5 March 1742 [sic]
258	viii	ZEBEDEE b. 26 Feb. 1743 [sic]
	ix	dau. d. Bridgewater 3 June 1749

References: MD 15:200(b. 1st 4 ch.; d. 1st wife); 16:44(2nd m.). VR BRIDGEWATER 1:165(b. Sarah Hooper), 300-4(b. ch.); 2:239(Sarah's 1st m.), 347(2nd m.), 559(d. 1st w. Sarah). VR TAUNTON 1:129(b. Lydia); 2:516(Lydia's 1st m.). BRIDGEWATER BY MITCHELL pp. 315-6. THE WILBORES OF AMERICA, John Reid Wilbor and Benjamin Franklin Wilbour, 1933, Boston, p. 42(m.&d. Lydia). Plymouth Co. PR 19:188(Joseph Pratt). Bristol Co. LR 62:293(Ebenezer Snow). Plymouth Co. LR 39:125, 60:45(Ebenezer Snow). Raynham Church records, Vol. I(d. Ebenezer). RAYNHAM VR pp. 88(int. 3rd m.), 152(d. Francis), 153(d. 2nd w. Sarah), 156(d. Ebenezer, Lydia).

NOTE: No proof found for children John, Eli, or Mary mentioned in BRIDGEWATER BY MITCHELL p. 316. (Also listed by J. H. Temple in HIST. OF NORTH BROOKFIELD, but he may have copied Mitchell). No deeds from Ebenezer to children except as noted above.

66 ELIZABETH SNOW[4] (Benjamin[3], Rebecca[2] Brown, Peter[1]) b. Bridgewater 5 May 1705; d. there 6 July 1755 in 51st yr.

She m. Bridgewater 4 May 1725 JOSEPH CARVER, b. ca. 1700; d. Bridgewater 24 Sept. 1778; son of Eleazer and Experience (Blake) (Sumner) Carver. He m. (2) int. Walpole 9 May 1756 Sarah Lyon.

The will of Joseph Carver of Bridgewater dated 20 June 1764, presented 28 Sept. 1778, names "loving wife"; son Robert; dau. Experience Lummis; son Joseph; dau. Elizabeth Packard; 2nd son Benjamin; and dau. Sarah Porter and grandson Abiezer Porter.

Children (CARVER) b. Bridgewater:

259 i   JOSEPH[5] b. 23 March 1727
260 ii   BENJAMIN b. 28 Feb. 1728/9
261 iii ELIZABETH b. 10 Sept. 1731
     iv   ABIEZER b. 14 Sept. 1734; d. Bridgewater 31 Aug.
          1755 in 21st yr. No PR.
262 v   SARAH b. 14 Feb. 1736/7
263 vi   EXPERIENCE b. 2 May 1739
264 vii ROBERT b. 2 June 1742
     viii REBECCA b. 28 Sept. 1744(not in father's will)

References: MD 15:200(b. 1st 5 ch.); 16:45(m). VR
            BRIDGEWATER 1:65-6(b. ch.); 2:73(m.),
444(deaths). BRIDGEWATER BY MITCHELL p. 130. THE
CARVER FAM OF NEW ENGLAND, Clifford N. Carver,
Rutland VT 1935 p. 67. Plymouth Co. PR #3610(Joseph Carver).
BRIDGEWATER EPITAPHS p. 74(d. Abiezer). NEHGR 88:226-7.
VR WALPOLE p. 103(int. his 2nd m.).

67 SARAH SNOW[4] (Benjamin[3], Rebecca[2] Brown, Peter[1]) b.
Bridgewater 20 Aug. 1706; d. there 28 April 1732.
       She m. Bridgewater ca. 1728 NATHANIEL PRATT, b.
Weymouth 23 March 1700/01; d. Bridgewater 24 Dec. 1749; son of
Joseph and Sarah (Benson) Pratt. He m. (2) Bridgewater 15 Jan.
1733/4 Sarah Allen who d. Bridgewater 29 Sept. 1744. He m. (3)
Bridgewater 5 Nov. 1745 Hannah Conant.
       The will of Benjamin Snow of Bridgewater dated 12 Sept.
1738, names grandson Seth Pratt, son of his dau. Sarah dec.
       No Plymouth Co. PR or LR for Nathaniel Pratt.

Children (PRATT) b. Bridgewater:

265 i   SETH[5] b. 21 June 1729
     ii   twin d. bef. 20 May 1732
     iii twin d. bef. 20 May 1732

References: VR BRIDGEWATER 1:271(b. Seth); 2:309(his 2nd, 3rd

m.), 542(d. Sarah, twins), 545(d. Nathaniel).   VR
WEYMOUTH   1:237(b. Nathaniel).   BRIDGEWATER   BY
MITCHELL pp. 288, 315. CONANT FAM p. 173. WEYMOUTH
BY CHAMBERLAIN 4:507. Plymouth Co. PR 9:83(Benjamin
Snow).

NOTE: No proof found for dau. Anna mentioned in
BRIDGEWATER BY MITCHELL p. 288. She is not mentioned in
the will of Benjamin Snow.

68   HANNAH RICKARD[4] (Rebecca Snow[3], Rebecca[2] Brown,
Peter[1]) b. Plymouth 25 Sept. 1693; d. East Bridgewater 17 Oct.
1771 ae 78.
     She m. Plympton 12 April 1720 JOSIAH BYRAM, b.
Bridgewater 3 May 1698; d. 1760 or 1761; son of Nicholas and
Mary (Edson) Byram.
     Josiah Byram of Bridgewater, gentleman, mortgaged his
dwelling house and land bounded by land of his father Nicholas
dec., signed 2 Aug. 1740 with wife Hannah releasing dower, ack.
14 Sept. 1740.
     Josiah Byram of Bridgewater, gentleman, sold to John
Codman of Charlestown, Suffolk Co. land, forge, tools, etc. with
wife Hannah releasing dower, signed 16 Dec. 1743, ack. Plymouth
same day.
     Josiah Byram of Bridgewater sold to Theophilus Byram land
in Bridgewater, "my homestead" 12 Sept. 1746, ack. 8 Nov. 1746.
He moved to New Jersey.
     No Josiah Byram PR in NJ Archives.
     No Plymouth Co. PR for Josiah Byram.

     Children (BYRAM) b. Bridgewater:

     266   i   SUSANNA[5] b. 27 April 1721
           ii   JOSIAH b. 5 March 1722/3; d.y.
     267 iii   THEOPHILUS   b. 8 Aug. 1725
     268   iv   MEHETABEL b. 25 May 1730
     269   v   REBECCA b. 26 Aug. 1732

References: VR BRIDGEWATER 1:50(b. Josiah), 64(b. ch.);
              2:443(d. Josiah).   VR EAST BRIDGEWATER p.

342(d. Hannah). VR PLYMPTON p. 255(m.). A GENEALOGY OUTLINE OF THE DESCENDANTS OF NICHOLAS BYRAM compiled by Thomas L. Byram, Brooklyn NY 1976, pp. 1-2. Plymouth Co. LR 33:193; 36:92; 38:159(Josiah Byram).

69 SAMUEL RICKARD[4] (Rebecca Snow[3], Rebecca[2] Brown, Peter[1]) b. Plymouth 21 May 1696; d. Plympton 21 Aug. 1768 ae 72y 2m 27d.

He m. Hingham 19 Oct. 1721 RACHEL WHITON (called Rachel Farrar in Plympton VR) b. Hingham 12 July 1700; d. Plympton 30 Jan. 1792 in 92nd yr.; dau. of Thomas and Joanna (May) (Gardner) Whiton. [Her mother later married Nathan Farrow 23 March 1711; this must be the source of the Farrar name in Plympton VR].

The first four children were bp. in Hingham, but their births are recorded in Plympton.

On 13 May 1754 Samuel Rickard of Plimpton deeded land in Plimpton to sons Lemuel, Samuel, Theophilus, and Lazarus.

The will of Samuel Rickard of Plimton, yeoman, dated 13 May 1754, presented 5 Sept. 1768, names wife Rachel; sons: Lemuel, Samuel, Theophilus, and Lazarus and daus. Elizabeth, Rachel, and Rebecca (no surnames).

Letters of administration were granted to Theophilus Rickard of Plimton, yeoman, on 5 Sept. 1768 as Samuel Rickard's will appointed son Lemuel sole exec., but he died bef. testator. On 20 May 1771 Theophilis Rickard rendered his account which included payments to Abner Harlow and wife Rachel and Elizabeth Everson [two of his sisters].

No Plymouth Co. PR for Rachel Rickard.

Children (RICKARD) b. Plympton:

270	i	LEMUEL[5] b. 6 Nov. 1722
271	ii	THEOPHILUS b. 26 Jan. 1725
272	iii	SAMUEL b. 12 Oct. 1727
273	iv	LAZARUS b. 29 May 1730
274	v	ELIZABETH b. 2 March 1732/3
275	vi	RACHEL b. 17 May 1736
	vii	REBECCA b. 17 April 1740; d. Plympton 24 Feb. 1757 16y 10m 6d

References: VR PLYMPTON pp. 162-6(b. ch.), 506(d. Rachel,
          Rebecca), 507(d. Samuel).   SAVAGE 4:533.
HINGHAM HIST 3:129, 290. Plymouth Co. LR 54:122(Samuel
Rickard).   Plymouth   Co.   PR   20:117(Samuel   Rickard);
#16924(Theophilis Rickard, adm.).

70 MEHITABELL RICKARD[4] (Rebecca Snow[3] Rebecca[2]
Brown, Peter[1]) b. Plympton 1 April 1707; d. Bridgewater bef. 20
May 1741.
      She m. Bridgewater 12 Nov. 1730 ARTHUR HARRIS, b.
Bridgewater 25 June 1708; d. there bef. 4 June 1750; son of Isaac
and Jane (Cooke) Harris, a descendant of Pilgrims James Chilton
and Francis Cooke. He m. (2) Bridgewater 20 May 1741 Bethiah
Hayward, dau. of Deacon Thomas Hayward by whom he had
Bethiah, Mehitabel, William, Abner, and Caleb.
      The will of Arthur Harris of Bridgewater, yeoman, dated 27
March 1750, presented 4 June 1750, names wife Bethiah exec.;
eldest son Benjamin, 2nd son Silas; Luie[sic] my eldest dau.; 2
youngest sons William and Caleb; 2 youngest daus. Bethia and
Mehitabell.

      Children (HARRIS) b. Bridgewater:

      276   i   BENJAMIN[5] b. 30 Sept. 1731
      277   ii   SILAS b. 8 Nov. 1734
            iii ARTHUR bp. E. Bridgewater 19 June 1737; d. bef.
                 27 March 1750 as not named in father's will.
      278   iv   LUCY b. 27 July 1739

References: VR BRIDGEWATER 1:132(b. Arthur, Benjamin),
          133(b. Lucy, Silas); 2:159(m.; his 2nd m.). VR EAST
BRIDGEWATER p. 61(bp. Arthur). MF 15:78-9. BRIDGEWATER
BY MITCHELL pp. 176-7.   GEN ADVERTISER 1:38(m.).
Plymouth Co. PR 12:141 (Arthur Harris).

71 ELEAZER RICKARD[4] (Rebecca Snow[3], Rebecca[2] Brown,
Peter[1]) b. Plympton 8 March 1709/10; d. Carver 7 Jan. 1784 ae 74y
9m 18d.
      He m. Plympton 2 Aug. 1739 MARY CHURCHILL, b.
Plympton 17 April 1720; d. Carver 27 July 1788 in 70th yr.; dau.

of Benjamin and Mary (Shaw) Churchill.

The will of Eleazer Rickard of Plimton, yeoman, dated 29 Oct. 1783, presented 1 March 1784, names wife; dau. Marcy Wright wife of James, Jr.; dau. Mary Chase wife of Consider; Sarah Wright wife of Parez; Kiziah Ransom wife of Joseph; grandson Lewis Chase son of Consider under 21; dau. Deborah Rickard; sons Eleazer, Abner, and Elijah.

No Plymouth Co. PR for Mary Rickard.

Children (RICKARD) b. Plympton:

279	i	MARCY[5] b. July 1740
280	ii	ELEAZER b. 22 July 1742
281	iii	ABNER b. 28 Sept. 1744
282	iv	MARY b. 29 Aug. 1747
283	v	SARAH b. 9 Oct. 1749
284	vi	KEZIAH b. 26 Aug. 1753
285	vii	ELIJAH b. 24 Jan. 1756
	viii	DEBORAH b. 26 May 1758; d. Carver 26 Aug. 1784 in 27th yr. No Plymouth Co. PR.

References: VR CARVER p. 165(deaths.). VR PLYMPTON pp. 59(b. Mary), 161-6(b. ch.), 371(m.). Plymouth Co. PR #16893(Eleazer Rickard).

FIFTH GENERATION

72   MARTHA SOULE[5] (Martha Tinkham[4], Ephraim[3], Mary[2] Brown, Peter[1]) b. Middleboro 11 April 1702; d. there 18 March 1772 in 70th yr.
   She m. Middleboro 25 April 1732 THOMAS TOMSON, b. Middleboro 29 July 1688; d. Halifax bet. 7 July 1759 and 7 April 1760; son of John and Mary (Tinkham) Tomson.
   See #42 for an account of this family.

References: MD   2:41(b. Thomas); 13:249(m.).   MF   3:55.
          MIDDLEBORO DEATHS p. 195. MIDDLEBORO VR 1:5(b. Thomas), 60(m.).

73   SARAH SOULE[5] (Martha Tinkham[4], Ephraim[3], Mary[2] Brown, Peter[1]) b. Middleboro 8 Oct. 1703; d. there 12 April 1743 in 39th yr.
   She m. Middleboro 18 Dec. 1728 JONATHAN SNOW, b. Bridgewater 27 Sept. 1703; d. Middleboro 17 Jan. 1783 in 81st yr.; son of Joseph and Hopestill (Alden) Snow.
   See #60 for an account of this family.

References: VR BRIDGEWATER 1:302(b. Jonathan). MD 5:40(m.).
          MF   3:56.   MIDDLEBORO   DEATHS   p.   166.
MIDDLEBORO VR 1:32(m.).

74   JOHN SOULE[5] (Martha Tinkham[4], Ephraim[3], Mary[2] Brown, Peter[1]) b. Middleboro 13 April 1705; d. there 19 Feb. 1750/1 in 46th yr.
   He m. Middleboro 12 April 1750 MARY LEACH "of Middleboro"; living 28 Feb. 1786 (deed). She m. (2) Middleboro 9 June 1752 Ephraim Wood by whom she had Ezra, Mary, Ephraim, Susanna, Huldah, and Jacob.
   On 10 July 1751 Mary Soule was appointed guardian of a minor son John, son of John Soule, dec., late of Middleboro. The account of Mary Wood, wife of Ephraim Wood, was made 23 June 1758. On 28 Feb. 1786 Ephraim Wood 2nd of Middleboro sold his homestead to Ebenezer Cox; signed by Ephraim Wood and Mary Wood.

Child (SOULE) b. Middleboro:

i   JOHN[6] b. 9 May 1751, posthumously

References: MD 18:83(m.). MF 3:56. MIDDLEBORO VR 1:108(m.),
          113(b. Mary), 114(b. John, Ezra), 131(b. Ephraim),
142(b. Susanna), 147(b. Huldah), 161(b. Jacob); 2:47 (int. Mary's
2nd m.). MIDDLEBORO DEATHS pp. 168, 233. Plymouth Co. PR
#18814(John Soule); #18815(gdn.). Plymouth Co. LR 65:210
(Ephraim Wood).

75   MARY SOULE[5] (Martha Tinkham[4], Ephraim[3], Mary[2] Brown,
Peter[1]) b. Middleboro 14 March 1709; d. there 7 Dec. 1794 ae 86,
widow.
      She m. Middleboro 14 Dec. 1731 OBADIAH SAMPSON, d.
Middleboro bef. 3 March 1766; son of Samuel and Mercy (Eddy)
Sampson.
      On 3 March 1766 John Sampson of Middleboro, husbandman,
was appointed to adm. the estate of Obadiah Sampson, late of
Middleboro. The inventory was dated 4 April 1766. On 18 April
1766 Issachar Fuller of Plimton was appointed guardian of Esther
Samson, over 14 years of age.
      On 8 June 1771 Ezekiel Samson of Plimpton, husbandman,
sold to John Samson of Middleborough all rights to land of his
father Obadiah Samson, dec.; wife Sarah renounced her dower.
      On 2 April 1778 John Samson of Middleborough,
husbandman, sold to Isaac Bryant land which his grandfather
Samuel Samson had given to his father Obadiah Samson; wife
Elizabeth Samson renounced her dower.

Children (SAMPSON) b. Middleboro:

    i   RUTH[6] b. ca. 1732*
    ii   ISRAEL b. 24 Oct. 1734; d. 23 Nov. 1734 ae 29d
    iii SAMUEL b. 16 Oct. 1735; d. 31 Aug. 1757
    iv   MARY (twin) b. 18 Nov. 1737; d. 12 May 1738
    v   MARTHA (twin) b. 18 Nov. 1737; d. 4 May 1738
    vi   OBADIAH b. 29 March 1739

vii   JOHN   b. 22 Nov. 1741
viii   EZEKIEL   b. 11 Aug. 1744
ix   ESTHER   b. 12 Nov. 1749

References: MD 4:70(b. Mary, Martha); 8:30(b. Samuel); 13:7 (b.&d. Israel), 249(m.); 15:120(b. Obadiah), 122 (b. John); 16:14(b. Ezekiel), 222(d. Mary, Martha); 18:85(b. Esther). MIDDLEBORO DEATHS pp. 149, 150. Plymouth Co. PR 17:157; 19:343, 405(gdn.); 20:537(Obadiah Sampson). MF 3:56-7. MIDDLEBORO VR 1:24(b. Mary, Martha), 44(b. Sam.), 60(m.; b.&d. Israel), 68(b. Obadiah), 70(b. John), 76(d. Mary, Martha), 79(b. Ezekial), 110(b. Esther). Plymouth Co. LR 56:85 (Ezekiel Samson); 60:57(John Samson).

*MF3 and (PLYMOUTH) ANC LANDMARKS 2:227 list her as dau. No proof seen.

76   JAMES SOULE[5] (Martha Tinkham[4], Ephraim[3], Mary[2] Brown, Peter[1]) b. Middleboro 15 April 1711; d. there 1 June 1793 in 83rd yr.

He m. Plympton 6 June 1744 DEBORAH HOLMES, b. prob. Plympton ca. 1717; d. Middleboro 7 Sept. 1791 in 75th yr.; dau. of John Holmes.*

On 17 April 1783 James Soule of Middleborough, yeoman, sold land in Middleborough to son John Soule of Middleborough, Gentleman.

James Soule was 2-0-2 in the 1790 census of Middleboro.

No Plymouth Co. PR for James Soule or other deeds to children.

Children (SOULE) b. Middleboro:

i   SARAH[6] b. 20 May 1745; d. 23 Dec. 1747 ae 2y 7m 3d
ii   MARTHA b. 3 Jan. 1746 [sic]; d. 26 March 1754 in 8th yr.
iii   JOHN b. 23 Dec. 1748
iv   DEBORAH b. 27 May 1750
v   RACHEL b. 26 March 1754; d. there 13 Dec. 1811 in 57th yr.; unm. No PR.

vi   JAMES b. 10 Nov. 1756; d. Middleboro 3 June 1828
      in 71st yr.; apparently unm. An account of the
      estate of James Soule dated 4 July 1837 includes a
      list of the heirs at law: Rebecca Washburn, wife of
      Sampson Washburn; Cyrus Soule; John Soule;
      Nathan Soule; James Soule; Mary Soule; Sarah
      Miller; Deborah Whitten wife of Joseph Whitten;
      Sarah Clark, wife of Samuel Clark; Elias Miller;
      Jacob Miller; and Saba Miller and Betsey Miller.

References: VR PLYMPTON p. 394(m.). MD 13:219(d. Deborah,
          Sarah, Martha); 14:134(d. of son James); 16:107(b.
Sarah); 17:19(b. Martha); 18:85(b. John, Deborah), 154(d. Martha;
b. Rachel); 19:175(b. James); 27:182(bp. 6 ch.). MIDDLEBORO
DEATHS pp. 168-70. MF 3:57. Plymouth Co. LR 62:66(James
Soule). Middleboro Mortality Recs p. 64. Plymouth Co. PR
79:254(son James Soule). MIDDLEBORO VR 1:80(int.), 86(b.
Sarah), 100(b. Martha), 106(d. Sarah), 110(b. John), 111(b. Deb.),
114(d. Martha; b. Rachel), 125(b. James).

*MF 3 says Deborah Holmes dau. of John & Joanna (_____)
Holmes (VR PLYMPTON p. 117), but this is questionable).
(PLYMOUTH) ANC LANDMARKS 2:140 says John and 2nd w.
Mercy (Ford) Holmes had Deborah 1717. That is also unlikely.
Mercy Ford was the only wife of John Holmes and they did not
have a dau. Deborah (NGSQ 74:101). She is more likely the
Deborah Holmes born Plymouth Jan. 1716/7 dau. of John & Sarah
(_____) Holmes.

77 RACHEL SOULE[5] (Martha Tinkham[4], Ephraim[3], Mary[2]
Brown, Peter[1]) b. Middleboro 16 Nov. 1719; d. there 4 Sept. 1778
in 59th yr.
      She m. Middleboro 6 June 1744 EBENEZER VAUGHAN, b.
Middleboro 7 Sept. 1722; d. there 28 May 1810 in 88th yr.; son of
Jabez and Deborah (Bennett) Vaughn. He m. (2) int. Bridgewater
25 Dec. 1778 Lucy Pratt of Bridgewater by whom he had
Ebenezer, Rachel, and Jabez.
      On 16 Aug. 1810 a committee was appointed to set off the
widow's dower to Lucy Vaughan from the real estate of Ebenezer
Vaughan of Middleborough, yeoman.

No known children by Rachel.

References: VR BRIDGEWATER 2:377(int. his 2nd int.). MD
2:158 (m. his par.); 4:68(b. Eben.); 18:78(m.);
31:137(b. ch. Eben.); 32:6(b. 3 ch. by Lucy). MIDDLEBORO
DEATHS p. 215. Plymouth Co. PR 43:297, #21519(Eben.
Vaughan). MIDDLEBORO BY WESTON p. 668. MF 3:57.
MIDDLEBORO VR 1:22(b. Eben.), 80(1st int.), 104(m.), 193(b.
Eben.), 201(b. Eben., Rachel, Jabez), 204(d. Rachel).

78   JOHN TINKHAM[5] (John[4], Ephraim[3], Mary[2] Brown, Peter[1])
b. Middleboro 8 May 1719; d. there 22 Aug. 1793 in 75th yr.
   He m. Middleboro 27 Jan. 1742/3 JERUSHA VAUGHAN, b.
Middleboro 11 Dec. 1721; d. there 25 Nov. 1787 in 66th yr.; dau. of
John and Jerusha (Wood) Vaughan.
   On 6 March 1784 John Tinkham of Middleboro, yeoman,
gave to eldest son Cornelius Tinkham land in Middleboro,
acknowledging the deed the same day. On 23 March 1784 he gave
to son Daniel Tinkham of Rochester land partly in Middleboro
and partly in Rochester that he bought of his sister Hannah
Weston, acknowledging his signature 5 April 1784.
   The will of John Tinkham of Middleboro, yeoman, dated 26
May 1788, presented 13 Sept. 1793, names sons Cornelius, Daniel,
John and Levi; daus. Hannah Tinkham, unm.; and Jael Cobb, wife
of John, were to have wearing apparel their mother and sister left
at their decease.

      Children (TINKHAM) b. or bp. Middleboro:

        i   JAEL[6] b. 24 Jan. 1743/4
        ii   CORNELIUS b. 20 Oct. 1745
        iii DANIEL b. 26 Jan. 1746/7
        iv   SUSANNA b. 27 Nov. 1748; d. June 1753 ae 4y 6m
        v   JOSEPH b. 18 Aug. 1750; d. June 1753 ae 2y 9m
        vi   ZENAS b. 29 Oct. 1752*; bp. 18 March 1753; d.
             June 1753 ae 7m
        vii JOHN b. 16 April 1754
        viii HANNAH b. 14 April 1756*; bp. 23 May 1756
        ix   HULDAH b. 30 July 1760*; bp. 12 Oct. 1760; d. 6
             Aug. 1787 ae 27y 7d. No PR.

    x   AMASA b. 25 July 1762*; bp. 5 Sept. 1762; d. 27
          Sept. 1778 ae 16y 1m 12d
   xi   LEVI b. 19 Oct. 1765*; bp. 13 April 1766

References: MD 4:70(m. her par.); 7:240(b. Jerusha); 15:100 (d.
Amasa), 101(d. Hannah, Huldah, Jerusha), 220(m.);
16:15(b. Jael); 18:152(b. Corn. thru Joseph). MIDDLEBORO
DEATHS pp. 202, 204, 206-7. Plymouth Co. PR 33:427(John
Tinkham). Plymouth Co. LR 68:265; 72:16(John Tinkham).
Middleboro First Church Bp. pp. 44(bp. Zenas, Hannah), 45(bp.
Huldah), 46(bp. Amasa, Levi. MIDDLEBORO VR 1:74(m.), 79(b.
Jael), 112(b. Corn., Daniel, Susanna, Joseph, John).

*The birthdates of Zenas, Hannah, Huldah, Amasa, and Levi come
from DAR application #266518 and are based on the family
records of the late Marinda Tinkham.

79 ESTHER TINKHAM[5] (John[4], Ephraim[3], Mary[2] Brown,
Peter[1]) b. Middleboro 26 April 1721; living 9 April 1782.
    She m. Middleboro 4 April 1746 ELISHA VAUGHAN, b.
Middleboro 4 Dec. 1723; living 9 April 1782; son of John and
Jerusha (Wood) Vaughan.
    On 3 April 1778, ack. 9 April 1782, Elisha Vaughan and
Esther his wife of Middleboro sold land in Middleboro to Isaac
Thomas including "the lot whereon we now dwell" and lot they
received by the will of their father John Tinkham, late of
Middleborough.
    There is an Elisha Vaughn 1-2-1 in 1790 census of
Washington Town, Berkshire Co. MA. He is not there in 1800
Census. No further record has been found.
    No Plymouth Co. PR for Elisha or Esther Vaughan.

    Children (VAUGHAN) b. Middleboro:

     i   SIMEON[6] b. 21 Jan. 1747
     ii   PRISCILLA b. 13 Oct. 1748
    iii   MARY b. 23 July 1750
    iv   JOANNA b. 6 Dec. 1752
     v   JOSEPH b. 2 Aug. 1756
    vi   AZUBA b. 3 Jan. 1759

     vii   ELISHA b. 3 May 1761
     viii   ELIZABETH b. 12 Dec. 1766

References: MD 4:70(m. his par.); 7:240(b. Elisha); 17:20(b. 1st 3
              ch.), 21(b. next 4 ch.); 24:39(b. Eliz.). TAG 23:31.
Plymouth Co. LR 61:156(Elisha Vaughan). MIDDLEBORO VR pp.
38(b. Elisha), 102(b. 7 ch.), 105(m.), 146(b. Eliz.).

80   HANNAH TINKHAM[5] (John[4], Ephraim[3], Mary[2] Brown,
Peter[1]) b. Middleboro 10 April 1723; d. there 14 April 1802 ae 79.
     She m. (1) Middleboro 28 July 1742 JOSEPH VAUGHAN, b.
Middleboro 26 Jan. 1718/9; d. there bef. 5 Feb. 1747; son of John
and Jerusha (Wood) Vaughan.
     Hannah Vaughn of Middleboro was appointed
administratrix of the estate of Joseph Vaughn late of Middleboro
dec. 5 Feb. 1747.
     She m. (2) int. Middleboro 8 July 1749 JOHN WESTON, b.
Plymouth 27 July 1695; d. Middleboro 18 Aug. 1768 ae 73; son of
Edmund and Rebecca (Soule) Weston, a descendant of Pilgrim
George Soule. He m. (1) Plympton 9 Nov. 1723 Content Jackson by
whom he had John and Eleazer.
     She m. (3) Middleboro 20 Dec. 1781, DAVID SEARS, b.
Yarmouth 2 Oct. 1710; d. Middleboro 20 Aug. 1788 ae 78 yrs.; son
of Josiah and Mercy (Howes) Sears. He m. (1) Plympton 29 Nov.
1733 Phebe Bryant by whom he had Abner, David and Zebedee.
Phebe d. 9 Oct. 1779 in 67th yr.
     On 31 Jan. 1771 Hannah Weston of Middleborough, widow,
sold to Thomas Blackman land in Middleborough; Zebulon
Vaughn quitclaimed all rights to this land.
     No Plymouth Co. PR for David Sears, Hannah Sears, or John
Weston.

     Children (VAUGHAN) b. Middleboro:

     i   ZEBULUN[6] b. 8 June 1744
     ii   JOHN b. 9 Feb. 1746

References: VR PLYMPTON p. 423(John's 1st m.). MD 2:80(b.
              John); 4:70(Joseph's par.); 7:240(b. Joseph); 13:6(ch.
by David & Phebe); 15:219(1st m.); 17:20(b. ch.). MIDDLEBORO

BY WESTON pp. 660-1. MIDDLEBORO DEATHS pp. 153(d. David, Hannah), 224(d. John). TAG 23:31. MF 3:41(does not have m. to Hannah). NGSQ 71:50. SEARS DESC pp. 68, 108. Plymouth Co. PR 11:35(Jos. Vaughn). MIDDLEBORO VR 1:38(b. Joseph), 73(1st m.), 102(b. ch.); 2:9(d. Hannah), 43(int. 2nd m.), 143(3rd m.). YARMOUTH VR 1:22(b. David). Plymouth Co. LR 64:258(Hannah Weston).

81   SUSANNAH TINKHAM[5] (John[4], Ephraim[3], Mary[2] Brown, Peter[1]) b. Middleboro 19 March 1724/5; d. there 21 June 1813 in 88th yr.

She m. prob. Middleboro ca. 1749 JAMES COBB, b. Middleboro 11 March 1726/7; d. there 14 Aug. 1773 in 47th yr.; son of James and Thankful (Thomas) Cobb.

On 23 April 1777 dower was set off to widow Susanna Cobb. The 6 Oct. 1777 div. of the estate names sons James Cobb and Seth Cobb; dau. Thankful Cobb, Susanna Pratt wife of Joseph Pratt, Asenath Cobb, Zilpah Cobb, Hannah Cobb, and Priscilla Cobb.

On 3 May 1787 Susanna Cobb, widow of James late of Middleboro dec., and Mary Weston, wife of Edmond, both of Middleboro, sold the rights of their father John Tinkham of Middleboro dec.

Sussanah Cobb was 0-0-2 in the 1790 census of Middleboro.

The will of Susanna Cobb, dated 6 Jan. 1803, proved 2 Aug. 1813, names son James Cobb; daus. Priscilla Cobb; Susanna Pratt, wife of Joseph; Zilpah Sampson, wife of Philemon; Asenath Leonard, wife of Archippas; and Thankful Cobb, dec.

Children (COBB) b. Middleboro:

    i   THANKFULL[6] b. 12 Oct. 1750; d. 24 Oct. 1778 in 29th yr. No PR.

    ii   JAMES b. 26 Oct. 1752

    iii   SUSANNAH b. 22 Nov. 1754

    iv   SETH b. 8 May 1757; d. 7 miles from Kings Ferry in Army 15 Jan. 1778 in 21st yr.

    v   ASENATH b. 28 April 1760

    vi   ZILPAH b. 31 Jan. 1762

    vii   HANNAH b. 19 Feb. 1768; d. 5 July 1778 in 11th yr.

viii   PRISCILLA b. 9 Sept. 1770; d. VT in 1851; unm.

References: MD 7:240(b. James); 16:134(b. 1st 2 ch.); 18:154 (b.
              Susanna); 20:35(b. Seth, Asenath); 23:44(b. Zilpah);
29:185(b. Hannah); 30:11(b. Priscilla). MIDDLEBORO DEATHS
p. 39. COBB FAM pp. 83, 127(acct. of fam. incl. d. of Priscilla).
Plymouth Co. LR 66:254(Susanna Cobb et al.). Middleboro
Mortality Records. MIDDLEBORO VR 1:38(b. James), 91(b.
Thankfull, James), 115(b. Susanna), 126(b. Seth, Asenath), 138(b.
Zilpah), 175(b. Hannah). Plymouth Co. PR 23:22; 24:453-5(James
Cobb); 45:61-2, 128, 246(Susanna Cobb).

82   ABAISHA TINKHAM[5] (John[4], Ephraim[3], Mary[2] Brown,
Peter[1]) b. Middleboro 23 May 1727; d. there 7 March 1811 in 84th
yr.
     He m. int. Middleboro 17 Aug. 1754 HANNAH BENSON, b.
Middleboro 30 May 1736; d. there 4 Dec. 1816 in 82nd yr.; dau. of
Caleb and Deborah (Barrows) Benson. The will of Caleb Benson
of Middleborough dated 27 Nov. 1782 names dau. Hannah
Tinkham.
     Abaisha Tinkham served as a Captain in the Revolution.
     Abisha Tinkham was 2-1-2 in the 1790 census of
Middleboro.
     The will of Abisha Tinkham of Middleboro, gentleman,
dated 21 Oct. 1803, proved 21 March 1811, names wife Hannah;
dau. Lucy Clark, wife of Elisha; grandson Abisha Clark; grandson
Elisha Clark 3rd, son of dau. Lucy; granddaus. Hannah, Lucy,
Charity, and Azuba Clark; son-in-law Elisha Clark of Middleboro
to be executor with Isaiah Standish of Rochester.

     Child (TINKHAM) b. Middleboro:

     i   LUCY[6] (named in will)

References: MD 14:246(b. Hannah). MIDDLEBORO DEATHS p.
              204. Plymouth Co. PR #20809(Abisha Tinkham);
30:262 (Caleb Benson). VR ROCHESTER 2:34(m. of Hannah's
par.). MIDDLEBORO VR 1:66(b. Hannah), 436(d. Hannah); 2:17(d.
Abiasha), 49(int.).

83 AMOS TINKHAM[5] (John[4], Ephraim[3], Mary[2] Brown, Peter[1])
b. Middleboro 10 July 1729; d. there 25 April 1776 in 47th yr.
    He m. Middleboro 27 Feb. 1752 SARAH TINKHAM, b.
Middleboro 9 April 1735; d. there 13 Feb. 1820 ae 85; dau. of Peter
and Eunice (Thomas) Tinkham. (See #97 iii)
    On 24 April 1753 Amos Tinkham of Middleboro,
husbandman, and wife Sarah sold to Joseph Bates Jr. of
Middleboro, cordwainer, 1/5 of land of their father Peter
Tinkham, acknowledging their signatures 30 Oct. 1761.
    Amos Tinkham left no will but on 3 June 1776 Sarah
Tinkham and Ichabod Wood Jr., both of Middleboro, were
appointed administrators on the estate of Amos Tinkham late of
Middleboro dec. On 1 July 1776 widow Sarah Tinkum gave her
bond as guardian to Squire Tinkham under 3 years, Cyrus under
8, Amos 11 and Seth over 14, children of Amos Tinkham late of
Middleboro, with Nehemiah Allen and Ichabod Wood Jr. as
sureties.
    On 15 Oct. 1782 Seth Tinkham of the territory of VT,
husbandman, sold all rights in the estate of his father Amos
Tinkham late of Middleboro to Ichabod Wood Jr. of Middleboro.
    On 3 May 1788 Amos Tinkham of Middleboro, blacksmith,
sold Ichabod Wood of Middleboro, Gent., his interest in the estate
of his father Amos Tinkham dec.
    Sarah Tinkham was 1-0-4 in the 1790 census of Middleboro.
Listed next to her was Cyrus Tinkham 1-1-1.

        Children (TINKHAM) b. Middleboro:

        i   EUNICE[6] b. 20 May 1753; d. 22 May 1756 ae 3y 2d
        ii   SARAH b. 4 April 1757
        iii ZILPAH b. 2 Aug. 1759
        iv   SETH b. 28 Sept. 1761
        v   AMOS b. 21 May 1765
        vi   CYRUS b. 1768 (based on age at death)
        vii SQUIRE b. 17 Oct. 1772
References: MD 20:36(b. Eunice), 38(b. Sarah); 22:148(b. Zilpah);
            23:44(b. Seth); 25:105(b. Amos); 32:89 (b. Squire).
MIDDLEBORO DEATHS pp. 202(d. Amos, Sarah), 206 (d. Eunice,
Cyrus). Plymouth Co. PR #20813, 20814(Amos Tinkham; gdn.).
Plymouth Co. LR 49:66(Amos Tinkham); 66:131(Seth Tinkham);

82:244(Amos Tinkham). MIDDLEBORO VR 1:77(b. Sarah), 99(d. Eunice), 127(b. Eunice), 129(b. Sarah), 132(b. Zilpah), 137(b. Seth), 157(b. Amos), 211(b. Squire).

84 MARY TINKHAM[5] (John[4], Ephraim[3], Mary[2] Brown, Peter[1]) b. Middleboro 17 Jan. 1731/2; d. there 6 Aug. 1808 in 77th yr.

She m. Middleboro 11 Sept. 1755 EDMOND WESTON, b. Middleboro 23 Feb. 1731; d. there 4 April 1814 in 83rd yr.; son of Edmund and Susanna (Jackson) Weston, a descendant of Pilgrim George Soule.

Edmund Weston served as a private in the Revolution.

On 3 May 1787 Mary Weston, wife of Edmond Weston of Middleboro, sold her rights to the estate of her father John Tinkham of Middleboro dec.

Edmund Weston was 2-1-3 in the 1790 census of Middleboro.

The will of Edmund Weston of Middleboro, gentleman, dated 8 Sept. 1813, proved 13 April 1814, names dau. Bethania; son Edmund long absent; sons Daniel, Abner and Thomas; grandchildren Hercules, Mary, Daniel, Lewis, Leviania, and Charles, all children of son Daniel Weston; and friend Isaac Thompson.

Children (WESTON) b. Middleboro:

i   SUSANNAH[6] b. 17 Aug. 1756; d. 26 March 1757 ae 7m 8d

ii   BETHANA b. 8 Nov. 1757; d. 5 June 1837 ae 78 yrs.; unm. The will of Bethania Weston of Middleborough dated 20 March 1837, proved first Tuesday of Aug. 1837, names Thomas Wood and Horatio W. Wood, children of Horatio G. Wood of Middleboro; Abner Weston, George H. Weston and Edmund Weston, children of nephew Abner Weston, dec. & grandchildren of bro. Abner Weston dec.; Lavinia Weston dau. of bro. Thomas Weston dec.; Sarah Weston dau. of brother Thomas Weston; rest to be divided into 3 parts; one-third to children of bro. Abner, one-third to children of bro. Daniel Weston dec.; and one-third divided bet. Abigail Wood wife of Horatio G. Wood, Thomas

Weston, Lavinia Weston, Henry Weston, and
Bethania Sproat wife of Earle Sproat children of
Thomas Weston dec.

- iii   ABNER   b. 28 March 1760
- iv   EDMOND   b. 2 Feb. 1763
- v   LAVINIA   b. 29 Sept. 1764
- vi   DANIEL   b. 18 Jan. 1768
- vii   THOMAS   b. 20 March 1770

References: MD 18:153(b. Susannah); 19:48(m.); 22:148(b. Bethana),
151(b. Abner); 23:70(b. Edmond); 24:40 (b. Lavina);
29:186(b. Daniel, Thomas). MIDDLEBORO DEATHS pp. 224-5.
NGSQ 71:51. DAR PATRIOT INDEX p. 731. Plymouth Co. PR
45:336(Edmund Weston); 79:298(Bethania Weston). MIDDLEBORO
VR 1:113(b. Susanna), 120(m.), 131(b. Bethana), 135(b. Abner),
142(b. Edmond), 147(b. Lavinia), 175(b. Daniel, Thomas), 426 (d.
Mary). MF 3:135.

85   ZILPAH TINKHAM[5] (John[4], Ephraim[3], Mary[2] Brown,
Peter[1]) b. Middleboro 25 July 1737; d. there 26 Nov. 1818 ae 81.
She m. Middleboro 6 Sept. 1764 JOHN MILLER 3rd, b.
Middleboro 27 Nov. 1737; d. there 1 Dec. 1807 in 70th yr.; son of
John and Priscilla (Bennett) Miller; a descendant of Pilgrims John
Howland and Degory Priest.

John Miller was a Lt. in the Revolutionary War.

The will of John Miller 2nd of Middleboro, gentleman, dated
7 June 1794, presented 13 April 1808, names wife Zilpah; son John
3rd of Middleboro; dau. Hannah Shaw wife of Abraham 2nd of
Middleboro; dau. Lydia Wood wife of Jacob of Middleboro; dau.
Zilpah Porter wife of James of Middleboro; dau. Priscilla Miller;
dau. Minerva Miller; and mentions land which was part of estate
of John Tinkham, his father-in-law dec.

There is no Plymouth Co. PR for Zilpah Miller.

Children (MILLER) b. Middleboro:

- i   LYDIA[6]   b. 2 June 1766
- ii   ABISHAI   b. 17 Nov. 1767
- iii   ZILPHA   b. 3 Nov. 1769
- iv   JOHN   b. 24 July 1771

      v   PRISCILLA b. 16 April 1773
    vi   HANNAH b. 25 March 1765; [sic; should be 1775;
          d. 2 Oct. 1813, ae 48]. No PR.
   vii   SUSANNA b. 10 Dec. 1776
  viii   MINERVA b. 28 Feb. 1779

References: MIDDLEBORO VR 1:64(b. John), 151(b. ch.), 154 (m.).
              MD 13:251(m. John's parents); 14:244(b. John); 24:58
(b. ch.), 185(m.). MIDDLEBORO DEATHS p. 112. Plymouth Co.
PR 42:292(John Miller). DAR PATRIOT INDEX p. 469.

86   ISAAC TINKHAM[5] (Isaac[4], Ephraim[3], Mary[2] Brown, Peter[1])
b. Middleboro 21 April 1720; d. there 28 Oct. 1779 in 60th yr.
    He m. Halifax 14 June 1753 HANNAH ROBBINS, bp.
Middleboro 6 Sept. 1729; d. there 11 Jan. 1780 in 51st yr.; dau. of
John and Elizabeth (Thomas) Robbins. On 17 April 1762 Isaac
Tinkham and wife Hannah of Halifax and others sold land of
their father John Robbins dec.
    The will of Isaac Tinkham of Middleboro dated 1 July 1779,
proved 6 Feb. 1780, names wife Hannah and children Abijah;
Hannah wife of Seth Robbins; and Elizabeth, Abel, Esther,
Abigail, Huldah, and Content. On 2 Oct. 1780 Benjamin Thomas
of Middleboro posted his bond as guardian of Huldah Tinkham
under 14, dau. of Isaac Tinkham, late of Middleboro.

    Children (TINKHAM) b. Middleboro:

     i   ISAAC[6] b. 16 March 1754; prob. d.y.; not in
          father's will
    ii   ABIJAH b. 8 May 1755
   iii   HANNAH b. 13 Sept. 1756
   iv   ELIZABETH b. 27 June 1758
    v   ABEL b. 8 May 1760
    vi   ESTHER bp. 27 June 1762
   vii   ABIGAIL bp. 20 May 1764
  viii   HULDAH b. after 1766
   ix   CONTENT bp. 4 Aug. 1771

References: MD 1:246(m. her par.); 14:221(deaths); 20:35(b. Isaac),
              36(b. Abijah), 38(b. Hannah); 23:43(b. Eliz., Abel).

MIDDLEBORO DEATHS p. 203. Plymouth Co. PR 25:455-7(Isaac Tinkham); #20857(Huldah Tinkham). Plymouth Co. LR 47:267(Isaac Tinkham et al.). Middleboro First Church Bp. pp. 24(bp. wife Hannah), 46(bp. Esther, Abigail), 47(bp. Content). HALIFAX VR p. 35(m.). MIDDLEBORO VR 1:126(b. Isaac), 127(b. Abijah), 129(b. Hannah), 137(b. Eliz., Abel).

87   NOAH TINKHAM⁵ (Isaac⁴, Ephraim³, Mary² Brown, Peter¹)
b. Middleboro 25 July 1722; d. Halifax 12 June 1765 in 43rd yr.
      He m. Bridgewater 16 June 1751 SARAH PORTER, b. Abington 26 May 1723; d. Halifax 27 July 1795 in 73rd yr.; dau. of Samuel and Sarah (Joslyn) Porter.
      The will of Noah Tinkham of Halifax, yeoman, dated 7 June 1765, proved 5 Aug. 1765, names wife Sarah; sons Noah and Joseph; daus. Sarah and Mary; brother Isaac Tinkham was named executor.
      No Plymouth Co. PR for Sarah Tinkham.

      Children (TINKHAM) b. Halifax:

      i   MOSES⁶ b. 16 Nov. 1752; d. 13 May 1754
      ii   SARAH b. 20 April 1756; d. Halifax 12 June 1832 ae 76 yrs.; unm. The will of Sarah Tinkham of Halifax, singlewoman, dated 20 Jan. 1827, proved 7 Aug. 1832, leaves all to bro. Joseph Tinkham & after his death to go to Sarah wife of Seabury Hathaway until her oldest son arrived at age 21.
      iii   MARY b. 15 June 1758; d. Halifax 23 March 1814 in 56th yr.; unm. No PR.
      iv   NOAH b. 15 Sept. 1761
      v   JOSEPH b. 24 Nov. 1764

References: MD 3:157(d. Moses); 14:10(all d's.). VR ABINGTON
                  1:173(b. Sarah). VR BRIDGEWATER 2:370(m.).
HALIFAX VR pp. 4(d. Moses), 7(d. Sarah), 53(b. ch.), 58(int.).
Plymouth Co. PR 19:242-3(Noah Tinkham); 72:340; 75:191(Sarah Tinkham).

88   NATHAN TINKHAM⁵ (Isaac⁴, Ephraim³, Mary² Brown,

Peter[1]) b. Middleboro 18 April 1725; d. Pomfret VT 3 Oct. 1807 ae 82.

She m. Halifax 10 Dec. 1746 SARAH SOULE, b. Plympton 15 June 1727; d. Pomfret VT 28 Sept. 1807 ae 80; dau. of Zachariah and Mary (Eaton) Soule, a descendant of Pilgrims John Alden, Francis Eaton, George Soule, and Myles Standish.

On 9 Jan. 1799 Nathan Tinkham of Halifax, yeoman, sold his farm in Halifax to Abishai and Damaris Samson of Taunton. Sarah Tinkham relinquished her dower. In Feb. 1801 Nathan Tinkham of Randolph [the son] sold 17 acres in Randolph [VT] to Nathan Tinkham of Pomfret.

The will of Nathan Tinkham of Pomfret, Windsor Co. VT dated 24 June 1803, recorded 3 Nov. 1807, names wife Sarah; son Ephraim; dau. Ruth Tinkham; children of his dau. Sarah Churchill dec.; and sons Nathan and Isaiah. On 4 April 1809 order was given to divide the land among the children. Son Isaiah Tinkham of Pomfret paid the other children for their shares.

Children (TINKHAM) b. Halifax:

i	EPHRAIM[6] b. 21 April 1748
ii	RUTH b. 14 Aug. 1750
iii	SARAH b. 2 June 1753
iv	NATHAN b. 26 Jan. 1756
v	ISAIAH b. 19 Sept. 1757
vi	ZENAS b. 10 July 1763 (not named in will)

References: VR PLYMPTON p. 192(b. Sarah). HALIFAX VR pp. 34 (m.), 53(b. Ephraim), 54(b. last 5 ch.). Record of Deaths, Pomfret VT Vol. 1(d. Nathan, Sarah). MF 3:164. Plymouth Co. LR 85:252(Nathan Tinkham). MD 43:163-4(son Isiah). Randolph VT LR 2:367(Nathan Tinkham). Hartford VT Probate Dist. 3:446, 464, 506(Nathan Tinkham).

89 ABIJAH TINKHAM[5] (Isaac[4], Ephraim[3], Mary[2] Brown, Peter[1]) b. Middleboro 21 March 1727/8; d. there 5 Feb. 1776 in 48th yr.

She m. Middleboro 29 Nov. 1753 NATHAN COBB, b. Middleboro 24 Oct. 1728; d. there 29 Aug. 1818 ae 90; son of John and Mary (Connant) Cobb, a descendant of Pilgrim George Soule.

On 19 Jan. 1759 Nathan and Abijah Cobb sold land in Halifax which had belonged to "our honoured father Isaac Tinkham deceased" to Jacob Tomson.

On 4 Jan. 1774 Nathan and Abijah Cobb sold land to Daniel Thomas which Nathan had received from his father John Cobb.

No Plymouth Co. PR for Nathan Cobb.

No intrafamily Plymouth Co. LR.

Children (COBB) b. Middleboro:

i	JOHN[6]	b. 7 Oct. 1754; d. 7 Oct. 1760 ae 6y
ii	SUSANNA	b. 25 Oct. 1756
iii	ABIJAH	b. 7 Aug. 1761
iv	NATHAN	bp. 3 Nov. 1765
v	ISAAC	bp. 27 Sept. 1767

References: MD 4:73(m. his par.); 8:29(b. Nathan); 19:46(m.); 20:34(b. John, Susanna); 23:44(b. Abijah). MIDDLEBORO DEATHS pp. 39-40. Middleboro First Ch. Bp. pp. 46(bp. Nathan), 47 (bp. Isaac). COBB FAM p. 126. MF 3:46-7, 149. MIDDLEBORO VR 1:43(b. Nathan), 119(m.), 125(b. John), 126(b. Susanna), 138 (b. Abijah). Plymouth Co. LR 45:190-1; 57:250 (Nathan Cobb).

90 EPHRAIM TINKHAM[5] (Samuel[4], Ephraim[3], Mary[2] Brown, Peter[1]) b. Middleboro 30 April 1733; d. there 5 Nov. 1769 in 37th yr.

He m. Halifax prob. 5 Jan. 1758* SARAH STANDISH, b. Halifax 26 April 1736; d. poss. bef. 2 Dec. 1809 when John Wright administered the estate of Sarah Wright dec.; dau. of Moses and Rachel (Cobb) Standish, a descendant of Pilgrims John Alden, Myles Standish, and George Soule. She m. (2) Plympton 1 June 1773 Adam Wright by whom she had Benjamin.

On 28 Feb. 1770 Silas Tinkham of Middleboro was appointed administrator of the estate of Ephraim Tinkham of Middleboro yeoman dec. and on 21 June 1773 Sarah Wright petitioned to have a guardian appointed for "my four children, Abigail, Sarah, Ephraim and Samuel Tinkham." On 1 Oct. 1781 dower was set off from the estate of Adam Wright to his widow Sarah.

On 12 April 1791 Caleb Leach and Abigail his wife of Plymouth, Ephraim Tinkham and Samuel Tinkham, both of Middleboro sold to Peter Wood of Middleboro a piece of land in Plimton that their father Ephraim Tinkham purchased from their grandfather Samuel Tinkham.

Children (TINKHAM) b. Middleboro:

i ABIGAIL[6] b. 20 July 1758
ii SAMUEL b. 16 March 1760; d. 2 Aug. 1761
iii JOSHUA b. 24 April 1762; d. 24 Oct. 1762
iv SARAH b. 11 Sept. 1763
v EPHRAIM b. 2 Aug. 1765
vi SUSANNA b. 27 Aug. 1767; d. 3 Nov. 1769 ae 2y 2m 6d
vii SAMUEL b. 17 July 1769

References: MD 26:24(b. 6 ch.), 25(d. Susanna); 29:189(b. Samuel). VR PLYMPTON p. 429(2nd m.). HALIFAX VR pp. 36(m.), 42(b. Sarah).   MIDDLEBORO BY WESTON p. 666. MIDDLEBORO DEATHS pp. 205-6. Plymouth Co. PR 20:357, 380; 21:101(Ephraim Tinkham); #23498(Adam Wright); 43:77(Sarah Wright). Middleboro First Church Bp. p. 48(bp. Benj. Wright). MF 3:145, 155; 14:107-8. Plymouth Co. LR 77:166(Caleb Leach, etc.). MIDDLEBORO VR 1:162(b. 6 ch.; d. Sam.), 163(d. Susanna), 179(b. Sam).

*HALIFAX VR states that the marriage took place in 1759, however since it was recorded in the middle of marriages which took place in 1757 and 1758, and their intentions of marriage were published 19 Dec. 1757, the year of their marriage is more likely 1758.

91 SILAS TINKHAM[5] (Samuel[4], Ephraim[3], Mary[2] Brown, Peter[1]) b. Middleboro 25 April 1739; d. there 22 Jan. 1816 ae 77.
    He m. Plympton 20 Dec. 1771 LYDIA (SAVERY) SMITH, b. Middleboro 27 Feb. 1747; d. there 6 Nov. 1801 in 54th yr.; dau. of John and Mary (Thomas) Savery. She m. (1) Middleboro 26 Nov. 1767 Jabez Smith by whom she had Jabez. The will of John

Savory of Middleboro dated 20 May 1778 names wife Mary and dau. Lydia Tinkham.

The will of Silas Tinkham of Middleboro, yeoman, dated 16 Oct. 1812, presented 2 April 1816, names daus. Elizabeth Tinkham and Susanna Tinkham who were to have land; his father Samuel Tinkham dec.; dau. Lydia Soule wife of Thomas; and son John Tinkham 2nd who with friend Isaac Thompson Esq. was to be executor. On 26 May 1840 John Tinkham, Silas Tinkham, Amasa Merrill and wife Elizabeth, and Sarah B. Tinkham, all of Middleboro; Sophia Tinkham wife of John; and Sophia A. Tinkham dau. of John and Elizabeth Tinkham, of Middleboro, singlewoman, sold land and dwelling house formerly owned by Silas Tinkham late of Middleboro dec., which was given Elizabeth and her late sister Susannah by the will of the dec.

Children (TINKHAM) b. Middleboro:

i   ELIZABETH[6] b. 20 Feb. 1772
ii   JOHN b. 8 Aug. 1774
iii   SUSANNA b. 30 July 1778; d. Middleboro 30 Dec. 1823; unm. No PR.
iv   LYDIA b. 15 Aug. 1782

References: MD 8:250(m. her par.); 14:221(d. Silas, Lydia); 18:85(b. Lydia); 29:183(Lydia's 1st m.); 30:9(b. Jabez). VR PLYMPTON p. 413(m.). MIDDLEBORO DEATHS p. 204. MIDDLEBORO BY WESTON pp. 672, 667. NEHGR 41:387. Plymouth Co. PR 25:71(John Savory); #20913(Silas Tinkham). Plymouth Co. LR 199:137(John Tinkham). MIDDLEBORO VR 1:110(b. Lydia), 173 (Lydia's 1st m.), 246(b. Eliz., John), 247(b. Susan, Lydia); 2:9(d. Lydia).

92 SUSANNA WOOD[5] (Mary[4] Tinkham, Ephraim[3], Mary[2] Brown, Peter[1]) b. Middleboro 24 April 1724; d. there 24 Sept. 1786 in 63rd yr., widow of Capt. Samuel Smith.

She m. Middleboro 24 Dec. 1767 SAMUEL SMITH, b. Middleboro 30 Aug. 1714; d. there 16 Dec. 1781 in 68th yr.; son of Jonathan and Susanna (Thomas) Smith. He m. (1) Middleboro 23 Dec. 1738 Rachel Cobb, a descendant of Pilgrim George Soule, by whom he had William, Samuel, Cornelius, Susannah, Hannah,

Ebenezer, and Lucy.

The will of Samuel Smith of Middleboro dated 8 Dec. 1781, presented 6 Jan. 1783, names wife Susanna; sons William and Cornelius; dau. Susanna Smith unm.; Joanna Smith under 18; son Ebenezer; and grandsons Samuel and William Smith, sons of my son William.

No Plymouth Co. PR for Susanna Smith.

Child (SMITH) b. Middleboro:

    i   JOANNA[6] b. 18 June 1769; d. 23 Nov. 1785 in 16th yr.

References: MD 3:233(b. Samuel); 14:132(d. Joanna), 133(d. Susanna, Sam.); 27:132(b. Joanna); 29:184(m.). MIDDLEBORO DEATHS p. 163. MIDDLEBORO BY WESTON pp. 651, 659-60. Plymouth Co. PR 28:522-3(Sam. Smith). MF 3:151. MIDDLEBORO VR 1:18(b. Sam.), 69(b. Wm.), 100(b. Sam.), 101(b. Corn.), 114(b. Sus.), 125(b. Eben.), 136(b. Lucy), 170(b. Joanna), 173(m.).

93   HENRY WOOD[5] (Mary[4] Tinkham, Ephraim[3], Mary[2] Brown, Peter[1]) b. Middleboro 27 Feb. 1726/7; d. 26 Dec. 1806.

He m. Middleboro 1 Aug. 1754 LYDIA BENSON, b. Middleboro 27 Aug. 1736; d. 21 Feb. 1814; dau. of Samuel and Kezia (Barrows) Benson.

Henry Wood was 2-1-3 in the 1790 census of Middleboro.

Neither Henry nor Lydia Wood left probate records, but on 15 March 1791 Henry Wood of Middleboro gave land in that town to his son Enoch Wood of Middleboro and on 23 Aug. 1792 Henry, still of Middleboro, sold his homestead, with wife Lydia giving up her dower to Zachariah Weston of Middleboro.

Children (WOOD) b. Middleboro:

    i   DELIVERANCE[6] b. 25 March 1755; d. 19 Aug. 1769 ae 14y 4m 25d
    ii   MARY b. 16 May 1756
    iii HOPE b. 15 Oct. 1757
    iv SAMUEL b. 10 Sept. 1759

v   MARTHA   b. 9 April 1761
vi   DEBORAH   b. 13 May 1763
vii   KEZIAH   b. 6 Jan. 1765
viii   ENOCH (twin) b. 24 June 1769
ix   ELIJAH (twin) b. 24 June 1769
x   SUSANNA
xi   JOANNA   b. 9 April 1773
xii   HENRY   b. 14 Jan. 1779

References: MD 1:248(m. her par.); 15:120(b. Lydia); 18:153(b. Deliverance, Mary). MIDDLEBORO DEATHS p. 239 (d. Deliverance). WOOD OF MIDDLEBORO pp. 20-1(b. ch.). Plymouth Co. LR 71:260; 74:72; 78:125(Henry Wood). MIDDLEBORO VR 1:68(b. Lydia), 113(b. Deliverance, Mary).

NOTE: No proof found that this family moved to Winthrop ME.

94 MOSES WOOD[5] (Mary[4] Tinkham, Ephraim[3], Mary[2] Brown, Peter[1]) b. Middleboro 3 Feb. 1730/1; d. there 26 July 1779.
    He m. Middleboro 12 Jan. 1762 LYDIA WATERMAN, b. Middleboro 18 Aug. 1740; d. Winthrop ME 30 Oct. 1790; dau. of Joseph and Patience (Barrow) Waterman, a descendant of Pilgrims Isaac Allerton and Degory Priest.
    On 2 Aug. 1779 Lydia Wood of Middleboro, widow, was appointed administratrix of the estate of Moses Wood, late of Middleboro, blacksmith, and on 21 Nov. 1793 Ebenezer Wood of Middleboro was appointed administrator of the estate of Lydia Wood, late of Middleboro widow. There was no recorded division of the estate of either Moses or Lydia in Plymouth Co., but on 27 Dec. 1793 Joshua Waterman of Middleboro sold to Thomas and Andrew Wood of Middleboro land of "Isaiah Wood a minor, now residing in Winthrop, Lincoln Co. [ME] ... and son of Moses Wood late of Middleboro deceased."

    Children (WOOD) b. Middleboro:

    i   son[6] b. Sept. 1763; d. 16 Sept. 1763
    ii   MOSES b. 3 March 1765
    iii   DELIVERANCE   b. 28 Aug. 1769; d. 5 Oct. 1786
    iv   ISAIAH b. 3 July 1773

     v   BATHSHEBA b. 9 Sept. 1776; d. 20 March 1788. No PR.

References: MD 19:142(m.); 29:189(b. Moses, Deliverance). PN&Q 2:42(Rebecca (Perley) Wood's Bible). MIDDLEBORO DEATHS p. 240. WATERMAN GEN 1:94-5,183-4. WOOD OF MIDDLEBORO pp. 20, 22. Plymouth Co. PR 27:27; 28:234(Moses Wood); 27:462 (Lydia Wood). Plymouth Co. LR 75:239(Isaiah Wood). MIDDLEBORO VR 1:67(b. Lydia), 122(m.), 178(b. Moses, Delv.).

95 ELIZABETH TINKHAM[5] (Ebenezer[4-3], Mary[2] Brown, Peter[1]) b. Middleboro 13 Oct. 1704; d. Bridgewater 3 Feb. 1780.

    She m. Middleboro 28 March 1728 NATHANIEL HOOPER, b. Bridgewater 16 Nov. 1703; d. there 27 Oct. 1774; son of John and Sarah (Harden) Hooper.

    On 17 Nov. 1730 Nathaniel Hooper of Bridgewater and wife Elizabeth sold to their brother Peter Tinkham of Middleboro 1/6 of land of their father Ebenezer Tinkham dec.

    Nathaniel Hooper served in the French and Indian War at Fort Edward and at Halifax, Nova Scotia. He is called a bricklayer in various court records.

    On 17 Dec. 1764 Nathaniel Hooper sold to Ebenezer Hooper 33 acres in South Bridgewater, the northerly end of his homestead. On 15 April 1771 Nathaniel Hooper sold to Daniel Keith 7 acres in Bridgewater with wife Elizabeth renouncing dower.

    There is no Plymouth Co. PR for Nathaniel or Elizabeth Hooper, nor any deeds to children other than the above.

    Children (HOOPER) b. Bridgewater:*

i	ELIZABETH[6]	b. 13 April 1729
ii	MARY	b. 17 May 1731
iii	PATIENCE	b. 5 Feb. 1732/3
iv	NATHANIEL	b. 9 Feb. 1734/5
v	SARAH	b. 10 Feb. 1736/7
vi	ZILPHA	b. 1738
vii	EBENEZER	bp. June 1740
viii	LEMUEL	b. 1742; d. 6 Nov. 1758
ix	MILLICENT	b. 1744

x   child   d. 20 July 1746

References: MD 5:39(m.); 15:85(b. Nath.), 196(b. 1st 5 ch.). VR
         BRIDGEWATER   1:163-5(b. Nathaniel;   b. ch.);
2:494(d. Nathaniel), 495(d. Elizabeth). BRIDGEWATER BY
MITCHELL p. 195. HOOPER GEN, Charles Henry Pope &
Thomas Hooper, Boston 1908, pp. 16-18(b. Zilpha, Ebenezer,
Lemuel, Millicent, William). Plymouth Co. LR 42:201; 52:214;
56:73 (Nathaniel Hooper). MIDDLEBORO VR 1:31(m.).

*The first 5 children are in VR BRIDGEWATER, as well as the
death of the child in 1746. The others are from HOOPER GEN
without documentation, which also includes a possible son
William, who seems unlikely.

96   MARY TINKHAM[5] (Ebenezer[4-3], Mary[2] Brown, Peter[1]) b.
Middleboro 30 Jan. 1705/6; d. after 12 April 1757.
        She m. Middleboro 21 Aug. 1729 WILLIAM HACK of
Taunton, who d. bef. 7 July 1752; son of William Hack.
        On 27 May 1734 William Hack of Taunton and wife Mary
sold to their brother Peter Tinkham of Middleboro, 1/6 of land of
their father Ebenezer Tinkham.
        Mary Hack of Taunton widow was appointed administratrix
on the estate of her husband, William Hack late of Taunton dec.,
7 July 1752. On the same day she was appointed guardian to
Mary, Peter, and Susannah, children of the late William Hack.
Division of William Hack's real estate, 12 April 1757, names
widow Mary Hack, eldest son William, 2nd son Nathan, eldest dau
Mary Hack, 2nd dau. Susanna Hack, 3rd surviving son Peter, and
son Zephaniah who died after his father.

        Children (HACK) b. Taunton; all named in division:

        i   WILLIAM[6] b. ca. 1731
        ii   NATHAN b. 1733
        iii   ZEPHANIAH d. bet. 1752 and 1757
        iv   MARY b. aft. 7 July 1738
        v   SUSANNA b. aft. 7 July 1738
        vi   PETER b. aft. 7 July 1738

References: MD 5:39(m.). NEHGR 48:454. Bristol Co. PR 13:188-9;
        18:128; 124:45-7(William Hack). Plymouth Co. LR
42:202(Wm. Hack). MIDDLEBORO VR 1:31(m.).

97 PETER TINKHAM[5] (Ebenezer[4-3], Mary[2] Brown, Peter[1]) b.
Middleboro 5 Sept. 1709; d. there 10 Oct. 1745 in 37th yr.
        He m. Middleboro 1 April 1730 EUNICE THOMAS, b.
Middleboro 15 Feb. 1708/9; d. there 8 April 1778 in 70th yr.; dau.
of William and Sarah (Barden) Thomas. The will of David
Thomas of Middleboro dated 30 Aug. 1742 names his mother
Sarah Thomas and [his sister] Eunice, wife of Peter Tinkham.
        On 4 March 1745 Joseph Tinkham was appointed guardian
to Patience and Sarah Tinkham and Unise Tinkham was
appointed guardian to Peter Tinkham.
        Patience Tinkham of Middleboro sold to Joseph Bates Jr. of
Middleboro cordwainer 1/5 of the estate of her father Peter
Tinkham dec., land in Middleboro, signed 5 May 1753, ack. 6 Nov.
1753.
        The estate of Peter Tinkham of Middleboro was divided 12
March 1756 with 1/3 going to widow Eunis Tinkham; two shares
to only son Peter; and one share each to eldest dau. Eunis Bates,
2nd dau. Patience Eaton, and youngest dau. Sarah Tinkham.

        Children (TINKHAM) b. Middleboro:

        i   EUNICE[6] b. 6 July 1730
        ii   PATIENCE b. 9 April 1732
        iii   SARAH b. 9 April 1735
        iv   (son) b. 23 April 1739; d. 16 days
        v   PETER b. 24 June 1743

References: MD 2:43(m. her par.), 202(b. Eunice); 8:250(m.);
        15:101(d. Eunice), 102(d. Peter). MQ 43:114(b. 5 ch.;
d. son). MIDDLEBORO DEATHS pp. 201(d. Peter, Eunice); 207(d.
ch. iv). Plymouth Co. PR 8:539(David Thomas); 16:141;
#20897(Peter Tinkham). Plymouth Co. LR 42:203(Patience
Tinkham). THOMAS GEN p. 9. MIDDLEBORO VR 1:14(b.
Eunice), 47(m.), 77(b. ch.).

98   PATIENCE TINKHAM[5] (Ebenezer[4-3], Mary[2] Brown, Peter[1])
bp. Middleboro 11 April 1714; d. there 9 April 1791 in 74th yr.
She m. Middleboro 20 June 1744 EDMOND WOOD, b.
Middleboro 28 Nov. 1721; d. there 29 Dec. 1805 ae 84; son of
David and Joanna (Tilson) Wood.

On 16 March 1743 Patience Tinkham of Middleboro sold to
brother Peter Tinkham of Middleboro, 1/6 of land of her father
Ebenezer Tinkham, acknowledging the deed the next day.

Edmond Wood was a private in the Revolution.

The will of Edmond Wood of Middleboro, yeoman, dated 3
June 1791, codicil 10 April 1800, and both presented 4 Feb. 1806,
names sons Edmond, Joshua, Francis and Peter, each to have 1/4
of real estate; daus. Patience wife of James Smith, and Priscilla
wife of Perez Churchill, Jr.

Children (WOOD) b. Middleboro:

    i   PATIENCE[6] b. 9 May 1746
    ii   EDMOND b. 9 March 1747/8
    iii   PETER b. 24 Jan. 1749/50
    iv   PRISCILLA b. 4 Jan. 1752
    v   JOSHUA b. 27 Dec. 1753
    vi   FRANCIS b. 6 Sept. 1756

References: MD 3:235(b. Edmund); 15:107(d. Edmund), 109 (d.
          Patience); 16:15(int.), 20(m.); 17:21(b. 1st 2 ch.), 22(b.
Peter); 18:153(b. last 3 ch.). DAR PATRIOT INDEX p. 757.
Plymouth Co. PR #23342(Edmond Wood). Plymouth Co. LR
42:203(Patience Tinkham). MIDDLEBORO VR 1:21(b. Edmond),
80 (int.), 85(m.), 102(b. Patience), 103(b. Edmond, Peter), 113 (b.
Joshua, Francis), 114(b. Priscilla); 2:12(d. Edmond).
MIDDLEBORO DEATHS p. 234(d. Edmund, Patience).

99   PRISCILLA TINKHAM[5] (Ebenezer[4-3], Mary[2] Brown, Peter[1])
bp. Middleboro 22 April 1716; living 20 May 1758 (deed).
She m. ca. 1733 JOHN WOODS, b. Bridgewater 1 Oct. 1710;
living 24 April 1772 (deed) and prob. living 14 April 1779 (when
his son was still called Jr.); son of Francis and Sarah (Harden)
(Hooper) Woods.

On 12 Feb. 1755 John Wood of Bridgewater   and   wife

Priscilla, who deeded to Peter Tinkham now dec. 1/6 of land of Ebenezer Tinkham late of Middleboro dec., and "that deed not likely to be recorded," quitclaimed their rights to heirs of Peter Tinkham.

On 20 May 1758 John Woods of Bridgewater and wife Priscilla sold 22 acres in Bridgewater to James Hooper of Bridgewater.

On 1 Oct. 1761 Ebenezer Jones of Easton sold to John Woods of Bridgewater, yeoman, his homestead of over 28 acres in Easton.

On 24 March 1767 John Woods of Easton sold 20 acres in Easton to John Woods Jr. and on 15 July 1769 John Woods of Easton sold the tract he bought from Ebenezer Jones to Ebenezer Woods of Easton. [While they are not called sons, they are obviously his sons.]

On 14 April 1779 John Woods Jr. of Easton with wife Rachel sold 20 acres "conveyed to my honored father from Wm. Pratt."

No Bristol Co. or Plymouth Co. PR for John or Priscilla Woods.

Children (WOODS) b. Bridgewater:

i	ANNA[6] b. 21 July 1734; d. 30 Oct. 1734
ii	MARY b. Oct. 1735
iii	WILLIAM b. 12 May 1737; d. 14 May 1737
iv	PRISCILLA b. 19 Dec. 1738
v	JOHN b. 28 Jan. 1740
vi	SARAH b. 19 Feb. 1742
vii	EBENEZER (twin) b. 14 Sept. 1745
viii	PATIENCE (twin) b. 14 Sept. 1745
ix	ABIGAIL b. 8 July 1747
x	FRANCIS b. 2 Nov. 1750
xi	SILAS b. 6 April 1752
xii	JOSEPH b. 9 March 1756

References: VR BRIDGEWATER 1:358(b. John; b. ch.); 2:586(d. Anna, William). VR EAST BRIDGEWATER pp. 147-8(b. ch.). BRIDGEWATER BY MITCHELL p. 372. Plymouth Co. LR 49:65, 124(John Woods). MD 15:85(b. John). Bristol Co. LR 49:304; 54:515(John Woods); 59:464(John Woods Jr.).

100 JEREMIAH TINKHAM[5] (Jeremiah[4], Ebenezer[3], Mary[2] Brown, Peter[1]) b. Middleboro 20 Feb. 1712/3; d. there 4 June 1790 in 77th yr.

He m. ca. 1739 NAOMI WARREN, b. 1716; bp. Scituate 8 Sept. 1717; d. Middleboro 21 June 1795 ae 79y 4m 11d; dau. of John and Naomi (Bates) Warren, a descendant of Pilgrim Richard Warren.   The will of John Warren of Middleboro dated 21 Jan. 1768 names dau. Naomi wife of Jeremiah Tinkham.

The will of Jeremiah Tinkham of Middleboro, yeoman, dated 2 June 1790, proved 5 July 1790, names wife Naomi; son Jeremiah; son Elisha who is to have the legacy given his mother by the will of her father John Warren, late of Middleboro; sons James and Jesse; daus. Anna Warren, Abigail Tinkham, and Huldah Tinkham; grandson Tiler Tinkham, son of Ebenezer Tinkham "the second of the name in said Middleboro."

No Plymouth Co. PR for Naomi Tinkham.

Children (TINKHAM) b. Middleboro:

i	JEREMIAH[6] b. 27 Oct. 1740	
ii	ELISHA b. 18 Aug. 1742	
iii	JOANNA b. 6 Dec. 1743; d. 2 June 1761 in 18th yr.	
iv	JAMES b. 8 May 1745	
v	ABIGAIL b. 25 Dec. 1746	
vi	ANNA b. 9 Oct. 1748	
vii	JESSE b. 25 July 1750	
viii	BENJAMIN b. 6 Jan. 1755; d. 23 Aug. 1775 ae 20y 7m 17d	
ix	HULDAH b. 8 Dec. 1756; d. Middleboro 25 May 1835 in 79th yr.; unm. Administration of the estate of Huldah Tinkham of Middleborough was dated 7 July 1835.	
x	EBENEZER b. 26 Aug. 1758	

References: MD 15:100(d. Benj.), 101(d. Huldah, Jeremiah), 102(d. Naomi, Joanna), 220(b. 1st 3 ch.); 20:36 (b. 6 ch.), 38(b. Eben.). MIDDLEBORO DEATHS pp. 201-2. Plymouth Co. PR 20:59(John Warren); 31:218-21(Jeremiah Tinkham); 71:334; 77:447; 78:412(Huldah Tinkham).   VR SCITUATE 1:401(bp. Naomi). MIDDLEBORO VR 1:76(b. 1st 3 ch.), 127(b. 6 ch.), 129 (b.

Eben.); 2:29(d. Huldah).

101 EBENEZER TINKHAM[5] (Jeremiah[4], Ebenezer[3], Mary[2]
Brown, Peter[1]) b. Middleboro 16 Dec. 1714; d. there 17 Nov. 1801
in 87th yr.
    He m. Plympton 22 Feb. 1738/9 HANNAH SHAW, b.
Plymouth ca. 1716; d. Middleboro 15 Sept. 1794 in 79th yr.; dau. of
Benoni and Lydia (Waterman) Shaw. On 19 Feb. 1754 Ebenezer
Tinkham of Middleboro and wife Hannah sold their rights to land
of their father Benoni Shaw dec., late of Plympton.
    The will of Ebenezer Tinkham of Middleboro, yeoman, dated
3 April 1795, proved 6 Jan. 1802, names eldest son Isaac and his
son Ebenezer; granddaus. Mary Wood, wife of Andrew; and
Priscilla Wood, wife of Enoch; daus. Rebecca Thomas, wife of
David; Lucy Fuller, wife of Issacher; Ruth Tinkham unm.; Betty
Tinkham, wife of Ebenezer Tinkham; and Lydia Thomas, wife of
Zebulon who "hath removed a great distance from me."

    Children (TINKHAM) b. Middleboro:

i	REBECCA[6]	b. 20 Dec. 1739
ii	ISAAC	b. 26 Nov. 1741
iii	ZEBEDEE	b. 24 Jan. 1744
iv	HANNAH	b. 26 July 1747
v	LYDIA	b. 4 Dec. 1749
vi	LUCIA	b. 22 April 1752

vii   RUTH   b. 17 April 1755.   The will of Ruth
        Tinkham of Middleboro "feme sole" dated 24 Sept.
        1805, proved 16 Oct. 1805, names niece Ruth
        Barrows, wife of Josiah; niece Hope Tinkham, dau.
        of bro. Zebedee Tinkham; sisters Rebeckah
        Thomas, Lydia Thomas, Lucy Fuller, and Betty
        Tinkham; and brother-in-law Ebenezer Tinkham.
viii   ELIZABETH b. 4 April 1757
ix   PRISCILLA b. 5 June 1760; d. 3 July 1770 ae 10y
        28d

References: MD 14:246(b. Rebecca); 15:100-1(deaths), 223(b. Isaac);
               16:108(b. Zeb.); 20:36-8(b. ch.); 22:149 (b. Priscilla).
Plymouth Co. PR 37:547-9(Eben. Tinkham);   #20901(Ruth

Tinkham). SHAW GEN pp. 10, 25-6. Plymouth Co. LR 45:64(Ebenezer Tinkham). MIDDLEBORO VR 1:66(b. Rebecca), 78(b. Isaac), 87(b. Zeb.), 127(b. Hannah, Lydia, Lucia), 128 (b. Ruth), 129(b. Eliz.), 132(b. Priscilla); 2:9(d. Eben.). WATERMAN GEN 1:35-6.

102 THOMAS MACOMBER[5] (Joanna Tinkham[4], Ebenezer[3], Mary[2] Brown, Peter[1]) b. Marshfield 28 April 1710; d. there 8 Jan. 1748/9 in 39th yr.

He m. Marshfield 9 May 1745 MARCY TILDEN, b. 1722; bp. Scituate 9 Sept. 1722; d. prob. Islesboro ME after 1781; dau. of Samuel and Desire (Oldham) Tilden, a descendant of Pilgrim Henry Samson. She m. (2) Marshfield 1 Jan. 1761 David Thomas by whom she had John and David. The will of Samuel Tilden of Marshfield dated 6 April 1757 names wife Desire; dau. Mercy Macomber and others.

On 26 Jan. 1748 admin. on the estate of Thomas Macomber late of Marshfield dec. was granted to his father Thomas Macomber of Marshfield and on 27 Jan. 1748 widow Mercy Macomber of Marshfield was appointed guardian of William and Thomas Macomber, minor sons of Thomas Macomber Jr.

Children (MACOMBER) b. Marshfield:

    i   WILLIAM[6] b. 1 May 1746
    ii   THOMAS b. 2 Aug. 1748

References: MD 19:16-21(prob.). MARSHFIELD VR pp. 96(b. Wm., Thomas), 97(d. Thomas), 148(2nd m.), 172(m.), 405 (d. Thomas). THOMAS GEN p. 172(Mercy living 1781). Plymouth Co. PR 11:128, 181-2(Thomas Macomber); 21:605(Samuel Tilden). VR SCITUATE 1:359(bp. Marcy). MF 20:1:44.

103 SARAH MACOMBER[5] (Joanna Tinkham[4], Ebenezer[3], Mary[2] Brown, Peter[1]) b. Marshfield 27 Oct. 1713; d. Pembroke 6 Jan. 1786.

She m. ca. 1738 JOSIAH BARKER, b. Scituate or Pembroke ca. 1717; d. Pembroke 15 June 1774; son of Ebenezer and Deborah (Randall) Barker.

The will of Josiah Barker of Pembroke, gentleman, dated 10

April 1774, presented 4 July 1774, names wife Sarah; sons Ebenezer and Thomas exe.; and daus. Deborah Randall, Joanna Tilden, Ursula Crooker, Sarah Little, and Lydia Barker. On 3 March 1781, Robert Barker of Pembroke, exe. of the estate of Thomas Barker, was empowered to sell part of Josiah's estate to pay the debts, the dec. Thomas had purchased his brother Ebenezer's portion of the estate and had promised to pay the debts.

The will of Sarah Barker of Pembroke, widow, advanced in age, dated 10 Oct. 1785, presented 1 March 1786, names dau. Sarah Little executor; dau. Lydia Sprague; 8 (unnamed) children of son Ebenezer dec.; 6 (unnamed) children of son Thomas dec.; and daus. Deborah Randall, Joanna Tilden, and Ursula Crooker.

Children (BARKER) b. Pembroke:

i	EBENEZER[6] b. 3 Aug. 1739
ii	DEBORAH b. 5 Oct. 1741
iii	THOMAS b. 29 Oct. 1743
iv	JOANNA b. 2 Sept. 1745
v	SARAH b. 14 Sept. 1747; d. Pembroke 2 March 1748
vi	URSULA b. 5 March 1749
vii	SARAH b. 6 Aug. 1751
viii	LYDIA b. 6 Feb. 1754

References: NEHGR 53:426-9. BARKER GEN pp. 170, 176-7. Plymouth Co. PR #921, 21:363(Josiah Barker); #942 29:471(Sarah Barker). VR PEMBROKE pp. 24-6((b. ch.). HINGHAM HIST 2:21.

104 ELIZABETH MACOMBER[5] (Joanna Tinkham[4], Ebenezer[3], Mary[2] Brown, Peter[1]) b. Marshfield 22 Feb. 1715; d. there 16 March 1800 in 85th yr.

She m. Marshfield 20 March 1740 JOB WINSLOW, b. prob. Marshfield ca. 1715; d. there 19 May 1787 in 72nd yr.; son of Gilbert and Mercy (Snow) Winslow, a descendant of Pilgrim Richard Warren. The will of Gilbert Winslow of Marshfield dated 26 May 1731 names wife Mercy and son Job.

On 20 Dec. 1787 Daniel Lewis, housewright of Marshfield, and wife Marcy, and Charles Hatch of Scituate and wife Joanna, divided equally the estate of their father Job Winslow late of Marshfield dec., reserving to their mother widow Elizabeth Winslow her thirds.

No Plymouth Co. PR for Job or Elizabeth Winslow.

Children (WINSLOW) b. Marshfield:

    i   MERCY[6] b. 11 March 1741
    ii   BENJAMIN b. ca. 1745; d. 4 Dec. 1761 in 17th yr.
    iii JOANNA b. 18 March 1755

References: MARSHFIELD VR pp. 77(b. Mercy, Joanna), 171(m.), 414(d. Job, Elizabeth, Benj.). Plymouth Co. LR 68:103(Daniel Lewis, etc.). Plymouth Co. PR 6:45(Gilbert Winslow).

105 ONESIMUS MACOMBER[5] (Joanna Tinkham[4], Ebenezer[3], Mary[2] Brown, Peter[1]) b. Marshfield 18 June 1720; d. there 26 Aug. 1749 in 30th yr.

He m. Marshfield 15 Jan. 1744 LUCY BARKER of Hingham; d. after 7 March 1794; dau. of Francis and Mary (Jacob) Barker. In the marriage record Lucy is mistakenly called Lydia. She m. (2) Marshfield 9 Jan. 1759 Simeon Curtis of Hanover by whom she had Lucy, Mary, and Barker.

On 2 Nov. 1749 Thomas Macomber of Marshfield, yeoman, gave his bond as administrator on the estate of Onesimus Macomber late of Marshfield, husbandman, dec.

There is no Plymouth Co. PR for Lydia Curtis, but on 4 March 1794 she was named in the will of her second husband, Simeon Curtis of Hanover.

Children (MACOMBER) b. Marshfield:

    i   THOMAS[6] b. 31 May 1746
    ii   ONESIMUS b. 20 July 1748

References: MD 19:16-21(probate). MARSHFIELD VR pp. 96(b. ch.), 147(2nd m.), 172(m.), 405(d. Onesimus). BARKER GEN p. 169. HANOVER FIRST CH p. 202(d. Simeon Curtis). Plymouth Co. PR #13485 (Onesimus Macomber);

#5516(Simeon Curtis). HANOVER VR p. 120(m.).

106 ELIZABETH TINKHAM[5] (Shuball[4], Ebenezer[3], Mary[2] Brown, Peter[1]) b. Middleboro 1 Oct. 1719; d. ae 63 (no date given in record).

    She m. Middleboro 16 Sept. 1735 LEMUEL DUNHAM; living 24 June 1763 (deed); son of Eleazer Dunham.

    On June 1752, acknowledged 17 June 1752, Lemuel Dunham of Middleborough sold to Isaac Billington land in Middleboro.

    On 24 June 1763 Lemuel Dunham of Middleborough, cordwainer, sold to Samuel Snow of Middleborough a tract of land in Middleborough; Elizabeth Dunham released her dower.

    There is no Plymouth or Berkshire County probate for either Lemuel or Elizabeth, but on 7 Jan. 1817 Samuel Meritt of Sandisfield posted bond as administrator of the estate of Manassah Dunham of Otis, with Gamaliel Dunham and Zina Downs both of Sandisfield as sureties. On 6 March 1823 distribution of Manassah's personal estate was made to his brothers and sisters: Isaac, Joseph and Ephraim Dunham, Betsey wife of Allan Butler, Priscilla Marcy wife of (blank) Marcy, and children and heirs of Ebenezer Dunham dec.

    Children (DUNHAM) b. Middleboro:

i	EBENEZER[6] b. 4 Jan. 1737/8
ii	PRISCILLA b. 28 June 1740
iii	ISAAC bp. 24 Oct. 1742
iv	LEMUEL b. 14 July 1746
v	JOSEPH b. 21 April 1749
vi	EPHRAIM b. 23 Jan. 1752
vii	MANASSETH b. 25 Feb. 1755
viii	ELIZABETH b. 1 June 1757
ix	GAMALIEL b. 28 Sept. 1759

References: MD 4:69(b. Eben.); 13:251(m.); 15:120(b. Priscilla); 16:134(b. 5 ch.), 135(b. Gamaliel). DUNHAM GEN p. 143. Berkshire Co. PR #3480 (Manassah Dunham). MIDDLEBORO VR 1:24(b. Eben.), 62(m.), 68(b. Priscilla), 77(b. son), 91(b. 3 ch.), 92(b. 3 ch.). Plymouth Co. LR 49:120; 59:27(Lemuel Dunham). Middleboro First Ch Bp. p. 38(bp. Isaac).

107 JOSEPH TINKHAM[5] (Shuball[4], Ebenezer[3], Mary[2] Brown, Peter[1]) b. Middleboro 16 Dec. 1721; d. there 28 April 1767 ae 45y 4m 1d.

He m. Middleboro 5 June 1740 AGNES MAC FUN, b. Middleboro 23 June 1721; apparently living 7 Sept. 1779; dau. of Robert and Joanna (Parlow) (Tinkham) MacFun (see #24). She m. (2) Middleboro 22 May 1769 Samuel Benson. She apparently m. (3) Middleboro 7 Sept. 1779 Stephen Ellis.

Joseph Tinkham was a Capt. in the expedition against Fort William Henry in 1757.

The will of Joseph Tinkham of Middleboro Esq. dated 24 Feb. 1767, proved 22 May 1767, names wife Agness; son Shubael; grandson Ebenezer Tinkham; 4 youngest sons Joseph, Perez, Moses, and Seth; eldest dau. Priscilla, wife of John Benson; dau. Betty, wife of Abiel Wood; and dau. Susannah Tinkham. On 2 April 1774 the estate was divided bet. Perez Tinkham, Seth Tinkham, and Joseph Tinkham.

On 1 Nov. 1782 Seth Tinkham of Pownalborough, Lincoln Co. [ME] sold land in Middleboro which had belonged to his father Joseph Tinkham late of Middleboro dec., mentioning his brothers Joseph, and Perez, to Abiel Wood of Pownalborough ME.

Children (TINKHAM) b. Middleboro:

i	PRISCILLA[6] b. 9 Aug. 1741
ii	SHUBAEL b. 26 March 1743
iii	ELIZABETH b. 26 July 1746; d. there 28 June 1748 ae 1y 11m 2d
iv	EBENEZER b. 28 July 1748; d. there 19 Sept. 1749 ae 1y 1m 22d
v	ELIZABETH b. 14 June 1750
vi	JOSEPH b. 12 Feb. 1753
vii	PEREZ b. 1 June 1755
viii	MOSES b. 20 Jan. 1758; d. there 18 July 1771 in 14th yr.
ix	SETH b. 13 Feb. 1761
x	SUSANNA b. 23 June 1763

References: MD 6:180(b. Agnes); 15:100(d. Ebenezer), 101(d. Eliz.), 102(d. Joseph, Moses), 218(m.), 223(b. 1st 2 ch.);

17:19(b. Eliz.); 18:151(b.&d. Eben.); 20:36(b.& d. Eliz.; b. Joseph, Perez), 38(b. Moses); 22:149(b. Seth); 23:71 (b. Susanna). MASS OFFICERS IN THE FRENCH & INDIAN WARS 1748-1763, Nancy S. Voye, 1975, #5685. Plymouth Co. PR 19:465-7, #20879(Joseph Tinkham). Plymouth Co. LR 62:21(Seth Tinkham). MIDDLEBORO BY WESTON p. 660. MIDDLEBORO VR 1:33(b. Agnes), 72(m.), 78(b. Priscilla, Shubael), 101(b. Eliz.), 111(b.&d. Eben.), 127(b.&d. Eliz.; b. Joseph, Perez), 129(b. Moses), 132(b. Seth), 143(b. Susanna), 167(d. Joseph); 2:139(her 3rd m.). TAG 51:216(2nd & 3rd m.). MIDDLEBORO DEATHS pp. 201(d. Joseph), 202(d. Eliz., Eben., Moses). WATERMAN GEN 1:333.

108 SARAH TINKHAM[5] (Shuball[4], Ebenezer[3], Mary[2] Brown, Peter[1]) b. Middleboro 23 Feb. 1723/4; d. there 28 Sept. 1772 ae 48y 6m 22d "wife of Thomas Blackman."

She m. (1) prob. Middleboro bef. 8 Nov. 1751 (deed) WILLIAM RANSOM, b. Plympton 9 May 1720; d. bet. 24 April 1756 and 24 Feb. 1757 (2nd m.); son of Robert and Sarah (Thomas) Ransom.

She m. (2) Middleboro 28 July 1757 THOMAS BLACKMAN, b. Dorchester 30 Dec. 1713; living Middleboro 1766; son of Thomas and Mary (Horton) Blackman. He m. (1) Stoughton 2 Jan. 1734/5 Mary Pitcher by whom he had children including Hannah and Thomas.

On 8 Nov. 1751, ack. 24 April 1756, William and Sarah Ransom sold 13 acres in Middleboro to Lemuel Ransom.

On 24 Feb. 1757 Joseph Tinkham of Middleboro, gentleman, gave his bond to administer the estate of William Ransom late of Middleboro, dec., husbandman. On 28 Jan. 1762 Thomas Blackman, weaver of Middleboro, gave his bond as guardian of Samuel and Sarah Ransom, minor children of William Ransom late of Middleboro dec. On 29 June 1773 Samuel Ransom, minor son of William Ransom late of Middleboro, petitioned to have "my uncle Lemuel Ransom" of Middleboro appointed his guardian.

The will of Perez Tinkham of Middleboro dated 17 Nov. 1760 names sister Sarah Blackman and others.

There are no Plymouth Co. PR for Thomas or Sarah Blackman.

Children (RANSOM) b. Middleboro:

    i   ZILPHA[6] b. 4 Aug. 1742
    ii   JOSEPH b. 31 July 1744; apparently d.y.
    iii SARAH b. 14 April 1752
    iv   SAMUEL b. 9 March 1755

Children (BLACKMAN) b. Middleboro:

    v   SUSANNA b. 27 April 1758
    vi   ELIZABETH b. 20 April 1761
    vii ELIJAH b. 26 Jan. 1764
    viii ROSEANNAR (dau.) b. 18 June 1766

References: MD 2:53(b. William); 15:218(b. Zilpha); 16:14(b. Joseph); 18:155(b. Ransom ch.); 19:174(2nd m.); 22:147(b. Susanna); 23:46(b. Eliz.), 70(b. Elijah), 71(b. Rosennar). VR PLYMPTON p. 160(b. Wm.). MIDDLEBORO DEATHS pp. 21, 140 (d. date for Wm. is wrong as the battle was in 1757 & PR confirms 1757). Plymouth Co. PR #16478, 16480, 16482(Wm. Ransom); 16:29(Perez Tinkham). Plymouth Co. LR 45:75(William Ransom). THOMAS GEN p. 8. MIDDLEBORO VR 1:72(b. Zilpha), 79(b. Joseph), 115(b. Sarah, Sam.), 124(2nd m.), 130(b. Susanna), 139(b. Eliz.), 143(b. last 2 ch.), 168(d. Sarah). DORCHESTER VR 1:60(b. Thomas). STOUGHTON VR pp. 32(m.), 36(b. Hannah), 38(b. Thos.), 44(b. Hannah).

109 PRISCILLA TINKHAM[5] (Shuball[4], Ebenezer[3], Mary[2] Brown, Peter[1]) b. Middleboro 10 June 1726; d. there 5 April 1769 ae 43, widow of Wm.
    She m. (1) Middleboro ca. 1743 JOHN COBB, b. Middleboro 31 May 1722; d. there 22 June 1750 in 29th yr.; son of John and Joanna (Thomas) Cobb, a descendant of Pilgrim George Soule.
    She m. (2) Middleboro 11 April 1751 WILLIAM CUSHMAN, b. Plympton 13 Oct. 1715; d. Middleboro 27 Aug. 1768 ae 52y 10m 3d; son of Ichabod and Patience (Holmes) Cushman, a descendant of Pilgrim Isaac Allerton. He m. (1) Middleboro 25 Dec. 1735 Susanna Sampson by whom he had Joseph, Joanna, William, Zenas and Noe (or Noah).
    The will of John Cobb of Middleboro dated 14 June 1750, presented 11 July 1750, names wife Priscilla; only son John; and only dau. Martha under 18. On 14 March 1752 William Cushman

was appointed guardian of John and Martha Cobb.

On 2 Jan. 1769 a petition was presented asking that the will of William Cushman late of Middleboro not be approved as he was not of sound mind when he signed it.

The will of Priscilla Cushman of Middleboro, widow, dated 18 March 1769, presented 1 May 1769, names son John Cobb; dau. Martha Eaton wife of Lot; dau. Priscilla Cushman; sons Isaac, Andrew and Perez Cushman; daus. Susanna Cushman and Patience Cushman, whose father William Cushman is dec.; dau.-in-law [step-dau.] Joanna Thomas, wife of Ebenezer; and [step-sons] Joseph, Zenas, William and Noah Cushman. John Weston of Middleboro, gentleman, was named executor.

The division of the estate of William Cushman late of Middleboro dec. was dated 28 March 1771 and names oldest son Joseph, sons Zenas and Noah, daus. Patience Cushman and Priscilla Cushman, son William Cushman, daus. Joanna Thomas wife of Ebenezer Jr., dau. Susanna Cushman, and sons Isaac, Andrew and Perez.

Children (COBB) b. Middleboro:

  i   JOHN[6] b. 9 Nov. 1745
  ii   MARTHA b. 9 June 1748

Children (CUSHMAN) b. Middleboro:

  iii   PRISCILLA b. 23 Oct. 1751
  iv   ISAAC b. 27 Feb. 1754
  v   SUSANNA b. 13 Jan. 1756
  vi   ANDREW b. 26 March 1757
  vii   PEREZ b. 26 Jan. 1759
  viii PATIENCE b. 16 Sept. 1764
  ix   WELTHEA b. 13 Sept. 1767; d. 3 June 1768 ae 8m
        20d

References: MD 6:226(b. John); 13:251(Wm's 1st m.); 16:134(b. Cobb ch.); 18:84(2nd m.), 154(b. Priscilla), 155 (b. Isaac, Susanna); 20:35(b. Andrew); 25:106(b. Welthea); 26:25(d. Wm.). VR PLYMPTON p. 87(b. Wm.). MIDDLEBORO DEATHS pp. 39, 49. MIDDLEBORO BY WESTON pp. 660-2. CUSHMAN GEN pp. 127,

135, 167. Plymouth Co. PR 20:236(Priscilla Cushman); 20:504, #5903(William Cushman); 12:55(John Cobb), #4549(John & Martha Cobb). MF 3:45, 46, 148, 149; 17:127-8. MIDDLEBORO VR 1:45(b. Joseph), 62(1st m. Wm.), 65(b. Joanna), 69(b. Wm.), 76(b. Zenas), 86(b. Noe), 110(2nd m.), 115(b. Priscilla, Isaac, Susanna), 126(b. Andrew), 138(b. Perez, Patience), 159 (b. Welthea), 163(d. Wm., Welthea).

110 EBENEZER TINKHAM[5] (Shuball[4], Ebenezer[3], Mary[2] Brown, Peter[1]) b. Middleboro 2 Jan. 1728/9; d. prob. Boston bef. 17 May 1751.

He m. Boston 3 Oct. 1749 ABIGAIL CLARK, b. ca. 1732; d. Middleboro 14 Oct. 1752 in 20th yr., "widow of Ebenezer."

On 17 May 1751 Joseph Tinkham of Middleboro, yeoman, was appointed administrator (in Suffolk Co.) of the estate of his brother Ebenezer Tinkham.

On 10 Feb. 1752 appraisers were appointed on the real estate of Ebenezer Tinkham late of Boston dec. The inventory taken 11 Feb. 1752 includes his homestead farm, Winnetuxet meadow etc. Joseph Tinkham administrator made oath to the inventory 20 Feb. 1752.

No known children.

References: BOSTON VR 28:265(m.). Plymouth Co. PR 12:431
            (Ebenezer Tinkham). MIDDLEBORO DEATHS p.
202(d. Abigail). Suffolk Co. PR #9757(Ebenezer Tinkham).

111 PETER RAYMOND[5] (Mercy Tinkham[4], Peter[3], Mary[2] Brown, Peter[1]) b. Middleboro 27 March 1718; d. Newark, Essex Co. NJ bet. 21 March and 16 April 1760.

He m. ca. 1739 CHRISTIANA MAC HAAN, d. Springfield Township, Essex Co. NJ bet. 6 July and 4 Sept. 1800; dau. of Duncan and Patience (Lawrence) MacHaan.

On 3 July 1739 Peter Raymond of Middleborough sold to John Douglas Jr. land which did originally belong to his great grandfather Ephraim Tinkham of Plymouth, dec.

The will of Peter Raymond of Newark NJ, carpenter, dated 21 March 1760, proved 16 April 1760, names wife Christianna; eldest son Edward, eldest dau. Mercy Bedford; 2nd son James; youngest son Seth; daus. Hannah, Susannah, Rebeckah and Rachel.

A codicil dated the same day mentions an unborn child. He named son-in-law Jonas Bedford and Ebenezer Byram his executors.

The will of Christianny Raymond of Springfield Township, Essex Co. NJ, dated 6 July 1800, proved 4 Sept. 1800, names son James Raymond, dau. Massey (or Mercy) Bedford and dau. Susannah Oakley.

Mercy[6] Bedford is one of the few women listed as a qualifying ancestor in the DAR PATRIOT INDEX.

Children (RAYMOND) first two b. Middleboro:

i	MERCY[6] b. 3 June 1740
ii	MC KAHAN b. 13 March 1742/3 (not in father's will)
iii	EDWARD
iv	JAMES b. ca. 1746
v	SETH
vi	HANNAH
vii	SUSANNAH
viii	REBECKAH
ix	RACHEL
x	child b. Newark, NJ 1760

References: MD 15:121(b. Mercy), 221(b. McKahan). MIDDLEBORO BY WESTON pp. 654, 658. NJ ARCH 1:32:264(Peter's will); 1:38:292-3(Christiana's will). DAR PATRIOT INDEX p. 49. MQ 44:80-4. MIDDLEBORO VR 1:69(b. Mercy), 75(b. McKahon). Plymouth Co. LR 33:60(Peter Raymond).

112 JOANNA BATES[5] (Joanna Tinkham[4], Peter[3], Mary[2] Brown, Peter[1]) b. Middleboro 28 May 1718; d. bet. 9 June 1757 and 19 Feb. 1758 (2nd m.).

She m. Middleboro 19 Aug. 1735 JOHN JACKSON, b. Middleboro 11 Sept. 1716; d. Sidney ME 29 June 1810 ae 93; son of John and Mary (Smith) Jackson. He m. (2) Middleboro 19 Feb. 1758 Jemima Jackson by whom he had John and Pharez.

On 11 April 1748 John Jackson of Middleboro, cordwainer, sold to Samuel Smith of Middleboro all his rights of his grandfather John Smith of Middleboro, acknowledging the deed 19 April 1748.

On 19 May 1779 John Jackson of Middleboro, cordwainer, and wife Jemima sold his homestead in Middleboro to Ziba Eaton. John Jackson was 2-0-1 in the 1790 census of Vassalborough ME.

On 7 April 1791 John Jackson sold land in Vassalborough to Pharez Jackson. On 28 July 1791 he sold land to John Jackson Jr.

There are no probate records for John or Joanna Jackson in Plymouth County, nor any will in Maine.

Children (JACKSON) b. Middleboro:

i	MARY[6]	bp. 16 Sept. 1736
ii	SUSANNA	bp. 3 April 1737
iii	JOANNA	bp. 21 Jan. 1738/9
iv	MERCY	bp. 28 June 1741
v	PRISCILLA	bp. 17 April 1743
vi	AZUBA	bp. 5 May 1745
vii	LUSANNA	bp. 26 April 1747
viii	CONTENT	bp. 25 Dec. 1748

References: MD 2:158(m. his par.); 3:233(b. John); 13:251(m.).
MIDDLEBORO BY WESTON p. 660. New Bedford Mercury Obits(d. John). Plymouth Co. LR 40:216; 62:65(John Jackson). Middleboro First Church Bp. pp. 32(bp. Mary), 33(bp. Susanna), 34(bp. Joanna), 36(bp. Mercy), 38(bp. Priscilla), 40(bp. Azuba), 42(bp. Lusanna, Content). MIDDLEBORO VR 1:18(b. John), 120(2nd m.), 62(m.). Lincoln Co. ME LR 4:136(to Pharez Jackson), 136(to John Jackson). MAINE FAMILIES IN 1790 5:166-70(suggests other poss. children by second wife).

113 MERCY BATES[5] (Joanna Tinkham[4], Peter[3], Mary[2] Brown, Peter[1]) b. Middleboro 8 Aug. 1719; d. bet. 23 July 1768 when she signed a deed and 27 July 1773 when her father made his will.

She m. Middleboro 7 Oct. 1735 HEZEKIAH PURRINGTON of Truro, b. Truro 26 Sept. 1715; d. Middleboro 30 May 1765 in 50th yr.; son of Hezekiah and Mary (Scammon) Purrington.

The will of Hezekiah Purrington of Middleboro dated 26 Feb. 1764, presented 7 Oct. 1765, names wife Mercy; son Hezekiah; dau. Mercy (no last name) and sons Samuel, Joseph, Nathaniel, Seth, Eleazer, Silvenus and Joshua, who has a set of tools and a

trade; dau. Mary under 18; wife Mercy executor.
No Plymouth Co. PR for Mercy Purrington.

Children (PURRINGTON) all b. prob. Middleboro:

    i   MERCY[6] bp. 8 May 1737
    ii   HEZEKIAH bp. 13 May 1739
    iii   JOSHUA bp. 19 April 1741
    iv   SAMUEL bp. 28 Jan. 1742/3
    v   JOHN bp. 4 Dec. 1744 (not in will)
    vi   JOSEPH bp. 20 July 1746
    vii   NATHANIEL bp. 24 July 1749
    viii SETH bp. 25 Aug. 1751
    ix   ELEAZER bp. 12 Nov. 1752
    x   MARY (named in will)
    xi   SILVANEUS bp. 23 Jan. 1757

References: MD 9:56(bp. Hez.); 13:251(m.); 14:84(d. Hez.). TRURO
VR p. 14(b. Hezekiah) . MIDDLEBORO BY
WESTON pp. 657, 665. Plymouth Co. PR 19:285(Hezekiah
Purrington). Middleboro First Church Bp. pp. 33(bp. Mercy),
34(bp. Hezekiah), 35(bp. Joshua), 38(bp. Sam.), 40(bp. John), 42(bp.
Jos., Nathaniel), 43(bp. Seth), 44(bp. Eleazer), 45(bp. Silvanus).
ME NH GEN DICT p. 571. MIDDLEBORO VR 1:62(m.).

114 JOSEPH BATES[5] (Joanna Tinkham[4], Peter[3], Mary[2] Brown,
Peter[1]) b. Middleboro 18 March 1721/2; d. Hartland VT 27 Aug.
1789 ae 67.

He m. Middleboro 16 Nov. 1749 EUNICE TINKHAM, b.
Middleboro 6 July 1730; d. there 14 Oct. 1785 in 56th yr.; dau. of
Peter and Eunice (Thomas) Tinkham, a descendant of Pilgrim
Peter Brown (see #97i).

On 1 June 1786 Joseph Bates of Middleboro sold to Israel
Smith 30 acres abutting the home place of Thomas Bates.

Joseph Bates was a sergeant in the Revolutionary War and
was dismissed from the Middleboro Church to Hartland VT in
1787.

The will of Joseph Bates of Hartland, Windsor Co. VT dated
18 Aug. 1789, presented 22 Sept. 1789, names sons Jacob, Silvanus,
Eliphalet, Thomas and Joseph; daus. Elizabeth Briant, Sarah Cobb

and Mary Bates; with son Jacob Bates as executor.

Children (BATES) b. Middleboro:

      i   PETER[6] b. 22 Dec. 1750
     ii   JOANNA b. 2 Aug. 1752; d. 25 Jan. 1785 in 34th yr.; unm. No PR.
   iii   ELIZABETH b. 20 July 1754
   iv   SARAH b. 26 Feb. 1756
    v   JOSEPH b. 1758; d. 14 May 1758 ae 2m 11d
   vi   SAMUEL b. 15 June 1759; d. 17 May 1760 ae 11m 2d
  vii   JOSEPH b. 5 March 1762
 viii   JACOB b. 3 June 1764
   ix   ZILPAH bp. 31 May 1767; d. 26 Jan. 1769 ae 3y 2m
    x   ELIPHELET b. 5 March 1769
   xi   THOMAS b. 11 July 1771
  xii   MARY b. 25 Jan. 1776
 xiii   SILVANUS b. 25 May 1778

References: MD 12:68(d. Eunice), 69(d. 3 ch.); 18:82(m.), 152(b. 1st 3 ch.), 153(b. Sarah); 22:147(b. Sam.); 23:70(b. Jacob); 26:26(b. Joseph, Eliphelet); 30:15 (b. Thomas); 32:8(b. Mary), 87(b. Silvanus). MIDDLEBORO BY WESTON p. 659. MIDDLEBORO DEATHS pp. 13-4. DAR PATRIOT INDEX p. 43. Hartland VT PR 1:128(Joseph Bates). Middleboro First Church Bp. p. 47(bp. Zilpah). Middleboro Mortality Records. MIDDLEBORO VR 1:77(b. Eunice), 108(m.), 112(b. Peter), 113(b. Joanna, Eliz., Sarah), 131(b. Sam.), 143(b. Jacob), 164(b. Joseph, Eliphelet), 188(b. Thomas), 203(b. Mary), 209(b. Silvanus). Plymouth Co. LR 71:131(Joseph Bates).

115 THOMAS BATES[5] (Joanna Tinkham[4], Peter[3], Mary[2] Brown, Peter[1]) b. Middleboro 9 Nov. 1724; d. there 2 April 1821.

He m. Plymouth 23 May 1782 SUSANNA CORNISH, b. Plymouth 4 March 1755; d. Middleboro 15 June 1823 ae 69 yrs.; dau. of Benjamin and Rhoda (Swift) Cornish.

Thomas Bates of Middleboro, husbandman, sold to Josiah Clark of Middleboro land in Winnetuxet meadow of his father Joseph Bates, signed 21 July 1786, ack. 7 July 1789.

Thomas Bates of Middleboro, yeoman, sold to Isaac Thomson of Middleboro land in Middleboro on which his father Joseph Bates last dwelt, with wife Susanna giving up dower, signed 2 Nov. 1796; ack. 20 March 1797 by Thomas.

Susanna Bates, wife of Thomas, joined the Middleboro First Church 12 July 1807. That record indicates that her husband's father was Joseph Bates and his mother Joanna Tinkham.

No Plymouth Co. PR for Thomas or Susanna Bates.

Children (BATES) b. Middleboro:

i	THOMAS[6]	b. 24 Aug. 1782
ii	JOSEPH	b. 6 July 1784
iii	BENJAMIN	b. 4 Oct. 1786
iv	HANNAH	b. 30 Nov. 1788
v	STEPHEN	b. 23 Nov. 1790
vi	MARY	b. 15 Nov. 1792

References: MD 18:214(b. Susanna); 29:90(int.); 32:137(b. Thomas, Joseph), 141(b. Benj.); 34:157(b. last 3 ch.). MIDDLEBORO DEATHS p. 14. MIDDLEBORO BY WESTON p. 672 (Susanna adm.; d. Susanna). Plymouth Co. LR 68:258; 83:147 (Thomas Bates) . (PLYMOUTH) ANC LANDMARKS 2:71. MIDDLEBORO VR 1:214(b. Thomas, Joseph), 218(b. Benj.), 238(b. last 3 ch.). PLYMOUTH VR pp. 185(b. Susanna), 385(m.).

NOTE: While he was age 57 at mar. & 97 at death this identification seems correct. The deed under #114 shows he was living in Middleboro in 1786 and the church record supports this identification.

116 PRISCILLA BATES[5] (Joanna Tinkham[4], Peter[3], Mary[2] Brown, Peter[1]) b. Middleboro 6 Jan. 1726/7; d. there 18 Dec. 1806 in 80th yr.

She m. int. Middleboro 21 July 1750 EBENEZER COX, bp. Middleboro 27 Sept. 1730; d. there 8 Oct. 1774 in 45th yr.; son of John and Hannah (Smith) Cox.

On 5 Dec. 1774 Elisha Cox of Middleboro gave his bond as administrator of the estate of Ebenezer Cox late of Middleboro, yeoman, dec., with Joseph Bates Jr. and Samuel Raymond, both of

Middleboro, as sureties. On 5 April 1779 Silas Tinkham, yeoman, of Middleboro gave his bond as guardian to Daniel and Timothy Cox minors over 14, sons of Ebenezer Cox late of Middleboro, yeoman, dec. On 12 June 1779 Priscilla Cox, widow, posted bond as guardian to her children Priscilla Cox Jr., John Cox and Patience Cox, all children of Ebenezer Cox under 14 years of age.

The rest of the children are named in a deed 14 Jan. 1789 in which Elisha and Ebenezer Cox, both of Middleboro, "owners of 7/9 of the homestead of our father Ebenezer Cox dec. with Elisha owning 4/9 and Ebenezer 3/9, divided the land with proviso that Elisha engages to purchase of sister Patience (no surname) and my brother John Cox their rights." No deed was found showing the transfer from Patience and John to Elisha.

Children (COX) all b. prob. Middleboro:

   i   LEVI[6] b. ca. 1751; d. 12 Nov. 1774 in 23rd yr. No PR.
   ii   ELISHA b. bef. 1765
   iii   EBENEZER b. 19 Feb. 1759
   iv   DANIEL b. bef. 1765
   v   TIMOTHY b. bef. 1765
   vi   PRISCILLA b. after 1765
   vii JOHN b. 16 Feb. 1772
   viii JOSEPH b. 1773; d. 24 Nov. 1778 in 6th yr.
   ix   PATIENCE b. after 1765

References: MD 12:198(d. Eben.), 199(d. Pris., 2 ch.); 33:77 (b. John).   MIDDLEBORO DEATHS p. 47. MIDDLEBORO BY WESTON pp. 659, 662. Plymouth Co. PR #5140, 5155(Ebenezer Cox & gdn.). Plymouth Co. LR 77:28(Elisha & Ebenezer Cox). Middleboro First Ch. Bp. p. 25(bp. Eben.). Middleboro Mortality Recs. MIDDLEBORO VR 1:222(b. John), 250(b. Eben.); 2:44(int.).

117 MARTHA TINKHAM[5] (Samuel[4], Peter[3], Mary[2] Brown, Peter[1]) b. Middleboro 23 Aug. 1720; d. there 20 March 1744 ae 23y 10m 25d.

She m. Middleboro 1 June 1742 NATHANIEL WOOD, b. Middleboro 18 April 1725; d. there 25 June 1803 ae 78 yrs.; son of

Deacon Samuel and Elizabeth (Smith) Wood. He m. (2) Middleboro 19 June 1744 Mary Winslow by whom he had Seth, Martha, Nathaniel, Elizabeth, Anna, Sarah, William, Mary, Ezra, Rebeckah, and Lucia.

Nathaniel Wood was a Captain in the Rev. War and moved to Woodstock VT in 1783.

On 16 Feb. 1780 Nathaniel Wood of Middleborough, gentleman, sold land in Middleborough to David Thomas.

On 14 Sept. 1795 Nathaniel Wood of Woodstock in the county of Windsor in Vermont, yeoman, sold to Thomas Sturtevant land in Middleborough.

No Plymouth Co. PR for Nathaniel Wood.

Child (WOOD) b. Middleboro:

i   JOSHUA[6] b. 17 March 1743/4; d. 20 Oct. 1744 ae 7m 3d

References: MD 9:48(b. Nath.); 15:219(m.); 16:15(2nd m.), 18 (d. Joshua, Martha), 20(b. Joshua, Seth); 48:139-40(Wood). MIDDLEBORO DEATHS pp. 232, 233(d. Nath., Martha; moved to VT). DAR PATRIOT INDEX p. 758. WOOD OF MIDDLEBORO pp. 44-5. Middleboro Mortality Recs p. 89. MIDDLEBORO VR 1:49(b. Nath.), 73(m.), 80(2nd m. int.), 83(d. Martha, Joshua), 84(b. Joshua, Seth), 85(2nd m.), 103(b. Martha, Nath.), 113(b. Anna), 114(b. Eliz., Sarah), 131(b. Wm., Mary), 142(b. Ezra), 147(b. Rebeckah), 161(b. Lucia). Plymouth Co. LR 70:236; 85:233(Nathaniel Wood).

118 PETER TINKHAM[5] (Samuel[4], Peter[3], Mary[2] Brown, Peter[1]) b. Middleboro 16 May 1722; d. there bet. 4 Nov. 1754 and 17 Nov. 1756.

No marriage record found for Peter Tinkham or any record of a wife in his deeds.

On 8 April 1754 Peter Tinkham Jr. of Middleboro sold to Nathan Cobb land in Middleboro where he lived which came to him from the estate of his father Samuel Tinkham dec., acknowledging the deed 4 Nov. 1754.

On 17 Nov. 1756 Samuel Tinkham Jr. of Middleboro, yeoman,

was appointed to administer the estate of Peter Tinkham late of Middleboro, yeoman, and on the same day Samuel signed a bond as administrator of "his brother Peter deceased." On 2 May 1757 Samuel was appointed guardian to Keziah Tinkham, minor dau. of Peter Tinkham late of Middleboro dec.

Child (TINKHAM) b. prob. Middleboro:

    i   KEZIAH[6] b. after 1740

References: Plymouth Co. PR #20881(Keziah Tinkham); #20894 (Peter Tinkham). Plymouth Co. LR 51:98(Peter Tinkham).

119 SAMUEL TINKHAM[5] (Samuel[4], Peter[3], Mary[2] Brown, Peter[1]) b. Middleboro 13 March 1723/4; d. there 28 March 1796 ae 72y 4d.

He m. (1) Middleboro 5 April 1745 HOPE COBB, b. Middleboro 10 Nov. 1727; d. there 3 June 1760 ae 33; dau. of Gershom and Melatiah (Smith) Cobb.

He m. (2) Middleboro 6 Nov. 1760 PATIENCE SIMMONS, b. Middleboro 21 Feb. 1722/3; d. there 3 Nov. 1814 in 92nd yr.; dau. of Aaron and Martha (Cobb) Simmons, a descendant of Pilgrim George Soule (see #19).

The will of Samuel Tinkham of Middleboro, yeoman, dated 2 June 1788, presented 2 May 1796, names wife Patience; nephew Joseph Besse Jr.; Lazarus Tinkham, son of James Tinkham of Middleboro, "he being named to bear up the name of my only son Lazarus deceased."

The will of Patience Tinkham of Middleboro, widow of Samuel late of Middleboro dec., dated 3 Jan. 1814, presented 9 Nov. 1814, names niece Abigail Thomas of Middleboro; Nelson Wood of Middleboro gent.; and Hope Southworth, wife of Seth of Middleboro gent.

Children (TINKHAM) one by 1st wife, other by 2nd wife; b. and d. Middleboro:

    i   LAZARUS[6] b. 28 Feb. 1745/6; d. Nov. 1762 in 17th yr.

ii   HOPE   b. 7 May 1764; d. 7 Dec. 1774 ae 10y 7m

References: MD 5:40(b. Patience); 6:229(b. wife Hope); 14:221(d.
              wife Hope; Lazarus); 15:101(d. dau. Hope), 102(d.
Patience), 103(d. Samuel); 16:16(int. 1st m.), 20(b. Lazarus), 108(1st
m.); 23:71(b. Hope); 24:132(2nd m.). MIDDLEBORO DEATHS pp.
202-3.   Plymouth   Co.   PR   35:505-6   (Samuel   Tinkham);
45:527(Patience Tinkham). Middleboro Mortality Recs p. 77 . MF
3:46.   MIDDLEBORO   VR   1:32(b. Patience), 38(b. Hope), 85(b.
Lazarus), 87(1st m.), 144(b. Hope), 152 (2nd m.); 2:16(d. Patience).

120 MERCY TINKHAM[5] (Samuel[4], Peter[3], Mary[2] Brown, Peter[1])
b. Middleboro 24 Aug. 1726; d. there 16 Feb. 1811 ae 85.
     She m. (1) Middleboro 30 Nov. 1741 EPHRAIM DONHAM,
living 12 June 1748 (when dau. Mercy was bp.), but apparently
dead by 25 Sept. 1750.
     She m. (2) Middleboro 4 March 1756 JOSEPH BESSE of
Wareham, b. ca. 1735; d. Middleboro 1 March 1814 in 80th yr.; son
of Benjamin and Martha (_____) Besse.
     On 25 Sept. 1750 Mercy Donham of Middleboro sold to
Ebenezer Tinkham her share of her father Samuel Tinkham's
estate, acknowledging her signature 22 March 1756 as Mercy
DONHAM.
     No Plymouth Co. PR for Ephraim Donham, Joseph or Mercy
Besse.

          Children (DONHAM) b. Middleboro:

          i   MARY[6] b. 18 April 1742
          ii   PHILEMON b. 20 Dec. 1744
          iii   LYDIA   b. 23 March 1747/8

          Children (BESSE) first bp. Wareham, rest bp. Middleboro:

          iv   HOPE bp. 10 April 1757
          v   JOSEPH bp. 3 July 1759
          vi   KEZIAH bp. 3 May 1761
          vii   MARTHA bp. 26 Sept. 1762
          viii PATIENCE bp. 11 May 1766

References: MD 15:219(1st m.), 221(b. Mary); 16:19(b. Philemon),
            134(b. Lydia); 19:48(2nd m.). MIDDLEBORO BY
WESTON pp. 654, 662-3. MIDDLEBORO DEATHS p. 20.
WAREHAM CH RECS p. 60(bp. Hope). DUNHAM GEN p. 143.
DESCENDANTS OF ANTHONY BESSE 1609-1656, Florence
Besse Ballantine, 1965, pp. 8, 13, 18. Middleboro First Church Bp.
pp. 45(bp. Joseph), 46(bp. Keziah, Martha, Patience). Plymouth
Co. LR 47:49(Mercy Donham). MIDDLEBORO VR 1:73(1st m.),
75(b. Mary), 84(b. Philemon), 91 (b. Lydia), 120(2nd m.).

121 DEBORAH TINKHAM[5] (Samuel[4], Peter[3], Mary[2] Brown,
Peter[1]) b. Middleboro 7 Sept. 1728; living 28 July 1761.
       At the Sept. 1752 Plymouth County Court Deborah Tinkham,
"Singlewoman" of Middleboro accused Samuel Snow of
Middleboro of being the father of the child borne of her body on
the tenth day of May last.
       At the March 1756 Plymouth County Court Deborah
Tinkham of Middleboro was fined for fornication. This time she
did not name the father.
       On 1 Jan. 1760 Deborah Tinkham of Middleboro sold to
Ebenezer Tinkham of Middleboro land in the 26 Men's Purchase
which was laid out to her in the division of the estate of her
father Samuel Tinkham dec. Deborah acknowledged the deed 28
July 1761.
       There is no Plymouth Co. probate for Deborah or further
LR. Apparently Deborah never married.

       Child (SNOW) b. Middleboro to Samuel Snow and Deborah
Tinkham:

       i   SAMUEL[6] b. 10 May 1752

       Child (TINKHAM) b. Middleboro to Deborah Tinkham:

       ii   EBENEZER b. 30 Dec. 1756

References: MD 18:154(b. Sam.); 22:148(b. Eben.). PLYMOUTH
            CO CT RECS 5:30, 80. Plymouth Co. LR
47:52(Deborah Tinkham). MIDDLEBORO VR 1:114(b. Sam.),
132(b. Eben.).

122   GIDEON TINKHAM⁵ (Samuel⁴, Peter³, Mary² Brown, Peter¹)
b. Middleboro 24 April 1731; living there April 1779.
     He m. Middleboro 1 Nov. 1753 MERCY THOMAS, b.
Middleboro 12 May 1733; living 14 Aug. 1764; dau. of William and
Mary (Bates) Thomas.   The will of William Thomas of
Middleborough dated 21 Aug. 1762 names wife Mary and dau.
Mercy Tinkham.
     On 30 May 1754 Gideon Tinkham of Middleboro,
housewright, sold land of his father Samuel Tinkham, with wife
Mercy releasing her dower, to Nathan Cobb. On 1 April 1762,
Gideon Tinkham of Middleboro, sold to Silvanus Thomas his
homestead where he dwelled with buildings, etc., with Mercy
quitclaiming her dower rights, both acknowledging the deed 14
Aug. 1764.
     In October 1771 Gideon Tinkham of Middleboro,
husbandman, was sued for debt and in April 1779 Gideon
Tinkham, Middleboro, labourer, was sued again.
     No Plymouth Co. PR for Gideon or Mercy Tinkham.

     Children (TINKHAM) b. Middleboro:

         i   DAVID⁶ b. 5 Aug. 1754; d. 10 Aug. 1775 ae 21y 5d.
              No PR.
        ii   PETER b. 20 Jan. 1758
       iii   LYDIA b. 24 June 1759

References: MD 12:231(b. Mercy); 19:46(m.); 20:35(b. 1st 2 ch.);
             22:149(b. Lydia). MIDDLEBORO DEATHS p. 202
(d. David). THOMAS GEN p. 14. TAG 51:146. Plymouth Co. LR
51:99; 52:128(Gideon Tinkham). PLYMOUTH CO CT RECS 8:389;
9:66. MIDDLEBORO VR 1:54(b. Mercy), 119(m.), 126(b. David,
Peter), 132(b. Lydia).

123   JOANNA TINKHAM⁵ (Samuel⁴, Peter³, Mary² Brown,
Peter¹) b. Middleboro 15 May 1734; living there 9 May 1757.
     She m. Middleboro 11 Oct. 1750 JONATHAN REED, b.
Middleboro 22 Oct. 1725; living 21 Aug. 1769 (when named in the
will of his aunt Anna Warren); son of William and Elizabeth
(_____) Reed.
     On 9 May 1757 Jonathan Reed and wife Joanna of

Middleboro sold to Ebenezer Tinkham of Middleboro, part of the homestead of their father Samuel Tinkham late of Middleboro, dec.

On 2 Sept. 1783 John Shaw 2nd of Middleboro administered the estate of Jonathan Reed Jr. late of Middleboro dec., gave bond, with Joshua White Esq. and Jonathan Fuller physician, all of Middleboro as sureties. On 2 Sept. 1783 James Reed infirm, only surviving brother of dec. and greatest creditor, appointed John Shaw 2nd administrator of estate of Jonathan Reed Jr., the widow and her father and her now lawful husband refusing to act.

On 12 June 1785 John Shaw 2nd of Middleboro, yeoman, administrator of the estate of Jonathan Reed Jr. of Middleboro, sold real estate reserving the widow's dower, and on 4 July 1786 Jonathan Reed of Middleboro, yeoman, sold land to John Shaw 2nd of Middleboro, innholder, acknowledged 17 Oct. 1787.

Children (REED) b. prob. Middleboro:

    i   JONATHAN[6]
    ii   JAMES

References: MD 13:6(b. Jonathan); 18:83(m.); 40:126-7(Reed family).   HALIFAX VR pp. 8(int.), 20(m.). Plymouth Co. PR #16629(Jonathan Reed). Plymouth Co. LR 47:50 (Jonathan Reed); 67:77(John Shaw 2nd); 71:14(Jonathan Reed). MIDDLEBORO VR 1:59(b. Jonathan), 109(m.).

124 KEZIA TINKHAM[5] (Samuel[4], Peter[3], Mary[2] Brown, Peter[1]) b. Middleboro 15 Aug. 1738; d. Bridgewater 8 Feb. 1823 "wife of Jonathan Ames."

She m. Bridgewater 17 Nov. 1757 JONATHAN AMES, b. Bridgewater 10 June 1707; d. there 4 Nov. 1775 "husband of Kezia"; son of John and Sarah (Washburn) Ames, a descendant of Pilgrim Francis Cooke.

On 31 Dec. 1759 Jonathan Ames of Bridgewater and wife Kezia sold to Ebenezer Tinkham land of her father Samuel Tinkham dec.

The will of Jonathan Ames of Bridgewater, yeoman, dated 11 Oct. 1775, presented 4 Dec. 1775, names wife Kezia executrix;

son Jonathan under 21 to have land my father bought of Solomon and David Perkins; 3 daus.: Kezia, Lusannah and Molly to have land in Tittecut.

On 3 Oct. 1788 Thaddeus Howard of Bridgewater and wife Kezia, Molly Ames of Bridgewater, singlewoman, and Ebenezer Tinkham of Middleboro, yeoman, and wife Susanna, sold to Josiah Dean of Raynham land in Bridgewater which was laid out to John Ames in 1754. The deed was acknowledged the next day by Ebenezer and Susannah Tinkham.

No Plymouth Co. PR for Kezia Ames.

Children (AMES) b. Bridgewater:

i	JONATHAN[6] b. 26 March 1759
ii	KEZIAH b. 4 Nov. 1761
iii	SUSANNAH b. 4 July 1763
iv	MOLLEY b. 5 Feb. 1765

References: VR BRIDGEWATER 1:33-6(b. Jonathan;   b. ch.); 2:32(m.), 431(d. Jonathan, Keziah). Plymouth Co. PR 28:404(Jonathan Ames). Plymouth Co. LR 47:51(Jonathan Ames); 72:79(Thaddeus Howard). MF 12:285-6.

125 BATHSHEBA TINKHAM[5] (Seth[4], Peter[3], Mary[2] Brown, Peter[1]) b. Middleboro 10 July 1726; living 6 May 1794 when she rendered an account on Sam Hayford's estate.

She m. (1) Halifax 1 March 1776 SAMUEL HAYFORD (or HEAFORD) of Hardwick, b. Pembroke 8 Aug. 1734; d. bef. 3 May 1783; son of Daniel and Deliverance (Boles) Hayford. He m. (1) Plympton 31 Jan. 1754 Rebecca Waterman, a descendant of Pilgrim William Bradford, by whom he had Deliverance, Abigail, Ann, Mercy Freeman, Rebecca, and Molly Waterman (who d.y.). He m. (2) Hanover 27 Nov. 1768 Diadama Bishop by whom he had Molly Waterman.

Samuel Heiford, his wife Rebecca and their children Abigail, Anna, Mary Freeman, and Rebecca, who came from Pembroke, were warned from Hanover 16 Feb. 1767.

She m. (2) Hardwick 3 May 1783 SAMUEL WORK of Leicester, who d. bef. 6 May 1794.

On 8 April 1784 Samuel Work and wife Bathsheba of

Leicester gave their bond as administrators of the estate of Samuel Hayford late of Hardwick dec. On 6 May 1794 Bathsheba rendered an account on the estate.

Samuel and Bathsheba had no children.

No Worcester Co. PR for Samuel or Bathsheba Work.

References: MD 4:21; 7:50. VR HARDWICK p. 271(2nd m.). VR PEMBROKE p. 104(b. Sam., b. ch. by 1st m.). VR PLYMPTON p. 330(Sam. 1st m.). DAR PATRIOT INDEX p. 316. PLYMOUTH CO CT RECS 3:246. Worcester Co. PR #28504(Samuel Hayford). WATERMAN GEN 1:169-70. HANOVER FIRST CH 1:95(Sam. 2nd m.). HANOVER VR p. 122 (Sam. 2nd m.).

126 MERCY TINKHAM[5] (Seth[4], Peter[3], Mary[2] Brown, Peter[1]) b. Middleboro 25 July 1732; d. there 29 April 1761 in 29th yr.

She m. Middleboro 8 April 1756 WOODWARD TUCKER, b. Milton 28 May 1733; d. Middleboro 12 April 1761 in 28th yr.; son of Benjamin and Sarah (Woodward) Tucker.

On 16 May 1758 Woodward Tucker of Middleboro, husbandman, and wife Mercy sold to Seth Tinkham Jr. of Middleboro laborer 1/6 of land in Middleboro of their father Seth Tinkham late of Middleboro dec., acknowledging the deed 6 Feb. 1769.

Administration on the estate of Woodward Tucker of Middleboro, yeoman, dec. was granted to Benjamin Tucker of Middleboro on 12 May 1761. Although there are no records in his estate to show his children, receipts of heirs of Benjamin Tucker, for the estate of Woodward Tucker, dated 21 May 1781, name Daniel Tucker, laborer, and Jesse Tinkham, laborer, and his wife Betty Tinkham, all of Middleboro.

Children (TUCKER) b. Middleboro:

    i   BETTY[6] b. 14 Dec. 1757
    ii DANIEL bp. 25 May 1760

References: MD 22:148(b. Betty); 24:57(m.). MIDDLEBORO VR 1:132(b. Betty), 150(m.). MIDDLEBORO DEATHS p. 211. Plymouth Co. PR 16:203; 17:38; 28:193(Woodward Tucker).

Plymouth Co. LR 48:40(Woodward Tucker). Middleboro First Ch.
Bp. p. 45 (bp. Daniel). VR MILTON p. 61(b. Woodward).

127 SETH TINKHAM[5] (Seth[4], Peter[3], Mary[2] Brown, Peter[1]) b.
Middleboro 13 Nov. 1734; d. there 13 Feb. 1808 in 74th yr.

He m. Halifax 22 Oct. 1761 EUNICE SOULE, b. Plympton 1
Feb. 1735/6; d. Middleboro 10 May 1808 in 72nd yr.; dau. of
Zachariah and Mary (Eaton) Soule, a descendant of Pilgrims
Francis Eaton and George Soule. On 1 Dec. 1784 Seth Tinkham of
Middleboro and wife Eunice and others sold land of (brother)
James Soule, with part set off (as dower) to Mary Soule.

On 29 Oct. 1787 Seth Tinkham of Middleboro, yeoman, sold
to Ebenezer and Zebedee Tinkham, both of Middleboro, part of
land in the 26 Men's Purchase "originally Peter Brown's and
afterwards Peter Tinkham's" with wife Eunice releasing dower.

No probate was found in Plymouth Co. for either Seth or
Eunice Tinkham, but it appears they had only one child who lived
to adulthood for on 20 April 1790 Seth Tinkham of Middleboro,
yeoman, sold to Hazael Tinkham of Middleboro, laborer, land and
the westerly end of his dwelling house, with wife Eunice giving
up her dower rights. The deed was acknowledged the same day.

Child (TINKHAM) b. Middleboro:

i   HAZAEL[6] (son) b. 20 April 1763

References: MD 19:142(m.); 23:71(b. Hazael). VR PLYMPTON p.
192(b. Eunice). MF 3:165; 9:114. MIDDLEBORO
DEATHS pp. 204, 206. Plymouth Co. LR 68:80; 68:127; 70:140
(Seth Tinkham). MIDDLEBORO VR 1:122(m.), 144(b. Hazael);
2:13(d. Seth, Eunice).

128 ELIZABETH TINKHAM[5] (Helkiah[4-3], Mary[2] Brown, Peter[1])
b. Plymouth 5 July 1713; living 25 April 1748 (rec. bond).

She m. Plymouth 3 July 1741 JONATHAN SANDERS of
Wareham, b. Plymouth 17 Nov. 1713; d. prob. bef. 25 April 1748
(not mentioned in bond); son of Henry and Ann (Bates) Sanders.

On 25 April 1748 Elizabeth Sanders received a bond from
her brother Isaac Tinkham for her part of her father's estate (see
#31).

No Plymouth Co. PR for Jonathan or Elizabeth Sanders.

Children (SANDERS) b. Plymouth:

    i   MARY[6] b. 22 March 1741/2
    ii   ELIZABETH b. 12 Aug. 1744
    iii JONATHAN b. 5 Feb. 1746/7; d. 1 Oct. 1747

References: MD 2:227(b. Jonathan); 15:162(b. ch.; d. Jonathan); 16:255(m.). NEHGR 127:253-4. (PLYMOUTH) ANC LANDMARKS 2:264. Plymouth Co. LR 39:118(Isaac Tinkham). PLYMOUTH VR pp. 25(b. Jonathan), 126(b. ch.; d. son Jonathan), 150(m.).

129 ISAAC TINKHAM[5] (Helkiah[4-3], Mary[2] Brown, Peter[1]) b. Plymouth 27 Dec. 1715; living 4 May 1752 (2nd m.).
    He m. (1) Duxbury 26 July 1739 KEZIAH WORMALL, b. Duxbury 21 Feb. 1717/8; d. prob. Plymouth bet. 11 Aug. 1749 and 4 May 1752; dau. of Ebenezer and Elizabeth (Briggs) Wormall.
    He m. (2) Plymouth 4 May 1752 REMEMBRANCE (JACKSON) (NASH) (WALKER) COOPER; dau. of Abraham and Remembrance (Morton) Jackson. She m. (1) Plymouth 20 Feb. 1723/4 Joseph Jackson by whom she had Joseph. She m. (2) Plymouth 3 April 1732 Giles Gnash [sic]. She m. (3) int. Plymouth 5 Nov. 1736 John Walker. She m. (4) int. Plymouth 17 Aug. 1743 John Cooper.
    Isaac Tinkham, his wife Kezia and their family who came out of Plymouth the latter end of May last past, warned out of Duxborough to depart 31 March 1743.
    On 25 March 1749 Isaac Tinkham of Plymouth, fisherman, signed and acknowledged a deed to Samuel Nelson of Plymouth of all the real estate of widow Elizabeth Tinkham, with Keziah giving up her dower 11 Aug. 1749.
    No Plymouth Co. PR for Isaac or Remembrance Tinkham nor Plymouth Co. LR for Isaac Tinkham with wife Remembrance.

Children (TINKHAM) b. Plymouth all by first wife:

    i   BRIGGS[6] b. 21 June 1740

ii   ELIZABETH b. 26 April 1743
iii   ISAAC b. 22 Oct. 1745

References: MD 13:173(b. ch. Joseph Jackson); 14:70(1st m. Rem.),
74(2nd m. Rem.); 16:88(b. Briggs), 89(b. last 2 ch.),
169(int. 2nd m. Rem.), 170(2nd m. Rem.); 17:131 (int. 4th m. Rem.),
138(int. 3rd m. Rem.); 18:30(int. 1st m. Isaac). VR DUXBURY pp.
206(b. Keziah), 321(1st m.). Plymouth Co. LR 40:95 (Isaac
Tinkham). PLYMOUTH CO CT RECS 2:230. PLYMOUTH VR
pp. 93(Keziah's 1st m.), 102(Keziah's 2nd m.), 141(b. ch.), 147 (2nd
m.), 158(int. Keziah's 4th m.), 163(int. Keziah's 3rd m.).

130 ZEDEKIAH TINKHAM[5] (Helkiah[4-3], Mary[2] Brown, Peter[1])
b. Plymouth 11 July 1721; living 17 Dec. 1792 (deed).
   He m. Plymouth 6 Dec. 1753 MERCY TINKHAM, b.
Plymouth 8 May 1726; living 17 Dec. 1792; dau. of Caleb and
Mercy (Holmes) Tinkham, a descendant of Pilgrim Peter Brown
(see #144).
   Zedekiah Tinkham of Plymouth, yeoman, sold to William
Watson of Plymouth land in Plymouth, 4 1/4 acres set off from
his mother's thirds. Zedekiah and Mercy signed 20 Nov. 1783, he
ack. 19 Dec. 1783.
   Zedekiah Tinkham was 1-0-3 in 1790 census of Plymouth.
   In the 17 Dec. 1792 deed under #35 he is called "Helkiah"
Tinkham. This is surely an error for Zedekiah.
   No Plymouth Co. PR for Zedekiah or Mercy.

   Child (TINKHAM) b. Plymouth:

   i   SARAH[6] b. 8 May 1768

References: MD 14:114(b. Mercy); 16:165(int.); 22:178(b. Sarah).
          Plymouth Co. LR 62:153(Zedekiah Tinkham).
PLYMOUTH VR pp. 121(b. Mercy), 223(b. Sarah), 348(m.).

131 MARY TINKHAM[5] (Helkiah[4-3], Mary[2] Brown, Peter[1]) b.
Plymouth 14 Sept. 1724; living 12 April 1761 when she was bp. in
Halifax Church.
   She m. (1) Plymouth 28 Oct. 1746 BENJAMIN EATON, b.
poss. Plymouth ca. 1698; d. Kingston 3 March (or May) 1751 in

53rd yr.; son of Benjamin and Mary (Coombs) Eaton, a descendant
of Pilgrims Francis Eaton and Degory Priest. He m. (1) Plympton
7 July 1726 Marcy Sturtevant by whom he had Ruth, Jabesh,
Noah, Mary and Seth. He m. (2) Kingston 27 Jan. 1742/3 Mary
Tilson by whom he had Thaddeus.

She m. (2) Kingston 28 Jan. 1760 ANDREW BEARCE, prob.
the one b. Plympton 8 Dec. 1716; son of Shubael and Thankful
(Ford) Bearce. He m. (1) Bridgewater 15 July 1736 Margaret
Dawes of Bridgewater by whom he had Lois, Margaret, Ruth,
Lydia, Experience, Deborah, Abthiah, and Andrew.

In 1748 Mary, wife of Benjamin Eaton of Kingston, was to
receive payment from her brother Isaac Tinkom as her share of
the estate of their father Helkiah Tinkom.

Division of Benjamin Eaton's estate was recorded 2 May
1757, allowing the widow Mary Eaton her dower; eldest son Noah
2/6 parts plus 1/5 of the share of Thadeus dec.; and Seth, James,
and Benjamin each received shares.

Children (EATON) b. prob. Kingston, but bp. Halifax:

  i   HANNAH[6] bp. 22 Nov. 1747; d. bef. 2 May 1757
  ii   BENJAMIN bp. 19 March 1748/9 (see MF 9:110-1
       for an additional generation)
  iii THADDEUS bp. 19 May 1751 "after his father's
       death"; d. bef. 2 May 1757

References: MD 16:100(1st m. Andrew); 17:5(1st m.); 18:119 (int. 1st
          m.); 27:121(bp. Mary; bp. Bearce ch.), 180(bp. Eaton
ch.). MF 9:34-5. HALIFAX VR pp. 44(b. Bearce ch.), 55(int.
Andrew's 1st m.), 60(int. 2nd m.). MA MARR 2:9 (1st m.). VR
BRIDGEWATER 2:48(1st m. Andrew). VR KINGSTON pp.
171(2nd m.), 214(2nd m. Benj.), 344(d. Benj.). VR PLYMPTON p.
312(1st m. Benj.). PLYMOUTH VR p. 154(m.).

NOTE: The only Plymouth Co. PR for Andrew Bearce is #1750
where George Wm. Munro of Halifax posted bond 5 April 1803 as
adm. of estate of Andrew Berce late of Halifax, yeoman; and
34:284 acct. of same dated 7 May 1804 which doesn't mention
widow or children. The estate was insolvent.

132   MARTHA TINKHAM[5] (Helkiah[4-3], Mary[2] Brown, Peter[1]) b. Plymouth 29 Dec. 1726; d. after 4 March 1756, prob. the Thomas Silvester's wife who d. Plymouth 29 Sept. 1763.

She m. Plymouth 23 April 1750 THOMAS SYLVESTER prob. the one who d. Plymouth 21 April 1786. He m. (2) Plymouth 24 July 1766 Elizabeth Dunham.

No Plymouth Co. PR for Thomas Sylvester.

Children (SYLVESTER) b. Plymouth:

    i   THOMAS[6] b. 11 Feb. 1750/1
    ii   SARAH b. 5 June 1753
    iii   HANNAH b. 4 March 1756

References: MD 16:166(int.), 169(m.); 18:212(b. ch.); 26:86 (int. 2nd m.). PLYMOUTH CH RECS 1:393(d. wife); 415(d. Thomas). PLYMOUTH VR pp. 146(m.), 183(b. ch.), 351(his 2nd m.).

133   RUTH TINKHAM[5] (Helkiah[4-3], Mary[2] Brown, Peter[1]) b. Plymouth 9 July 1729.

She apparently m. Plymouth 13 April 1766 ISAAC MORTON, b. Plymouth 8 May 1725; son of Thomas and Abigail (Pratt) Morton. He m. (1) Plymouth 19 March 1746 Meriah Lewen by whom he had Hannah, Hannah, Sarah, Isaac, and Abner.

No known children.

References: MD 13:33(ch. by 1st m.), 116(b. Isaac); 17:6(his 1st m.); 26:86(int.). PLYMOUTH VR pp. 69(b. Isaac), 154(his 1st m.), 382(m.).

134   LYDIA TINKHAM[5] (Helkiah[4-3], Mary[2] Brown, Peter[1]) b. Plymouth 10 March 1734/5; prob. the one who d. Plymouth 28 Aug. 1817 ae 80 "from the alms house."

She m. Plymouth 12 July 1756 JOHN JONES who was living 30 Jan. 1776.

On 3 Oct. 1763 Lidia Jones, wife of John of Liverpool NS, and her children who came from Liverpool Sept. last, were warned out of Plymouth; on 30 Jan. 1776 John Jones and wife Lydia and their children John Jr., Benjamin, and Lydia, who came from Plymouth were warned out of Mansfield.

There is no Plymouth Co. PR for John or Lydia Jones, but there was a John Jones listed in the 1771 tax list in Plymouth.

Children (JONES) b. Plymouth, except John b. Liverpool, NS and Ebenezer b. Kingston:

     i   JOHN[6] b. 2 March 1759; d. 22 Oct. 1761
    ii   child d. 13 Oct., 1760
   iii   JOHN b. 14 Jan. 1763
   iv   BENJAMIN b. 20 May 1767
    v   EBENEZER b. 14 Sept. 1769; prob. the John Jones child who d. 15 Sept. 1770
   vi   LYDIA b. 13 Nov. 1771
  vii   EBENEZER b. 12 Sept. 1774; prob. the John Jones child who d. 8 Sept. 1775

References: MD 19:9(b. ch.; d. ch. John). PLYMOUTH CH RECS 1:391(d. ch.), 399(d. ch.), 404(d. ch.); 2:665 (d. Lydia). NEHGR 126:98(b. John). THE MASS. TAX VALUATION LIST OF 1771, Bettye Hobbs Pruitt, Ed., Boston, 1978, p. 654. PLYMOUTH CO CT RECS 3:118. Bristol Co. Court of Sessions 1746-77, p. 592(warning).

135 JACOB CURTIS[5] (Mary Tinkham[4], Helkiah[3], Mary[2] Brown, Peter[1]) b. Plymouth 11 Oct. 1710; d. there bef. 22 Jan. 1752.

He m. Plymouth 7 May 1731 FEAR DUNHAM, b. Plymouth 13 March 1707/8; d. Liverpool NS 13 Sept. 1774; dau. of Eliazer and Meriam (Phillips) Dunham. She m. (2) Plymouth 13 June 1752 William Gammons by whom she had a dau. Rebecca.

On 22 Jan. 1752 Fear Curtis, widow of Jacob Curtis, late of Plymouth, mariner, was appointed administratrix on his estate. The account of 31 Jan. 1752 mentions but does not name three small children.

Children (CURTIS) b. Plymouth:

     i   ELIZABETH[6] b. 24 May 1732
    ii   SARAH b. 14 July 1734
   iii   CALEB b. 13 July 1737; d. 29 July 1740

    iv   FEAR b. 12 May 1740
    v   JACOB b. 10 Aug. 1742
    vi   MARY b. 19 March 1744/5
    vii   HANNAH b. 24 April 1747

References: Plymouth Co. PR 12:428-9(Jacob Curtis). MD 5:53 (b.
              Fear); 14:73(m.); 15:42(b. ch.); 18:141(int. 2nd m.);
19:7(b. Rebecca). DUNHAM GEN p. 160. Simeon Perkins Diary(d.
Fear). TAG 54:227-9. PLYMOUTH CH RECS 1:437(bp. Eliz.,
Caleb), 443(bp. Hannah). PLYMOUTH VR pp. 37(b. Fear), 96(m.),
114(b. ch.; d. son Jacob), 175(her 2nd m.).

136 MARY CURTIS[5] (Mary Tinkham[4], Helkiah[3], Mary[2] Brown,
Peter[1]) b. Plymouth 21 Dec. 1714; prob. d. there bet. 27 Aug.
1735(b. of Experience) and 18 April 1736(when Marcy, wife of
Nathaniel was bp.).
     She m. int. Plymouth 2 Jan. 1733 NATHANIEL
CHURCHILL, b. Plymouth 19 Dec. 1712; d. there 15 April 1794 ae
82; son of Stephen and Experience (Ellis) Churchill.   He
apparently m. (2) ca. 1736 Mercy _____ who was bp. in the First
Plymouth Church 18 April 1736 as Marcy, wife of Nathaniel.
Nathaniel apparently had Eleazer, Mary, Nathaniel, and Mary by
the 2nd wife.
     On 16 Feb. 1733 Nathaniel Churchell, cordwainer, and wife
Mary signed a release to Ruth Tinkham, widow, for their share of
Hilkiah Tinkcom's estate.
     No Plymouth Co. PR for Nathaniel Churchill.

     Child (CHURCHILL) b. Plymouth:

       i   EXPERIENCE[6] b. 27 Aug. 1735

References: MD 12:13(b. Nath.), 147(release); 15:44(b. ch.);
             17:134(int.).   PLYMOUTH CH RECS 1:422(d.
Nath.), 441(bp. Eleazer, Mary), 448(bp. Mary); 2:523(bp. wife
Mercy). CHURCHILL FAM pp. 12, 25. PLYMOUTH VR pp. 50(b.
Nathaniel), 116(b. Experience).

137 SARAH CURTIS[5] (Mary Tinkham[4], Helkiah[3], Mary[2] Brown,
Peter[1]) b. Plymouth 19 Aug. 1717; living 10 April 1734.

She m. Plymouth bet. 29 Dec. 1733 (int.) and 10 April 1734 WILLIAM GRIFFING (or GRIFFITH).

On 10 April 1734 William Griffeth of Plymouth, hatter, and wife Sarah signed a release to Ruth Tinkcom, widow, for their part of the estate of Hilkiah Tinkcom.

There is no Plymouth Co. PR for William Griffing nor any Plymouth Co. LR after 1734.

No known children.

References: MD 12:147-8(release); 17:134(int.). PLYMOUTH VR p. 161(int.).

138   EDWARD TINKHAM[5] (John[4], Helkiah[3], Mary[2] Brown, Peter[1]) b. Plymouth 2 Feb. 1719/20; d. Yarmouth, Nova Scotia 10 May 1793.

He m. Plymouth 29 Sept. 1742 LYDIA RIDER, b. Plymouth 4 Feb. 1721/2; d. Yarmouth NS bef. 6 June 1807; dau. of Benjamin and Hannah (Rider) Rider.

On 1 Aug. 1746, ack. same day, Edward Tinkham of Kingston, nailer, sold to Benjamin Lothrop the whole of the real estate that his father John Tinkham late of Kingston died seized of; Lydia also signed deed with a mark.

In 1762 Edward Tinkham moved to Yarmouth, Nova Scotia.

On 28 Nov. 1770 Edward Tinkham of New Yarmouth NS, husbandman, sold a farm in Kingston that he bought of James Low, Seth Chipman and Michael Sampson, acknowledging the deed at Plymouth the next day.

Lydia Tinkham of Yarmouth, posted bond 15 Jan. 1794 as administratrix of the estate of Edward Tinkham, late of Yarmouth.

On 28 Jan. 1794 the estate of Edward Tinkham, late of Yarmouth, was partitioned with one-third set off to widow Lydia Tinkham; 2/5 of rest to eldest son Seth Tinkham; 1/5 to dau. Hannah Bartlett, wife of Lemuel; 1/10 each to grandchildren Hannah and Ebenezer Tinkham, children of Stephen Tinkham dec.; and 1/5 to Lydia Perry wife of Nathaniel.

On 6 June 1807 the estate of Lydia Tinkham late of Yarmouth dec. was divided to: heirs of Seth Tinkham, dec.; heirs of Stephen Tinkham dec.; heirs of Lydia Perry, dec., and to Lydia Bartlett.

Children (TINKHAM) first 2 b. Kingston; last 2 b. Yarmouth
NS:

i	SYLVANUS[6] b. 1 Aug. 1743; prob. d.y.
ii	REBECCA b. 11 June 1745; prob. d.y.
iii	SETH
iv	HANNAH
v	STEPHEN
vi	EDWARD b. 24 Oct. 1762; d. 17 June 1780
vii	LYDIA b. 11 March 1765

References: MD 13:169(b. Lydia); 17:4(m.). VR KINGSTON p.
145(b. 1st 2 ch.). YARMOUTH NS HERALD GEN
#64 20 Sept. 1898(last 5 ch. incl. b. of Edward & Lydia).
Yarmouth NS PR(Edward Tinkham). Plymouth Co. LR 38:104;
57:251(Edward Tinkham). PLYMOUTH VR p. 74(b. Lydia),
152(m.).

139 JOHN TINKHAM[5] (John[4], Helkiah[3], Mary[2] Brown, Peter[1])
b. Kingston 1721; d. there 15 Sept. 1748 ae 26y 9m 29d.

He m. Kingston 2 Feb. 1747/8 SARAH EVERSON, b.
Kingston 17 Dec. 1727; d. after 8 Aug. 1762 (birth of last child);
dau. of John and Silence (Staples) Everson. She m. (2) Kingston
5 Oct. 1749 Charles Cooke, a descendant of Pilgrim Francis Cooke,
by whom she had Hannah, Asenath, John, Zadoc, Hannah, Zenus,
Francis, Anne, and Sarah. The division of the estate of Mr. John
Everson mentions widow Silence Everson and dau. Sarah Cook
wife of Charles Cook of Halifax.

On 30 Nov. 1748 Sarah Tinkham, widow of Kingston,
administratrix on the estate of John Tinkham late of Kingston
dec., gave her bond with Ebenezer Fuller and John Everson both
of Kingston as sureties. On 15 Feb. 1759 Ebenezer Fuller of
Kingston was appointed guardian of Joseph Tinkham, minor son
of John late of Kingston dec.

Children (TINKHAM) b. Kingston:

i	ANNE[6] b. 3 Jan. 1748/9; d. 6 Jan. 1754 ae 6y 3d
ii	JOSEPH (twin?)

References: VR KINGSTON pp. 71(b. Sarah), 145(b. Anne), 291
            (m.), 386(d. John, Anne). Plymouth Co. PR #20874
(John Tinkham); #20878(gdn. Joseph Tinkham); 28:22(John
Everson). MF 12:442-3.

140 EPHRAIM TINKHAM[5] (John[4], Helkiah[3], Mary[2] Brown,
Peter[1]) b. Kingston 25 March 1724; living 1768.
    He m. int. Kingston 8 Dec. 1750 SARAH FULLER, b.
Plympton 27 Jan. 1727/8; dau. of Seth and Deborah (Edwards)
Fuller, a descendant of Pilgrims John Billington, Francis Eaton,
and Samuel Fuller.
    On 29 Nov. 1752 Ephraim Tinkham was ordered warned out
of Kingston, having moved there last May, living with his brother
Edward.   He was said to be in Chebogue and the owner of a
schooner in 1768 and prob. returned to Kingston. He may be the
one listed as a non-resident owner of property in the 1771 Tax list
for Plympton.
    No known children.

References: VR KINGSTON p. 291(int.). VR PLYMPTON p.
            107(b. Sarah).   MF 10:41.   YARMOUTH NS
HERALD GEN #64 20 Sept. 1898. PLYMOUTH CO CT RECS
3:14.

141 ANN TINKHAM[5] (John[4], Helkiah[3], Mary[2] Brown, Peter[1]) b.
Kingston 6 Aug. 1726; d. after 11 Sept. 1758 (deed).
    She m. Kingston 22 Oct. 1747 SAMUEL FULLER, b.
Plympton 14 May 1724; d. bef. 9 May 1758; son of Benjamin and
Mary (Samson) Fuller, a descendant of Pilgrims John Billington,
Francis Eaton, and Samuel Fuller.
    On 9 May 1758 Anne Fuller, administratrix on the estate of
her husband Samuel Fuller late of Plimton dec., posted bond with
Benjamin Weston and John Fuller sureties.
    On 11 Sept. 1758 Anne Fuller of Plympton, administratrix of
the estate of Samuel Fuller, sold land to John Faunce.
    No Plymouth Co. PR or LR for Ann Fuller.

    Children (FULLER) b. Plympton:

        i   MARY[6] (or MOLLY) b. 23 Nov. 1748

    ii   RUBY b. 20 Jan. 1750/1
    iii   BENJAMIN b. 10 Dec. 1752
    iv   SILVANUS b. 16 March 1755
    v   ANNA b. 4 May 1757

References: VR KINGSTON p. 228(m.). VR PLYMPTON p. 107(b.
           Samuel, 103-7(b. ch.). MF 10:45-6. Plymouth Co.
PR #8284(Samuel Fuller). Plymouth Co. LR 45:133(Anne Fuller).

NOTE: Possibly Ann m. (2) Plympton 3 May 1762 Thomas Harlow
(VR PLYMPTON). If so, they had Thomas 12 July 1768.

142 JOSEPH TINKHAM[5] (John[4], Helkiah[3], Mary[2] Brown, Peter[1])
b. Kingston 14 May 1728; living Plympton 18 Jan. 1779.
    He m. int. Kingston 15 Sept. 1750 DEBORAH FULLER bp.
Plympton 4 Nov. 1733; dau. of Seth and Deborah (Edwards)
Fuller, a descendant of Pilgrims John Billington, Francis Eaton,
and Samuel Fuller.
    Joseph can be followed through a series of warnings out: 18
Jan. 1750 he was warned out of Plympton to return to Kingston,
having come there 1 Dec. late; on 13 June 1766 he was warned out
of Plymouth with his wife and family, having come from
Kingston; and on 18 Jan. 1779 he was warned out of Plympton to
Kingston.
    No Plymouth Co. PR for Joseph Tinkham.

    Children (TINKHAM) b. Kingston:

    i   JOHN[6] b. 9 Nov. 1754
    ii   JOSEPH b. 26 May 1757
    iii LEVI b. 17 Feb. 1762
    iv SETH b. 22 March 1764

References: VR KINGSTON pp. 145(b. ch.), 291(int.).   VR
           PLYMPTON p. 104(bp. Deborah). PLYMOUTH CO
CT RECS 3:47, 239, 360. MF 10:42; 21:55-6.

143 JACOB TINKHAM[5] (Jacob[4], Helkiah[3], Mary[2] Brown, Peter[1])
b. Plymouth 28 Feb. 1723/4; living 1754.
    He m. Plymouth 5 Feb. 1746/7 LYDIA DONHAM, b.

Plymouth 8 Feb. 1724/5; dau. of Josiah and Ruth (Kempton) Donham.

No Plymouth Co. PR or LR for Jacob or Lydia Tinkham.

Children (TINKHAM) b. Plymouth:

    i   HANNAH⁶ b. 31 Oct. 1747
    ii   LYDIA b. 15 Nov. 1749
    iii MARY b. 28 Nov. 1751
    iv   JACOB b. 10 Sept. 1754

References: MD 4:110(b. ch.); 16:172(m.); 18:119(int.). DUNHAM
              GEN pp. 160-1. PLYMOUTH VR pp. 33(b. ch.),
61(b. Lydia), 149(m.).

144 MARCY TINKHAM⁵ (Caleb⁴, Helkiah³, Mary² Brown,
Peter¹) b. Plymouth 8 May 1726; living 17 Dec. 1792 (deed).
      She m. Plymouth 6 Dec. 1753 ZEDEKIAH TINKHAM, b.
Plymouth 11 July 1721; living 17 Dec. 1792 (deed); son of Helkiah
and Elizabeth (Heister) Tinkham, a descendant of Pilgrim Peter
Brown.
      See #130 for an account of this family.

References: MD 5:99(b. Zedekiah). PLYMOUTH VR pp. 41(b.
              Zedekiah), 348(m.).

145 FEAR TINKHAM⁵ (Caleb⁴, Helkiah³, Mary² Brown, Peter¹)
b. Plymouth 5 Nov. 1731; d. there 29 Dec. 1766.
      She m. Plymouth 9 Dec. 1756 JOSIAH WATERMAN, b.
Plympton 2 Aug. 1728; d. Plymouth 13 April 1817 ae 84; son of
Josiah and Joanna (Bryant) Waterman. He m. (2) Kingston 27 July
1769 Lydia (Chandler) Everson by whom he had Chandler and
Ebenezer.
      Josiah Waterman served with the forces against Crown Point
in 1755. On 20 Oct. 1766 Josiah Waterman, laborer, and Fear
Waterman of Plymouth sold to Samuel Bryant of Plymouth,
mariner, land which came to them by heirship from their
grandfather Nathaniel Holmes.
      On 20 Oct. 1766 Josiah Waterman of Plymouth, laborer, and
wife Fear, sold to Samuel Bryant of Plymouth all rights to real

estate of their grandfather Nathaniel Holmes.

On 15 Dec. 1766 Fear, wife of Josiah Waterman, was bp. "upon a sick bed."

Josiah Waterman, his wife Lidia and their sons Joshua, Josiah, and Chandler "who came from Plymouth about the 10th day of Dec. 1767" were warned from Kingston 5 Dec. 1770.

On 13 March 1781 Joshua Waterman and Josiah Waterman Jr., both of Kingston, sold to Benjamin Smith of Duxbury, cordwainer, 4 acres in Plymouth that came to them from their uncle Nathaniel Tinkham.

No Plymouth Co. PR for Josiah or Fear Waterman.

Children (WATERMAN) b. Plymouth:

    i   JOSHUA[6] b. 1 Dec. 1757
   ii   JOSIAH b. 19 Jan. 1760
  iii   JERUSHA b. 19 June 1763; prob. d.y.; (not in warning or deed)
   iv   LUCY b. 5 June 1775 [sic; should be 1765 as she d. 20 Jan. 1839, ae 73 yrs 7 mos]
    v   FEAR b. 1 Nov. 1767 [sic.; prob. 1766 as her mother d. 29 Dec. 1766]; prob. d.y.

References: MD 21:19(b. 1st 3 ch.); 25:139(int.). VR KINGSTON pp. 156(b. Lucy, Fear), 300(his 2nd m.). MA MARR 2:16(m. - he is called Joseph). WATERMAN GEN 1:81, 165-6. PLYMOUTH CO CT RECS 3:304. Plymouth Co. LR 61:37(Joshua Waterman, etc.); 62:273(Josiah Waterman). Plymouth Third Church records(bp. Fear). PLYMOUTH VR pp. 203(b. 1st 3 ch.), 348(m.).

146 SARAH TINKHAM[5] (Caleb[4], Helkiah[3], Mary[2] Brown, Peter[1]) b. Plymouth 28 Dec. 1733; d. bef. 4 Nov. 1757 (2nd m.).

She m. Plymouth 13 Nov. 1749 BENJAMIN SMITH of Plymouth; living 23 June 1776 (warning). He m. (2) Plymouth 4 Nov. 1757 Sarah Doten by whom he had Sarah, William, Nathaniel, Samuel, Susanna, John, John, and Betty.

Sarah Smith, the wife of Benjamin Smith, was received into the Third Church of Plymouth 19 July 1761 and her children Sarah and William were bp. the same day.

On 2 July 1765 Benjamin Smith of Plymouth, mariner, was appointed guardian for his son Benjamin, a minor, and on the same day he was chosen guardian by his dau. Mary Smith, a minor over 14, for estate which came from their grandfather Caleb Tinkham late of Plymouth, mariner.

On 23 June 1776 Benjamin Smith from Plymouth and wife Sarah were warned from Duxbury.

On 19 June 1781 Benjamin Smith of Duxbury, cordwainer, sold to Cornelius Cobb land in Plymouth, part of which he had received from his uncle Nathaniel Tinkham dec., part was his sister's share, and part was land he bought of Joshua and Josiah Waterman of Kingston. His wife Sarah released her dower.

No Plymouth Co. PR for Benjamin Smith.

Children (SMITH) b. Plymouth:

    i   MARY[6] b. ca. 1750; bp. 17 July 1761
    ii   BENJAMIN b. ca. 1755 (ae 76 when he d. Duxbury 5 Feb. 1831)

References: MD 16:166(int.), 169(m.); 17:3(2nd m.). VR DUXBURY p. 419(d. son Benj.). Plymouth Co. PR #18440 (Smith gdn.). Plymouth Co. LR 61:37(Benj. Smith). MQ 49:24(Sarah adm. 3rd church), 83(bp. Sarah, Wm., Nathaniel). Plymouth Third Church Records(bp. ch.). PLYMOUTH CO CT RECS 3:360 (warning). PLYMOUTH VR pp. 146(m.), 152(his 2nd m.).

147 ELEANOR (or NELLIE) TINKHAM[5] (Caleb[4], Helkiah[3], Mary[2] Brown, Peter[1]) b. Plymouth ca. 1740; d. after 19 Aug. 1805.

She m. Plymouth 21 Feb. 1758 SAMUEL BRYANT, prob. the one b. Plympton 18 Nov. 1736 to Samuel and Tabitha (Ford) Bryant; d. Plymouth 21 June 1800.

Samuel Bryant served in the Revolutionary War.

On 7 Nov. 1787 Samuel Bryant of Plymouth, mariner, and wife Eleanor sold to Joseph Warren Nelson land which he bought of Josiah Waterman and his wife Fear in 1766. On 28 June 1794 Eleanor Bryant wife of Samuel, about 60 years old, was bp. and admitted to the Plymouth Church.

On 27 Dec. 1799 Patience Tinkham of Plymouth, seamster,

deeded moveable properties to niece Sarah Tinkham and nieces Patience Bryant and Lucy Bryant, daus. of Samuel Bryant of Plymouth.

On 19 Aug. 1805, ack. same day, Eleanor Bryant of Plymouth, widow, sold to Samuel Holmes land in Plymouth with dwelling house which she bought of Sarah Tinkham on 9 May 1804.

There is no Plymouth Co. PR for Samuel Bryant.

Children (BRYANT) b. Plymouth:

   i   SARAH[6] b. 23 Dec. 1758
   ii   SAMUEL b. 14 April (blank)
   iii LYDIA (listed in VR without a date)
   iv PATIENCE
   v   LUCY

References: MD 20:71(b. 1st 3 ch.); 25:141(int.). PLYMOUTH CH RECS 2:482(Eleanor joined Ch.), 622(d. Sam.). Plymouth Co. LR 66:266(Samuel Bryant); 88:125(Patience Tinkham); 103:252(Eleanor Bryant). PLYMOUTH VR pp. 201(b. 1st 3 ch.), 349(m.). VR PLYMPTON p. 49(b. Samuel). MSSR 2:736. NEHGR 154:237-8(Bryant Fam.).

147A   SARAH TINKHAM[5] (Ebenezer[4], Helkiah[3], Mary[2] Brown, Peter[1]) b. Plymouth 22 Nov. 1733: d. Plympton 28 Aug. 1767 in 34th yr.

She m. Plympton 1 Feb. 1759 BENJAMIN BRYANT, b. Plympton 25 Dec. 1734; d. there 2 May 1824 ae 89y 3m 28d; son of Nathaniel and Zerviah (Curtis) Bryant. He m. (2) Plympton 13 Sept. 1768 Sarah Harlow by whom he had Abigail, Benjamin, and Nathaniel.

No Plymouth Co. PR for Benjamin Bryant.

Children (BRYANT) b. Plympton:

   i   MOLLEY[6] b. 5 Nov. 1759
   ii   CONSIDER b. 6 Dec. 1764
   iii ASAPH b. 12 Feb. 1767

References: VR PLYMPTON pp. 44(b. Benjamin), 44-8(b. ch.),
            270(m.), 452(d. Benjamin, 455(d. Sarah). HARLOW
GEN p. 230. NEHGR 154:242(Bryant fam.).

148 MARY TINKHAM[5] (Ebenezer[4], Helkiah[3], Mary[2] Brown,
Peter[1]) b. Plymouth 9 April 1739; d. there 22 May 1790 ae 51.
        She m. Plymouth 3 Feb. 1760 JOSEPH MITCHELL, b. ca.
1737; d. Plymouth 30 Dec. 1791 ae 54.
        Mary, wife of "Jo." Mitchell of Liverpool, Nova Scotia and
her children were warned out of Plymouth 3 Oct. 1763. Joseph
Mitchell "who came ... from Nova Scotia ... in November last" was
warned from Plymouth 22 Dec. 1763.
        On 29 Nov. 1793 Thomas Pope was ordered to administer the
estate of Joseph Mitchell late of Plymouth. The account includes
gravestone for Mr. & Mrs. Mitchell (this could be the gravestone
on Burial Hill.) A slip of paper in the estate lists the heirs: Joseph
Mitchell; Ebenezer Mitchell; the heir of Mary Pope dec., wife of
Thomas; Nancy Churchill, wife of Lewis; Betsy Pomeroy, wife of
Ebenezer of Suffield CT; and Priscilla Mitchell.

        Children (MITCHELL) b. Plymouth:

        i   JOSEPH[6] b. 14 Nov. 1760
        ii   JAMES b. 23 March 1763
        iii   EBENEZER b. 23 Aug. 1765
        iv   MARY b. 3 Feb. 1768
        v   NANCY
        vi   ELIZABETH (or BETSY)
        vii   PRISCILLA

References: MD 21:164(b. 4 ch.). PLYMOUTH CO CT RECS 3:118,
            206. (PLYMOUTH) BURIAL HILL p. 66(d. Mary,
Joseph). Plymouth Co. PR #14089(Joseph Mitchell). PLYMOUTH
CH RECS 1:417(d. Mary), 419(d. Joseph). PLYMOUTH VR pp.
211(b. 1st 4 ch.), 350(m.).

149 PHEBE TINKHAM[5] (Ebenezer[4], Helkiah[3], Mary[2] Brown,
Peter[1]) b. Plymouth 12 July 1746; d. there 11 June 1809 "aged."
        She m. (1) Plymouth 4 May 1766 ENOCH RANDALL, b.
Plymouth; d. there 29 June 1779; son of Doughty and Elizabeth

(Tilson) Randall.

She m. (2) Plymouth 13 Jan. 1782 BENJAMIN CHURCHILL
Jr., b. Plymouth 17 Nov. 1748; d. there 1 Sept.
1802; son of Benjamin and Ruth (Delano) Churchill, a descendant of Pilgrim
Edward Doty.

Phebe Churchill of Plymouth, widow, sold to son Benjamin
Churchill Jr., mariner, lands in Plymouth, signed 24 March 1809,
ack. same day.

No Plymouth Co. PRs for Enoch Randall, Benjamin or Phebe
Churchill.

Children (RANDALL) b. Plymouth:
    i   ENOCH[6] b. 26 July 1767
    ii   PHEBE b. 9 Aug. 1769
    iii LUCY b. 1 Sept. 1771
    iv   WILLIAM b. 7 Aug. 1773
    v   MERCY b. 2 April 1777

Children (CHURCHILL) b. Plymouth:

    vi   NATHAN
    vii BENJAMIN b. 16 Dec. 1785

References: MD 14:243(b. Benjamin); 23:186(b. Randall ch.);
        26:86(int. 1st m.); 28:71(int. 2nd m.). PLYMOUTH
CH RECS 1:409(d. Enoch); 2:501(2nd m.), 627(d. Benjamin), 657 (d.
Phebe). (PLYMOUTH) ANC LANDMARKS 2:55 (names son
Nathan), 210. PLYMOUTH VR pp. 109(b. Benjamin), 236(b.
Randall ch.), 254(int. 1st m.), 364(2nd m.), 382(1st m.), 407(b.
Churchill ch.). Plymouth Co. LR 112:58(Phebe Churchill). MF
11:2:83.

150 SUSANNAH TINKHAM[5] (Ebenezer[4], Helkiah[3], Mary[2]
Brown, Peter[1]) b. Plymouth 15 Sept. 1748; living 1776.

She m. (1) Plymouth 30 Oct. 1768 THOMAS FARMER.

She apparently m. (2) Plymouth 4 Nov. 1786 GEORGE
PRICE. He m. (1) Plymouth 23 Feb. 1773 Abigail Thomas by
whom he had Jenna, Sarah, and George.

No Plymouth Co. PR or LR for Thomas or Susannah Farmer.

Children (FARMER) b. Plymouth:

   i   child[6] d. 6 Aug. 1769
   ii   THOMAS b. 8 June 1770
   iii MARY b. 15 Jan. 1776

References: MD 22:181(b. Thomas, Mary). (PLYMOUTH) ANC
            LANDMARKS 2:105. PLYMOUTH CH RECS
1:398(d. child); 2:495(1st m.). PLYMOUTH VR pp. 227(b. last 2
ch.), 235(b. Price ch.), 358(1st m.), 360(George's 1st m.), 387(2nd
m.).

NOTE: (PLYMOUTH) ANC LANDMARKS 2:105 gives Thomas &
Susanna Farmer a dau. who m. George Price. This doesn't seem
likely, as she would have been too young. However, there is a
Susanna Farmer 0-1-2 in 1790 census of Plymouth.

151 PRISCILLA TINKHAM[5] (Ebenezer[4], Helkiah[3], Mary[2] Brown,
Peter[1]) b. Plymouth 26 July 1755; apparently d. Duxbury 1 Oct.
1808 (as Priscilla Coomer).
      She m. (1) Plymouth 21 Aug. 1778 WILLIAM ANDERSON.
      She m. (2) Plymouth 16 March 1780 WILLIAM COOMER of
Duxbury; prob. son of William and Mabel (Kempton) Coomer.
      William Coomer was 1-1-3 in the 1790 census of Duxbury.
      In 1803 the Selectmen of Duxbury petitioned for a guardian
for William Coomer.
      No Plymouth Co. PR or LR for William Anderson.

   Child (COOMER) b. Duxbury:

   i   child[6] d. 1784 ae 7d

References: MD 27:178(int.). Plymouth Co. PR #4942(Coomer).
            PLYMOUTH CH RECS 2:499(m.), 500(2nd m.). VR
DUXBURY p. 363(d. Priscilla, child). PLYMOUTH VR pp.
143(m. of 2nd husband's par.), 362(1st m.), 363(2nd m.).

152 EBENEZER COBB[5] (Ruth Tinkham[4], Helkiah[3], Mary[2]
Brown, Peter[1]) b. Plymouth 4 March 1723/4; d. Kingston 10 Nov.
1782 ae 58.

He m. Kingston 30 Oct. 1747 [sic, but note b. of 1st ch.] JERUSHA CUSHMAN, b. Kingston 15 Jan. 1727/8; d. after 1790 (census); dau. of Robert and Mercy (Washburn) Cushman, a descendant of Pilgrims Isaac Allerton, John Billington, and John Howland. The 2 May 1760 settlement of the estate of Robert Cushman mentions dau. Jerusha Cobb.

Ebenezer Cobb served as a Sergeant in the Revolution.

On 12 April 1783 widow Jerusha Cobb gave her bond as administratrix on the estate of her late husband Ebenezer Cobb Jr. late of Kingston, yeoman, dec. The latest reference in probate papers for Jerusha was 1 Dec. 1783.

Jerusha Cobb was 0-0-2 in the 1790 census of Kingston.

There is no Plymouth Co. PR for Jerusha Cobb.

Children (COBB) b. Kingston:

i	RUTH[6]	b. 30 Aug. 1747
ii	SYLVANUS	b. 30 Oct. 1748
iii	ELEANOR	b. 5 Sept. 1750
iv	MARY	b. 25 Nov. 1751
v	FRANCIS	b. 2 Nov. 1753
vi	MELATIAH	b. 1 April 1755
vii	ELISHA	b. 15 Oct. 1756
viii	JERUSHA	b. 31 Oct. 1757
ix	JOSEPH	b. 2 Aug. 1759; d.y.
x	EBENEZER	b. 27 Sept. 1760
xi	MERCY	b. 24 Aug. 1762
xii	WILLIAM	b. 20 Aug. 1764
xiii	FEAR	b. 19 Aug. 1766
xiv	JOSEPH	b. 11 March 1768
xv	ZENAS	b. 2 Feb. 1772

References: VR KINGSTON pp. 41-3(b. ch.), 55(b. Jerusha), 193 (m.), 328(d. Ebenezer). Plymouth Co. PR 15:497(Robert Cushman). DAR PATRIOT INDEX p. 140. CUSHMAN GEN p. 144. MF 17:104; 21:84-5.

153   CALEB TINKHAM[5] (Peter[4], Helkiah[3], Mary[2] Brown, Peter[1]) b. Plymouth ca. 1739; d. Middleboro 5 July 1798 in 60th yr.*

He m. Middleboro 27 May 1764 DEBORAH BABBITT, b.

Berkley 25 April 1747; d. Middleboro 15 Sept. 1815; dau. of
Benjamin and Abiah (_____) Babbitt.
 Caleb Tinkham was a Pvt. in the Rev. War.
 Caleb Tinkham was 3-1-9 in the 1790 census of Middleboro.
 On 19 July 1793 Caleb Tinkham of Middleboro, cordwainer,
and wife Deborah sold to William Sturbridge Jr. a lot in 16
Shilling Purchase in Middleboro.
 On 3 Nov. 1800 "Helkiah" Tinkham of Freetown, mariner,
sold to Benjamin Tinkham of Middleboro, yeoman, all interest in
the real estate of his father Caleb Tinkham, late of Middleboro;
Arthur Tinkham was a witness.
 No Plymouth Co. PR for Caleb or Deborah Tinkham.

 Children (TINKHAM) b. Middleboro:

i	ARTHUR[6]	b. 1766(yr. from MF. Soc. App. paper).
ii	MARY	
iii	BARBARA	
iv	BIAH	
v	HEZEKIAH (or HELKIAH)	
vi	HANNAH	
vii	CALEB	
viii	ACHSA	
ix	PHEBE	
x	BENJAMIN	b. 15 Aug. 1782
xi	BETSY	

References: MD 24:56(m.). MIDDLEBORO DEATHS p. 208.
     Tinkham ms. p. 80(list of ch.). DAR PATRIOT
INDEX p. 680. Mortality Recs 1667-1854 Middleboro MA p. 75.
Berkley VR Index Births, p. 2(b. Deborah). MIDDLEBORO VR
1:149(m.). Plymouth Co. LR 77:124(Caleb Tinkham);
91:10(Helkiah Tinkham).

*While he is the right name and age to be the son of Caleb
Tinkham (#35), the fact that he didn't share in the division of
Caleb's estate makes it unlikely he is Caleb's son. The data on the
children is from the Tinkham Ms. and no proof has been found
except the deed. No other deeds selling Caleb's land. No births of
ch. in IGI.

154 JOHN TOMSON[5] (John[4], Mary Tinkham[3], Mary[2] Brown, Peter[1]) b. Plympton 18 Feb. 1724/5; d. 18 Jan. 1777, frozen to death while traveling from Plymouth to Plympton. He m. int. Halifax 2 March 1760 ELIZABETH FULLER, b. Middleboro 15 Aug. 1729; d. bef. 30 March 1779; dau. of Ebenezer and Elizabeth (Short) Fuller, a descendant of Pilgrim Samuel Fuller. The will of Ebenezer Fuller dated 12 July 1785 names dau. Elizabeth Thompson and grandson Thaddeus Thompson.

The petition of Ebenezer Fuller, dated 30 March 1779 at Halifax, asks the court to appoint Freeman Waterman guardian of his grandchildren, the children of John Tomson 2nd late of Halifax, who died leaving a widow and 6 minor children, since which time the widow has died. Freeman Waterman's bonds as guardian of Thaddeus and Susannah, both over 14, and Nathan, Stephen, Elizabeth and Zacheus, all under 14, children of John Tomson late of Halifax dec., were dated 5 April 1779. On 3 May 1779 Ebenezer Fuller petitioned the court to appoint Jacob Soule to settle the estate of his (Ebenezer's) dau., the widow Betty Tomson of Halifax.

On 3 May 1779 Jacob Soule of Halifax was appointed administrator of the estate of Betty Tomson of Halifax, widow.

On 6 June 1785 the estate was divided bet. eldest son Thaddeus Tomson and Susanna Tomson, Nathan Tomson, Zacheus Tomson, Elizabeth Tomson, and Stephen Tomson.

Children (TOMSON) b. Halifax:

   i   SUSANNA[6] bp. 17 May 1761
   ii   THADDEUS bp. 25 July 1763 (called Eliphalet in bp. rec.)
   iii NATHAN bp. 19 Jan. 1766
   iv ZACHEUS bp. 27 March 1768
   v   ELIZABETH bp. 27 Oct. 1770
   vi STEPHEN b. ca. 1774

References: MD 3:14(b. Eliz.); 27:183(bp. 1st 5 ch.). Plymouth Co. PR #20586; 23:159; 24:252; 29:305-7(John Tomson); #20619(gdns.); #20522; 27:19; 29:307-8(Betty Tomson). HALIFAX VR p. 60(int.). MIDDLEBORO VR 1:56(b. Eliz.). MF 10:73.

155 ELIZABETH TOMSON⁵ (John⁴, Mary Tinkham³, Mary²
Brown, Peter¹) b. Plympton 7 Aug. 1726; living 11 Jan. 1768 when
child bp.
    She m. Halifax 30 Sept. 1743 SAMUEL FULLER, b.
Middleboro 29 Jan. 1717/18; living 11 Jan. 1768 (ch. bp.); son of
Isaac and Mary (Pratt) Fuller, a descendant of Pilgrim Samuel
Fuller.
    On 2 Feb. 1752 Samuel & Elizabeth Fuller of Halifax sold to
Ebenezer Fuller Jr. of Halifax land in Middleboro "being part of
land formerly Dr. Isaac Fuller's." They also sold to Ebenezer
Fuller Jr. land in Halifax in 1757 and land lying partly in
Plympton and partly in Middleboro in 1765.
    No Plymouth Co. PR for Samuel Fuller.
    See MF 10 SAMUEL FULLER for an additional generation.

    Children (FULLER) b. Halifax:

        i   ZADOCK⁶ b. 19 Sept. 1744
        ii   ELIZABETH b. 28 Dec. 1745
        iii   JOHN b. 30 March 1748
        iv   HULDAH bp. 3 June 1750*
        v   MARTHA bp. 25 Aug. 1754
        vi   LYDIA bp. 10 Aug. 1760
        vii   SAMUEL bp. 20 Nov. 1763
        viii   LEMUEL bp. 11 Jan. 1768

References: MD 27:122(bp. all ch.). MF 10:34-5. HALIFAX VR
            pp. 33(m.), 50(b. 1st 3 ch.). VR PLYMPTON p.
105(b. Huldah). Plymouth Co. LR 50:246-9(Samuel Fuller).
MIDDLEBORO VR 1:38(b. Sam.).

*NOTE: VR PLYMPTON gives b. of Huldah as 1 June 1752.

156 LYDIA TOMSON⁵ (John⁴, Mary Tinkham³, Mary² Brown,
Peter¹) b. Plympton 13 Aug. 1730; d. Middleboro 29 Aug. 1771 in
42nd yr.
    She m. Halifax 20 Dec. 1764 ISAAC SOULE, b. Middleboro
2 Jan. 1731/2; d. there 3 Sept. 1808 in 77th yr.; son of Jacob and
Mary (Thomas) Soule, a descendant of Pilgrim George Soule. He
m. (2) Middleboro 12 Nov. 1772 Lydia (Randall) Wood by whom

he had Faith, Thomas, Isaac, Ezra, and Betty.
No Plymouth Co. PR for Isaac Soule nor Plymouth Co. LR
for Lucy or Lydia Soule.

Children (SOULE) b. Middleboro:

    i   MARY[6] b. 7 Dec. 1766; d. 26 Jan. 1772 ae 5 yrs.
    ii   LUCY b. 6 July 1768; d. 16 Oct. 1852 ae 84y 3m
        10d; unm. On 1 March 1853 Joshua Eddy was
        appointed administrator of the estate of Lucy
        Soule of Middleborough.
   iii   LYDIA b. 22 Dec. 1770; d. 29 Nov. 1817 in 47th yr.

References: MD 9:46(m. her par.); 14:244(b. Isaac); 30:9(b. Mary,
        Lucy); 32:8(b. Lydia), 9(b. Faith, Thomas), 138(b.
Ezra, Betty). MF 3:139. HALIFAX VR p. 32(m.). MIDDLEBORO
DEATHS pp. 168, 170. MIDDLEBORO VR 1:65(b. Isaac), 182(b.
Mary, Lucy), 203(b. Lydia, Faith, Thomas), 204(d. Lydia, Mary; b.
Isaac), 215(b. Ezra, Betty). Plymouth Co. PR 12:489(Lucy Soule).

157 JOHN TOMSON[5] (Shubael[4], Mary Tinkham[3], Mary[2] Brown,
Peter[1]) b. Middleboro 11 June 1717; d. there 22 June 1766 ae 49.
    He m. (1) Halifax 4 June 1741 LYDIA WOOD, b. Middleboro
1 July 1722; d. there 28 Jan. 1761 in 39th yr.; dau. of Elnathan and
Mary (Billington) Wood, a descendant of Pilgrim John Billington.
The will of Elnathan Wood of Middleborough dated 1 April 1752
names dau. Lydia Tomson.
    He m. (2) Plympton 10 Aug. 1762 SARAH (BRYANT)
SOULE, b. Plympton 31 Oct. 1731; d. Halifax 20 Aug. 1805; dau.
of George and Sarah (Ripley) Bryant. She m. (1) ca. 1751
Zachariah Soule by whom she had Jabez, Sarah, and Abigail. She
m. (3) Halifax 22 Jan. 1771 Reuben Tomson by whom she had
Joanna.
    The will of John Tomson of Middleboro, yeoman, dated 12
May 1766, presented 4 Aug. 1766, names wife Sarah who is to have
the goods she brought with her; son Shubael to have land of his
father Shubael; sons Isaac, John, and Ezra; daus. Susanna Thomas,
Lidia Tomson, Sarah Tomson, Fear Tomson, Priscilla Tomson, and
youngest dau. Mary Tomson.

Children (TOMSON) all but last by 1st wife, b. Middleboro:

i   SHUBAEL[6] b. 11 March 1741/2
ii   SUSANNA b. 1 Nov. 1743
iii ISAAC b. 1 Feb. 1745/6
iv   JOHN b. 6 May 1748
v   EZRA b. 4 July 1750
vi   LYDIA b. 21 June 1752
vii SARAH b. 6 Oct. 1754; d. there 10 Nov. 1777 ae
     23y 1m 4d; unm.
viii UZZA b. 10 Dec. 1756; d. 11 June 1758 ae 18m 1d
ix   FEAR b. 6 Nov. 1757
x   PRISCILLA b. 11 April 1760
xi   MARY b. 27 Dec. 1763

References: MD 4:68(b. Lydia); 14:219-20(deaths); 15:220(b. Shubael), 221(b. Susanna); 20:35(b. Isaac, John, Ezra), 36(b. Lydia, Sarah); 23:43(b. Uzza, Fear, Priscilla; d. Uzza), 71(b. Mary). HALIFAX VR p. 33(m.). VR PLYMPTON pp. 49(b. Sarah), 410(2nd m.). MIDDLEBORO DEATHS pp. 194-5. Plymouth Co. PR 13:34(Elnathan Wood); 19:382(John Tomson). MF 3:163; 21:33-4. Middleboro Mortality Recs. p. 74(d. dau. Sarah). MIDDLEBORO VR 1:22(b. Lydia), 75(b. Shubael, Susanna), 99(d. Lydia), 122(b. Isaac, John, Ezra), 127(b. Lydia, Sarah), 137 (b. Uzza, Fear, Priscilla; d. Uzza), 144(b. Sarah), 163(d. Lydia).

158 THOMAS TOMSON[5] (Shubael[4], Mary Tinkham[3], Mary[2] Brown, Peter[1]) b. Middleboro 28 July 1721; d. Bridgewater 8 Feb. 1756.

He m. Bridgewater 31 Oct. 1745 JANE WASHBURN, b. Bridgewater 28 March 1722; d. there 22 March 1793 in 71st yr.; dau. of John and Margaret (Packard) Washburn, a descendant of Pilgrim Francis Cooke. The will of John Washburn of Bridgewater dated 3 April 1746 names dau. Jane (no surname).

On 5 April 1756 Josiah Edson gave his bond as administrator of estate of Thomas Tomson late of Bridgewater, cordwainer, dec. No Plymouth Co. PR for Jane Tomson.

Children (TOMSON) b. Bridgewater:

   i   MARY[6] b. 20 July 1746
   ii   ABISHA b. 6 Aug. 1747
   iii JANE b. 14 Feb. 1748/9
   iv PEGGY b. 1750; d. 15 Oct. 1750 ae 15d
   v   MARGARET b. 3 Sept. 1751
   vi BETHIA b. 15 Nov. 1755

References: VR BRIDGEWATER 1:314(b. ch.), 330(b. Jane); 2:368(m.), 566(deaths). Plymouth Co. PR 10:318 (John Washburn); #20651(Thomas Tomson).

NOTE: VR BRIDGEWATER records the death of a child of Thomas Tomson on 25 Feb. 1755.

159 PETER TOMSON[5] (Thomas[4], Mary Tinkham[3], Mary[2] Brown, Peter[1]) b. Middleboro 8 Oct. 1733; d. Halifax 21 June 1800 in 67th yr.

He prob. m. (1) int. Halifax 8 Nov. 1761 REBECCA STURTEVANT of Halifax, b. Middleboro 17 Aug. 1737; d. bef. 14 June 1753 (2nd m.).

He m. (2) Halifax 14 June 1763 REBECCA THOMAS, b. Middleboro 17 Aug. 1737; d. Halifax 16 Oct. 1792 in 56th yr.; dau. of Samuel and Lydia (Richmond) Thomas, a descendant of Pilgrim Thomas Rogers.

On 20 May 1801 Asaph Thomson of Halifax sold for 600 dollars "paid me by my brethen namely Levi Thomson, Ezekiel Thomson and Eliab Thomson all of said Halifax...the property that my honoured father Peter Thomson late of Halifax deceased" gave him.

No Plymouth Co. PR for Peter or Rebecca Tomson or Samuel or Lydia Thomas.

Children (TOMSON) b. Halifax:

   i   LEVI[6] b. 6 Jan. 1764
   ii   EZEKIAL b. 4 May 1766
   iii ELIAB b. 8 Dec. 1768
   iv ASEPH b. 2 Sept. 1771

References: MD 8:250(b. Rebecca); 14:8(d. Peter), 9(d. Rebecca).
HALIFAX VR pp. 6(d. 2nd wife Rebecca), 31(2nd
m.), 37 (b. ch.), 62(int. 1st m.). MF 3:180; 19:206. THOMAS GEN
p. 101. Plymouth Co. LR 90:276(Asaph Tomson). MIDDLEBORO
VR 1:46(b. Rebecca).

160 FRANCIS TOMSON[5] (Thomas[4], Mary Tinkham[3], Mary[2]
Brown, Peter[1]) b. Halifax 15 March 1734/5; d. Middleboro 17 Dec.
1798 ae 63y 9m 2d.

He m. (1) Halifax 19 May 1761 REBECCA SNOW, b.
Bridgewater 16 Oct. 1734; d. Middleboro 27 Aug. 1766 in 32nd yr.;
dau. of Jonathan and Sarah (Soule) Snow, a descendant of
Pilgrims Peter Brown and George Soule (see #240).

He m. (2) Middleboro 17 Dec. 1769 MARY BUMPAS, b. ca.
1745; d. Middleboro 17 Dec. 1829 in 85th yr.; prob. the one b.
Middleboro 1 Feb. 1745 to Joseph and Mehitable (Tupper) Bumpas.

Francis Tomson was 3-1-3 in the 1790 census of Middleboro.

The will of Francis Thomson of Middleboro dated 20 Nov.
1798, presented 31 Dec. 1798, names wife Mary; son Elias; dau.
Zilpah Cushman, wife of Noah; sons Thomas and Ruel; dau.
Cynthia Cox, wife of John; and dau. Molley Tomson unm.

There is no Plymouth Co. PR for widow Mary Tomson.

Children (TOMSON) 1st 3 by first wife, b. Middleboro*:

    i   MARTHA[6] b. 5 Nov. 1761; d. 26 Feb. 1771 ae 9y
          3m 21d
    ii   ZILPAH b. 3 March 1763
    iii   ELIAS b. 18 June 1766
    iv   THOMAS b. 8 Oct. 1770
    v   CYNTHIA b. 1773
    vi   RUELL b. 1777 (yr. of b. from d. records)
    vii   MARY (or MOLLY) b. 1781
    viii FRANCIS b. 1785; d. 9 April 1787 ae 2y 5m 25d

References: MD 14:218(d. Francis, son Francis), 219(d. Mary,
Martha), 220(d. Rebecca); 15:219(m. Mary's par.);
22:147(b. Mary); 26:24(b. Martha, Zilpah, Elias), 25 (d. Rebecca,
Martha); 29:189(b. Thomas). HALIFAX VR pp. 31 (1st m.), 61(1st
m. int.). VR BRIDGEWATER 1:303(b. Rebecca). MIDDLEBORO

DEATHS pp. 195(d. Francis, Rebecca, Mary, Martha), 196(d. Reuel). Plymouth Co. PR 36:473(Francis Thomson). MF 3:181. Middleboro Mortality Recs. p. 73. MIDDLEBORO VR 1:161 (b. Martha), 162(b. Zilpah, Elias), 163(d. Martha), 179(b. Thomas), 268(d. Francis); 2:68(int. 2nd m.), 161(2nd m.).

*Last 4 ch. from THOMSON GEN & MF 3:181. MF 3 also lists a Rebecca d.y. (Ruell called s. of Francis and Mary in death record.)

161 NATHAN TOMSON[5] (Thomas[4], Mary Tinkham[3], Mary[2] Brown, Peter[1]) b. Halifax 10 Dec. 1736; d. Middleboro 7 May 1808 in 72nd yr.

He m. Halifax 27 Oct. 1761 MARY HARLOW, b. Plymouth 5 May 1739; d. Norton 30 Sept. 1806 in 66th yr.; dau. of Robert and Susanna (Cole) Harlow; a descendant of Pilgrims Isaac Allerton and Richard Warren.

The will of Esther Soule of Middleborough, spinster, dated 16 Oct. 1792, names nephew Nathan Tomson.

On 7 Sept. 1801 Nathan Tomson and wife Mary sold land in Halifax which he had received from his father Thomas Tomson to Isaiah Ripley Jr.

No Plymouth Co. PR for Nathan or Mary Tomson nor Plymouth Co. LR to daus.

Children (TOMSON) b. Halifax:

    i   SARAH[6] b. 16 Aug. 1762
   ii   SUSANNAH b. 16 May 1764

References: MD 13:166(b. Mary); 19:140(Esther Soule will). HALIFAX VR pp. 31(m.), 39(b. ch.), 61(int.). MIDDLEBORO DEATHS p. 195. MF 3:181. VR NORTON p. 396(d. Mary). Plymouth Co. LR 91:114-5(Nathan Tomson). PLYMOUTH VR p. 69(b. Mary). HARLOW GEN pp. 182-3.

162 JAMES TOMSON[5] (Thomas[4], Mary Tinkham[3], Mary[2] Brown, Peter[1]) b. Halifax 11 Nov. 1739; living 1800 census.

He m. Bridgewater 14 Nov. 1765 ABIGAIL ALLEN, b. Bridgewater 12 Oct. 1744; living 4 Dec. 1792; (d. Salem NY according to MF 3:181); dau. of Nathan and Rebecca (Reed) Allen, a descendant of Pilgrim Francis Cooke.

On 22 April 1771 James Thomson, yeoman of Bridgewater, Plymouth Co., bought 51 acres of land in Brookfield from Samuel Gilbert.

On 6 May 1776 James Tomson Jr., yeoman of Brookfield, Worcester Co. bought land in Brookfield from Nathan Allen Jr.

James Thompson was 1-2-4 in the 1790 census of Brookfield.

On 4 Dec. 1792 James Tomson and wife Abigail of Brookfield sold two parcels of land in Brookfield, 48 acres and 4 acres to Abner Fisk.

On 23 Feb. 1793 David Rice of Salem NY sold 88 acres in Salem to James Thomson of Brookfield MA.

The 1800 census of Salem NY has James Thompson over 45; 2 males under 10; 1 male 10-16; 1 female under 10; 3 aged 10-16; 1 aged 16-24 and 1 aged 26-45.

No Washington Co. PR for James Tomson or further LR.

Children (TOMSON) from Thomson Gen. & MF 3:181:*

i	PHEBE[6] b. 11 Oct. 1766
ii	ABIGAIL b. 20 Nov. 1767
iii	CYRUS b. 21 Dec. 1774
iv	AZOR b. 1775-1780 (based on census records)
v	BELA b. 16 March 1779
vi	NATHAN b. 13 Oct. 1784
vii	REBECCA
viii	BELINDA b. 1790

References: VR BRIDGEWATER 1:26(b. Abigail); 2:368(m.). MF 3:181; 12:523-4. THOMSON (JOHN) DESC pp. 39-40. WATERMAN GEN 1:685. Worcester Co. LR 64:475; 116:55; 117:60(James Tomson).

*No births in Bridgewater or Brookfield VR or IGI.

NOTE: VR BROOKFIELD has the following marriages which are probably the children:
Nabby Thomson & Stephen Estee 10 Feb. 1790
Phebe Thomson & Dennison Ruggles of Salem NY 11 Jan. 1792
Cyrus Thomson of Salem NY & Polly Waterman 12 Jan. 1801

Azor Thompson of Salem NY & Hannah Hall 9 Feb. 1802

163   JACOB TOMSON[5] (Jacob[4], Mary Tinkham[3], Mary[2] Brown, Peter[1]) b. Halifax 9 July 1736; d. there 12 Nov. 1815 in 80th yr.

He m. Middleboro 15 April 1756 WAITSTILL MILLER, b. Middleboro 24 Feb. 1739/40; d. Halifax 18 July 1807 in 68th yr.; dau. of John and Waitstill (Clap) Miller. The will of John Miller the second of Middleboro, husbandman, dated 16 May 1759 names dau. Waitstill, wife of Jacob Tomson.

On 3 March 1777 Jacob Tomson of Halifax sold to Ephraim Tomson of Halifax all his rights to land and buildings given him by his aunts Martha Tomson and Sarah Tomson in their wills.

No Plymouth Co. PR nor LR for Jacob Tomson.

Children (TOMSON) b. Halifax:

i	HULDAH[6]	b. 17 May 1757
ii	EZRA	b. 14 April 1760
iii	JENNETT	b. 23 June 1763; d. 16 July 1830 in 68th yr.; unm. No PR.
iv	MARTHA	b. 20 Dec. 1764
v	JACOB	b. 25 Oct. 1769
vi	MARGARET MILLER	b. 22 April 1771

References: MD 13:249(m. her par.); 14:7(d. Jacob, Jennett), 9(d. Waitstill); 24:57(m.). MQ 43:114. HALIFAX VR p. 54(b. ch.). MIDDLEBORO VR 1:77(b. Waitstill), 150(m.). Plymouth Co. PR 15:286-7(John Miller). Plymouth Co. LR 62:224(Jacob Tomson).

164   EBENEZER TOMSON[5] (Jacob[4], Mary Tinkham[3], Mary[2] Brown, Peter[1]) b. Halifax 14 Oct. 1737; d. there 10 May 1832 in 95th yr.

He m. Wareham 1 May 1760 ELIZABETH BESSE, b. Wareham 11 March 1741; d. Halifax 31 Aug. 1820 in 80th yr.; dau. of David and Dinah (Muxom) Besse.

No Plymouth Co. PR for Ebenezer or Elizabeth Tomson nor Plymouth Co. LR to his children.

Children (TOMSON) b. Halifax:

    i   NATHANIEL[6] b. 11 May 1761
    ii   REBECCA b. 20 June 1764
   iii ASENATH b. 3 Sept. 1767; d. 10 Sept. 1842; unm.
   iv ELIZABETH b. 28 June 1771
    v CHARITY b. 24 June 1775

References: MD 14:6(d. Ebenezer, Eliz.); 27:183. WAREHAM CH
          RECS p. 74(bp. Eliz.). HALIFAX VR pp. 48(b. 1st
2 ch.), 49(b. last 3 ch.). MF 12:524-5. WAREHAM VR p. 5(b.
Elizabeth).

165 EPHRAIM TOMSON[5] (Jacob[4], Mary Tinkham[3], Mary[2]
Brown, Peter[1]) b. Halifax 1 Aug. 1748; d. Marlow NH 28 July
1820.

    He m. (1) int. Bridgewater 30 Dec. 1769 JOANNA THAYER,
b. ca. 1747; d. Halifax 7 Feb. 1789 in 43rd yr.; dau. of Jonathan
and Rachel (Holbrook) Thayer.

    He m. (2) Bridgewater 12 Jan. 1791 MOLLY WASHBURN, d.
Marlow NH 18 July 1822; dau. of Josiah and Phebe (Hayward)
Washburn.

    On 8 Feb. 1796 Josiah Washburn of Bridgewater and
Ephraim Thompson of Halifax bought 100 acres in Marlow NH.

    On 10 Feb. 1796, acknowledged 15 Feb. 1796, Ephraim
Tomson of Halifax, yeoman, sold land to Azariah Hayward;
signed by Ephraim Tomson and Mary Tomson. On 15 April 1797
Ephraim Thompson of Marlow and Josiah Washburn bought 200
more acres in Marlow from Caleb Hunt.

    In the 1800 census of Marlow NH Ephraim Thompson had 1
male 10-16; 1 male 16-25; 1 male over 45; 2 females 0-10; 1 female
10-16; and 1 female 26-45.

    On 31 July 1806 Ephraim Thompson, with wife Mary
signing, sold half the 100 acre plot "he now lives on."

    In the 1810 census of Marlow NH Ephraim Thomson had 1
male 0-10; 1 male 26-45; 1 male over 45; 3 females 0-10; 2 females
26-45.

    In the 1814 tax list for Marlow NH Ephraim Thomson is
listed as is his sons Francis and Silas and his son-in-law John
Winch.

    No Cheshire Co. NH PR for Ephraim Tomson.

Children (TOMSON) first 6 by Joanna b. Halifax; rest by Mary with first 2 b. Halifax:

i EPHRAIM[6] b. 2 Nov. 1771
ii HANNAH b. 23 Jan. 1773
iii SILAS b. 3 April 1778
iv RHODA b. 27 Oct. 1780
v DAVID b. 11 April 1783
vi FRANCIS b. 2 Aug. 1785
vii BETHIAH b. 19 July 1793
viii ROXANNA (or ROSANNA)
ix MARY b. NH ca. 1796 (the 1850 census of Canadice, Ontario Co. NY gives her age as 54, born NH.)
x PHEBE*
xi SALLY*

References: MD 14:7(d. Joanna). HALIFAX VR p. 29(b. ch.). VR BRIDGEWATER 2:368(1st m. int.), 372(2nd m.). Plymouth Co. LR 80:1(Ephraim Tomson). Marlow NH TR 2:334(tax list). THE HISTORY OF HANCOCK, NEW HAMPSHIRE, William W. Hayward, Lowell MA, 1889, p. 927(d. Ephraim, Molly). Cheshire Co. NH LR 26:311(Azariah Hayward); 28:95(Caleb Hunt); 50:114 (Ephraim Tomson). A GENEALOGY OF JOHN THOMSON, Ignatius Thomson, Taunton, 1841 p. 42. WARE GENEALOGY, Emma Forbes Ware, Boston, 1901, p. 208. MF 12:525-6.

*Daus. Phebe and Sally are listed in the THOMSON GEN and are consistent with the young daus. in the 1810 census record.

166 DANIEL TOMSON[5] (Jacob[4], Mary Tinkham[3], Mary[2] Brown, Peter[1]) b. Halifax 24 Oct. 1750; living Bridgewater 7 May 1794 (petition).
He m. (1) int. Halifax 6 April 1772 FEAR LYON, b. Middleboro 25 July 1749; living 3 April 1789; poss. d. Bridgewater 29 Dec. 1792 "_____ wife of Daniel Thompson"; dau. of Jedidiah and Mary (Cushman) Lyon, a descendant of Pilgrim Isaac Allerton. The will of Jedediah Lyon of Middleborough, yeoman, dated 3 April 1789 names wife Mary and dau. Fear Tomson.

He m. (2) Bridgewater 8 April 1794 SARAH SNOW, b. Bridgewater 23 March 1758; living 15 Nov. 1826; dau. of John and Hannah (Harlow) (Willis) Snow, a descendant of Pilgrims Isaac Allerton, Peter Brown and Richard Warren. (See #214).

On 8 May 1777 Daniel Tomson of Halifax sold to Jacob Tomson of Halifax his homestead in Halifax "on which I dwell" with wife Fear releasing her dower, acknowledging the deed 20 June 1777.

Daniel Tomson was 1-1-3 in the 1790 census of Bridgewater.

On 7 May 1794 Daniel Tomson of Bridgewater on behalf of wife Sarah, dau. of John Snow of Bridgewater, dec. petitioned to be appointed administrator of the estate of John Snow.

No Plymouth Co. PR for Daniel Tomson.

Children (TOMSON) all by Fear b. Halifax:

i	SAMUEL[6] b. 9 Dec. 1773
ii	MOLLY b. 20 Aug. 1778
iii	PHEBE b. 17 Jan. 1781
iv	FEAR b. 27 Jan. 1785*
v	DANIEL b. 27 April 1787**

References: VR BRIDGEWATER 1:303(b. Sarah); 2:367(2nd m.). MD 15:220(m. her par.); 16:244(b. Fear). HALIFAX VR pp. 55(b. ch.), 65(int.). Plymouth Co. LR 59:33; 76:177(Daniel Tomson). MIDDLEBORO VR 1:96(b. Fear). Plymouth Co. PR 42:53-4 (Jedediah Lyon); #18688(John Snow). A GENEALOGY OF JOHN TOMSON, Ignatius Thomson, Taunton, 1841, p. 32(b. of all ch.). MF 17:131.

*Her death certificate says she d. 10 July 1874, age 89 yr. 5 mo. 3 d.; dau. of Daniel and Fear Thompson (Mass. Deaths 266:314).

**The 1850 census of Buckfield, Oxford Co. ME gives his age as 63, which agrees with the birthdate in THOMPSON DESC.

167 JOHN TINKHAM[5] (John[4-3], Mary[2] Brown, Peter[1]) b. Dartmouth 10 May 1743; d. New Bedford 2 June 1810.

He m. Berkley 16 Jan. 1772 MARY MIRICK, living 28 Sept. 1824.

John Tinkum was 2-3-2 in the 1790 census of New Bedford.

On 7 April 1811 dower was set off to widow Mary Tinkham from the real estate of John Tinkcom late of New Bedford dec.; administrator was Bartholomew Akin.

No children are mentioned in the probate but they are found in deeds. On 28 Sept. 1824 Ebenezer Tinkham of Fairhaven bought land in Fairhaven from Mary Tinkham, Eliza Tinkham and Pamela Tinkham, all of Fairhaven singlewomen, with widow Mary Tinkham releasing her dower and on 11 March 1831 Ebenezer bought various properties in Fairhaven from William Haskins and wife Hannah, who was dau. of the late John Tinkham of Taunton, being her share of her father's property. Both deeds were recorded in 1852.

Children (TINKHAM) b. prob. in that part of Dartmouth which later became Fairhaven:

i	EBENEZER[6]	b. 1783
ii	HANNAH	
iii	MARY	
iv	ELIZA	
v	PAMELA	

References: VR NEW BEDFORD p. 171(d. John). VR DARTMOUTH 2:500(m.). Bristol Co. PR 46:365(John Tinkham). Bristol Co. LR New Bedford Registry 21:554; 23:5(Ebenezer Tinkham grantee). MD 51:42(m.).

168   AMY (or ALMY) TINKHAM[5] (John[4-3], Mary[2] Brown, Peter[1]) b. Dartmouth 15 Sept. 1745; d. Fairhaven 3 Jan. 1833 ae 87.

She m. int. Dartmouth 1 Nov. 1774 EPHRAIM TRIPP, b. bef. 1750 (over 80 in 1830 census of Fairhaven); d. bet. 25 May 1833 (date of will) and 18 Dec. 1837 (date will proved); son of Benjamin and Esther (_____) Tripp.

On 10 Oct. 1800 Ephraim Tripp of New Bedford, cooper, sold land to Marmaduke Tinkham of New Bedford, mariner, with wife Ame signing. On 1 Oct. 1823 Ephraim Tripp of Fairhaven, yeoman, and wife Amey signed and acknowledged a deed to Stephen Hathaway of Fairhaven, land in Fairhaven which descended to Amey from her father (unnamed) and her sister

Abigail Tinkham.

The will of Ephraim Tripp dated 25 May 1833, proved 18 Dec. 1837, does not mention any children, but mentions Phebe Tripp, wife of Thomas; nephew Ebenezer Tripp.

No known children.

References: VR DARTMOUTH 2:507(int.). New Bedford Mercury Obits p. 343(d. Amy). Bristol Co. PR 78:316 (Ephraim Tripp). Bristol Co. LR 105:107; 114:182(Ephraim Tripp). TG 4:94.

169 MARY TINKHAM[5] (John[4-3], Mary[2] Brown, Peter[1]) b. Dartmouth 4 Sept. 1747; living Fairhaven 22 March 1817.

She m. Dartmouth 18 June 1767 THOMAS TRIPP, b. ca. 1743; d. New Bedford bef. 17 Sept. 1812 (inv. ordered); son of Benjamin and Esther (_____) Tripp.

Thomas Tripp was 4-3-4 in the 1790 census of New Bedford suggesting there may be more children, especially daus.

On 17 Jan. 1792 Thomas Tripp, cooper, deeded his share of John Tinkham's land to Benjamin Tripp and John Tripp, seaman, all of New Bedford.

In deeds dated 24 April 1797 and 25 April 1797 Thomas Tripp and Ephraim Tripp (see #168) and other heirs of their grandfather Benjamin Tripp sold family land in Westport.

Inventory of the estate of Thomas Tripp late of New Bedford dec., was taken at Fairhaven 26 Sept. 1812 and sworn by Mary Tripp administratrix. An account dated 6 Oct. 1812 mentions housekeeping expenses for the administratrix but does not mention children.

On 7 Nov. 1815 Gilbert Tripp of Fairhaven, mariner, with wife Sally, sold land in Fairhaven to John Tripp of Fairhaven, seaman. On 8 Nov. 1815 Gilbert Tripp of Fairhaven and wife Sally sold a tract in Fairhaven to James and Francis Tripp of Fairhaven.

On 22 March 1817 Mary Tripp of Fairhaven, widow, sold to Thomas Tripp of Fairhaven, yeoman, land in Fairhaven from the division of her father John Tinkham and her part of the dower of her late mother Mary Tinkham, all the real estate she now owns and all her furniture and other personal estate, acknowledging the deed the same day.

Thomas Tripp had one male 26-45; 2 females under 10; one female 26-45 and one female over 45 in the 1820 census of Fairhaven. This must be son Thomas with his mother Mary being the woman over 45 who had deeded everything to Thomas in 1817.

On 9 April 1833 Ephraim Tripp, John Tripp, Gilbert Tripp, James Tripp, Thomas Tripp and Mary Read of Fairhaven; Henry Gidley, Thomas Gidley, Samuel Gidley and Benjamin Gidley of Dartmouth; Ezekiel Tripp and wife Roby Tripp of Westport, heirs of Lydia Tripp of Westport, dec. sold their interests in 20 acres in Westport owned by Lydia Tripp to Humphrey Tripp of Westport. [Lydia Tripp was the sister of Thomas Tripp.]

Children (TRIPP) b. prob. Dartmouth:

    i   JOHN[6] b. ca. 1769
   ii   GILBERT b. ca. 1772; d. Fairhaven 22 Dec. 1852 ae 80y 7m
  iii   THOMAS b. ca. 1775 (based on age at d.)
  iv   JAMES b. ca. 1778
   v   FRANCIS b. ca. 1782

References: VR DARTMOUTH 2:513(m.). Bristol Co. PR 47:495, 507(Thomas Tripp). Bristol Co. LR 75:520(Thomas Tripp); 76:476; 77:474(heirs); 99:135, 137(Gilbert Tripp); 102:185(Mary Tripp). Fairhaven VR 2:30:75(d. Gilbert). Bristol Co. LR, New Bedford Registry 12:233(Ephraim Tripp etc.). Massachusetts Deaths 2:65(d. son Thomas).

NOTE: The Mary Read in the 9 April 1833 deed may be a dau.

170 BARBARA TINKHAM[5] (John[4-3], Mary[2] Brown, Peter[1]) b. Dartmouth 14 July 1749; d. bef. 6 May 1794.

She m. int. Berkley 20 Aug. 1774 SAMUEL MIRICK, d. bef. 22 April 1786 (deed).

On 6 May 1788 appraisers were appointed for the real estate of Samuel Mirick late of Berkley dec. intestate and dower was set off to widow Barbara Mirick.

Barbara Mirick was 0-0-2 in the 1790 census of Berkley.

On 14 March 1792 Barbara Mirick of Berkley, widow, sold to John Tinkcom of New Bedford, yeoman, 2 lots in New Bedford, part of the real estate whereof John Tinkcom late dec. died seized of, acknowledging her signature 6 Nov. 1792.

John Tinkham presented his account on 3 Oct. 1797 as administrator of the estate of Barbara Mirick late of Berkley dec.

Child (MIRICK) b. prob. Berkley:

    i   HANNAH[6]

References: VR DARTMOUTH 2:334(int.). Bristol Co. PR 30:226, 237(Sam. Mirick); 35:163-164(Barbara Mirick). Bristol Co. LR 78:438(Barbara Mirick). Berkley VR typescript, marriages, p. 12(int.).

171 DEBORAH TINKHAM[5] (John[4-3], Mary[2] Brown, Peter[1]) b. Dartmouth 22 May 1751; d. bef. 6 May 1794.

She was prob. the one who filed intentions to marry Dartmouth 11 July 1772 with William Allen of Dartmouth but he apparently died bef. the marriage could take place.

She m. int. Dartmouth 13 Aug. 1774 WILLIAM WAGGENNOR, d. bef. 22 April 1786 (deed).

In an indenture of 22 April 1786 Deborah Waggoner was called widow.

The inventory of the estate of William Waggenor was taken 1 May 1787 and on the same day Deborah Waggenor, administratrix to said William, mariner, filed her account.

On 6 May 1794 Ephraim Tripp of New Bedford, yeoman, was appointed guardian to Samuel and William Waggoner, both over 14 "being both at sea," children of William Waggoner late of New Bedford dec., and on 4 Nov. 1794 John Tinkham of New Bedford, yeoman, was appointed guardian to William Waggoner a minor over 14, son of William Waggoner late of New Bedford and his wife Deborah.

On 25 Feb. 1804 Samuel Waggoner of New Bedford, mariner, sold to John Tripp of New Bedford land in New Bedford, part of the estate of his grandfather John Tinkham dec., with wife Jain signing.

Children (WAGGONNER) b. prob. New Bedford:

   i   SAMUEL[6] b. New Bedford 20 Aug. 1777
   ii   WILLIAM

References: VR DARTMOUTH 2:33(int. to Wm. Allen), 523(int.).
              VR NEW BEDFORD 1:499(b. Sam.). Bristol Co. PR
29:272-3(William Waggenor); 130:316(gdn.). Bristol Co. LR
74:264(indenture); 83:314(Samuel Wagoner).

172 HANNAH TINKHAM[5] (John[4-3], Mary[2] Brown, Peter[1]) b.
Dartmouth 3 Dec. 1754; d. Berkley 19 Sept. 1801 in 46th yr.
    She m. Berkley 18 Jan. 1781 JOSEPH PAUL, b. Berkley 23
"Jan. or June" 1757; d. there 7 May 1816 ae 60; son of John and
Love (Caswell) Paul. He m. (2) Berkley 15 Dec. 1803 Silence
French.
    On 23 Dec. 1789 Hannah Paul of Berkley, spinster, and
Joseph Paul of Berkley, yeoman, sold to Benjamin Tripp of New
Bedford, cooper, two lots in New Bedford which were set off to
them in a division of the estate of John Tinkham late of
Dartmouth dec., acknowledging their signatures 10 March 1790.
    The will of Joseph Paul of Berkley dated 26 Jan. 1816,
presented 4 June 1816, names wife Silence; son Ephraim; daus.
Amey Haskins and Phebe Tripp who were to have the things that
belonged to their mother.
    On 23 Dec. 1816 Gideon Haskins and wife Amey of Middle-
boro and Thomas Tripp and wife Phebe of Fairhaven sold to
Ephraim Paul of Berkley 2/3 of a lot in Berkley and Taunton
which was owned by Joseph Paul and his wife Hannah dec.

Children (PAUL) b. Berkley:

   i   ANNE (or AMEY)[6] b. 17 Aug. 1782
   ii   PHEBE b. 19 March 1784
   iii EPHRAIM b. 8 May 1789

References: VR DARTMOUTH 2:345(m.). Berkley VR Index(b.
             ch.; his 2nd m.). Bristol Co. PR 52:167(Jos. Paul).
Bristol Co. LR 69:242(Hannah Paul); 102:472(Gideon Haskins).
BERKLEY MASS CEMETERY INSCRIPTIONS, Gail E. Terry,

Bowie MD 1997, p. 73(d. Joseph, Hannah).

173 MARMADUKE TINKHAM[5] (John[4-3], Mary[2] Brown, Peter[1])
b. Dartmouth; d. Fairhaven bef. 11 April 1816.
    He m. Fairhaven 20 April 1794 MARY REED, b. ca. 1767; d.
Fairhaven 2 April 1850 ae 83; dau. of Charles and Zilpha (Myrick)
Read.
    On 10 Oct. 1800, ack. same day, Marmaduke Tinkham of
New Bedford, mariner, sold to Ephraim Tripp of New Bedford,
cooper land in New Bedford, wife Polly gave up dower.
    On 3 May 1803 (ack 5 Dec.) Marmaduke Tinkham of New
Bedford, mariner, sold land in New Bedford to Gilbert Tripp.
    On 11 April 1816 a committee was appointed to inventory
the estate of Marmaduke Tinkham late of Fairhaven, yeoman,
dec. On 7 May 1816 Mary Tinkham of New Bedford widow was
appointed admin. to Marmaduke Tinkham late of Fairhaven and
made oath to the inventory.
    No Marmaduke Tinkham deeds to children.

    Children (TINKHAM) b. Fairhaven:

        i   MARMADUKE (?)[6]
        ii   PAMELIA b. ca. 1806; (ae 45 when she m. Dec.
               1851)

References: VR DARTMOUTH 2:500(m.).   Fairhaven VR
             2:19:15(d. Mary); 3:12:36(m. Pamelia). Bristol Co.
PR 51:244; 52:42 (Marmaduke Tinkham).   Bristol Co. LR 81:169;
84:427(Marmaduke Tinkham).

174 HULDAH TINKHAM[5] (John[4-3], Mary[2] Brown, Peter[1]) b.
Dartmouth ca. 1758; d. Berkley 4 Feb. 1843 in 86th yr. (g.s.)
    She m. New Bedford 16 Oct. 1794 GILBERT TOWNSEND, b.
Berkley 9 June 1760; d. there 23 Sept. 1817 in 58th yr. (g.s.); son of
Nathaniel and Abigail (Briggs) Townsend.
    John Haskins, Ephraim Paull and Edmund Anthony were
appointed 29 Oct. 1817 to inventory the estate of Gilbert
Townsend late of Berkley, yeoman, dec. Administratrix Huldah
Townsend made oath to inv. 7 Nov. 1817.
    Hulday Townsend of Berkley sold to Thomas Tripp of

Fairhaven land in Fairhaven, part of John Tinkham's homestead farm 20 Feb. 1817, ack. 6 April 1819.

Huldah Townsend of Berkley sold to Nathaniel Townsend of Berkley, yeoman, land in Fairhaven, her share in estate of her father John Tinkham all she owned in Fairhaven, signed and ack. 4 June 1838.

Child (TOWNSEND) b. prob. Berkley:

i   NATHANIEL[6] b. 25 May 1796 (from g.s.)

References: VR DARTMOUTH 2:503(m.). VR NEW BEDFORD 2:557(m.). Bristol Co. PR 54:192, 195(Gilbert Townsend). Bristol Co. LR 106:332(Huldah Townsend). Berkley VR Index p. 277(b. Gilbert). Bristol Co. So. Registry 10:220(Huldah Townsend). Townsend Family Cem., Berkley(g.s. of Gilbert, Huldah, Nathaniel).

175 SUSANNA TINKHAM[5] (John[4-3], Mary[2] Brown, Peter[1]) b. Dartmouth; living 30 March 1818 (ack. deed).

She m. New Bedford 25 Nov. 1802 JOHN HASKINS of Taunton; living 30 March 1818 (ack. deed).

In 1803 John Haskins of Taunton, yeoman, and wife Susanna, sold to Marmaduke Tinkham of New Bedford, mariner, part of the real estate which John Tinkham late of New Bedford died seized of, as divided among the heirs on 22 April 1786. John and Susanna acknowledged their signatures at Freetown 30 March 1818.

No known children.

References: VR NEW BEDFORD 2:249(m.). Bristol Co. LR 90:233, 234(Susanna Haskins); 105:247(John & Susanna Haskins).

176 WILLIAM TABER[5] (Mary Tinkham[4], John[3], Mary[2] Brown, Peter[1]) b. Dartmouth 24 Feb. 1741; d. Hoosick, Rensselaer Co. NY 1 July 1810.

He m. Dartmouth 7 Dec. 1769 MARTHA HART, b. Dartmouth 5 May 1746; d. Hoosick NY 11 March 1810; dau. of Luke and Mary (Huddlestone) Hart, a descendant of Pilgrim

Francis Cooke. The will of Luke Hart of Dartmouth dated 23 May 1777 names wife Mary and dau. Martha Taber, wife of William.

On 8 May 1806 William Taber of New Bedford, yeoman, sold to Luke and Joseph Taber both of New Bedford, yeomen, his homestead farm in New Bedford, with Martha also signing.

Children (TABER) b. prob. Dartmouth:

i	RUTH[6] (twin) b. 19 July 1770
ii	PHEBE (twin) b. 19 July 1770
iii	LUKE (twin) b. 12 Jan. 1773
iv	JOSEPH (twin) b. 12 Jan. 1773
v	SYLVANUS b. 24 Feb. 1775
vi	MARY b. 10 May 1777
vii	JONATHAN b. 17 Nov. 1779
viii	ESTHER b. 5 July 1782
ix	WILLIAM b. 19 Sept. 1788

References: VR DARTMOUTH 1:108(b. Martha);   2:491(m.). Bristol Co. PR 26:216(Luke Hart). Bristol Co. LR 86:399 (William Taber). TABER DESC pp. 12, 25(b. ch.).

NOTE: List of children is from TABER DESC. Not found in VR.

177 ELIZABETH TABER[5] (Mary Tinkham[4], John[3], Mary[2] Brown, Peter[1]) b. Dartmouth 5 Feb. 1743; d. after 11 Oct. 1826.

She m. Dartmouth 25 April 1784 LUKE HART, b. Dartmouth 6 April 1744; d. Hoosick, Renssellaer Co. NY bet. 20 Aug. 1810 and 22 Oct. 1818; son of Luke and Mary (Huddlestone) Hart, a descendant of Pilgrim Francis Cooke.

On 29 May 1792 Luke Hart of Dartmouth and wife Elizabeth sold land in Dartmouth. On 5 Jan. 1799 Luke Hart and Seth Hart, both of Cambridge, Washington Co. NY, sold a lot in Dartmouth that Luke Hart of Dartmouth dec. gave to Luke in his will. The deed was signed by Luke, Seth, and Elizabeth Hart.

On 20 Aug. 1810 Luke Hart of Hoosac, Ransellier Co. NY sold land in Dartmouth and his share of swamp that he and his two brothers Jonathan and Seth bought in 1782, with Elizabeth signing, and he acknowledged it the same day at Cambridge "Luke

Hart a deaf and dumb man." On 30 Sept. 1826 Elizabeth Hart of Hoosac, widow, sold, to Luke Taber of Fairhaven a swamp in New Bedford lying in common with Vollentine Bradford, Sybil Brightman, Hannah Brightman & Joseph Taber, which fell to her from her mother late dec., and her share that fell to her from her sister Jemima Shearman late dec.; acknowledged 11 Oct. 1826 in NY.

On 22 Oct. 1818 Seth Hart of White Creek, Washington Co. NY was granted administration on the estate of Luke Hart of the town of Hoosick, Rensselaer Co. NY. Petition mentions he died without children and that he left a widow, his wife Elizabeth Hart, who had renounced her right to administer.

References: VR DARTMOUTH 1:108(b. Luke); 2:223(m.). TABER
            DESC p. 12. Bristol Co. LR 71:179; 78:233; 91:554;
121:376(Luke & Elizabeth Hart).   Rensselaer Co. NY PR(Luke Hart).   MF 12:529.

178   RUBY TABER[5] (Mary Tinkham[4], John[3], Mary[2] Brown, Peter[1]) b. Dartmouth 22 March 1745/6; d. Rochester 16 Dec. 1821 ae 75y 8m.

She m. Dartmouth 23 April 1769 DAVENPORT BRIGHTMAN, b. ca. 1746; d. Fairhaven 3 May 1821 ae 75; prob. son of William and Hannah (Davenport) Brightman.

The will of Davenport Brightman of Rochester, yeoman, dated 3rd day 2nd month 1816, presented 2 July 1821, names wife Ruby, sons Charles and John; daus. Sybil Brightman and Hannah Brightman unm. On 4 July 1821 James Taber of Fairhaven Esq., administrator on the estate of Davenport Brightman, posted bond with will annexed and the sons waived the provisions of the will asking to share equally with other heirs. No division was found.

The will of Rube Brightman of Rochester, widow of Davenport dec., dated 24 Oct. 1821, presented 21 Jan. 1822, bequeaths property to sons Charles and John and to daus. Sibel and Hannah. James Taber was to be executor.

Children (BRIGHTMAN) first 3 b. New Bedford, rest b. Rochester:

i   AMOS[6] b. 11 April 1770 (not in wills)

ii   SYBIL b. 28 Aug. 1772
iii   JOSEPH b. 29 Aug. 1775 (not in wills)
iv   CHARLES b. 7 Jan. 1778
v   TABER b. 21 May 1782 (not in wills)
vi   JOHN b. 7 Aug. 1784
vii   HANNAH b. 11 Nov. 1786

References: TABER DESC pp. 12, 26. VR DARTMOUTH 2:82(m.). VR NEW BEDFORD 1:67(b. Amos), 68(b. Sybil, Joseph). VR ROCHESTER 1:60(b. ch.); 2:356(d. Ruby; Davenport). New Bedford Mercury Obits(d. Davenport). Plymouth Co. PR #2958 (Davenport Brightman); 2960(Rube Brightman).

179 HANNAH TABER[5] (Mary Tinkham[4], John[3], Mary[2] Brown, Peter[1]) b. Dartmouth 30 Aug. 1750; d. Hoosick Township NY 23 Feb. 1825 ae 73y 6m.

     She m. int. Dartmouth 10 Dec. 1768 EDWARD ELDREDGE, b. Dartmouth 1747 (pens. rec.); living Hoosick NY 26 Dec. 1832. He m. (2) after 23 Feb. 1825 Ruth _____.

     Edward Eldredge served in the Rev. War.

     Edward Eldridge was 1-4-4 in the 1790 census of New Bedford.

     On 19 Feb. 1799 Edward Eldredge of the town of Saratoga in the County of Saratoga [NY] purchased land in Hoosick, Rensselaer Co. NY.

     Edward and Hannah Eldridge of Hoosuck, Ranseler Co. NY sold to Wm. K. Potter of Dartmouth 35 acres at Dartmouth: The whole of Hannah's share in lot of her father Joseph Taber dec., signed 10 Jan. 1800, ack. same day by Edward and 25 Jan. 1800 by Hannah.

     Edward Eldridge and wife Hannah of Hoosuck, Rensalear Co. NY sold to Valentine Bradford of Fairhaven all right title and interest in swamp in New Bedford given to Hannah by her mother Mary Taber in her last will and share from sister Jemima Shearman dec., signed 7 Oct. 1818, ack. same day by both.

     Edward Eldridge and wife Hannah of Hoosuck, Ranselar Co. NY sold to James Gifford of Dartmouth, land in Dartmouth 1/4 of land of Jemima Shearman late dec., signed 24 Sept. 1818, ack. same day by both.

On 19 April 1820 Edward Eldridge of Hoosick, Rensselaer Co. sold land in Hoosick to Joseph Eldridge of Hoosick. On the same day, Edward Eldridge sold land to Edward Eldridge Jr. of Hoosick.

On 11 Dec. 1828 Edward Eldridge of Hoosick and wife Ruth sold land to Edward Jr. and Joseph Eldridge of Hoosick.

Rev. War Pension application of Edward Eldredge, resident of Hoosick, Rensselaer Co. NY, ae 85, dated 26 Dec. 1832, states he was born Dartmouth in 1747. On 5 Nov. 1834 Ruby Eldridge ae 65 years deposed she remembered her father being absent a number of months as a soldier in the Rev. War.

No Rensselaer Co. NY PR for Edward Eldredge.

Children (ELDREDGE) b. Dartmouth:

    i   RUBY[6] b. ca. 1769; unm. in 1834
    ii   EDWARD b. ca. 1788 (bur. near his father)
   iii JOSEPH

References: VR DARTMOUTH 2:176(int.; b. Edward). TABER DESC p. 12. Bristol Co. LR 79:235; 104:549; 107:40(Edward Eldridge). Rev. War Pension R3281. Cem. & Death Records, Hoosick Township p. 117(d. Hannah). Rensselaer Co. LR 2:348-9; 16:68-9, 287; 201:150-151(Edward Eldridge).

180 JEMIMA TABER[5] (Mary Tinkham[4], John[3], Mary[2] Brown, Peter[1]) b. Dartmouth 17 Dec. 1753; d. there 14 July 1810 in 59th yr.

She m. New Bedford 21 Nov. 1802 ABRAHAM SHEARMAN, b. Dartmouth 11 Feb. 1744; d. Fairhaven 9 Sept. 1826; son of Abraham and Susanna (Delano) Shearman. He m. (1) int. Dartmouth 10 Aug. 1771 Peace Taber* by whom he had Ruth, Abraham, and Thomas.

There are no Bristol Co. probate or land records for Jemima Shearman; no probates for Abraham. Abraham and Jemima apparently had no children for Jemima's estate was divided among her sisters.

References: VR DARTMOUTH 1:219(b. Abraham). VR NEW BEDFORD 2:474(m.). SHERMAN DESC pp. 443-4.

*Jemima is not a sister of Peace Taber as shown in SHERMAN DESC and she did not m. 1st a Tobey. Peace Taber was b. 1744 to Thomas and Ruth (Bennett) Taber.

181 ELIJAH ELLIS[5] (Martha[4] Tinkham, John[3], Mary[2] Brown, Peter[1]) b. aft. 1755; living 1810 (census); d. bef. 1820 (when his widow Rebecca is listed in census).

He m. Dartmouth 30 Sept. 1798 REBEKAH SHEARMAN, living Fairhaven 1820 (census).

On 30 Sept. 1799 Elijah Ellis of New Bedford, yeoman, mortgaged land and dwelling house in New Bedford, all his share as contained in division deed bet. his brothers Seth, John, Luke and himself signed 15 April 1788; with wife Rebecca also signing. Elijah acknowledged the deed 1 Oct. 1799.

Elijah Ellis had one male 26-45, one female 26-45 and one female under 10 in the 1800 census of New Bedford. He was also in the New Bedford census of 1810 with an implied family of a wife and one son and two daus. Rebecca Ellis was in the 1820 census of Fairhaven with the implied children.

Neither Elijah nor Rebekah Ellis left any Bristol Co. PRs.

Children (ELLIS) b. New Bedford:

    i   dau.[6] b. ca. 1799 (implied by census rec.)
    ii   son b. 1800-1810 (implied by census rec.)
    iii   MARY C. b. 1800-1810 (implied by census rec.)*

References: VR DARTMOUTH 2:179(m.). Bristol Co. LR 78:310
            (Elijah   Ellis).   MSSR   5:300(Elijah   Ellis).
Massachusetts Death Records 76:208(d. Mary C.).

*She d. Marion, Plymouth Co. 16 Nov. 1853 (as Mary C. Hammond) and her d. cert. calls her dau. of Elijah and Rebecca Ellis.

182 LUKE ELLIS[5] (Martha Tinkham[4], John[3], Mary[2] Brown, Peter[1]) b. aft. 1755; d. after 10 June 1836.

He m. (1) Berkley 3 Dec. 1780 NAOMI BRIGGS, b. Berkley 17 April 1762; d. bef. 11 March 1784; dau. of Joseph and Abigail (Cole) Briggs.

He m. (2) Dartmouth 11 March 1784 ELISABETH

MACOMBER, b. ca. 1764; d. Fairhaven 2 June 1838 ae 74.

Luke Ellis was Pvt. in Rev. War.

Luke Ellis was 1-1-4 in the 1790 census of Rochester.

Luke Ellis of New Bedford, cordwainer, sold to "my brother Seth Ellis of New Bedford" 7 acres in New Bedford from his homestead farm, signed 12 Dec. 1792 by Luke and Elizabeth Ellis; ack. 27 Feb. 1794.

Luke Ellis of Fair Haven, cordwainer, sold to Abraham Tinkham of Rochester, yeoman, his homestead and dwelling house in Fair Haven 27 Dec. 1813, signed by Luke and Elizabeth, ack. 27 Dec. 1813.

Luke Ellis is in the 1820 census of Fairhaven with 2 males over 10, under 16; 1 male over 16, under 18; 1 female over 16, under 26; 1 female over 26, under 45; and 1 female over 45.

On 26 Jan. 1829 Luke Ellis of Fairhaven, cordwainer, deeded 15 acres in Fairhaven to Benjamin R. Ellis.

Luke Ellis of Fairhaven, yeoman, sold to Savery Wing land in Fairhaven reserving use of lane, barn etc. during his life, wife Elizabeth releases dower, signed 10 June 1836, ack. 16 June 1836.

A petition of May 1864 names the relatives of Naomi Ellis as brother Joseph P. Ellis of Antwerp, Jefferson Co. NY; brother Benjamin R. Ellis of Croghan NY; sister Sarah Maxim, widow of New Bedford; sister Lavinia Hammond of Philadelphia NY; sister Mary Bennett of Jamestown IA; Harvey Farrington and George B. Farrington, only surviving children of sister Deborah M. Farrington, dec., of Brooklyn NY; William Washburn of CA; Charles Washburn of MA and James Washburn of CA only children of sister Eliza Washburn dec.

No Bristol Co. PR for Luke or Naomi Ellis.

Children (ELLIS) all by Elisabeth:

    i   NAOMI[6] b. 1784; d. New Bedford 29 March 1864 ae 79; unm.*

    ii   ELIZA b. Jan. 1787 (based on age at death)

    iii MARY (or POLLY) b. 1789 (based on age in 1860 census)

    iv LOVINA b. 1793 (based on age in 1850 census)

    v   SARAH b. Feb. 1795 (based on age at death)

    vi DEBORAH MACOMBER b. ca. 1799 (based on age

at death)
vii   JOSEPH P. b. 13 May 1803
viii   BENJAMIN R. b. 1805 (based on ae in 1850 census)
ix   CHARLES F. b. 1810; d. Philadelphia NY 12
       March 1851 ae 41; unm.

References: VR DARTMOUTH 2:179(both m.). Bristol Co. LR
          72:383; 96:246; 140:389(Luke Ellis). DAR PATRIOT
INDEX p. 219. Berkley VR Index(b. Naomi). New Bedford
Mercury Obits 1807-1845 p. 126(d. Elizabeth). CLEMENT
BRIGGS OF PLYMOUTH COLONY AND HIS DESCENDANTS,
Edna Anne Hannibal, 1966, pp. 79, 80. Bristol Co. So. Registry
2:324(Luke Ellis). FAIRHAVEN VR 1:152(census). MSSR
5:310(Luke Ellis). Massachusetts Deaths 103:226(d. Eliza);
174:116(d. Naomi); 328:96 (d. Sarah).

*Naomi's d. cert. says she is dau. of Luke & Elizabeth Ellis.

183 THANKFUL ELLIS[5] (Martha Tinkham[4], John[3], Mary[2]
Brown, Peter[1]) b. New Bedford ca. 1763; d. Fairhaven 10 May 1850
ae 86.
       She m. Fairhaven 11 Dec. 1817 JACOB KINNEY, b.
Dartmouth 9 Sept. 1749; d. bef. 5 May 1829, son of Thomas and
Mary (Jenney) Kinney, a descendant of Pilgrim Francis Cooke.
He m. (1) Dartmouth 20 Nov. 1777 Parnel Hammond by whom he
had Jacob and other children.
       The will of Jacob Kinney dated 9 April 1825, proved 5 May
1829, names wife Thankful and several children by the first wife.

       No children.

References: VR DARTMOUTH 1:143(b. Jacob); 2:283(his 1st m.).
          FAIRHAVEN VR 1:28(m.). Bristol Co. PR
67:125(Jacob Kinney). Massachusetts Death Records 48:57(d.
Thankful).

184 CHARLES TINKHAM[5] (Peter[4], John[3], Mary[2] Brown, Peter[1])
b. Dartmouth 16 June 1747; d. Rochester 18 Nov. 1822 ae 77.
       He m. int. Rochester 22 Aug. 1772 JANE ELLIS, b. ca. 1750;
d. May 1832; dau. of John and Maria (Landers) Ellis.

Charles Tinkham was 2-2-4 in the 1790 census of Rochester. The will of Charles Tinkham of Rochester dated 17 Sept. 1822, presented 8 Nov. 1822, names wife Jane; daus. Eunice, Betsey while single, and Jane; sons Abraham and Andrew; grandson Charles Peirce; son Charles executor.

No Plymouth Co. PR for Jane Tinkham.

Children (TINKHAM) b. Rochester:*

i	ABRAHAM[6]	b. 5 March 1773
ii	CHARLES	b. 20 Aug. 1775
iii	ANDREW	b. 4 April 1777
iv	EUNICE	b. 2 Aug. 1782
v	BETSEY	b. 21 Jan. 1788
vi	JANE	b. 20 March 1793

References: VR ROCHESTER 1:293(b. ch); 2:204(int.). Plymouth Co. PR #20824(Chas. Tinkham). NEHGR 120:288-9(d. Jane).

*Tinkham ms. p. 97 says "an old letter" from Charles[6] in Mattapoisett to his brother Andrew in Maine proves they had brothers Sylvanus and Pardon in Maine, however since they were not mentioned in their father's will, it seems unlikely that Sylvanus and Pardon were his children.

185 EPHRAIM TINKHAM[5] (Peter[4], John[3], Mary[2] Brown, Peter[1]) b. Dartmouth 27 Jan. 1750/1; d. Rochester 27 Aug. 1796.

He m. Dartmouth 12 June 1774 ELIZABETH JONES, b. ca. 1750; d. Rochester 2 March 1841 ae 91y 2m 6d.

Ephraim Tinkham was a Pvt. in Rev. War.

Ephraim Tinkham was 1-2-3 in the 1790 census of Rochester.

On 31 May 1837 Elizabeth Tinkham ae 87 living at Rochester applied for pension for service of Ephraim Tinkham who was living in Rochester when he enlisted; Elizabeth d. 2 March 1841. Includes depositions of Abraham Tinkham of Rochester; brother Hezekiah Tinkham of Montpelier, Co. of Washington (age 79 on 8 Oct. 1838), and sister Elizabeth Tinkham of New Bedford (in 84th yr. 12 Dec. 1838).

The 1840 census of Rev. War Pensioners lists Elizabeth Tinkham of Rochester, ae 90, living with Levi Handy.

No Plymouth Co. PR for Ephraim or Elizabeth Tinkham.

Children (TINKHAM) b. Rochester:

   i   EPHRAIM[6] b. 20 Dec. 1779
   ii   ABIGAIL b. April 1785
   iii THANKFUL b. 15 Feb. 1793

References: VR DARTMOUTH 2:499(m.). VR ROCHESTER 1:293(b. Ephraim, Abigail), 294(b. Thankful); 2:440(d. Ephraim, Eliz.). DAR PATRIOT INDEX p. 680. Rev. War Pension #W14024(Ephraim Tinkham). 1840 CENSUS OF REV WAR PENSIONERS p. 30.

186 SARAH TINKHAM[5] (Peter[4], John[3], Mary[2] Brown, Peter[1]) b. Dartmouth 14 Dec. 1753; d. Nantucket 30 Nov. 1838 ae 86y 3m.

She m. Dartmouth 30 April 1772 GEORGE WHIPPEY of Sherburne, Nantucket Co. b. ca. 1745; d. New Bedford 5 April 1823 ae 78y 1m.

The will of George Whippey of New Bedford, cooper, dated 31 Aug. 1818, presented 6 May 1823, names wife Sarah; Betsey Tinkham sister of his wife Sarah to have all real and personal estate after death of Sarah, then to go to his nearest relations on Island of Nantucket. Letter of adm. granted to Sarah on the same day. Inventory of the estate of George Whippey late of New Bedford, mariner, was dated 18 April 1823.

On 28 June 1836 Sally Whippey of New Bedford, widow, sold to Alfred C. Briggs of New Bedford, land in New Bedford; ack. next day.

Children (WHIPPEY) b. prob. New Bedford:

   i   SARAH[6] b. ca. 1784; d. New Bedford 7 Sept. 1818 ae 34y
   ii   BETSEY b. ca. 1790; d. New Bedford 22 July 1810 in 21st yr

References: VR DARTMOUTH 2:536(m.). VR NANTUCKET

5:603(d. Sarah). VR NEW BEDFORD 3:181(d. dau. Sarah, Betsey). NEHGR 100:285. New Bedford Mercury Obits 1807-1845 pp. 360(d. George, Betsey), 361(d. dau. Sarah). Bristol Co. PR 60:300, 324(George Whippey). Bristol Co. LR 150:522(Sally Whippey).

187 HEZEKIAH TINKHAM[5] (Peter[4], John[3], Mary[2] Brown, Peter[1]) b. prob. Rochester 8 Oct. 1759; d. East Montpelier, Washington Co. VT 26 Oct. 1843 ae 85.

He m. New Bedford 23 Jan. 1807 LYDIA BENNETT, b. ca. 1769; d. Montpelier VT 10 March 1840 ae 71 yrs.; dau. of Robert and Meribah (Cook) Bennett.

Hezekiah Tinkham of New Bedford, yeoman, sold to Elias Terry of New Bedford, mariner, several lots and buildings in New Bedford, 54 acres, 4 acres he bought of Wm. Jenne and 10 acres which came to him by his wife Lydia in division of estate of her father Robert Bennett of New Bedford, signed by Hezekiah and Lydia 24 Oct. 1807, ack. 24 Oct. 1811.

Hezekiah Tinkham of Montpelier, yeoman, and wife Lydia and Rhoda Bennett of Montpelier, spinster, sold 2/6 of real estate in Fairhaven of their mother Meribah Bennett deceased's dower in estate of her husband Robert Bennett, signed 29 Sept. 1829, ack. 3 Oct. 1829.

The pension papers for Elizabeth Tinkham, widow of Ephraim Tinkham, contain a deposition by Hezekiah Tinkham of Montpelier, Co. of Washington, VT dated 17 Oct. 1838 states he was "of the age of 79 years old on the eighth day of Oct. 1838," that Ephraim Tinkham was his brother and that when he returned from whaling off the coast of Brazil in 1776 he found his brother had enlisted in the army.

In the 1840 census of Rev. War pensioners Hezekiah Tinkham, ae 81, was living in Montpelier VT with Hezekiah Tinkham.

The estate of Hezekiah Tinkham was proved in Washington Co. VT 3 Feb. 1844. The estate was insolvent. Henry Tinkham was listed as a creditor.

On 11 April 1844, rec. 12 April 1844, Henry Tinkham of Montpelier purchased quitclaim from Perkins and Lovisa Richardson of Marshfield, Washington Co. VT for property deeded to Hezekiah Tinkham in 1812. The deed mentions Lovisa

Tinkham now Richardson.

Children (TINKHAM):

   i   HENRY⁶
   ii   LOVISA
   iii HEZEKIAH

References: VR NEW BEDFORD 2:551(m.). Bristol Co. LR 98:515; 149:384(Hezekiah Tinkham). Washington Co. VT PR m. 70-3(Hezekiah Tinkham). Rev. War Pension W14024. Montpelier VT LR 13:94(Hezekiah Tinkham). THOMAS COOKE OF RHODE ISLAND, Jane F. Fiske, Boxford 1987, 1:252. 1840 CENSUS OF REV WAR PENSIONERS p. 64. Tinkham Cem., East Montpelier VT(g.s. Hezekiah).

188 EUNICE TINKHAM⁵ (Peter⁴, John³, Mary² Brown, Peter¹) b. Dartmouth or Rochester; living 8 Dec. 1814.
    She m. New Bedford 15 Nov. 1798 JOHN BLACKMER, living 3 June 1823. Joseph Blackmore of Dartmouth, yeoman, was appointed guardian to John Blackmore minor over 14, son of Stephen late of Dartmouth dec., signed 3 Oct. 1789. (This may refer to the John Blackmer who m. Eunice.)
    On 7 Dec. 1814 John Blackmer of Rochester, laborer, sold to Abraham Tinkham of Rochester land in Rochester deeded to me by Salsbury Blackmer, signed by John and Eunice Blackmer, ack. next day. On 3 June 1823 John Blackmer of Rochester, laborer, sold to John Blackmer Jr. of Rochester, ack. same day.
    No Plymouth Co. PR for John Blackmer.

Child (BLACKMER):

   i   JOHN⁶

References: VR NEW BEDFORD 2:58(m.). Plymouth Co. LR 124:344; 150:31(John Blackmer). Bristol Co. PR 129:455 (gdn.).

189 REUBEN TINKHAM⁵ (Peter⁴, John³, Mary² Brown, Peter¹) b. Rochester 6 May 1768; d. Rochester 2 Aug. 1857.

He m. int. Rochester 17 April 1790 MARY DEXTER, b. ca. 1750; d. Rochester 16 April 1837 ae 82 "Mary wf Reuben" (perhaps an exaggeration?).

Reuben Tinkham was 1-0-4 in the 1790 census of Rochester. No Plymouth Co. PR or LR for Reuben Tinkham.

Children (TINKHAM) b. Rochester:

    i   HEZEKIAH[6] b. 29 Jan. 1791
    ii   MARY b. 23 June 1793
    iii REUBEN b. 3 June 1795
    iv   SARAH b. 7 Oct. 1798

References: VR ROCHESTER 1:293-4(b. ch.); 2:304(int.).   New Bedford Mercury Obits 1807-1845 p. 339(d. Mary). Tinkham ms., Horace W. Tinkham, 1921, p. 103(d. Reuben).

190 ELIZABETH TINKHAM[5] (Hezekiah[4], John[3], Mary[2] Brown, Peter[1]) b. Swansea 11 May 1746; d. NY 30 March 1810*.

She m. Glocester RI 27 Oct. 1768 STEPHEN SMITH, b. Glocester RI 20 May 1750; d. NY 29 Aug. 1817*; son of Stephen Smith.

Stephen Smith Jr. had 1 m over 16, 2 under 16, 1 female over 16 and 1 under in 1774 census of Glocester RI.

Stephen Smith was a Rev. War soldier.

Stephen Smith deeded ten acres to his brother Esek Smith of Glocester on 9 Dec. 1784, his wife Elizabeth yielded her dower rights.

He is apparently the Stephen Smith who was 1-3-3 in the 1790 census of Glocester RI.

When Esek Smith adm. the estate of Obadiah Lewis Jr. of Glocester and in May 1796 petitioned the General Assembly of RI for the sale of the land of Obadiah Lewis, who had died in Nov. 1793, the proceeds were to go to the wife and two children of Obadiah. In the petition Esek Smith stated his own brother was the father of Obadiah Lewis's widow. He added that the widow had since remarried and with her husband and her two children had moved to Cooperstown where she had been joined by the father. Glocester deeds identify her as Mary wife of Obadiah Lewis.

The will of Stephen Smith [the son] dated 16 Oct. 1820, proved 28 May 1832, names wife Ruth; brothers and sisters: Hezekiah Smith, Oliver Smith, Betsey Smith, Naomy Hopkins and Abigail Round; sister's son Otis Lewis and his sister Hannah Lewis. A petition of Ruth Smith, widow of Stephen Smith sworn 12 April 1832, stated that Stephen died in Hartwicke, Otsego Co., NY 6 April 1832 and that he left no children, father or mother surviving, that the heirs and next of kin of dec. are your petitioner; Hezekiah Smith and Oliver Smith, who were brothers; Betsey Smith a sister; Jarvis Smith who is dead was also a brother and left: Chester Smith, Daniel Ward (?) and wife Sally, Benjamin Buel and wife Susan, Henry Beldenkirk (?) and wife Zinella (?), James L. Smith and Chauncey Smith; Abigail wife of William Rounds, a sister also dead who left children Eliza, Harriet, John, Lenny (?), and Stephen Rounds; Mary Hawkins wife of Rufus Hawkins also a sister and also dead and left Henry Fields and wife Hannah who reside in Otsego and Amasa Hawkins and Rufus Hawkins who reside in Onondaga Co. NY, Jeremiah Hopkins and wife Naome of Cateraugus Co. NY.

Children (SMITH) first 6 b. Glocester RI:

i	STEPHEN[6] b. 3 Aug. 1771
ii	HEZEKIAH b. 12 May 1773
iii	NAOMI b. 29 March 1775
iv	MARY
v	JARVIS b. 30 Oct. 1778
vi	BETSEY b. 1783; d. Hartwick NY 29 Nov. 1850; unm.
vii	OLIVER
viii	ABIGAIL

References: RIVR Glocester 3:1:34(m.). Glocester RI LE 11:51 (Stephen Smith). Otsego NY PR 1:681(Stephen Smith). RHODE ISLAND HISTORY pp. 22-6. RI 1774 CENSUS p. 137.

*Dates of b. & d. for Stephen & Elizabeth are apparently from their tombstones.

NOTE: Mary apparently married Obadiah Lewis and Rufus Hawkins. Her son Otis Lewis mentioned in the will was dead at the time of probate and the Hannah Lewis in the will is apparently the Hannah wife of Henry Fields in the petition.

191 JOANNA TINKHAM[5] (Hezekiah[4], John[3], Mary[2] Brown, Peter[1]) b. ca. 1750; d. Foster RI 22 Feb. 1838 ae 87y 6m 3d (g.s.).
        She m. OBEDIAH ESTEN of Foster RI, b. ca. 1749; d. there 7 Aug. 1842 ae 93y 1m 19d (g.s.); son of Henry Esten.
        Obediah Esten had one male over 16, one male under 16; one female over 16 and one female under 16 in the 1774 census of Glocester RI.
        On 1 Aug. 1774 Obadiah Esten of Glocester and wife Joanna sold five acres in Glocester to George Bowen. On 28 April 1775 Obadiah and Joanna Esten deeded land to Abin Luther of Killingly.
        On 1 Feb. 1788 Asa Balloo of Foster sold 16 acres in Foster to Obadiah Esten of Foster.
        Obediah Esten was 1-2-6 in the 1790 census of Foster RI.
        On 18 Feb. 1793 Obadiah and Joanna Esten deeded land to Theophilus Esten.
        On 2 Feb. 1807 Obadiah Estin of Foster, yeoman, deeded land in Foster to son Henry Eastin. He deeded more land to Henry on 10 April 1810.
        On 28 Aug. 1815 Obadiah Eastin of Foster, yeoman, deeded part of his home lot in Foster to Stephen Eastin of Foster, laborer. On 27 March 1819 he deeded more land to Stephen. On 10 Aug. 1840 he deeded more land in Foster to Susanna Eastin, widow of Stephen Eastin.
        Joanna filed a deposition in 1836 for her sister Renew (Tinkham) Smith, when the latter filed for a pension on the Rev. War services of her husband, Esek Smith.
        No PR for Obadiah Esten.

        Children (ESTEN) b. prob. Foster RI:

i	STEPHEN[6] b. ca. 1776 (based on age at d.)
ii	HULDAH (called "of Obediah" in mar. rec.)
iii	MERCY (called "of Obediah" in mar. rec.)
iv	HANNAH (called "of Obediah" in mar. rec.)

v   STEPHEN   b. 1793 (g.s.)

References: Foster RI LE 1:111(Asa Ballou), 601; 2:497; 3:437;
          5:126, 545; 10:174(Obadiah Esten). Glocester RI LE
9:464(Obadiah Esten). RIVR Foster 3:4:12(daus. ms.). Gravestones
on Esten farm in Foster RI(d. Joanna, Obediah, Stephen).
Providence RIVR 10:102(d. Henry). RHODE IS 1774 CENSUS p.
132.

192 RENEW TINKHAM[5] (Hezekiah[4], John[3], Mary[2] Brown,
Peter[1]) b. Glocester RI ca. 1751; d. there after 1841.
      She m. Glocester RI Nov. 1776 ESEK SMITH of Glocester RI;
d. Glocester RI 11 Feb. 1817; son of Stephen Smith.
      In 1758 (after his father died) Esek Smith, son of Stephen
Smith, was put out to Zebedee Hopkins Jr.
      Eseek Smith was 2-1-3 in the 1790 census of Glocester RI.
This may imply he had daus.
      Renew Smith was 85 in 1836 when she applied for a Rev.
War pension on her husband's service. The pension papers give
date of marriage and death of Esek.

      Children (SMITH) b. Glocester RI:

      i   ARNOLD[6] b. 1 Aug. 1779
      ii   GEORGE   b. ca. 1781; (ae 55 in 1836 when he
            deposed in support of the pension application)

References: RIVR Glocester 3:1:62(b. Arnold). RHODE ISLAND
          HISTORY 22:24-9(Smith Fam.). Rev. War Pension
R9728(Esek Smith).

193 JOHN TINKHAM[5] (Hezekiah[4], John[3], Mary[2] Brown, Peter[1])
d. Greenfield NY bef. 10 Oct. 1803.
      He m. FREELOVE _____.
      John Tinkham was a soldier in the Rev. War.
      On 20 Nov. 1790 John Tinkham deeded land to George Peirce
with Freelove Tinkham his wife giving up dower.
      John Tinkum was 1-0-2 in the 1790 census of Glocester RI.
      John Tinckum had 1 male under 10, 1 male 26-45, 1 fem.
10-16, 1 fem. 26-45 in 1800 census of Greenfield, Saratoga Co. NY.

On 10 Oct. 1803 Samuel Tinckom of Greenfield (relationship not stated, but surely his brother) was given administration of the estate of John Tinckom, blacksmith of Greenfield, during the minority of his dau. Sally.

Children (TINKHAM):

    i   son[6] (implied in Census Record) d.y.
   ii   SALLY

References: Glocester RI LE 11:592(John Tinkham). Saratoga Co. NY PR 1:212(John Tinkham).

194 SARAH TINKHAM[5] (Hezekiah[4], John[3], Mary[2] Brown, Peter[1]) b. ca. 1755; d. Glocester RI (rec. in Providence Patriot of 3 Nov. 1830).
    She m. ca. 1773 STEPHEN IRONS of Glocester RI, b. 23 May 1751; d. Glocester RI 13 June 1826 ae 75y 20d (g.s.); son of Samuel and Hannah (Waterman) Irons.
    Stephen Irons was 2-1-3 in the 1790 census of Glocester RI.
    On 16 April 1813 Stephen Irons deeded land to son Thomas Irons.
    The will of Stephen Irons of Glocester, yeoman, dated 2 Feb. 1819, proved 26 Aug. 1826, names wife Sarah; dau. Isabel Tyler and her children; son Nicholas Irons; and excludes son Thomas and his heirs because they have already received their portion.*
    The will of Sarah Irons of Glocester, widow of Stephen Irons, dated 15 Sept. 1830, proved 4 Dec. 1830, names Isabel Irons, dau. of son Thomas; dau. Isabel, wife of Thomas Tyler. Samuel Steere of Glocester to be executor.*

Children (IRONS) b. prob. Glocester RI:

    i   NICHOLAS[6] b. 10 Sept. 1774
   ii   ISABEL b. ca. 1783
  iii   THOMAS b. ca. 1791 (based on age on g.s.)

References: Benns Grave Records 1:89(d. Stephen & Thomas). Glocester RI LE 17:334(Stephen Irons). Glocester RI PR 4:132(Stephen Irons), 231(Sarah Irons). WATERMAN GEN

3:49-50. RI ROOTS 26:2:8(b. ch.).

*Although not called deceased in the wills of his father or mother, Thomas Irons died bef. his parents.

195 NEHEMIAH TINKHAM[5] (Hezekiah[4], John[3], Mary[2] Brown, Peter[1]) b. Glocester RI in 1766; d. there 17 Feb. 1813.
    He m. bef. 1796 LYDIA LEWIS* who d. Glocester RI 11 Jan. 1815.
    Nehemiah Tinkham was 1-1-4 in the 1790 census of Glocester RI.
    The will of Nehemiah Tinkham of Glocester, blacksmith, dated 1 Dec. 1812, proved 20 March 1813, names wife Lydia; dau. Hannah Steere wife of Hosea; son Peter; daus. Betsey and Ruth; sons Nehemiah, Cyrus, John, Daniel and William. Daniel and William were under age at their father's death. Widow Lydia Tinkham and Hosea Steere were named guardians to Ruth, Nehemiah, Cyrus and John Tinkham.
    On 23 March 1815 Daniel Tinkham sold land given him and his brother William Tinkom in will of father Nehemiah Tinkom.

    Children (TINKHAM) b. Smithfield RI:

        i   PETER[6]
        ii   BETSEY
        iii DANIEL
        iv   WILLIAM
        v   HANNAH b. 14 March 1796
        vi   RUTH
        vii NEHEMIAH b. 28 Nov. 1799
        viii CYRUS b. 18 June 1801
        ix   JOHN
References: Tinkham ms p. 90(b. Nehemiah, Cyrus; name of wife). Harmony RI Cem. Recs. Glocester RI PR 3:345(Nehemiah Tinkham). RIVR 14:38(d. Nehemiah). Glocester RI LE 18:12(Daniel Tinkham). REPRESENTATIVE MEN AND OLD FAMILIES OF RI, J. H. Beers Co., Chicago 1908, 1:353(b. Nehemiah).

*Tinkham ms. says Lydia Lewis b. 23 Nov. 1780, but that doesn't seem possible unless she is 2nd wife. It would appear Nehemiah married bef. 1790.

196 DANIEL TINKHAM[5] (Hezekiah[4], John[3], Mary[2] Brown, Peter[1]) b. Glocester RI 30 April 1767; d. Sumnerville MI 1 Nov. 1853 ae 84y 6m.

He m. Smithfield RI ca. 1789 ADAH WINDSOR, b. Smithfield RI 8 Nov. 1768; d. Spafford NY 28 Feb. 1851 ae 82y 3m 19d; dau. of John and Mercy (Smith) Windsor.

In the 1800 census for Greenfield, Saratoga Co. NY Daniel Tinkham had 4 males under 10, one 26-45, one female under 10, one female 16-26 and one female 26-45.

On 11 April 1804 Daniel Tinkham bought 100 acres in Aurelius, Onondaga Co. NY. He sold this tract 3 March 1810, with wife Adah participating, to Jonathan Berry.

In the 1810 census of Onondaga Co. Daniel Tinkham had 2 males under 10, 3 males 10-16, 1 male 16-25, 1 male 26-45, 3 females under 10, 1 female 16-26 and 1 female 26-45.

On 6 April 1839 Daniel Tinkham sold 209 acres in Spafford NY to son Zenas.

In the 1850 census of Spafford, Onondaga Co. NY Daniel Tinkhum, laborer, ae 82, born RI and wife Ada, ae 82, born RI are living with their son Zenus, ae 45, born NY and his family.

No Saratoga Co. NY LR for Daniel Tinkham.

Children (TINKHAM) last 6 b. NY:

i	JOHN K.[6] b. 26 Dec. 1790; d. Spafford NY 6 Nov. 1813; unm.
ii	MERCY b. 3 Sept. 1792
iii	RUSSELL b. 21 July 1794
iv	STEPHEN b. 21 June 1796
v	ALANSON b. 5 Oct. 1798
vi	RELLY b. 28 Dec. 1800
vii	PRAXANA b. 22 Feb. 1803
viii	ZENAS b. 18 April 1805
ix	ALMEDA b. 27 Dec. 1807
x	CYNTHIA b. 29 April 1810
xi	ADAH b. 17 April 1813; d. Spafford NY 12 July 1814

References: HISTORY OF SPAFFORD, ONONDAGA CO. with
gen. notes, G. K. Collins, 1917, pp. 255-6(b. ch.; d.
wife Adah, John). CASS CO MI CEM RECS 4:81(d. Daniel).
RIVR Smithfield 3:6:122(b. Adah). TINKHAM: A
BIOGRAPHICAL INDEX, Kenneth Ira Tinkham, Centralia WA,
1986, p. 56. Onondaga Co. NY LR C:420; Q465; 73:388(Daniel
Tinkham).

NOTE: The Tinkham genealogy says Daniel Tinkham went to
Springfield VT bef. moving to NY. While no proof was found, the
statement appears true.

197 SAMUEL TINKHAM⁵ (Hezekiah⁴, John³, Mary² Brown,
Peter¹) b. Glocester RI in 1769; d. Portland NY 20 June 1841 ae 70
(g.s.).
 He m. Glocester RI ca. 1790 MARY WILLIAMS, b.
Providence RI 23 May 1767; d. Portland NY 30 July 1850 ae 84
yrs. (g.s.); dau. of John and Mary (_____) Williams.
 The 1800 Greenfield, Saratoga Co. NY census lists Samuel
Tinkham with 2 m under 10, 1 26-45, 2 fem. under 10, 1 26-45. In
the 1820 census of Chautauqua NY Samuel was over 45, as was his
wife, and he had one male over 26; one female 10-16 and one
female under 10.
 Neither Samuel nor Mary Tinkham left probate or land
records in Chautauqua Co., but in 1859 Hezekiah Tinkcom of
Westfield, Chautauqua Co. NY, aged 68 signed his will, being
apparently their son.

 Children (TINKHAM) first 2 b. Glocester RI, rest b. Saratoga
Co. NY:

  i HEZEKIAH⁶ b. 1791
  ii WATERMAN b. 3 Feb. 1794
  iii CELESTIA b. 17 Nov. 1797 (on g.s.)
  iv ZENESIA b. ca. 1799
  v WEST b. ca. 1801; d.y.
  vi JOHN b. ca. 1804(1850 census of Chautauqua)
  vii AMANDA b. ca. 1805*

      viii   MARY b. ca. 1807*
      ix   SARAH b. ca. 1809*
      x   HARRIET b. ca. 1811

References: NYGBR 58:373(d. Amanda, Mary, Sally). Portland
            Evergreen Cem., Chautauqua Co., NY(d. Sam.,
Mary, Celestial). TINKHAM: A BIOGRAPHICAL INDEX,
Kenneth I. Tinkham, Centralia WA, pp. 244-5.

*Amanda, Mary and Sarah are bur. in the same plot in the
Mayville, Chautauqua Co. NY Cem. Amanda, wife of Stephen
Hoxie, d. 25 Aug. 1840 ae 35y 6m; Mary, wife of Joseph Starr, d.
10 June 1837 ae 30y 19d; and Sally, wife of Amos Carver, d. 15
March 1844 ae 33.

198 PHILIP TINKHAM[5] (Hezekiah[4], John[3], Mary[2] Brown, Peter[1])
b. Glocester RI.
      He m. EUNICE WATERMAN, dau. of John and Martha
(Dyer) Waterman.
      There are two men named Philip Tinkham in the 1800 census
of Glocester RI. One has one male 26-45 and one female 26-45.
The other has 1 male under 10, one male 26-45, 2 females 10-16
and one female 26-45.
      Nothing further has been found on this family.

References: ROGER WILLIAMS OF PROVIDENCE RI, Bertha
            Williams Anthony, 1966, 2:53(m.; parents of
Eunice).

199 BETHIAH HAYWARD[5] (Bethiah Snow[4], William[3], Rebecca[2]
Brown, Peter[1]) b. Bridgewater 7 April 1722; living 13 April 1773
(deed).
      She m. West Bridgewater 19 July 1743 THOMAS WILLIS of
Taunton, d. aft. 13 April 1773 (deed); son of Thomas and
Elizabeth (Glading) Willis. The will of Thomas Willis of Taunton,
yeoman, dated 27 March 1724/5 names wife Elizabeth; sons
Thomas (eldest), Abraham (2nd) and Silas (3rd) Willis all under 14
and his daus.
      Thomas Willis and wife Bethia, both of Taunton, sold to
John Snow of Bridgewater land in Bridgewater of their father

Elisha Hayward dec.; signed and ack. 9 Nov. 1752.

Thomas and Silas Willis of Taunton, yeomen, and children of Thomas Willis of Taunton dec., being brothers to Abraham Willis of Taunton, dec., divided his inheritance 30 April 1756.

On 2 Oct. 1764 Thomas Willis of Taunton was put under guardianship as non compos mentis. On 7 Feb. 1765 his wife Bethiah was the first to sign a petition requesting the discharge of the guardians, which was granted 25 April 1765.

Thomas Willis of Taunton, yeoman, sold to Richard Williams of Raynham, 9 acres in Taunton; signed and ack. 16 Aug. 1768. Bethia Willis discharged her dower rights to this land 21 Dec. 1769.

On 13 April 1773, ack. same day, Thomas Willis of Taunton, yeoman, and his wife Bethiah sold land in Taunton to Timothy Smith.

There is no Bristol Co. PR for Thomas or Bethiah other than the guardianship.

Apparently no children.*

References: VR WEST BRIDGEWATER p. 178(m.). Bristol Co. LR 42:23(Thomas & Silas Willis); 51:294(Thomas Willis), 583(Bethia Willis); 55:289(Thomas & Bethiah). Plymouth Co. LR 47:99(Thomas Willis). Bristol Co. PR (alphabetical files) (Thomas Willis guard.).

*It is possible that the Bethiah Willis who m. Amasa Richard 14 May 1779 is a dau. but no proof found (Easton Marriages p. 24).

200 NAOMI HAYWARD[5] (Bethiah Snow[4], William[3], Rebecca[2] Brown, Peter[1]) b. Bridgewater 25 March 1726; d. West Bridgewater 23 Dec. 1807 in 82nd yr.

She m. Bridgewater 24 March 1746/7 JOSEPH ALGER, b. Bridgewater 26 April 1723/4[sic]; d. West Bridgewater 29 Nov. 1790; son of Joseph and Mary (Ames) Alger.

Letters of administration of the estate of Joseph Alger of Bridgewater, yeoman, on estate of Joseph Alger late of Bridgewater dec. was dated 7 Feb. 1792. Account includes paying "Ebenezer Alger one of the heirs." On 6 Dec. 1790 "aged widow" Neomia Alger refused to administer.

No Plymouth Co. PR for Naomi Alger.

Children (ALGER) b. Bridgewater:

i EDWARD[6] b. 9 Aug. 1750; d. 17 Sept. 1750.
ii BETHIA b. 4 Sept. 1752
iii MARY b. 9 Sept. 1754
iv HANNAH b. 13 March 1757
v SILENCE b. 23 May 1759
vi JOSEPH b. 1 June 1762
vii SUSANNAH b. 21 May 1767
viii EBENEZER b. West Bridgewater 4 Sept. 1770

References: VR BRIDGEWATER 1:22-5(b. Joseph; b. ch.); 2:24 (m.), 427(d. Edward). VR WEST BRIDGEWATER p.12(b. Ebenezer). BRIDGEWATER BY MITCHELL p. 90. A GENEALOGICAL HISTORY OF THAT BRANCH OF THE ALGER FAMILY WHICH SPRINGS FROM THOMAS ALGER OF TAUNTON AND BRIDGEWATER IN MASSACHUSETTS 1665-1876, Arthur M. Alger, Boston 1876, pp. 7, 9. Plymouth Co. PR #222 (Joseph Alger).

201 EZRA HAYWARD[5] (Bethiah Snow[4], William[3], Rebecca[2] Brown, Peter[1]) b. Bridgewater 16 Nov. 1729; d. there 8 May 1808.

He m. Bridgewater 11 Oct. 1757 LYDIA LEE who d. Bridgewater 25 March 1816.

On 3 Jan. 1762 the selectman of Bridgewater declared Ezra Hayward non compos and appointed Abner Hayward his guardian. On 2 Jan. 1764 Jacob Hayward was appointed successor guardian. His land was sold in 5 sales to pay his debts.

Children (HAYWARD) b. Bridgewater:

i BETHIAH[6] b. 3 Sept. 1758
ii EZRA b. 25 March 1764
iii LYDIA b. 10 Feb. 1767
iv CHARLES b. 17 June 1769
v CYRUS b. 19 Sept. 1772
vi SARAH b. 20 March 1777

References: VR BRIDGEWATER 1:144-54(b. ch.); 2:171(m.), 485(d. Ezra), 486(d. Lydia). Plymouth Co. PR 16:234, 235,

259; 18:161, 24:337(Ezra Hayward).   Plymouth   Co. LR 68:219(to John Hayward).

202 ISRAEL ALGER[5] (Susanna   Snow[4], William[3], Rebecca[2] Brown, Peter[1]) b. Bridgewater ca. 1725; d. there 3 May 1755.
He m. Bridgewater 28 May 1747 ABIEL LATHROP, b. Bridgewater 7 Dec. 1729; d. there 1 Sept. 1803 ae 73; dau. of Samuel and Abial (Lassell) Lathrop. She m. (2) Bridgewater 6 Jan. 1756 Jonathan Bozworth as his second wife by whom she had Mary, Jonathan, Molly, Sarah, Chloe & Israel.   She m. (3) int. Bridgewater 12 Oct. 1768 Joseph Ames as his third wife by whom she had James, Olive & Fisk.
The will of Israel Alger, husbandman of Bridgewater, dated 12 March 1755, presented 2 June 1755, names wife Abiel as executrix, she to have stock and moveables.   No children mentioned.
Abiel Bosworth, widow of Bridgewater, administratrix gave bond on estate of Jonathan Bosworth of Bridgewater dec. on 1 June 1767 with Daniel and Isaac Lathrop of Bridgewater as sureties.
Abiel Ames, administratrix   on the estate of Jonathan Bosworth late of Bridgewater, gave account 9 Oct. 1769.
The will of Joseph Ames of Bridgewater, yeoman, dated 1 Dec. 1788, proved 7 June 1790, names wife Abiel to have "furniture she brought to me at the time or our intermarriage." The will names dau. Olive Alger; dau. Phebe Howard; children of son Ebenezer Ames dec. namely Ambrose, Charles, Silence, Walter, William, and Ebenezer; sons Elijah Ames and Nathaniel Ames; son Zephaniah Ames dec.; dau. Susanna Copeland; son Joseph Ames; daus. Bethia Fobes, Sarah Williams, and Olive Alger; and sons Fisk and James Ames.
The will of Abial Ames of Bridgewater, dated 10 Nov. 1802, proved 3 Oct. 1803, names son Jonathan Bosworth; sons James Ames, Fisk Ames; dau. Olive Alger, wife of Joseph; granddau. Tiley Alger, dau. of Joseph to have my gold beads; dau. Sally Lothrop, wife of Barnabas; dau. Chloe Tolman, wife of Daniel; son Fisk Ames executor.

Child (ALGER) b. Bridgewater:

i   SARAH[6] b. 21 Dec. 1754; d. 6 March 1755

References: VR BRIDGEWATER 1:25(b. Sarah), 202(b. Abiel);
            2:23(m.), 32(int. 3rd m.), 59(her 2nd m.), 427(d.
Israel), 428(d. Sarah), 430(d. Abiel). BRIDGEWATER BY
MITCHELL pp. 89, 101, 233. LO-LATHROP GEN p. 331.
Plymouth Co. PR 13:500(Israel Alger); 31:198-201(Joseph Ames);
20:270(Jonathan Bosworth); #2328(Jonathan Bosworth);
#352(Abial Ames).

203 DANIEL ALGER[5] (Susanna Snow[4], William[3], Rebecca[2]
Brown, Peter[1]) bp. W. Bridgewater 24 Sept. 1727; d. there 29 March
1786 (VR) or bef. second Tues. of April 1786 (deeds).
    He m. Easton 1 Dec. 1749 SUSANNA FOBES who was living
28 April 1786; dau. of Benjamin and Martha (Hunt) Fobes.
    On 21 March 1786 Daniel Alger of Bridgewater, yeoman, and
wife Susanna, sold land to son Daniel Alger of Easton, yeoman; to
son Benjamin Alger and to son Israel Alger. On the same date he
gave land in Easton to daus. Kezia, Chloe, and Martha. All deeds
say James Alger appeared on the second Tues. of April 1786 and
swore that he saw Daniel Alger, since dec., sign the deeds.
    Letters of administration of the estate of Daniel Alger of
Bridgewater, yeoman, on estate of Daniel Alger of Bridgewater,
yeoman, dated 1 May 1787; widow Susanna Alger requested
Daniel Alger be appointed administrator as eldest son, dated 28
April 1786. No Plymouth Co. PR for Susanna Alger.

Children (ALGER) b. Bridgewater:

    i   "first born" (dau.)[6] b. 24 July 1749; d. same day
   ii   daughter b. 15 June 1750; d. 16 June 1750
  iii   DANIEL b. 10 June 1751
   iv   SUSANNA b. 21 June 1753
    v   ISRAEL b. 26 June 1755
   vi   KEZIA b. 19 Aug. 1757
  vii   BENJAMIN b. 19 Jan. 1760
 viii   CHLOE (twin) b. 13 Nov. 1761
   ix   SILVIA (twin) b. 13 Nov. 1761

x   NATHAN b. 10 Oct. 1763
xi   MARTHA b. 27 Jan. 1766
xii DAVID b. 25 June 1768
xiii ABIEL b. 22 June 1772

References: VR BRIDGEWATER 1:22-5(b. ch.); 2:23(m.), 427(d.
Daniel), 428(d. 1st 2 ch.). BRIDGEWATER BY
MITCHELL pp. 89, 90. Plymouth Co. PR #207(Daniel Alger).
Plymouth Co. LR 66:136(to Daniel), 137(to Benj.), 138(to daus.; to
Israel).

204 JAMES ALGER[5] (Susanna Snow[4], William[3], Rebecca[2] Brown,
Peter[1]) bp. W. Bridgewater 23 March 1728/9; d. there 20 May 1810
in 82nd yr.
      He m. Bridgewater 8 Nov. 1750 MARTHA KINGMAN, b.
Bridgewater 24 Sept. 1732; d. there 23 Aug. 1813 ae 80; dau. of
Jonathan and Mary (Keith) Kingman.
      James Alger was a Corporal in the Rev. War.
      The will of James Alger, gentleman of Bridgewater, dated 8
Nov. 1791, presented 2 July 1810, names wife Martha; dau. Nancy
Keith, wife of Amos; Parnal and James Keith; granddau. Olive
Dunbar; sons Abiezer and James; Abiezer executor.
      No Plymouth Co. PR for Martha Alger.

      Children (ALGER) b. Bridgewater:

      i   NANCY (ANNA)[6] b. 10 Dec. 1752
      ii   ALICE b. 27 May 1755
      iii ABIEZER b. 25 July 1757
      iv   MARTHA b. 23 Oct. 1760
      v   PHEBE b. 2 April 1763
      vi   JAMES bp. West Bridgewater 13 Oct. 1765; d.y.
      vii JAMES b. 22 Oct. 1770
           + 3 others who died in infancy

References: VR BRIDGEWATER 1:22-4(b. ch. except 1st James),
197(b. Martha); 2:24(m.), 428(d. James, Martha). VR
WEST BRIDGEWATER p. 184(d. James, Martha).
BRIDGEWATER BY MITCHELL pp. 89, 226. BRIDGEWATER
EPITAPHS pp. 51(d. James, Martha). DAR PATRIOT INDEX p.

8. Plymouth Co. PR 43:230 (James Alger).

205 WILLIAM SNOW[5] (William[4-3], Rebecca[2] Brown, Peter[1]) b. Bridgewater 10 Aug. 1723; d. there 14 May 1755 in ye 32d year of age.

He m. Bridgewater 7 Nov. 1743 HANNAH HILL, b. Bridgewater 14 July 1725; dau. of Nathaniel and Hannah (Conant) Hill.

No Plymouth Co. PR for William or Hannah Snow.

Children (SNOW) b. Bridgewater:

i	child[6]	d. 19 Nov. 1744
ii	CALVIN	b. 20 Jan. 1749
iii	SALOME	b. 5 March 1751
iv	WILLIAM	b. 1 Jan. 1754

References: VR BRIDGEWATER 1:157(b. Hannah), 300-4(b. ch.); 2:350(m.), 559(d.William, child). BRIDGEWATER BY MITCHELL pp. 191, 317.

206 SETH SNOW[5] (William[4-3], Rebecca[2] Brown, Peter[1]) b. Bridgewater 7 Aug. 1725; d. Augusta, Oneida Co. NY bet. 20 Jan. and 7 July 1812.

He m. prob. Bridgewater ca. 1749 BETTY SPRAGUE, b. Bridgewater 10 May 1731; d. there 24 March 1797 "w. Seth."; dau. of Jonathan and Lydia (Leavit) Sprague. The will of Jonathan Sprague dated 8 Nov. 1748 names dau. Betty Sprague.

On 29 Sept. 1798 Seth Snow of Bridgewater sold 44 1/2 acres in Bridgewater to [son] Simeon Snow. No wife mentioned in deed.

The will of Seth Snow the 1st of Augusta, Oneida Co. NY, dated 20 Jan. 1812, proved 7 July 1812, names sons Simeon, Seth and Jonathan Snow; daus. Huldah, wife of Jonathan Snow; Sally wife of Joshua Richmond and Bethia wife of Asaph Larabee; granddaus. Betsey Larabee and Patty Ranken; dau. Susannah wife of Mathew Rankin to have balance of estate and they to be execs.

Children (SNOW) first 5 b. Bridgewater:

i	SIMEON[6]	b. 25 Nov. 1750

       ii   BETTY b. 9 Nov. 1752
       iii   SETH b. 28 April 1755
       iv   JONATHAN   b. 22 May 1757
       v   LYDIA b. 6 June 1759; d. 3 Sept. 1760
       vi   HULDAH (named in will)
       vii   SUSANNAH (named in will)
       viii SALLY (named in will)
       ix   BETHIA (named in will)

One of the children of Seth "Dropt Down Dead" in 1759 (prob. Betty).

References: VR BRIDGEWATER 1:300-4(b. ch.); 306(b. Betty); 2:559(d. Lydia, ch.), 560(d. Betty). BRIDGEWATER BY MITCHELL pp. 317, 321. Oneida NY Co. PR 1:336(Seth Snow). Plymouth Co. PR 14:137-9(Jonathan Sprague). Plymouth Co. LR 85:55(Seth Snow).

NOTE: The Eunice Snow who m. Alfred Edson in 1796 and d. in 1797 is prob. a dau. of Seth.

207 JAMES SNOW[5] (William[4-3], Rebecca[2] Brown, Peter[1]) b. Bridgewater 4 April 1729; d. there 1762 (according to Edson Gen.).
       He m. Bridgewater 10 Jan. 1758 MARY EDSON, b. Bridgewater; d. Stafford CT 13 Sept. 1803; dau. of Nathan and Mary (Sprague) Edson.
       Mary Snow of Stafford, Toland Co. CT, widow, sold to Caleb Fobes 2nd of Bridgewater, husbandman, land in South precinct of Bridgewater and half a dwelling house that belonged to her late husband Mr. James Snow late of Bridgewater dec., signed 23 Sept. 1796, ack. 19 Oct. 1796 at So. Brimfield, Hampshire Co.
       No Plymouth Co. or CT PR for James Snow; no CT PR for Mary Snow.

       Children (SNOW) b. Bridgewater:

       i   ELIAB[6] b. 16 April 1759
       ii   JAMES b. 5 April 1761; d. 9 March 1762

References: VR BRIDGEWATER 1:301(b. Eliab, James); 2:348(m.),

559(d. son James). BRIDGEWATER BY MITCHELL pp. 155, 317. Plymouth Co. LR 82:269(Mary Snow). EDSON FAMILY HISTORY AND GENEALOGY, Carroll Andrew Edson, Ann Arbor MI, p. 249.

NOTE: No proof found for dau. Eunice as stated in EDSON GEN. She is unlikely. She might be a dau. of Seth Snow #206.

208 MARY SNOW[5] (William[4-3], Rebecca[2] Brown, Peter[1]) b. Bridgewater 12 Aug. 1731; d. there Dec. 1811 ae 79 (wife of Lt. Samuel).

She m. Bridgewater 11 May 1758 SAMUEL DUNBAR, b. Bridgewater 8 March 1736/7; d. there 14 Oct. 1814 as Lt. ae 78; son of Samuel and Melatiah (Hayward) Dunbar, a descendant of Pilgrim Richard Warren.

No Plymouth Co. PR for Samuel or Mary Dunbar or meaningful LR.

Children (DUNBAR) b. Bridgewater:

i ELIJAH[6] b. 23 April 1759
ii OLIVER b. 20 Jan. 1761; d. 12 Oct. 1776 in 16th yr.
iii LEMUEL b. 9 March 1763
iv SAMUEL b. 13 June 1765; d. 28 Sept. 1776 in 14th yr.
v ALPHEUS b. 28 Feb. 1769; d. 25 Sept. 1770 in 2nd yr.

References: VR BRIDGEWATER 1:92-6(b. Samuel; b. ch.); 2:116 m.), 459-60(deaths). BRIDGEWATER BY MITCHELL pp. 150-1.

209 BETTY SNOW[5] (Eleazer[4], William[3], Rebecca[2] Brown, Peter[1]) b. Bridgewater 9 March 1729; d. after 22 Dec. 1768.

She m. (1) Bridgewater 31 Dec. 1750 NATHAN AMES, b. Bridgewater 4 July 1722; d. there 13 March 1756; son of Thomas and Mary (Hayward) Ames.

She m. (2) Bridgewater 29 Sept. 1757 WILLIAM TOLMAN, b. Dorchester 12 Aug. 1719; bur. Bridgewater or Sharon 3 Aug. 1763; son of Samuel and Experience (Clapp) Tolman. He m. (1) Sharon 1 Nov. 1744 Mary Savel, who d. 3 July 1755, by whom he had

William, Mary, Experience, Elizabeth, and Samuel.
She m. (3) Bridgewater 22 Dec. 1768 MICAH WHITE, b.
Braintree 10 Dec. 1721; d. Bridgewater 11 March 1805 ae 86; son
of Thomas and Mary (Bowditch) White. He m. (1) Weymouth 10
Sept. 1746 Susanna Eager/Ager by whom he had Susanna, Lot,
Susanna, Micah, Ebenezer, Hannah, and Rebecca.

The will of Nathan Ames of Bridgewater, yeoman, dated 12
March 1756, presented April 1756, names brother Joseph Ames of
Bridgewater exec.; wife Betty; son Nathan under 21; dau. Sarah
Ames; my mother Mary Ames.

Micah White was 1-0-2 in the 1790 census of Bridgewater.

On 6 May 1805 administration of the estate of Micah White
of Bridgewater, yeoman, was granted to Micah White of
Randolph, Norfolk Co.

No Plymouth Co. PR for William Tolman or Betty White.

Children (AMES) by first m. b. Bridgewater:

   i   SARAH[6] b. 7 Jan. 1752
  ii   NATHAN b. 24 Nov. 1753

Children (TOLMAN) by second m. b. Sharon:

  iii   DANIEL b. 1759; bp. Sharon 3 Feb. 1760
  iv   REUBEN b. ca. 1761

Child (WHITE):

  v   (?) BETSY

References: VR BRIDGEWATER 1:34(b. Nathan; son Nathan),
           35(b. Sarah); 2:33(1st m.), 372(2nd m.), 397(3rd m.),
431(d. Nathan), 565(d. William), 577(d. Micah). VR SHARON pp.
141(William's 1st m.), 190(d. William). VR WEYMOUTH 2:214
(Micah's 1st m.). Plymouth Co. PR 14:342(Nathan Ames); 39:7;
40:504 (Micah White). BRIDGEWATER BY MITCHELL pp. 101,
315, 332, 351. Plymouth Co. PR 14:342(Nathan Ames).
BRAINTREE RECS p. 709(b. Micah). Genealogies of the Families
of Braintree MA 1640-1850, Waldo C. Sprague (microfilm), card
5468 R(Micah White). DORCHESTER VR 1:66(b. Wm. Tolman).

NOTE: Waldo Sprague lists a possible dau. Betsy for Micah & Betty.

210 REUBEN SNOW[5] (Eleazer[4], William[3], Rebecca[2] Brown, Peter[1]) b. Bridgewater 16 April 1731; d. Mansfield 1 Sept. 1817 in 87th yr.
He m. Bridgewater 5 May 1768 HANNAH WILLIS, b. Bridgewater 15 June 1748; d. Mansfield 20 Oct. 1821 in 75th yr.; dau. of Stoughton and Hannah (Harlow) Willis, a descendant of Pilgrims Isaac Allerton and Richard Warren.
Reuben Snow of Mansfield, yeoman, bought land and dwelling house in Easton from heirs of Phinehas Briggs of Norton 7 April 1773.
Reuben Snow was 2-3-3 in 1790 census of Manfield.
The will of Reuben Snow of Mansfield, yeoman, dated 20 Aug. 1811, presented 4 Nov. 1817, names wife Hannah; sons Reuben, Simeon, Levi; dau. Rhoda "singlewoman" and son Asahel (exec.).

Children (SNOW) first b. Bridgewater, others b. Mansfield:

    i   RHODA[6] b. 20 March 1769; unm. 20 Aug. 1811 (will)
   ii   REUBEN b. 6 Aug. 1771
  iii   ASAHEL b. 4 Nov. 1774
  iv   SIMEON b. 4 Oct. 1777
   v   LEVI b. 7 Aug. 1784

References: MD 36:31(Bible rec.). VR BRIDGEWATER 1:303(b. Rhoda), 352(b. Hannah); 2:350(m.). VR MANSFIELD pp. 58(b. Reuben, Asahel, Simeon, Levi), 217(d. Reuben, Hannah). BRIDGEWATER BY MITCHELL p. 317. Bristol Co. LR 54:153(Reuben Snow). Bristol Co. PR 55:272 (Reuben Snow).

211 ELEAZAR SNOW[5] (Eleazer[4], William[3], Rebecca[2] Brown, Peter[1]) b. Bridgewater 30 Oct. 1734; d. there 1 Feb. 1797 in 64th yr.
He m. Bridgewater 13 Jan. 1757 MARY WOOD, b. Bridgewater Oct. 1735; d. Brockton 18 Feb. 1824 ae 90; dau. of

John and Priscilla (_____) Wood.

The will of Eleazer Snow of Bridgewater, gentleman, dated 6 Jan. 1797, proved 5 June 1797, names wife Mary; sons Eleazer and Jonathan to have land; son Silas to have homestead farm; daus. Mary, wife of Seth Snow, Jr.; Priscilla, wife of Simeon Snow; Sarah, wife of Ezekiel Merritt; Mercy, wife of Nathaniel Willmarth; Betty Snow; Zerviah Snow; and Phebe Snow.

Children (SNOW) b. Bridgewater:

i	MARY[6] b. 25 Oct. 1757	
ii	ELEAZAR b. 8 April 1759	
iii	PRISCILLA b. 12 April 1761	
iv	JONATHAN b. ca. 1763 (d. Brockton 11 Aug. 1838 in 75th yr.)	
v	BETTY (named in will)	
vi	SARAH (named in will)	
vii	ZERVIAH (named in will)	
viii	MERCY (named in will)	
ix	PHEBE (named in will)	
x	SILAS b. 7 May 1776	

References: VR BRIDGEWATER 1:301-3(b. 1st 3 ch.), 358(b. Mary); 2:347(m.), 558(d. Eleazer). VR BROCKTON p. 361(deaths). BRIDGEWATER BY MITCHELL p. 372. Plymouth Co. PR 36:169(Eleazer Snow).

212 MERCY SNOW[5] (Eleazer[4], William[3], Rebecca[2] Brown, Peter[1]) b. Bridgewater 22 March 1737; d. Sharon 16 July 1829 in 94th yr.; "widow of Elijah."

She m. (1) Bridgewater 28 Feb. 1760 JACOB JOHNSON of Stoughton, b. Hingham 31 Jan. 1734/5; d. Sharon 1 April 1777 ae 43; son of Joshua and Lydia (Ward) Johnson.

She m. (2) Sharon 22 May 1789 ELIJAH CAPEN, bp. Dorchester 7 June 1724; d. by 29 Oct. 1802; son of Preserved Capen. He m. (1) Sharon 2 Sept. 1743 Elizabeth Bird by whom he had Elijah, Damaris, Mary, Elijah, Sarah, Sarah, Samuel, and Eunice.

On 6 June 1777 Mercy Johnson, widow, and Elijah Hewins were appointed to administer the estate of Jacob Johnson of

Stoughtonham.

On 29 May 1778 Job Swift as named guardian for Oliver, Jacob, David, and Mercy Johnson, children of Jacob Johnson.

On 24 Sept. 1788, ack. 28 Oct. 1791, Job Swift of Fairlee, Orange Co., VT, husbandman, appointed Job Swift of Sharon, Suffolk Co., yeoman, power of attorney regarding his being guardian of heirs of Jacob Johnson late of Sharon.

Elijah Capen is apparently the man of that name in Sharon 26 April 1801 who was incapable of caring for himself. A guardian was appointed and the inventory was approved 3 Nov. 1801. The account of 5 March 1805 includes expenditures for him up to 29 Oct. 1802. On 5 May 1801 John Morse was appointed guardian for Elijah Capon of Sharon who was non compos mentis. The inventory of his estate was sworn 12 Nov. 1801.

Children (JOHNSON) b. Sharon except Jacob:

i	OLIVER[6] bp. 20 July 1761
ii	JACOB b. Stoughton 17 Dec. 1763
iii	DAVID b. 21 July 1766
iv	MERCY bp. 2 Aug. 1773

References: VR BRIDGEWATER 2:203(1st m.). VR SHARON pp. 41(b. David), 42(bp. Massa), 43(bp. Oliver), 81(2nd m.; 1st m. Elijah). STOUGHTON VR pp. 93(b. son Jacob), 173(1st m. int.). Suffolk Co. PR 76:161(Jacob Johnson); 77:660-1(guardianships). HINGHAM HIST 2:386(b. Jacob). DORCHESTER CH RECS (bp. Elijah). Norfolk Co. PR #3148; 7:259, 342; 11:265(Elijah Capon). SHARON EPITAPHS, William Mann, Boston, 1908, p. 112(d. Jacob). THE CAPEN FAMILY, Rev. Charles A. Hayden, Minneapolis, Minn., 1919, p. 50(Capen children).

213 DANIEL SNOW[5] (Eleazer[4], William[3], Rebecca[2] Brown, Peter[1]) b. Bridgewater 30 April 1742; d. Readfield ME bef. 21 April 1818 ae 77.

He m. Bridgewater 19 April 1764 HANNAH DUNBAR, b. Bridgewater 17 Oct. 1743; d. there 15 Sept. 1812; dau. of Samuel and Melatiah (Hayward) Dunbar, a descendant of Pilgrim Richard Warren. The will of Samuel Dunbar of Bridgewater, yeoman, dated 4 May 1780, names granddau. Sarah Snow.

Sarah Snow and Azel Snow were appointed administrators of the estate of Daniel Snow late of Readfield. The account of his estate made by "Sarah Hill late Sarah Snow" on 29 Feb. 1820 mentions a journey to Bridgewater to get some of the estate appraised.

No Plymouth Co. PR for Hannah Snow.

Children (SNOW) b. Bridgewater:

i	HANNAH[6]	b. 24 April 1765
ii	DANIEL	b. 18 Feb. 1767
iii	SYLVIA	b. 31 March 1769; d. 6 April 1814. No PR.
iv	SARAH	b. 27 April 1771; d. 14 Jan. 1779
v	MELATIAH	b. 14 March 1773; d. 24 Sept. 1775
vi	NATHAN	b. 22 Aug. 1776
vii	CYRUS	b. 15 Aug. 1778
viii	SARAH	b. 13 June 1780
ix	MELATIAH	b. 3 Aug. 1782

References: VR BRIDGEWATER 1:93(b. Hannah), 300-4(b. ch.); 2:347(m.), 559(d. Hannah; d. ch.). VR WEST BRIDGEWATER p. 217(d. Melatiah, Sarah). BRIDGEWATER BY MITCHELL p. 150. Kennebec Co. ME PR(Daniel Snow). Plymouth Co. PR 29:519-521(Samuel Dunbar). New Bedford Mercury Obits p. 312(d. Daniel).

NOTE: "Daniel Snow late Bridgewater 77 at Reedfield Mass. P.I. May 1818." (New Bedford Mercury Obits p. 312).

214 SARAH SNOW[5] (John[4], William[3], Rebecca[2] Brown, Peter[1]) b. Bridgewater 23 March 1758; living 15 Nov. 1826 (brother John's will).

She m. Bridgewater 8 April 1794 DANIEL TOMSON, b. Halifax 24 Oct. 1750; living 7 May 1794; son of Jacob and Mary (Howard) Tomson, a descendant of Pilgrims Peter Brown and Francis Cooke (see #166).

On 7 May 1794 Daniel Tomson of Bridgewater on behalf of wife Sarah, dau. of John Snow of Bridgewater, dec. petitioned to be appointed administrator of the estate of John Snow.

The will of her brother John Snow (#215) dated 15 Nov. 1826, mentions sister Sarah Thompson.

No known children.

References: VR BRIDGEWATER 2:367(m.). Plymouth Co. PR #18688 (John Snow); 70:500(brother John Snow). HALIFAX VR p. 51(b. Daniel).

215 JOHN SNOW[5] (John[4], William[3], Rebecca[2] Brown, Peter[1]) b. Bridgewater 4 Jan. 1762; d. there 12 Oct. 1831 in his 70th yr.

He m. (1) Bridgewater 5 May 1784 MARY AMES, b. Bridgewater 8 Oct. 1756; d. there 12 Feb. 1819; dau. of James and Betty (Ames) Ames. On 5 Jan. 1789 a committee was to view the property of James Ames of Bridgewater, yeoman, dec. and divide it bet. the widow and Mary Snow the wife of John Snow the only child and heir of James Ames.

He m. (2) Bridgewater 4 June 1821 HANNAH (HAYWARD) PERKINS, b. Bridgewater 15 Nov. 1770; living 15 Nov. 1826; dau. of Edmund and Anna (Snell) Hayward. She m. (1) int. Bridgewater 5 July 1794 Nathaniel Perkins.

The will of John Snow of West Bridgewater, yeoman, dated 15 Nov. 1826, presented 5 Dec. 1831, names wife Hannah; sons David, John Jr., George; dau. Sally Dunbar, wife of William; grandson Charles Snow, son of Charles dec.; dau. Lucy Randall, wife of Benjamin; sister Sarah Thompson to have a room in my house; son David exec.

No Plymouth Co. PR for Mary Snow.

Children (SNOW) b. Bridgewater:

i	DAVID[6] b. 6 April 1785
ii	JOHN b. 11 Aug. 1787
iii	SARAH b. 27 July 1789
iv	CHARLES b. 24 July 1791
v	GEORGE b. 1 June 1794
vi	LUCY b. 22 Feb. 1798

References: VR BRIDGEWATER 1:34(b. Mary), 147(b. Hannah), 300-4(b. ch.); 2:292(int. Hannah's 1st m.), 348(1st m.), 349(2nd m.), 559(d. Mary). BRIDGEWATER BY MITCHELL pp. 101, 317. Plymouth Co. PR 31:4-5(James Ames); 70:500 (John Snow). BRIDGEWATER EPITAPHS p. 13(d. John).

216 JOSEPH SNOW[5] (Joseph[4-3], Rebecca[2] Brown, Peter[1]) b. Bridgewater 26 March 1715; d. Providence RI 10 April 1803 in 89th yr. and 58th of his ministry.

He m. (1) Providence RI 1 Nov. 1737 SARAH FIELD, b. Providence RI 9 Aug. 1710; d. there 19 July 1753 ae 42y 11m; dau. of Zachariah and Abigail (_____) Field.

He m. (2) Boston 14 March 1754 REBECCA GRANT, b. ca. 1726; d. Providence RI 30 Sept. 1774 ae 48y.

He m. (3) Providence RI 24 Oct. 1775 MARGARET PROCTOR, b. ca. 1734; prob. the one b. Boston 25 Sept. 1734; dau. of Benjamin and Margaret (Langden) Proctor; d. Attleboro 21 April 1817 in 83rd yr.

In a series of deeds Joseph Snow of Providence, clerk, deeded land to his children. To dau. Rebecca & son-in-law James Munro of Providence on 26 Nov. 1773; to son Josiah Snow of Providence, housewright, on 28 Dec. 1773 and 12 Oct. 1775; to son Joseph Snow of Providence, merchant, on 26 Nov. 1773; to son Samuel Snow of Providence 28 Aug. 1775.

Joseph Snow became insolvent in 1791 and there is no probate.

Children (SNOW) 9 by 1st wife, rest by 2nd, b. Providence RI:

i	SARAH[6] b. 27 Oct. 1738; d. there 23 April 1752 ae 13y 5m 26d
ii	JOHN b. 3 Feb. 1740
iii	JOSEPH b. 22 Sept. 1741; d. 10 Oct. 1741 ae 7d
iv	JOSEPH b. 2 Sept. 1742
v	LYDIA b. 8 Jan. 1744; d. 22 March 1763
vi	SUSANNAH b. 14 Oct. 1745; d. 21 March 1766
vii	ELIZABETH b. 10 Oct. 1747
viii	ABIGAIL b. 26 March 1749; d. 10 Aug. 1752 ae 3y 4m 15d
ix	JOSIAH b. 24 Feb. 1750
x	REBECCA b. 13 Feb. 1756
xi	SAMUEL b. 1 Aug. 1758

xii   EDWARD b. 9 May 1760; d. Providence 27 March
        1772 ae 13y
xiii   BENJAMIN b. 6 Dec. 1761

References: RIVR Providence 2:1:174(all 3 m.), 246(b. ch.), 274(d.
          Sarah, Lydia, Susanna); 14:291(d. Joseph, Margaret,
Edward). BOSTON NEWS OBITS 3:391(d. Rebecca, Edward).
Benns Grave Records 4:65(d. Sarah; dau. Sarah, Abigail), 66(d. son
Joseph). BOSTON VR 24:218(b. Margaret). Providence RI LE
20:160(to Rebecca), 218(to Josiah), 336(to Joseph), 338(to Josiah),
534(to Samuel); 22:618, 620(insolvent).

217 ELIZABETH SNOW[5] (Joseph[4-3], Rebecca[2] Brown, Peter[1]) b.
Bridgewater 4 May 1719; d. Providence RI 18 Dec. 1750 ae 31y 7m
14d.
        She m. (1) Providence RI 12 Jan. 1735/6 JOHN FIELD, b. ca.
1708; d. St. Eustatius, West Indies 5 April 1738; son of Zachariah
and Abigail (_____) Field.
        She m. (2) Providence RI 13 Sept. 1743 EZRA DEAN, b.
Plainfield CT 18 Nov. 1718; d. Pawtuxet, Cranston RI 14 Dec.
1806 in 89th yr.; son of Jonathan and Sarah (Olcott) (Douglas)
Dean. He m. (1) Joanna Fellows by whom he had Jonathan. He
m. (3) Rebecca _____ by whom he had Elizabeth, Alma, Sarah,
William, Ruth and apparently others who d.y. He m. (4)
Providence RI 20 April 1774 Phebe (Aborn) Waterman.
        On 8 Nov. 1731 John Field late of Bridgewater now resident
in Providence sold land in Bridgewater.
        Elizabeth Field, widow of Capt. John Field of Providence,
mariner, who d. 5 April 1738 intestate, was appointed
administratrix 15 July 1738.
        Ezra Dean rendered account of the administration of his
wife Elizabeth who was the widow and administratrix of her
former husband John Field, late of Providence, mariner, on 24
Dec. 1744.
        On 1 May 1748 Anna, James and Sybil the children of Ezra
Dean were bp. at Plainfield CT.
        On 3 Feb. 1753 Ezra Dean of Providence, blacksmith, sold
land in Providence to Peter Cook; wife Rebekah signed and
acknowledged.
        Ezra Dean appeared on the tax rolls of East Greenwich RI

from 1754 to 1771.

On 3 Oct. 1776 Ezra Dean of West Greenwich, yeoman, sold land in West Greenwich to Jonathan Dean; wife Phebe signed and acknowledged.

On 9 Jan. 1807, by recommendation of the majority of the heirs, Capt. Joshua Davis of North Kingstown was appointed to administer the estate of Capt. Ezra Dean of Cranston, but he declined and David Martin of Providence was appointed administrator. No accounting or distribution.

Child (FIELD) b. Providence RI:

    i   JOHN[6] bp. ca. 1738; apparently d.y. as not named in will of his grandfather Joseph Snow (#55).

Children (DEAN) b. perhaps Providence RI but bp. Plainfield CT:

    ii   ANNA b. 1744; prob. d.y.
    iii JAMES b. 1746; lost at sea; unm. (according to Dean Gen.)
    iv SYBIL b. 1747

References: RIVR Providence 2:1:56(2nd m.), 70(1st m.), 174(m.), 266(d. John); 10:204(4th m.); 13:328(d. Ezra). FIELD GENEALOGY, Frederick Clifton Pierce, Chicago IL 1901, pp. 174, 240. Town of Providence RI Will book 3:334; 4:149. WEYBOSSET BRIDGE IN PROVIDENCE PLANTATIONS 1700-1790, Arthur E. Wilson, Boston 1947, p. 74(bp. son John). Benns Grave Records 4:82(d. Elizabeth). Plainfield CT VR 1:23(b. Ezra). TAG 57:48. Plymouth Co. LR 29:74 (John Field). NEHGR 70:179(bp. 3 ch.). GENEALOGY OF THE DEAN FAMILY, Arthur D. Dean, Scranton PA, 1903, pp. 46-60. Providence RI LE 13:165 (Ezra Dean). East Greenwich RI Tax Lists. West Greenwich RI LR 7:187(Ezra Dean). Cranston RI PR 2:4, 6(Ezra Dean).

NOTE: The Mayflower Society has accepted a line through a dau. Elizabeth Dean. According to one account dau. Elizabeth was born in 1752 which would be 2 yrs. after Elizabeth died.

218 SUSANNA SNOW[5] (Joseph[4-3], Rebecca[2] Brown, Peter[1]) b. Bridgewater 12 Dec. 1722; d. Providence RI 18 Feb. 1743 ae 22y 2m 6d.

She m. Providence RI 19 March 1740/1 MATTHEW SHORT, b. Biddleford ME 20 April 1719; son of Matthew and Margaret (Freeman) Short.

On 29 Jan. 1741/2 Mathew Short of Providence RI, blacksmith, sold to Joseph Snow of Providence 5/11 of real estate of his father Mathew Short late of Easton, dec.

Apparently no surviving children, as they are not named in her father's will.

References: RIVR Providence 2:1:174(m.). Benns Grave Records 4:82(d. Susanna). ME NH GEN DICT p. 632. Bristol Co. LR 33:126(Matthew Short).

219 DANIEL SNOW[5] (Joseph[4-3], Rebecca[2] Brown, Peter[1]) bp. W. Bridgewater 12 Nov. 1727; d. Providence RI 17 Nov. 1784 "in his 58th yr., leaves a wife and six children."

He m. (1) Providence RI 6 Feb. 1748/9 ELIZABETH SEARLE; dau. of Solomon and Elizabeth (Gladding) Searle.

He m. (2) Providence RI 11 Jan. 1767 SARAH SEARLE, b. ca. 1737; d. Providence RI 8 July 1821 in 85th yr.; dau. of Solomon and Elizabeth (Gladding) Searle.

Daniel Snow 1-0-1-3 in 1774 census of Providence RI.

In the 1782 census of Providence RI Daniel Snow had one male under 16; 6 females under 16; 2 females 22 to 50 and one male over 50.

On 10 Nov. 1784 Daniel Snow of Providence, mason, sold land in Providence to Joseph Snow of Providence, clerk; wife Sarah released her dower.

The will of Daniel Snow of Providence (no date recorded in rec. book), proved 6 Dec. 1784, gives his son Daniel his land and rest of estate to be equally divided among "all my children"; daus. Elizabeth, Susana, Lydia, Rebecca, and Sarah; with son Daniel. Execs. may sell part of real estate "for the better bringing up or education of" the children. Wife Sarah and brother Joseph Snow executors.

On 2 March 1801 William Richmond, guardian to Daniel Snow 2nd of Providence, petitioned to sell real estate of the late

Daniel Snow to pay debts. Also Sarah Snow, Elizabeth Sampson, Walter Paine, William Richmond guardian to Daniel Snow, Sally Snow and Rebecca Snow petitioned to have dower set off to Sarah Snow, widow of Daniel and divided among the rest of the heirs, of which Susanna Snow, since Susannah Crapon, dec., which Susanna died without issue, was one.

Sarah Snow, widow of Daniel Snow, late of Providence dec. petitioned for dower; John Perin and Lamuel Jackson 2nd, gdns. of Daniel Snow were cited in the matter 29 July 1811.

Children (SNOW) b. Providence RI:

i	ELIZABETH[6]
ii	SUSANNA
iii	LYDIA
iv	DANIEL b. 23 Nov. 1774
v	REBECCA
vi	SARAH (or SALLY) b. ca. 1781

References: RIVR Providence 2:1:174(m.); 14:291(d. Daniel), 292(d. Sarah); 15:555. Town of Providence RI will books 6:422:3(Daniel Snow). Providence RI LE 21:173 (Daniel Snow). Probate Proceeding Book 1:102; 2:111; 13:35; 21:303. Oakland RI Cem. Recs. NEHGR 127:305(1782 census).

220 JAMES SNOW[5] (Joseph[4-3], Rebecca[2] Brown, Peter[1]) b. Easton 30 Dec. 1730; d. Providence RI 8 Oct. 1812 in 82nd yr.

He m. Providence RI 26 March 1755 HANNAH SEARLE, b. ca. 1733; d. Providence RI 14 Nov. 1823 in 91st yr.; dau. of Solomon and Elizabeth (Gladding) Searle.

James Snow was a Deacon.

On 21 June 1786 James Snow of Providence gave land in Providence to dau. Mary Wardwell, wife of Stephen Wardwell of Providence, baker.

On 28 Dec. 1812 Hannah Snow, widow of James Snow, late of Providence, dec., requested that her son John Snow be appointed administrator of the estate of James Snow.

Edward Snow of Tiverton, merchant, mortgaged to Stephen Wardwell of Providence his right, title and interest in land belonging to his father James Snow, late of Providence, gent. 11

Feb. 1813.

On 12 July 1815 John Snow, administrator of the estate of James Snow, late of Providence, Esq. dec., conveyed to Stephen Wardwell, highest bidder at auction, land of the late James Snow.

Daniel Snow and John Snow, both yeomen of Providence, sold to Stephen Wardwell 2/7 of a piece of Providence land as heirs of their father dec., with wives Hannah and Hannah releasing dower 14 Feb. 1824.

James Snow, yeoman of Providence, sold to Stephen Wardwell of Providence 1/7 of a piece of land as heir of father James Snow, with wife Rachel releasing her dower 27 March 1824.

William D. Snow, Hannah Snow, Henry Greene and his wife Ann, and Joseph Snow, all of Providence, children of Joseph Snow, son of James Snow, late of Providence, dec. and heirs of said James, sold land to Stephen Wardwell 17 Feb. 1824.

Children (SNOW) b. Providence RI:

i   JAMES[6] b. ca. 1756; (d. there 13 Sept. 1825 in 70th yr.)

ii   DANIEL b. 1758 (Rev. War Pension)

iii   JOHN

iv   MARY

v   JOSEPH b. ca. 1765

vi   SALLY b. ca. 1767 (d. 27 June 1793 in 27th yr.; unm.)

vii   HANNAH (as dau. of Capt. James Snow m. 1794 Jonathan Crapon)

viii EDWARD b. ca. 1778; (d. Smithfield RI 2 May 1829 in 52nd yr.)

References: RIVR Providence 2:1:174(m.). RIVR 13:35(d. Hannah); 14:291(d. James), 292(d. Hannah); 15:349(m. Hannah); 19:141(d. Hannah). Providence RI Probate Proceeding Book 2:207-8(James Snow). Providence RI LE 21:405(to Mary); 37:56(John Snow); 47:265(William D. Snow etc.), 302(James Snow). Rev. War Pension S 21989(son Daniel Snow). Benns Grave Records 4:82(d. James, Hannah, son James, Sally). RIVR Bristol 6:1:48(par. of Hannah). Plymouth Co. PR #18684(James Snow).

221 RUTH SNOW[5] (James[4], Joseph[3] Rebecca[2] Brown, Peter[1]) b. Bridgewater 12 May 1720; d. Cornwall CT 4 June 1789.

She m. Bridgewater 20 April 1739 PEREZ BONNEY, b. Pembroke 10 March 1709; d. Goshen or Cornwall CT 9 or 29 May 1792; son of John and Elizabeth (Bishop) Bonney.

On 10 March 1760 Perez Bonney of Pembroke, yeoman, sold land to Ichabod Bonney and two lots to David Magoon.

The will of Peres Bonney of Goshen CT dated 12? June 1787, sworn 6 July 1792, names 4 sons Peres, Titus, Jairus and Asa to have all his estate in Cornwall, Goshen, etc. Son Joel to have 30 pounds if he shall see cause to come for it. Dau. Celia (no last name) to have room in the house if she never marries.

Children (BONNEY) b. Pembroke:

    i   JOEL[6] b. 14 Aug. 1740
   ii   PEREZ b. 13 July 1742
  iii   TITUS b. 1 June 1744
   iv   CELIA b. 16 April 1746; unm. in 1787
    v   JARVIS (or JAIRUS) b. 14 Feb. 1747
   vi   ASA b. 6 Sept. 1751

References: VR PEMBROKE pp. 38-45(b. Perez; b. ch.), 243(m.). VR WEST BRIDGEWATER p. 124(m.). BRIDGEWATER BY MITCHELL p. 316. Litchfield CT PR #858(Perez Bonney). A HISTORY OF CORNWALL CT, Edward C. Starr 1926 p. 436. (PLYMOUTH) ANC LANDMARKS 2:38(Eliz. Bishop m. Bonney). Plymouth Co. LR 50:101; 51:160(Perez Bonney).

222 MARY SNOW[5] (James[4], Joseph[3], Rebecca[2] Brown, Peter[1]) b. Bridgewater 28 Feb. 1724.

She m. bef. 19 March 1760 _____ FOSTER who has not been identified. (date of father's will).

223 NATHAN SNOW[5] (James[4], Joseph[3], Rebecca[2] Brown, Peter[1]) b. Bridgewater 9 July 1725; d. Plainfield 2 Aug. 1803 ae 78.

He m. Abington 20 Oct. 1748 MARY MANSFIELD, b. ca. 1729; d. Plainfield 22 Feb. 1810 ae 81; prob. dau. of Thomas & Mary (Ward) Mansfield.

Nathan Snow moved to Cummington about 1778.

The 1790 census of Cummington lists Nathan Snow, Nathan Snow Jr., and Jacob Snow.

On 1 June 1798, ack. 1 Aug. 1803, Nathan Snow of Cummington, gentleman, with the assent of his wife Mary, sold 39 acres in Cummington to Beriah Shaw.

No Hampshire Co. PR for Nathan Snow.

Children (SNOW) b. Abington:

i	NATHAN[6] b. 10 May 1751
ii	MARY b. 9 Dec. 1752
iii	ABIJAH b. 15 Dec. 1754
iv	JOHN b. 2 June 1757
v	JACOB b. 12 April 1759
vi	SUSANNAH b. 2 Jan. 1762
vii	SARAH b. 7 Feb. 1764
viii	CALVIN b. 26 Jan. 1766
ix	HANNAH bp. 22 May 1768

References: VR ABINGTON 1:213-4(b. ch.); 2:196(m.). BRIDGEWATER BY MITCHELL p. 316. Rev. War Pension S 14538(Jacob Snow). CUMMINGTON VR p. 249(census), xiii (move). Plainfield Church Records(d. Nathan, Mary). Hampshire Co. LR 20:696(Nathan Snow). HINGHAM HIST 3:51 (parents of Mary).

NOTE: The Ruth, d. Nath. Snow bp. Abington 30 Oct. 1774, may be another child.

224 ABIGAIL SNOW[5] (James[4], Joseph[3], Rebecca[2] Brown, Peter[1]) b. Bridgewater 27 May 1727; d. East Bridgewater 2 May 1810 a 83.

She m. (1) East Bridgewater 27 Nov. 1746 JOHN EGERTON, b. Halifax 24 April 1721; d. East Bridgewater 3 Jan. 1779 ae 58; son of Dennis and Experience (_____) Egerton.

She m. (2) Bridgewater 7 Nov. 1780 JONATHAN BEAL, b. Bridgewater 10 Dec. 1730; d. East Bridgewater 24 Aug. 1813 ae 83; son of Samuel and Mary (Bassett) Beal. He m. (1) Bridgewater 11 July 1751 Abigail Harlow who d. Bridgewater 26 Aug. 1779 by whom he had Joseph, Azariah, Nabby, Jonathan, Hannah,

Hannah, and Molly.

The will of Jonathan Beal of Bridgewater, yeoman, dated 9 Dec. 1809, presented 6 Sept. 1813, names wife Abigail who is to have support from portion given to my granddau. Nabby and the furniture she brought with her; son Joseph; 2nd son Azariah; son Jonathan; dau. Hannah, wife of Noah Hill; granddau. Nabby, dau. of Josiah Hill or if she does not survive to my dau. Nabby, wife of Josiah Hill. Josiah Hill was named exec.

No Plymouth Co. PR for John Egerton or Abigail Beal.

Children (EGERTON) by 1st m., b. East Bridgewater:

i	RUTH[6] bp. 8 Nov. 1747
ii	JOHN bp. 18 Nov. 1750
iii	JAMES bp. 25 March 1753
iv	WILLIAM bp. 20 April 1755; d.y.
v	JOSEPH bp. 25 April 1756; d. New York July or Aug. 1776 "belonging to the Continental Army."
vi	WILLIAM bp. 7 May 1758; d. East Bridgewater 9 March 1777 ae 19
vii	ABIGAIL bp. 28 Dec. 1760
viii	BENJAMIN bp. 20 March 1763
ix	HANNAH bp. 9 June 1765

References: VR BRIDGEWATER 1:47(b. Jonathan); 2:47(2nd m.; Jonathan's 1st m.). VR EAST BRIDGEWATER pp. 50(bp. ch.), 167(2nd m.), 202(1st m.), 337(d. Abigail, Jonathan), 350(d. John, Joseph, William). HALIFAX VR p. 47(b. John). BRIDGEWATER BY MITCHELL pp. 114, 160, 316. Plymouth Co. PR 45:84(Jonathan Beal).

225 SUSANNA SNOW[5] (James[4], Joseph[3], Rebecca[2] Brown, Peter[1]) b. Bridgewater 15 Feb. 1729; d. Springfield 7 Sept. 1761.

She m. Bridgewater 29 Sept. 1747 ABIJAH EDSON, bp. Bridgewater 31 Oct. 1725; d. Valley Forge PA 15 April 1778 age 52; son of Timothy and Mary (Alden) Edson; a descendant of Pilgrim John Alden. He m. (2) Hardwick 10 June 1762 Hannah Ruggles by whom he had Cushman, Nathaniel, Susanna, and Timothy Alden.

On 3 Sept. 1753 Timothy Edson gave 50 acres of land on the

West side of the Willamatic River to his son Abijah Edson.

On 20 Feb. 1772 Abijah Edson of Springfield, potter, bought land in Springfield from Nathaniel Church Jr. of Brattleboro VT.

No CT PR or Hampden or Hampshire Co. PR for Abijah or Susanna Edson.

Children (EDSON) first b. East Bridgewater, last b. Springfield, rest b. Stafford CT:

    i   ABIJAH[6] b. 10 April 1748
    ii   NATHAN b. 11 April 1750
   iii SAMUEL b. 25 March 1752
   iv JOSEPH b. ca. 1755; d. 2 Oct. 1777 in the Army
         vMARY b. 10 April 1757
   vi JAMES b. 19 April 1759
  vii SUSANNAH bp. 30 Sept. 1761; d. Springfield 1 Oct. 1761

References: VR BRIDGEWATER 2:121(m.). VR EAST BRIDGEWATER p. 48(bp. Abijah, son Abijah). VR HARDWICK pp. 39 (ch. by Hannah), 169(2nd m.). Stafford CT VR 2:346(Timothy Edson). EDSON FAMILY HISTORY AND GENEALOGY, Carroll Andrew Edson, ed. Ann Arbor MI 1970, pp. 86-7. Hampden Co. LR 10:602(Abijah Edson). Springfield First Church records pp. 13(bp. Susanna), 45(d. wife Susanna & dau. Susanna).

226 SARAH SNOW[5] (James[4], Joseph[3], Rebecca[2] Brown, Peter[1]) b. Bridgewater 6 April 1732; d. East Bridgewater 6 Sept. 1807.

She m. Bridgewater 18 Dec. 1751 BENJAMIN HARRIS, b. Bridgewater 30 Sept. 1731; d. East Bridgewater 13 Jan. 1803 ae 71; son of Arthur and Mehitable (Rickard) Harris, a descendant of Pilgrims Peter Brown, James Chilton, Francis Cooke, and Stephen Hopkins.

See #276 for details of this family.

References: VR BRIDGEWATER 1:132(b. Benjamin); 2:159(m.). VR EAST BRIDGEWATER pp. 355(d. Benjamin), 356(d. Sarah). MF 15:78.

227 JOHN SNOW[5] (James[4], Joseph[3], Rebecca[2] Brown, Peter[1]) b. Bridgewater 31 March 1736; d. Saybrook CT 7 July 1808 ae 72.

He m. Lyme CT 31 March 1763 HEPZIBAH HALL, b. Lyme CT 11 Dec. 1746; living 4 March 1809; dau. of Isaac and Sarah (Gates) Hall. The will of Isaac Hall dated 26 July 1778, proved 2 Sept. 1778, names among others dau. Hepzibah Snow.

John Snow of Lyme, New London Co. CT, refiner, sold to Nathaniel Lowden of Duxbury land in Bridgewater 5 Dec. 1763, ack. same day. On 19 June 1768 John and Hepzibah Snow received the covenant at the First Church, Lyme CT. As dau. Sarah was bp. at the First Church, Killingworth on 2 Oct. 1768, it would seem they moved to Killingworth between those dates. All the later children were bp. at the Killingworth Church. John Snow of Killingworth sold land to David LeBarron 12 March 1771. John Snow of Killingworth sold property in Killingworth to Elnathan Stevens 25 March 1771. John Snow of Killingworth bought land of Aaron Elliott April 1771.

On 23 April 1793 John Snow of Killingworth sold 3 acres in Killingworth to [son] William Snow. Witnesses included Abel and Rufus Snow.

On 6 Sept. 1808 John Snow of Saybrook was appointed administrator of the estate of John Snow of Saybrook. The estate was insolvent, but on 4 March 1809, the widow received payment for household furniture. Amounts were owed to James Snow, Arthur Snow, Luther Snow, and others.

Children (SNOW) first 3 b. Lyme; rest b. Killingworth CT:

i	JAMES[6] b. 29 April 1763 [sic]; d.y.
ii	WILLIAM b. 24 Aug. 1765
iii	SARAH b. 14 Sept. 1767
iv	JOHN b. 25 July 1769
v	MARY b. Aug. 1771
vi	ABEL b. 24 May 1773
vii	RUFUS b. 1 Dec. 1774; d. 6 July 1794 ae 19
viii	ARTHUR b. 20 March 1777
ix	LUTHER b. 26 May 1780
x	HEPHZIBAH b. 20 May 1782
xi	JAMES bp. 31 July 1785
xii	HEMAN bp. 8 June 1788

References: LYME CT VR p. 11(b. Hepzibah).   CT MARR 3:137.
              Killingworth CT LR 11:19, 61, 359; 14:229(John
Snow). Killingworth CT VR 2:124(b. 10 ch.). Plymouth Co. LR
51:242(John Snow).   Lyme CT PR, New London District #2373,
filed 1778(Isaac Hall).   First Church Lyme records 2:11(bp. James,
Wm.), 34(m.); 3:11(joined church).   First Church Killingworth
records 2:41(bp. Sarah), 42(bp. John), 43(bp. Mary, Abel), 57(bp.
Hephzibah), 73(bp. Rufus), 74(bp. Arthur), 76 (bp. Luther), 79(bp.
James), 82(bp. Heman), 108(d. Rufus).   SAYBROOK CT VR p.
574(d. John).   Saybrook CT PR #2161 (John Snow).

228 HOPESTILL WADE[5] (Rebecca Snow[4], Joseph[3], Rebecca[2]
Brown, Peter[1]) b. Bridgewater 13 June 1725; d. Stafford CT 3 Sept.
1749.
      She m. Bridgewater 25 Sept. 1748 ZEPHANIAH ALDEN, b.
Bridgewater 13 June 1724; d. prob. Stafford CT bef. 6 Feb. 1801;
son of Daniel and Abigail (Shaw) Alden, a descendant of Pilgrim
John Alden. He m. (2) Stafford CT 19 July 1750 Hannah Foster,
a descendant of Pilgrim Myles Standish. He m. (3) Stafford CT 8
April 1778 Ann Dimmock.
      The will of Zephaniah Alden of Stafford, County of
Tolland, dated 2 Feb. 1796, proved 6 Feb. 1801, names wife Ann;
the heirs of his brother Joseph Alden, the heirs of his brother
Daniel Alden; the heirs of his sister Abigail Whitman; his sister
Hannah Blodget; his nephew Zephaniah Alden and his nephew
Abishai, son of his brother Joseph Alden.
      No known children.

References: VR BRIDGEWATER 1:26(b. Zephaniah); 2:25(m.).
              Stafford CT VR 1:25(2nd m.), 45(d. Hopestill);
2:130(3rd m.). FOSTER GEN 1:141, 143. BRIDGEWATER BY
MITCHELL p. 319. Stafford CT PR #28 (Zephaniah Alden).

229 KEZIAH WADE[5] (Rebecca Snow[4], Joseph[3], Rebecca[2] Brown,
Peter[1]) b. Bridgewater 18 Oct. 1729; d. West Bridgewater 28 Nov.
1789 in 61st yr.
      She m. Bridgewater 6 March 1750/1 JOB PACKARD, b.
Bridgewater 5 June 1716; d. West Bridgewater 18 Oct. 1805 in 89th
yr.; son of Samuel and Elizabeth (Edson) Packard. He m. (1)

Rachel _____ by whom he had Job in 1749.

Job Packard, gentleman of Bridgewater, sold to Elijah Packard of Bridgewater gent. land in Bridgewater with wife Keziah releasing dower, signed 30 March 1764, ack. 13 April 1764.

Job Packard of Bridgewater gave to Josiah Snell of Bridgewater, gentleman, land Job bought, signed and ack. by Job 3 March 1788, also signed by Keziah.

No Plymouth Co. PR for Job or Keziah Packard.

No known children.

References: VR BRIDGEWATER 1:243(b. Job); 2:277(m.). VR WEST BRIDGEWATER p. 211(d. Job, Keziah). BRIDGEWATER BY MITCHELL pp. 264, 266, 335. Plymouth Co. LR 49:107; 68:69 (Job Packard).

230 DAVID WADE[5] (Rebecca Snow[4], Joseph[3], Rebecca[2] Brown, Peter[1]) b. Bridgewater 14 March 1732; d. after 26 March 1795; prob. bef. 1800 (not in census).

He m. Bridgewater 9 Sept. 1756 MARY LITTLEFIELD, b. Bridgewater 30 Sept. 1734; d. Easton 19 July 1818 age 84; dau. of Daniel and Rebecca (Williams) Littlefield.

David Wade of Bridgewater, yeoman, sold to Joseph Hayward of Bridgewater 9 acres in Easton with wife Mary giving up dower, signed 11 Jan. 1773; ack. by both 12 Feb. 1773.

David Wade of Easton, housewright, sold to Elijah Copeland of Easton 7 1/2 acres of land in Easton, signed 28 Oct. 1778 by David and Mary Wade; he ack. 9 Dec. 1778.

David Wade of Bridgewater, housewright, bought two pieces of land in Easton (72 acres) 23 March 1778.

David Wade of Easton, housewright, sold to Joseph Howard of Bridgewater 13 acres in Easton 13 March 1784 with wife Mary releasing dower; David ack. 15 March 1784.

David Wade was a Corporal in the Rev. War.

David Wade was 1-1-5 in 1790 census of Easton.

On 25 March 1795, ack. next day, David Wade of Easton, housewright, sold 22 acres in Easton to son David Wade Jr. of Easton.

No Bristol or Plymouth Co. PR for David Wade.

Children (WADE) b. Bridgewater:

    i   REBECCA[6] b. 2 July 1757
    ii   RHODA b. 3 July 1759; d. Bridgewater 17 Jan. 1761
    iii   SILENCE b. 9 July 1762
    iv   THOMAS b. 18 June 1764; d. Bridgewater 14 March 1768 in 4th yr.
    v   DAVID b. 20 Sept. 1766
    vi   THOMAS b. 15 Oct. 1769
    vii KEZIAH b. 4 June 1772
   viii MARY b. 1 July 1775

References: VR BRIDGEWATER 1:220(b. Mary), 301-4(b. ch.); 2:378(m.), 568(d. Rhoda, Thomas).   VR WEST BRIDGEWATER pp. 174(m.), 219(d. Thomas). BRIDGEWATER BY MITCHELL pp. 248, 336. EASTON HIST p. 670. Bristol Co. LR 61:530; 62:285, 286; 78:549(David Wade).   DAR PATRIOT INDEX p. 708. Easton Death Records at NEHGS SL/EAS/2 lb p. 67(d. Mary).

231 REBECCA WADE[5] (Rebeccah Snow[4], Joseph[3], Rebecca[2] Brown, Peter[1]) b. Bridgewater 29 July 1734; d. Stoughton 12 May 1806 ae 71.

    She m. Bridgewater 24 Nov. 1757 ELISHA DUNBAR, b. Bridgewater 18 June 1735; d. Stoughton 11 April 1798 ae 63; son of Elisha and Mercy (Hayward) Dunbar, a descendant of Pilgrim Richard Warren.

    Keziah and Rebecca, children of Elisha Dunbar, were bp. in the Fourth Church of Christ of Bridgewater [now in Brockton] 4 Oct. 1767.

    Elisha Dunbar was 1-0-2 in the 1790 census of Stoughton.

    No Plymouth Co. PR for Elisha or Rebecca Dunbar.   No Suffolk or Norfolk Co. PR for Elisha Dunbar.   No Plymouth Co. PR or deed selling land of her father Thomas Wade or indicating move to Stoughton.

Children (DUNBAR) b. Bridgewater:

    i   KEZIAH[6] b. 16 March 1762; d. Stoughton 17 Sept.

1818 ae 56; unm.

ii   REBECCA   b. 24 Feb. 1764

References: VR BRIDGEWATER 1:93(b. Elisha), 94(b. Keziah), 95(b. Rebecca); 2:114(m.). VR BROCKTON pp. 43(bp. Keziah), 44(bp. Rebecca). BRIDGEWATER BY MITCHELL pp. 150, 335. NEHGR 128:283(deaths).

232 HANNAH SNOW[5] (Isaac[4], Joseph[3], Rebecca[2] Brown, Peter[1]) b. Bridgewater 14 Nov. 1723; d. after 3 Aug. 1767.

She m. Bridgewater 25 Oct. 1759 JOSEPH ROBINSON, b. ca. 1722; d. East Bridgewater 11 April 1766 in 47th yr.; son of Gain and Margaret (Watson) Robinson. He m. (1) East Bridgewater 10 Oct. 1746 Abigail Keith; dau. of Joseph and Susanna Keith who d. East Bridgewater 27 Nov. 1757 by whom he had Joseph, Benjamin, Edward, Susanna, and Abigail.

Hannah Robinson of Bridgewater, widow, posted bond on the estate of Joseph Robinson, late of Bridgewater dec., blacksmith, on 21 May 1766 with sureties James and Alexander Robinson and Ephraim Spooner.

The account of James Robinson and Hannah Robinson, administrators on the estate of Joseph Robinson late of Bridgewater, includes setting off the widow's dower dated 3 Aug. 1767.

No Plymouth Co. PR for Hannah Robinson or LR for Joseph or Hannah Robinson.

Children (ROBINSON) b. East Bridgewater:

i   ISAAC[6] b. 23 June 1760; lost at sea. No PR.
ii   HANNAH b. 16 March 1763; d. in 1803; unm. No PR.
iii   SNOW b. 8 May 1765; d. West Point NY 1783 ae 19

References: VR BRIDGEWATER 1:281(b. ch.); 2:327(m.). VR EAST BRIDGEWATER pp. 117(bp. ch.), 386(d. Joseph, Snow). BRIDGEWATER BY MITCHELL pp. 300, 316. ROBINSON GENEALOGY, DESCENDANTS OF GAIN AND MOSES ROBINSON, Vol. II, p. 50. Plymouth Co. PR #17116; 19:494(Joseph Robinson).

233   ISAAC SNOW[5] (Isaac[4], Joseph[3], Rebecca[2] Brown, Peter[1]) b. Bridgewater 16 Feb. 1726; d. Haverhill bet. 12 March 1789 & 4 May 1789.

He m. (1) Bridgewater 8 Sept. 1748 ELIZABETH BOWDITCH (BONDAGE (BONDAGE in VR) b. Braintree 7 March 1724; d. Haverhill 4 Nov. 1783; dau. of John and Mary (Hersey) Bowditch.

He m. (2) Haverhill 7 July 1785 HANNAH HUNKINS, b. Haverhill 13 Oct. 1739; living 12 March 1789; dau. of Robert and Hannah (Muzzey) Hunkins.

The will of Isaac Snow of Haverhill, blacksmith, dated 12 March 1789, proved 4 May 1789, names wife Hannah; children: Mary, wife of Jonathan Kimball; Elizabeth, wife of Thomas Hall; Hannah, wife of William Sawyer; James Snow; Sarah, wife of Richard Kimball; Joseph Snow; grandson James, son of dau. Judith Kimball dec.; grandson Isaac Snow, son of Isaac dec.; and Susannah Snow.

Children (SNOW) first b. East Bridgewater, rest b. Haverhill:

i	MARY[6]	bp. 16 July 1749
ii	ELIZABETH	b. 9 April 1751
iii	HANNAH	b. 31 March 1753
iv	ISAAC	b. 17 Nov. 1754; d. 31 March 1756
v	JAMES	b. 21 Sept. 1756
vi	ISAAC	b. 14 April 1758; d. 25 April 1759
vii	SARAH	b. 14 Dec. 1759
viii	JOSEPH	b. 1 Sept. 1761; d. 18 June 1791 ae 29
ix	JUDITH	b. 23 April 1763
x	ISAAC	b. 21 March 1765
xi	SUSANNA	b. 16 Feb. 1767

References: VR BRIDGEWATER 2:348(2nd m.).   VR EAST BRIDGEWATER   p.   125(bp.   Mary).   VR HAVERHILL   1:179(b.   Hannah),   281-2(b.   ch.);   2:294(m.), 475(deaths). BRIDGEWATER BY MITCHELL pp. 119, 317. Essex Co. PR #25822(Isaac Snow). NEHGR 79:180. BRAINTREE RECS p. 754(b. Elizabeth).

234   MARTHA SNOW[5] (Isaac[4], Joseph[3], Rebecca[2] Brown, Peter[1]) b. Bridgewater 15 Nov. 1728; d. East Bridgewater 30 Aug. 1781.

She m. Bridgewater 16 March 1749/50 Capt. SIMEON WHITMAN, b. Bridgewater 9 Sept. 1728; d. there 31 Oct. 1811 ae 83; son of Thomas and Jemima (Alden) Whitman, a descendant of Pilgrim John Alden. He m. (2) Bridgewater 6 Nov. 1783 Sarah (Vinal) Byram, widow of Seth Byram.

Simeon Whitman was a Sgt. in Rev. War.

On 4 Nov. 1811 Sarah Whitman waived right to administer the estate of her late husband Simeon Whitman dec. Isaac Whitman, gentleman, administrator with William Michell of Bridgewater and Aaron Hobart of Abington, Esq., posted bond on 4 Nov. 1811 on estate of Simeon Whitman late of Bridgewater, gentleman, dec. Dower set off to widow Sarah Whitman 3 Dec. 1811.

No Plymouth Co. PR for Martha Whitman.

Children (WHITMAN) b. Bridgewater:

i	ISAAC[6] b. 25 Sept. 1750
ii	SIMEON b. 26 Jan. 1753
iii	THOMAS b. 6 June 1755
iv	JOSEPH b. 31 Dec. 1757
v	MARTHA b. 3 Nov. 1760
vi	SYLVIA bp. East Bridgewater 14 April 1765; d. 6 Dec. 1808 ae 44; unm.
vii	HULDAH bp. East Bridgewater 11 June 1769

References: VR BRIDGEWATER 1:342-4(b. Simeon; b. 1st 5 ch.); 2:402(m.), 579(d. Simeon). VR EAST BRIDGEWATER pp. 142(bp. Huldah), 145(bp. Sylvia), 401(d. Sylvia), 402(d. Martha). BRIDGEWATER BY MITCHELL p. 316. BRIDGEWATER EPITAPHS pp. 204, 205. DAR PATRIOT INDEX p. 739. Plymouth Co. PR #22793 (Simeon Whitman). MD 32:158(d. Martha).

235 PETER SNOW[5] (Isaac[4], Joseph[3], Rebecca[2] Brown, Peter[1]) b. Bridgewater 25 July 1731; d. Crown Point NY in 1760.

He m. ca. 1754 EUNICE ATHERTON apparently the one b. Lancaster 20 Jan. or 28 Nov. 1733; d. Harvard 17 Dec. 1767; dau. of Benjamin and Eunice (_____) Atherton. She m. (2) Harvard

18 Jan. 1762 John Farwell by whom she had Eunice.

On 18 July 1760 Eunice Snow, widow, Nathaniel Whittemore and Oliver Atherton, yeomen, all of Harvard, posted bond for Eunice Snow to administer the estate of her husband Peter Snow late of Harvard, axsmith, dec.

An account of the estate was rendered by John Farwell and Eunice his wife, formerly Eunice Snow on 20 Sept. 1762.

On 8 April 1768 Mr. Oliver Atherton was appointed guardian to Peter Snow only child of Peter Snow dec., "whereas ye within named Eunice dyed ye 17th Day of Decmr 1767." Oliver Atherton was an uncle of Peter Snow.

No Plymouth Co. LR for Peter Snow.

Children (SNOW) b. Harvard:

    i   JUDITH[6] b. 17 Dec. 1755; d. there 12 Oct. 1756 ae
         10m
   ii   PETER b. 9 Sept. 1759

References: VR HARVARD pp. 96(b. Judith, Peter), 214(her 2nd m.), 267(d. Eunice), 304(d. Judith).   VR LANCASTER p. 49(b. Eunice).   Worcester Co. PR A54946, A54947(Peter Snow).

236 JUDITH SNOW[5] (Isaac[4], Joseph[3], Rebecca[2] Brown, Peter[1]) b. Bridgewater 7 Dec. 1736; d. Hartland, Windsor Co. VT 26 May 1807.

She m. Bridgewater 20 April 1756 JOHN BARRELL, bp. Scituate 31 March 1734; d. Hartland, Windsor Co. VT 20 July 1804; son of William and Abigail (Bowker) Barrell.

On 1 Dec. 1760, ack. 20 May 1761 by John, John Barrell of Bridgewater, cordwainer, sold to Colbun Barrell of Scituate, shop joyner, all his housing and land where he dwells in Bridgewater, signed by John and Judith.

On 14 May 1765 John Barrell, wife Judith, ch. Mary and Judith and Simon Prouty, servant from Bridgewater were warned from Harvard.

On 19 Aug. 1765, ack. 28 Nov. 1765, John Barrell of Harvard sold his house lot in Harvard.

On 14 Oct. 1765 John Barrell of Harvard, Worcester Co.,

cordwainer, sold land in Bridgewater to Nathan Whitman.

On 1 Nov. 1765, ack. 24 Feb. 1766, John Barrell of Harvard, cordwainer, sold property in Harvard to Joseph Wilder of Lancaster.

On 24 June 1777 John Barrell of Hartford [VT] bought 50 acres in Hartland from Nathaniel Killam.

John Barrell was 1-0-2 in the 1790 census of Springfield Town VT.

No Hartland VT LR for John Barrell selling land there.

No Windsor Co. VT PR for John Barrell.

Children (BARRELL) first 3 b. Bridgewater:
    i   MOLLY (or MARY)[6] b. 1 Oct. 1757
    ii   JOHN b. 11 March 1760; prob. the John who d. Bridgewater 7 March 1762 as he is not in warning.
    iii   JUDITH bp. E. Bridgewater 1 May 1763
    iv   NABBY (or ABIGAIL) b. Harvard 19 Feb. 1765
    v   JOHN b. 1766 (based on age at d.)
    vi   EDMUND b. ca. 1768*

References: VR BRIDGEWATER 1:39(b. Molly, John); 2:40(m.), 434(d. John). VR EAST BRIDGEWATER p. 19(bp. Judith). VR HARVARD p. 15(b. Nabby). VR SCITUATE 1:24(bp. John). Plymouth Co. LR 47:16; 51:75(John Barrell). Worcester Co. LR 55:312, 331(John Barrell). WORCESTER CO MA WARNINGS 1737-1788, Worcester MA, 1899 p. 21. Hartland VT VR 2:81(d. Judith, John). Hartland VT LR 2:54(Nath. Killam). Walker Cem. Rec., Hartland VT(d. John).

*Edmund Barrell mar. Olive Buck in Hartland VT 9 Aug. 1789 (VR 4:34) and is surely a son.

237 SAMUEL SNOW[5] (Jonathan[4] Joseph[3], Rebecca[2] Brown, Peter[1]) b. Bridgewater 20 Sept. 1729; d. Middleboro 22 June 1781 in 51st yr.

He m. Middleboro 8 Dec. 1763 JEDIDIAH BUMPAS (the mar. rec. calls him Samuel Shaw), b. Middleboro 11 Sept. 1742; d. there 26 Dec. 1838 ae 96 yrs.; dau. of Joseph and Mehitable (Tupper) Bumpas.

In the Sept. 1752 Court; Deborah Tinkham, "singlewoman"

charged Samuel Snow of Middleboro, labourer, as being the father of her child born on the tenth day of May last.

On 9 March 1756 Mehitable Bumpas, widow of Middleboro, posted bond as guardian of minor dau. Jedidiah, dau. of Joseph Bumpas, late of Middleboro dec.

Samuel and Jedidiah Snow sold to Joseph Bumpas on 8 March 1767 land set out to Jedidiah in the division of the estate of James Bumpas. This would be Jedidiah's part of the property left to the four children of "cousin" Joseph Bumpas dec. by James Bumpas in 1750.

No Plymouth Co. PR for Samuel Snow.

Child (SNOW) by Deborah Tinkham, b. Middleboro:

    i   SAMUEL[6] b. 10 May 1752 (VR says 10 May 1753)

Children (SNOW) b. Middleboro:

    ii   MOSES b. 1 Sept. 1764
    iii   AARON b. 7 June 1767
    iv   LAVINIA b. 22 Feb. 1770
    v   EZEKIAL b. 31 May 1772
    vi   DANIEL b. 3 July 1774
    vii   JANE d. 21 Aug. 1778, ae 1y 8m

References: MD 15:7(d. Samuel, Jane); 22:147(b. Jedidiah); 24:185(m.); 32:9(b. 1st 5 ch. by Jedidiah). MIDDLEBORO DEATHS pp. 166-7. MF 3:181. TAG 43:72, 216. Plymouth Co. LR 60:1(Samuel Snow). Plymouth Co. PR #3265(Bond of Mehitable Bumpas). PLYMOUTH CO CT RECS 3:30. MIDDLEBORO VR 1:114(b. of ch. Sam.), 130(b. Jedidiah), 154(m.), 203(b. 1st 4 ch.), 204(b. Daniel).

238 JESSE SNOW[5] (Jonathan[4], Joseph[3], Rebecca[2] Brown, Peter[1]) b. Bridgewater 8 Feb. 1730/1; d. Hardwick June 1825 ae 96y.

He m. Middleboro 19 May 1757 MARY EATON, b. Middleboro 14 May 1735; d. Hardwick 5 Feb. 1813 in her 78th yr.; dau. of Barnabas and Mehitabel (Alden) Eaton, a descendant of Pilgrims John Alden, John Billington, Francis Eaton, and Samuel Fuller.

On 27 Dec. 1769 Jesse Snow of Middleboro, husbandman, sold to Isaiah Keith of Bridgewater land in the 16 Shilling Purchase in Middleboro with wife Mary Snow giving up dower.

In April 1771 Jesse Snow of Hardwick, husbandman, attached Henry Leonard Jr. of Middleboro for trespass on note.

Jesse Snow was a Pvt. in the Rev. War.

Jesse Snow was 3-1-3 in the 1790 census of Hardwick.

On 21 Oct. 1790 Barnabas Eaton deeded land to "my six daughters" including Mary but did not give their last names.

On 8 March 1805 and 9 April 1811 Jesse Snow sold tracts of land in Hardwick to Apollos Snow. These deeds were not recorded until 9 April 1827 after Jesse died.

No Worcester Co. PR for Jesse Snow.

Children (SNOW) first 6 b. Middleboro; last 2 b. Hardwick:

i	SARAH[6] b. 20 March 1758
ii	BETHANIAH b. 6 Sept. 1760
iii	LAVINIA b. 9 April 1762
iv	SALOME b. 27 April 1764
v	APOLLOS b. 28 May 1767
vi	REBECKAH b. 16 May 1769
vii	JESSE b. 29 Sept. 1771
viii	MARY b. 7 March 1775

References: MD 19:176(b. Sarah); 12:152(b. Bethaniah), 153(b. Lavinia); 24:131(m.). VR HARDWICK pp. 105(b. last 2 ch.), 324(d. Jesse, Mary). MF 9:57-8; 21:53-4. DAR PATRIOT INDEX p. 631. Plymouth Co. LR 58:188(Jesse Snow). PLYMOUTH CO CT RECS 8:364. MIDDLEBORO VR 1:65(b. Mary), 125(b. Sarah), 136(b. Bethania, Lavinia), 151(m.). Worcester Co. LR 255:271, 276 (Jesse Snow).

239 SARAH SNOW[5] (Jonathan[4], Joseph[3], Rebecca[2] Brown, Peter[1]) b. Bridgewater 3 Dec. 1732; d. there 5 March 1758.

She m. Bridgewater 15 Nov. 1753 NATHANIEL PACKARD, b. Bridgewater 2 Aug. 1730; d. Lebanon NH bet. 30 April 1806 (will) and 4 Oct. 1814(probate); son of Zachariah and Abigail (Davenport) Packard. He m. (2) Bridgewater 17 Oct. 1758 Anna Slone by whom he had David, Sarah, Zechariah, Nathaniel,

William, Absolom, Barnabas, Abigail, and Betty.

Nathaniel Packard of Bridgewater, gentleman, sold to Oakes Angier land in Bridgewater with wife Anna releasing dower, signed 25 April 1785.

The will of Nathaniel Packard of Lebanon, Grafton Co. NH dated 30 April 1806, proved 4 Oct. 1814, names wife Anna; sons David and William; sons Zadoc, Ichabod, Nathaniel, Absolom; Hannah dau. of son Barnabas late of Bridgewater; dau. Abigail, wife of Frederick Cook; dau. Sarah, wife of Andrew Belcher; dau. Betty; Nathaniel son of dau. Sarah Belcher; and Anna Trufrell(?) dau. of said Betty.

Children (PACKARD) b. Bridgewater: (rest of ch. are by Anna)

i   ZADOK[6] b. 22 Sept. 1755
ii   ICHABOD b. 22 Aug. 1757

References: VR BRIDGEWATER 1:242(b. Ichabod), 246(b. Nathaniel), 250(b. Zadok); 2:280(m.; 2nd m.),534(d. Sarah). VR WEST BRIDGEWATER pp. 84(bp. Ichabod), 86(bp. Zadoc). BRIDGEWATER BY MITCHELL pp. 266, 270, 316. Plymouth Co. LR 64:58(Nathaniel Packard). Grafton Co. NH PR 3:152 (Nathaniel Packard). MF 3:182.

240 REBECCA SNOW[5] (Jonathan[4], Joseph[3], Rebecca[2] Brown, Peter[1]) b. Bridgewater 16 Oct. 1734; d. Middleboro 27 Aug. 1766 in 32nd yr.

She m. Halifax 19 May 1761 FRANCIS TOMSON, b. Halifax 15 March 1734/5; d. Middleboro 17 Dec. 1798 ae 63y 9m 2d; son of Thomas and Martha (Soule) Tomson; a descendant of Pilgrims Peter Brown, Francis Cooke, and George Soule.

See #160 for an account of this family.

References: HALIFAX VR pp. 31(m.), 46(b. Francis). MIDDLEBORO VR p. 195(d. Francis, Rebecca).

241 JONATHAN SNOW[5] (Jonathan[4], Joseph[3], Rebecca[2] Brown, Peter[1]) b. Bridgewater 10 March 1735/6; d. Brookfield 27 July 1822 "h. Betty."

He m. Bridgewater 8 Dec. 1761 BETTY PACKARD; d.

Brookfield 2 June 1816 "w. Jonathan."

On 30 March 1767 Jonathan Snow of Bridgewater, Plymouth Co. purchased land in Brookfield.

Ebenezer Vaughan of Middleboro attached Jonathan Snow of Brookfield, yeoman, on note dated 23 Dec. 1782.

Jonathan Snow was 1-0-4 in 1790 census of Brookfield so he probably had daus.

On 26 Nov. 1791 Jonathan Snow of Brookfield sold land to Jonathan Snow Jr. of Brookfield.

On 26 Nov. 1791 Jonathan Snow Jr. of Brookfield leased to Jonathan Snow of Brookfield, one half of all land conveyed to him by deed.

On 13 Aug. 1798 Jonathan Snow Jr. of Brookfield sold to Dwight Foster, Esq. land in Brookfield "which I hold by deed from my father Mr. Jonathan Snow of said Brookfield which deed is dated 26 Nov. 1791."

No Worcester Co. PR for Jonathan Snow.

Children (SNOW):

    i   JONATHAN[6] b. prob. Bridgewater 1762-1765 as he m. in 1790. In 1800 he was bet. 26 & 45; in 1810 over 45.

    ii   SUSANNA b. Brookfield 26 Sept. 1769*

References: VR BRIDGEWATER 2:349(m.). VR BROOKFIELD pp. 531(d. Betty), 532(d. Jonathan). Worcester Co. LR 56:259; 113:219(Jonathan Snow); 112:515; 133:550(Jonathan Snow Jr.). PLYMOUTH CO CT RECS 10:53.

*The death record of Susanna (Snow) Davis says she was born 26 Sept. 1769; died Warren 4 Dec. 1848, widow of Timothy Davis and dau. of Jonathan Snow (Mass. Deaths 41:339). Susanna married Timothy Davis 11 Oct. 1789 in Brookfield (VR p. 411).

NOTE: Jonathan is not the father of Rebecca Snow who was bapt. Hardwick in 1771, as stated in MF 3. Her parents were Jonathan and Mercy (Wing) Snow, a descendant of Pilgrim Stephen Hopkins.

242   RUTH SNOW[5] (Jonathan[4], Joseph[3], Rebecca[2] Brown, Peter[1])
b. Bridgewater ca. 1747; living 4 April 1793.
    She m. Middleboro 3 Dec. 1772 JOSHUA REED, b.
Middleboro 10 June 1745; living 4 April 1793; son of William and
Elizabeth (_____) Reed.
    Joshua Reed of Middleboro sold to brother Samuel Reed of
Middleboro his share of estate of his father William Reed, late of
Middleboro, signed 30 May 1782, wife Ruth quitclaimed her
dower, he ack. 23 Oct. 1783.
    Joshua Reed of Middleboro, joyner, sold to Samuel Reed of
Middleboro land in Middleboro which Samuel Bennett late of
Middleboro gave his dau. Eleanor Whitman bounded by land
Samuel Bennett gave his dau. Ruth Snow by his will, signed 23
May 1775 with wife Ruth giving up her dower; ack. by Joshua
Reed 30 Sept. 1776.
    Joshua Reed was 2-6-5 in the 1790 census of Middleboro.
    Joshua Reed of Middleboro, housewright, and wife Ruth
sold to Jesse Bryant of Middleboro the homestead where they
dwelt 4 April 1793, ack. same day.
    No Plymouth Co. PR for Joshua Reed.

    Children (REED) b. Middleboro:

        i   DARIUS[6] b. 14 Jan. 1774
        ii   LEVI b. 3 March 1775
        iii   JONAH b. 3 Jan. 1777
        iv   SARAH (twin) b. 3 Feb. 1779
        v   NOAH (twin) b. 3 Feb. 1779
        vi   DELIVERANCE b. 8 April 1781
        vii   WILLIAM b. 8 April 1783
        viii RUTH (twin) b. 5 April 1785
        ix   BETTY (twin) b. 5 April 1785
        x   JOSHUA b. 16 Feb. 1787
        xi   GEORGE b. 17 Sept. 1788

References: MD 17:21(b. Joshua); 33:39(b. ch.). MA MARR 2:79
          (Joshua Reed, Ruth Snow 2d). Plymouth Co. LR
67:82; 74:148(Joshua Reed). MIDDLEBORO VR 1:103(b. Joshua);
2:1(b. all ch.).

243   JOSEPH SNOW[5] (David[4], Joseph[3], Rebecca[2] Brown, Peter[1])
b. Bridgewater 27 June 1734; living 22 Nov. 1793.
      He m. (1) Bridgewater 7 Feb. 1759 RUTH SHAW, b.
Bridgewater 29 Jan. 1738; d. bef. 1 Dec. 1796; dau. of Zachariah
and Sarah (Packard) Shaw; a descendant of Pilgrim James Chilton.
The will of Zacharias Shaw of Bridgewater dated 5 April 1776
names wife Ruth, dau. Ruth Snow and others.
      He m. (2) Brookfield 1 Dec. 1796 RACHEL GILBERT; b. ca.
1708; d. Brookfield 1 May 1816 a 89 "mother of Joseph" (no doubt
meaning step-mother).
      On 22 Nov. 1793 Nathan Allen Jr. of Brookfield, gentleman,
sold land to Joseph Snow of Bridgewater, yeoman.
      No Worcester Co. PR for Joseph Snow.

      Children (SNOW) b. Bridgewater:

      i   SARAH[6] b. 8 Oct. 1759
      ii   DAVID b. 21 June 1761
      iii   DANIEL b. 27 Aug. 1763
      iv   RUTH b. 10 Nov. 1767; [sic] d. 10 Nov. 1769(bp. W.
             Bridgewater 17 Nov. 1765).
      v   MEHITABEL   b. 26 Nov. 1769 [sic] (bp. W.
             Bridgewater 29 Nov. 1767)
      vi   JOSEPH b. 2 May 1770 [sic] (bp. W. Bridgewater 3
             May 1772)
      vii   RUTH b. 26 Dec. 1770 [sic]; (bp. W. Bridgewater
             18 March 1770); d. there 8 Sept. 1844 ae 74y 8m
             14d; unm. No PR.
      viii   MOSES b. 5 June 1775

References: VR BRIDGEWATER 1:289(b. Ruth), 301-3(b. ch.);
             2:349(1st m.), 559(d. 1st dau. Ruth).   VR
BROOKFIELD pp. 411(2nd m.), 532(d. Rachel).   VR WEST
BRIDGEWATER pp. 99-100(bp. ch.), 217(d. 2nd dau. Ruth).
BRIDGEWATER BY MITCHELL pp. 305, 317. Worcester Co. LR
121:175(Nathan Allen Jr.). Plymouth Co. PR 31:115-6(Zacharias
Shaw).

244   JOANNA SNOW[5] (David[4], Joseph[3], Rebecca[2] Brown, Peter[1])
b. Bridgewater 27 Nov. 1735; d. East Bridgewater 23 Dec. 1802.

She m. Bridgewater 29 March 1759 NATHANIEL EDSON, b. Bridgewater 5 May 1728; d. there 19 March 1784 ae 56; son of Samuel and Mehitable (Brett) Edson.

Nathaniel Edson was a Deacon of the First Church of East Bridgewater.

The order to divide the estate of Nathaniel Edson late of Bridgewater, yeoman, gave widow Joanna her dower and divided the rest into 8 parts: 2 to eldest son Joel; one each to Mehitable, Eunice, Joanna, Lydia, Huldah and Nathaniel, all Edsons.

On 5 Oct. 1830 the probate court of East Bridgewater declared both Mehitable Edson and Lydia Edson non compos mentis.

Children (EDSON) b. Bridgewater:

i MEHITABLE[6] b. 24 Sept. 1760; prob. d. East Bridgewater Poor House in 1839 ae 78

ii JOEL b. 4 March 1763

iii EUNICE b. 4 April 1765

iv JOANNA b. 18 July 1767; d. West Bridgewater 27 Jan. 1846 ae 79y 6m; unm. No PR.

v NATHANIEL b. 4 Aug. 1769; d. 4 Oct. 1770

vi LYDIA b. 23 Sept. 1771; perhaps the Lydia Edson who d. East Bridgewater 21 June 1845 ae 75.

vii HULDAH b. 29 Aug. 1774; d. East Bridgewater 28 Feb. 1793 in 19th yr.

viii NATHANIEL b. 9 May 1777

References: VR BRIDGEWATER 1:101-5(b. ch.), 105(b. Nathaniel); 2:125(m.), 465(d. Nathaniel, son Nathaniel). VR EAST BRIDGEWATER p. 350(d. Joanna, daus.). VR WEST BRIDGEWATER p. 193(d. Joanna). BRIDGEWATER BY MITCHELL pp. 158, 316. EDSON FAMILY HISTORY AND GENEALOGY, Carroll Andrew Edson ed., Ann Arbor MI 1970? p. 85. Plymouth Co. PR 29:496(Nathaniel Edson); 69:389(Mehitable & Lydia Edson). MD 32:158(d. Nathaniel).

245 LYDIA SNOW[5] (David[4], Joseph[3], Rebecca[2] Brown, Peter[1]) b. Bridgewater 16 Feb. 1740; d. there 25 April 1771 ae 31 in childbirth.

She m. Bridgewater 11 Nov. 1764 JOHN WHITMAN, b. Bridgewater 17 March 1735; d. there 26 July 1842 ae 107y 3m 22d; son of John and Elizabeth (Cary) Whitman, a descendant of Pilgrim Myles Standish. He m. (2) Bridgewater 5 Aug. 1773 Abigail Whitman by whom he had Catherine, Bathsheba, Josiah, Alfred, Obediah, Nathaniel, Hosea, John, Abigail, Barnard, and Jason.

John Whitman was a Deacon and a Lt. in the Rev. War.

The will of John Whitman of Bridgewater "having arrived to a great age" dated 27 Aug. 1829, presented last Tuesday of Aug. 1842, names dau. Bathshebe to have moveables, etc. during her single life; son Alfred all real estate including "half the farm on which he and I live"; son James; dau. Lydia's heirs; son Josiah; son Obediah; Nathaniel (not called son); son Hoseah; son Bernard; son Jason; exec. son Alfred.

Account of Edmund Whitman of Cambridge, Middlesex Co., administrator dated 5 Feb. 1846 says "all heirs have relinquished legacies except heirs of Lydia Whitman and widow of Bernard Whitman."

No Plymouth Co. PR for Lydia Whitman.

Children (WHITMAN) b. Bridgewater:

    i   LYDIA[6] b. 29 July 1765
    ii   ELIZABETH b. 24 April 1767
    iii   JAMES b. 4 Feb. 1769
    iv   child b. 1771; prob. d.y.

References: VR BRIDGEWATER 1:342(b. Elizabeth), 343(b. John, ch. James, Lydia); 2:400(m.; his 2nd m.), 579(d. Lydia). VR EAST BRIDGEWATER p. 400(d. John), 401(d. Lydia). BRIDGEWATER BY MITCHELL pp. 316, 357. BRIDGEWATER EPITAPHS p. 221. DAR PATRIOT INDEX p. 739. HISTORY OF THE DESCENDANTS OF JOHN WHITMAN OF WEYMOUTH, MASS., Charles H. Farnam, New Haven 1889, pp. 258-62. Plymouth Co. PR #22759(John Whitman). MF 14:139.

246 RHODA SNOW[5] (David[4], Joseph[3], Rebecca[2] Brown, Peter[1]) b. Bridgewater 7 Oct. 1742; d. East Bridgewater 25 Feb. 1796 in ye 54th yr. of her age.

She m. Bridgewater 1 Sept. 1768 EZRA WHITMAN, b.
Bridgewater 7 May 1747; d. East Bridgewater 16 Jan. 1814 ae 66;
son of John and Hannah (Shaw) (Snow) Whitman. He m. (2)
Bridgewater 7 Nov. 1796 Thankful Freelove.

On 25 Feb. 1769 Ezra Whitman and Rhoda Whitman of
Bridgewater sold to Joseph Snow of Bridgewater 9 acres which
their parents David and Joanna Snow had recently given them.

The will of Ezra Whitman of Bridgewater, housewright,
dated 28 Sept. 1813, presented 7 Feb. 1814, names wife Thankful;
son Ezra; dau. Hannah Hayward; son David Snow Whitman;
grandson Ezra son of son Ezra; dau. Rhoda Totman; grandson
Calvin Whitman Keen, son of dau. Hannah by her first husband
Josiah Keen; grandson Luther Whitman, son of son Ezra;
granddau. Hannah Shaw Keen, dau. of Hannah; 2 grandsons
Luther and Ezra Whitman; Alfred Whitman, son of his brother
John Whitman to be guardian to his grandsons Luther and Ezra
and also exec.

No Plymouth Co. PR for Rhoda Whitman.

Children (WHITMAN) b. Bridgewater:

  i   EZRA[6] b. 5 Oct. 1769
  ii HANNAH b. 5 Oct. 1771
  iii DAVID SNOW b. 14 May 1774
  iv CALVIN b. 5 Oct. 1777; d. Bridgewater 18 July
      1794 in ye 17 year of his age
  v   RHODA b. 12 Nov. 1779

References: VR BRIDGEWATER 1:341-4(b.Ezra; b.ch.); 2:400 (m.;
          his 2nd m.). VR EAST BRIDGEWATER p. 399(d.
Ezra, Calvin), 402(d. Rhoda). BRIDGEWATER BY MITCHELL
pp. 316, 354, 358. BRIDGEWATER EPITAPHS pp. 222-3.
Plymouth Co. PR 45:232(Ezra Whitman). Plymouth Co. LR
56:111(Ezra Whitman).

247 JEMIMA SNOW[5] (Benjamin[4-3], Rebecca[2] Brown, Peter[1]) b.
Bridgewater 5 Jan. 1723; d. there 8 April 1763.

She m. Bridgewater 4 Dec. 1745 ELIJAH LEACH, b.
Bridgewater 7 July 1726; prob. d. bet. 4 March 1774 and 12 Dec.

1778; son of Samuel and Content (_____) Leach. He m. (2) int. Bridgewater 1 Oct. 1763 Ruth Prince.

On 13 Feb. 1767 Elijah Leach Sr. sold 50 acres to John Packard.

The widow Content Leach, Elijah Leach and his wife Ruth and children Elijah Jr. and Jemima "all of Bridgewater" were warned out of Halifax 23 March 1767.

His son is called Elijah Leach Jr. in a 4 March 1774 deed involving the guardianship for two daus. of Ebenezer Leach Jr., implying that his father is still alive.

Elijah Leach (the son) and wife Ruth of Halifax sold to Chipman Fuller of Halifax land in Middleboro 12 Dec. 1778, ack. same day.

No Plymouth Co. PR for Elijah or Jemima Leach.

Children (LEACH) b. Bridgewater:

i	ELIJAH[6] b. 20 Sept. 1746
ii	JEMIMA b. 12 May 1749
iii	NATHANIEL b. 10 Feb. 1751; d. 2 May 1751
iv	BARZILLA b. 21 May 1753; d. 6 Dec. 1753
v	BARZILLA b. 16 July 1756; d. 5 Sept. 1756

References: VR BRIDGEWATER 1:206-10(b. Elijah; b. ch.); 2:235(m.), 513(b. sons Barzilla), 515(d. Nathaniel), 517(d. Jemima). BRIDGEWATER BY MITCHELL pp. 239, 316. Plymouth Co. LR 55:91; 59:60; 66:266(Elijah Leach). PLYMOUTH CO CT RECS 3:240.

NOTE: Mitchell p. 239 says he moved to Westmoreland. No NH PR or LR was found for Elijah Leach and it seems doubtful that he moved there.

248 BENJAMIN SNOW[5] (Benjamin[4-3], Rebecca[2] Brown, Peter[1]) b. Bridgewater 25 Aug. 1724; living 1 Sept. 1788.

He apparently m. Duxbury 17 Sept. 1756 MERCY WADSWORTH, b. ca. 1738; d. there 23 Feb. 1778 ae 51 (Mary, w. Benjamin in town records, but Mercy in church record).

Benjamin Snow of Duxbury, yeoman, sold land to Silvanus Prior of Duxbury 19 Aug. 1788, ack. 1 Sept. 1788.

No Plymouth Co. PR for Benjamin Snow.

Children (SNOW) b. Duxbury:

    i   JEMIMA[6] b. 4 Aug. 1758; d. Duxbury 9 Nov. 1781
         ae 23y 3m 3d. No PR.
    ii   BENJAMIN b. 16 April 1763
References: VR DUXBURY pp. 159(b. ch.), 309(m.), 420(d. dau.
    Jemima). Plymouth Co. LR 71:38(Benj. Snow).

NOTE: Mercy Wadsworth is not dau. of John and Mary (Alden)
Wadsworth.

249 DANIEL SNOW[5] (Benjamin[4-3], Rebecca[2] Brown, Peter[1]) b.
Bridgewater 26 July 1726; d. Keene NH 15 May 1806 ae 80 (as
Deacon Daniel Snow).
    He m. Bridgewater 1 Feb. 1753 ABIGAIL FOBES, b.
Bridgewater 2 April 1728; d. Keene NH 29 March 1805 ae 75; dau.
of Joshua and Abigail (Dunbar) Fobes, a descendant of Pilgrim
Richard Warren.
    On 2 Jan. 1772 Daniel Snow of Bridgewater, blacksmith, and
wife Abigail sold 7 acres being the North lot in the estate of
Joshua Fobes, dec., late of Bridgewater to Daniel Fobes.
    On 11 June 1772 Daniel Snow of Bridgewater bought 62
acres in Keene NH from Ebenezer and Abigail Fisher of
Wrentham.
    In the 1790 census of Keene NH Daniel Snow is 2-1-2.
    No Cheshire Co. NH PR for Daniel Snow.

Children (SNOW) b. Bridgewater:

    i   ABIGAIL[6] b. 16 June 1754
    ii   DANIEL b. 12 April 1756
    iii   HOSEA b. 7 May 1758
    iv   JOSEPH b. 5 March 1760
    v   LUCY b. 17 Feb. 1762
    vi   BARZILLAI b. 15 May 1765
    vii   AZARIAH b. 24 June 1768
    viii JOHN b. 4 Aug. 1770

References: VR BRIDGEWATER 1:112(b. Abigail), 300-2(b. ch.);
2:347(m.). BRIDGEWATER BY MITCHELL pp.
163, 318. Plymouth Co. LR 65:138(Daniel Snow). HISTORY OF
CHESHIRE AND SULLIVAN COUNTIES (NH), D. Hamilton
Hurd, Philadelphia 1886, p. 81(d. Daniel, Abigail). Cheshire Co.
NH LR 3:17(Daniel Snow).

250 ELIJAH SNOW[5] (Benjamin[4-3], Rebecca[2] Brown, Peter[1]) b.
Bridgewater 6 Nov. 1728; d. there 1 July 1792 in 64th yr.
He m. (1) Bridgewater 9 Dec. 1767 SARAH DUNBAR, b.
Bridgewater 14 Sept. 1733; d. there 13 Feb. 1779; "w. Elijah"; dau.
of Samuel and Melatiah (Hayward) Dunbar, a descendant of
Pilgrims James Chilton and Richard Warren.
He m. (2) Bridgewater 7 Sept. 1780 SARAH SHAW, b. Bridge-
water 25 June 1734; dau. of Zechariah and Sarah (Packard) Shaw.
Elijah Snow was 1-1-1 in the 1790 census of Bridgewater.
The will of Elijah Snow of Bridgewater, yeoman, dated 17
Sept. 1791, sworn 6 Aug. 1792, names wife Sarah to have what she
brought with her; dau. Sarah Lothrop; grandson Elijah Lothrop to
have all real estate; and son-in-law Jacob Lothrop sole exec.

Children (SNOW) b. Bridgewater:

    i   SARAH[6] b. 18 May 1770
    ii   BENJAMIN d.y. (not in will)

References: VR BRIDGEWATER 1:96(b. 1st wife), 289(b. 2nd
wife), 303(b. dau. Sarah); 2:348(m.), 558(d. Elijah),
560(d. 1st wife). BRIDGEWATER BY MITCHELL pp. 150, 305,
318. Plymouth Co. PR #18669(Elijah Snow).

251 LUCY SNOW[5] (Benjamin[4-3], Rebecca[2] Brown, Peter[1]) b.
Bridgewater 27 May 1735; d. Easton 28 May 1774.
She m. Easton 25 June 1767 DAVID MAHURIN, b.
Bridgewater 18 Nov. 1726; living 28 March 1780; son of Hugh and
Mary (Snell) Mahurin. He m. (1) ca. 1749 Anna _____ who d.
Easton 30 Dec. 1765 by whom he had Sarah, Hannah, David,
Anna, Anna, Jonathan, and Susanna. He m. (3) Halifax 12 Jan.
1776 Ruth Dunbar by whom he had Ruth. He m. (4) Mansfield 26
Nov. 1778 Sarah Bassett.

David Mahurin of Easton, yeoman, sold to Gregory Belcher of Easton land in Easton 21 June 1773, both David & Lucia signed; David ack. 19 May 1779.

On 28 March 1780 David Mahurin sold land in Easton to Marlbury Williams and Josiah Williams.   David   and   Sarah Mehurin both signed deed.

No Bristol or Plymouth Co. PR for David Mahurin.   No Rutland Dist. VT PR for David Mahurin.

Child (MAHURIN) b. Easton:

i   SETH[6] b. 8 July 1769

References: VR   BRIDGEWATER   1:223(b.   David).   VR MANSFIELD p. 129(4th m.). HALIFAX VR pp. 8(int. 3rd m.), 20(3rd m.). Bristol Co. LR 59:381; 65:222(David Mahurin). NEHGR 136:24, 115-7. Marriages at Easton, Mass. (typescript by Lester Card)(m.). List of Easton Deaths Kept by Timothy Randall 1753-1783, pp. 8, 12(at NEHGS).

252 LEMUEL SNOW[5] (Solomon[4], Benjamin[3], Rebecca[2] Brown, Peter[1]) b. Bridgewater ca. 1729; d. Whately 11 Nov. 1777 ae 48.

He m. Stafford CT 11 Sept. 1750 MARGARET LILLIE, b. Woodstock CT 26 Aug. 1729; d. Windsor 3 Aug. 1810 ae almost 81; dau. of Samuel and Mehitable (Bacon) Lilly.

Lemuel Snow of Stafford CT, blacksmith, sold to Elijah Snow of Bridgewater land in Bridgewater as described in purchase dated 28 Jan. 1744/5, signed 3 April 1752, ack. same day in Plymouth.

Lemuel Snow of Bridgewater, blacksmith, sold to Josiah Hill of Bridgewater 30 acres bring the remainder of the homestead of Solomon Snow late of Bridgewater dec. Signed and ack. 2 Nov. 1751.

Lemuel Snow of Stafford   sold to Archibal Thomson of Bridgewater 1/3 lot at Buckhill Plain - called Snows lot 33. Signed and ack. 26 Jan. 1749/50 at Plymouth.

On 7 May 1761 Lemuel Snow of Stafford sold Daniel Munsell of Windsor CT 25 acres; ack. and recorded 20 May 1761.

Lemuel Snow was in Ashfield 9 Aug. 1770 when he was in court for non-payment of a note. Lemuel and Margaret Snow and children Barnis, Zephaniah, Sarah, Bathsheba, and Huldah were warned out of Whately on 4 May 1773, where he had been a resident since 15 Nov. 1772.

Children (SNOW) b. Stafford CT and Whately:
- i   MOLLEY[6] b. 17 Aug. 1751; d. 21 Aug. 1755
- ii   SARAH b. 1 June 1753; d. 10 Aug. 1755
- iii SOLOMON b. 21 Feb. 1755
- iv BERNICE (son) bp. 10 April 1757
- v   MOLLY bp. 17 Dec. 1758; perhaps the dau. b. _____ August _____; prob. d.y.
- vi ZEPHANIAH bp. 7 Dec. 1760
- vii SARAH b. 14 Feb. 1763
- viii BATHSHEBA b. 8 March 1765 (based on age at d.)
- ix HULDAH b. ca. 1770 (ae 50 in 1820; in warning)
- x   LEMUEL bp. Whately 20 Aug. 1774; d. 13 Sept. 1776 ae 2y

References: Stafford CT VR 1:25(m.); LR2:34(b. Molley), 37(b. Sarah); A:5(b. Solomon), 15(b. 2nd Sarah), 170(d. Molley, Sarah). Stafford CT Church Recs. p. 2(bp. Bernice), 4 (bp. 2nd Molly), 7(bp. Zephaniah). Court of Sessions, Northampton MA Vol. 13, p. 18(warning). Stafford CT LR 3:425(Lemuel to Daniel). Court of Common Pleas, Hampshire Co. MA. Plymouth Co. LR 46:235; 47:24; 51:249 (Lemuel Snow). Woodstock CT VR 1:45(b. Margaret). VR WINDSOR p. 146(d. Margaret). Whately Ch. Recs. unpaged(d. Lemuel, son Lemuel); 2:159(bp. son Lemuel). DAR Cem. Recs. Marsh Farm Cem., Sullivan Twp., Ashland Co. OH p. 43(d. Bathsheba). Rev. War Pension App. #S45187 for Aaron Allis (age Huldah in 1820). HISTORY OF THE TOWN OF WHATELY, MASS. 1661-1899, James M. Crafts, 1899, p.583(adds a dau. Lucinda).

253 BATHSHEBA SNOW[5] (Solomon[4], Benjamin[3], Rebecca[2] Brown, Peter[1]) b. Bridgewater ca. 1732; d. Ashford CT 22 June 1813 in 81st yr.

Almost surely she is the one who m. Ashford CT 17 Nov. 1763 BENJAMIN PRESTON "of Wellington" CT. She was "of Stafford." He was b. Windham CT 31 Dec. 1727; d. Ashford CT 1 Dec. 1798 ae 71; son of Benjamin and Deborah (Holt) Preston.

No CT PR for Benjamin Preston or Plymouth Co. LR for Benjamin or Bathsheba Preston.

Children (PRESTON) b. Ashford CT:

  i AMOS[6] b. 29 Dec. 1765; d. 31 July 1776
  ii OLIVER b. 13 Feb. 1768
  iii SOLOMON b. 10 Sept. 1770
  iv BENJAMIN b. 26 June 1773

References: GENEALOGY DATA ON EARLY ASHFORD, CONN. FAMILIES, Emily J. Chism, Hartford CT 1958. Ashford CT VR 2:55(m.; b. Benj.); 4:24(b. all ch.; d. Benj., Amos), 55(d. Bathsheba). Windham CT VR 1:90(b. Benjamin).

254 EBENEZER SNOW[5] (Ebenezer[4], Benjamin[3], Rebecca[2] Brown, Peter[1]) b. Bridgewater 16 Nov. 1729; d. Raynham bet. 9 March 1807 and 1 Jan. 1811.

He m. prob. Bridgewater ca. 1749 ELIZABETH HOOPER, b. Bridgewater 13 April 1729; living 9 March 1807; dau. of Nathaniel and Elizabeth (Tinkham) Hooper (see #95).

Ebenezer Snow of Raynham, husbandman, sold to Solomon Snow of Raynham, yeoman, his land and half his dwelling house 21 May 1758, ack. 1 Jan. 1771.

Ebenezer Snow and Solomon Snow of Raynham, yeoman, sold to Mesheck Wilbore, Jr. of Raynham 5 acres in Raynham 11 Feb. 1774, ack. 22 March 1775.

The will of Ebenezer Snow of Raynham, yeoman, advanced in age, dated 9 March 1807, presented 1 Jan. 1811, names wife Elizabeth; son Ebenezer executor; daus. Sarah Hall, Betsey Warren, and Zilpah Bolton; and grandson Nathan Snow.

Children (SNOW) b. Bridgewater:

  i "first ch."[6] b. 29 March 1750; d. 1 April 1750
  ii SARAH b. 13 July 1751
  iii BETTIE b. 19 June 1753
  iv LYDIA b. 27 March 1755
  v SUSANNAH b. 3 April 1757
  vi EUNICE b. 25 Feb. 1759

vii   EBENEZER (named in will)
viii   ZILPAH (named in will)

References: VR BRIDGEWATER 1:163(b. Elziabeth), 300-4(b. ch.);
2:559(d. 1st ch.). BRIDGEWATER BY MITCHELL
pp. 316-7. Bristol Co. LR 54:58; 56:366(Eben. Snow). Bristol Co.
PR 46:144(Ebenezer Snow). HOOPER GEN, Charles Henry Pope
and Thomas Hooper, Boston, 1908, pp. 16-7.

255 NATHANIEL SNOW[5] (Ebenezer[4], Benjamin[3], Rebecca[2]
Brown, Peter[1]) b. Bridgewater 6 June 1731; d. North Brookfield 1
May 1819.
    He m. (1) BETHIAH LEONARD, b. Raynham 20 April 1739;
d. bet. 10 Oct. 1759 and 1 Feb. 1770; dau. of Samuel and Abigail
(Shaw) Leonard. The division of the estate of Samuel Leonard Jr.
Esq. late of Raynham dec., dated 31 May 1758, allowed 1 Jan.
1782, mentions widow Abigail Leonard and sets off portion to
second dau. Bethiah, wife of Nathaniel Snow.
    He m. (2) int. Raynham 15 Sept. 1760 TABITHA HALL.
    Nathaniel Snow and wife Bethia of Raynham sold to
Amariah Hall of Raynham their part of the real estate of their
father Samuel Leonard of Raynham, dec., signed 8 May 1759, ack.
10 Oct. 1759.
    Nathaniel Snow of Raynham, innholder, sold to Philip King
of Raynham his mansion house in Raynham, with land he bought
of Mrs. Abigail Leonard in 1760, wife Tabitha signed, dated 1
Feb. 1770; ack. 11 Feb. 1770.
    Nathaniel Snow of Raynham, innholder, granted to Philip
King land adjacent to land conveyed today, which was set off to
his former wife Bethiah now dec., signed 1 Feb. 1770.
    Nathaniel Snow of Raynham, gentleman, in consideration of
a deed wherein his dau. Lois Snow of Raynham, singlewoman,
conveyed land to him today, quitclaims to her his curtesy in estate
of his first wife Bethiah what descended to him "as heir to my son
deceased (Nathaniel)" in the whole estate set forth to Bethia of
real estate of Samuel Leonard Esq., signed and ack. 19 March
1778.
    Joseph Hall of Taunton; Ebenezer Hall of Taunton;
Nathaniel Snow of Brookfield with wife Tabitha; Abial Dean of
Bristol Co. and wife Weltha; Jonathan Shaw Jr. of Raynham and

Seth Washburn of Raynham with wife Bethia sold to Ebenezer
Dean of Raynham our purchase right in swamp in Taunton,
originally that of George Hall, signed 22 Jan. 1783, ack. 20 June
1784 by Nathaniel Snow.
    Nathaniel Snow was 1-1-2 in the 1790 census of Brookfield.
No Worcester Co. PR for Nathaniel Snow.

Children (SNOW) by first wife:

    i   LOIS[6]
    ii   NATHANIEL

References: First Book of Raynham Records p. 21(b. Bethiah).
        Bristol Co. LR 43:545; 52:472, 473(Nathaniel Snow);
58:177-8(Joseph Hall etc.); 67:315(Nathaniel Snow). Bristol Co. PR
26:532-7(Samuel Leonard). HISTORY OF NORTH
BROOKFIELD, MASSACHUSETTS, J. H. Temple, North
Brookfield 1887, p. 736. RAYNHAM VR pp. 19(b.Bethiah), 87(int.
2nd m.).

256 CALEB SNOW[5] (Ebenezer[4], Benjamin[3], Rebecca[2] Brown,
Peter[1]) b. Bridgewater 8 June 1736; d. Plymouth VT 8 April 1819
ae 85.
    He m. Raynham 20 March 1760 LYDIA (WILBORE)
BARNEY; dau. of Ebenezer and Lydia (Deane) Wilbore. She m.
(1) int. Norton 9 Nov. 1754 Elijah Barney by whom she had
Hannah and Lydia. On 25 March 1763 Lydia Snow late Lydia
Barney rendered account on the estate of Elijah Barney.
    The division of real estate of Ebenezer Wilbore, late of
Raynham dec. to widow and children Elkenah, Bathsheba, Rachel,
Caleb Snow in right of wife Lydia and Elijah was dated 20 May
1763 (all were Wilbores unless otherwise stated.)
    Caleb Snow of Raynham, laborer, and wife Lydia sold to
Elijah Wilbore of Raynham land in Raynham set off to Lydia
from estate of her father Ebenezer Wilbore, signed 27 April 1762,
ack. 9 April 1763.
    Caleb Snow of Raynham, yeoman, sold to Mesheck Wilbore
of Raynham his homestead farm in Raynham 70 acres with
property rights and real and personal estate which he conveyed to
him in 1769, wife Lydia released dower, signed 26 July 1769;

acknowledged same day.

Caleb Snow of Raynham, husbandman, and wife Lydia sold to Jacob Wilbore of Raynham half their right in Norton to estate of Elisha Barney, late of Norton dec., signed 7 Sept. 1772, ack. same day.

In the 1790 census of Keene NH Caleb Snow is 2-0-2. In the 1800 census of Keene NH Caleb Snow is one male over 45, one female over 45 and a female 0-10.

No Windsor Co. VT PR for Caleb Snow.

Children (SNOW) b. prob. Raynham:

> i ELIJAH[6] b. ca. 1762*
> ii CALEB b. ca. 1766 (ae 52 on 10 April 1818; 54 on 1 Aug. 1820 pension application)**

References: VR NORTON pp. 15(b. Barney ch.), 186(int. her 1st m.). VR TAUNTON 2:445(m.). Bristol Co. PR 18:203-4(Elijah Barney); 19:181 (Eben. Wilbore). Bristol Co. LR 46:290; 52:185(Caleb Snow). Rev. War Pension Application #S42021. Plymouth VT Notch Cem.(d. Caleb).

*On 27 Oct. 1785 Elijah Snow of Raynham and his wife Lucy sold to her brother Ephraim Wilbore 5 acres in Raynham which belonged to her father Abijah Wilbore (Bristol Co. LR 66:277). On 29 May 1788 Elijah Snow of Westmoreland, Cheshire Co. NH and wife Lucy sold to Ephraim Wilbore their interest in the thirds of widow Phebe Wilbore, her mother (Bristol Co. LR 67:128). On 17 Nov. 1795 Caleb Snow of Plymouth VT sold 50 acres in Plymouth VT to Elijah Snow and on 5 March 1798 Elijah resold the same to Caleb (Plymouth VT LR 2:333, 3(1):27). (This would be the two brothers.)

**Caleb Snow Jr. of Keene, Cheshire Co. NH, yeoman, sold to Henry Wilbore of Raynham, land in Raynham 12 1/2 acres with dwelling house 6 Sept. 1790 (Bristol Co. LR 70:312).

257 SOLOMON SNOW[5] (Ebenezer[4], Benjamin[3], Rebecca[2] Brown, Peter[1]) b. Bridgewater 13 Dec. 1741; d. Raynham 30 May 1821 in 80th yr.

He m. Bridgewater 5 Oct. 1780 BETTIE (CARY) PERKINS, b. Bridgewater 1 Feb. 1754; d. Raynham 12 Jan. 1835 ae 80; dau. of Eleazer and Mary (Pratt) (Washburn) Cary; a descendant of Pilgrim Degory Priest. She m. (1) Bridgewater 9 July 1777 William Perkins.

See deeds with brother Ebenezer Snow (#254).

Solomon Snow of Raynham, yeoman, sold land in Middleboro to Theophilus Crocker of Middleboro 18 Feb. 1768, ack. 27 Aug. 1768.

Solomon Snow was 1-2-3 in 1790 census for Raynham.

Solomon Snow of Raynham, gentleman, and wife Betsy sold to James Warren of Raynham land in Raynham on 1 April 1813.

On 6 July 1821 Elizabeth Snow, widow of Solomon, late of Raynham, declined to administer estate and requested that William, son of dec., be appointed administrator. William Snow swore to the inventory 5 March 1822.

Children (SNOW) b. Raynham:

    i   ELIZABETH[6] (or BETSY) b. 3 Oct. 1786
    ii   SOLOMON b. 23 April 1789
    iii WILLIAM b. 15 July 1793

References: VR BRIDGEWATER 1:67(b. Bettie); 2:293(her 1st m.), 350(m.). BRIDGEWATER BY MITCHELL p. 316. CARY (JOHN) p. 94. Plymouth Co. LR 56:205(Solomon Snow). RIVR 14:291(d. Solomon); 19:141. Bristol Co. PR 58:273; 59:136 (Solomon Snow). Bristol Co. LR 95:260(Solomon Snow). RAYNHAM VR pp. 57(b.ch.), 75(d. Bettie), 91(int.).

257A REBECCA SNOW[5] (Ebenezer[4], Benjamin[3], Rebecca[2] Brown, Peter[1]) b. Bridgewater 5 March 1742/3; d. Raynham 18 Oct. 1811 ae 68.

She m. (1) Raynham 12 Jan. 1764 BENJAMIN JONES, b. Bristol 15 Feb. 1739/40; d. Raynham 8 Dec. 1773; son of Nathan and Bathsheba (Drown) Jones.

She m. (2) Raynham 16 Sept. 1784 NATHANIEL SHAW, b. prob. Taunton ca. 1724; d. Raynham 4 May 1804 ae 80; son of Samuel and Elizabeth (Hodges) Shaw. He m. (1) Raynham 10 Dec. 1745 Elizabeth Hall by whom he had Nathaniel, John, Betty, Asel,

Jairus, and Sarah.

On 10 April 1787 Francis and Asael Jones, both yeomen of Raynham, sold to Seth Washburn of Raynham a farm lately the property of Benjamin Jones, dec.; Rebecca Shaw waived her dower rights.

The will of Nathaniel Shaw dated 14 Aug. 1795, proved 22 Sept. 1804, names wife Rebecca; children Nathaniel, John, Betty, Asel, Jarius, and Sarah.

No Bristol Co. PR for Benjamin Jones.

Children (JONES) b. Raynham:

<blockquote>

i   FRANCIS[6] b. 6 Aug. 1764 (based on age at d.)

ii   ASAEL b. ca. 1765 (based on age at d.)

iii SALLY b. 5 Feb. 1768 (based on age at d.). The will of Sally Jones dated 22 April 1839, proved 10 Jan. 1845, names various Jones relatives and "cousin William Snow of Raynham." (see #257iii)

iv   REBEKAH b. ca. 1772; d. Raynham 24 Aug. 1820; unm.

</blockquote>

References: Raynham Church Rec.(1st m.). NEHGR 51:290(2nd m.); 113:140-1(Jones family). RIVR Bristol 6:1:85(b. Benjamin). Pleasant St. Cem., Raynham(d. Rebecca). RAYNHAM VR pp. 14(Nathaniel's 1st m.), 22-3(Nathaniel's ch.), 44(d. Nathaniel), 88(int. 1st m.), 168(d. Nathaniel), 169(d. Rebecca). Bristol Co. PR 40:535(Nathaniel Shaw). Bristol Co. LR 66:289(Francis & Asael Jones).

258 ZEBEDEE SNOW[5] (Ebenezer[4], Benjamin[3], Rebecca[2] Brown, Peter[1]) b. Bridgewater 26 Feb. 1743; d. Scituate RI 24 Nov. 1819 in 76th yr.

He m. _____ _____.

Zebadee Snow was 1-0-1-0 in the 1774 census of Scituate RI.

Zebedee Snow was 16-50 A in the 1777 Military Census of Scituate RI.

Zebedee Snow had 1 male under 15, 1 male 22-49, 1 female 22-49 and 1 female over 50 in the 1782 census of Cranston RI.

Zebadiah Snow was 1-3-2 in 1790 census of Scituate RI.

Zebadee Snow had 2 males 10-15, 1 male over 45 and one

female over 45 in the 1800 census of Scituate RI. In 1810 there
was one male over 45 and one female over 45.
No Scituate RI PR for Zebedee Snow.

Children (SNOW) b. prob. Scituate RI:

    i   ZEBEDEE[6] b. ca. 1774; d. Smithfield RI shortly
        bef. 11 Dec. 1815 in 42nd yr.; unm. The will of
        Zebedee Snow of Smithfield dated 28 Nov. 1815,
        left everything to friend Marcus Arnold.
   ii   SOLOMON (no proof found but implied in the
        1790 census)
  iii   WILLIAM CARTER b. ca. 1788; d. at sea 17 March
        1807 in 20th yr.; unm.

References: BRIDGEWATER BY MITCHELL p. 316(names 3 ch.).
RIVR 14:291(d. sons Zebedee, William); 19:140(d.
Zebedee & son Zebedee). NEHGR 128:55(1782 census). Smithfield
RI PR 3:583(Zebedee Snow). THE RHODE ISLAND 1777
MILITARY CENSUS, Baltimore, 1985 p. 88.

259 JOSEPH CARVER[5] (Elizabeth Snow[4], Benjamin[3], Rebecca[2]
Brown, Peter[1]) b. Bridgewater 23 March 1727; d. Foster RI 23 Dec.
1786 in 59th yr.
He m. Bridgewater 25 Dec. 1746 SARAH HARTWELL, b. ca.
1724; d. Scituate RI 27 June 1817 in 93rd yr., prob. dau. of Samuel
Hartwell.
Joseph Carver was 5-1-1-3in the 1774 census of Scituate RI.
Joseph Carver was an Ensign in the Rev. War.
The will of Joseph Carver of Foster, dated 19 Dec. 1781,
presented 8 Jan. 1787, names wife Sarah; sons Oliver, Salmon,
Joseph, and Bernice "if he ever comes home." The will mentions
cedar swamp in Bridgewater. The will also names daus. Hannah
(no surname given), Rhoda Barton, Sarah Hopkins, and Eunice
Carver; brother Robert Carver's children; and twin daus. of
Experience Leach.

Children (CARVER) first 4 b. Bridgewater:

    i   HANNAH[6] b. 19 May 1747

    ii   RHODA b. 9 Oct. 1749
    iii   OLIVER b. 12 May 1751
    iv   BERNICE (son) b. 8 Dec. 1753
    v   SARAH b. 1756
    vi   SALMON (son)
    vii   JOSEPH
    viii EUNICE

References: VR BRIDGEWATER 1:65-6(b. 1st 4 ch.); 2:73(m.).
BRIDGEWATER BY MITCHELL pp. 131, 178.
THE CARVER FAMILY OF NEW ENGLAND, Clifford N.
Carver, Rutland VT 1935 pp. 88-9. DAR PATRIOT INDEX p.
118. RIVR 14:255(d. Joseph, Sarah); 15:486(d. Joseph). Benns
Grave Recs 1:346; 4:86, 92. Foster RI PR 1:34(Joseph Carver).
NEHGR 88:319-20.

260 BENJAMIN CARVER[5] (Elizabeth Snow[4], Benjamin[3],
Rebecca[2] Brown, Peter[1]) b. Bridgewater 28 Feb. 1728/9; d.
Castleton VT 1 March 1804 ae 75 yrs.

    He m. ELIZABETH PORTER, b. Windsor CT 17 July 1738;
d. Castleton VT 31 Dec. 1822 ae 84 yrs.; dau. of Hezekiah and
Hannah (Ashley) Porter.

    On 4 June 1754 Benjamin Carver "of Bridgewater...now of
Windsor" bought land in Windsor. On 28 Feb. 1756 he bought
more land.

    On 1 April 1758 Hannah Porter, widow of Hezekiah Porter,
her son Hezekiah and her dau. Elizabeth and Elizabeth's husband
Benjamin Carver divided the estate of the late Hezekiah Porter.
On 28 July 1775 Hezekiah Porter sold to Benjamin Carver, both
of East Windsor, land held in dower by Hannah Porter. The deed
mentions Benjamin's wife Elizabeth was Hezekiah's sister.

    On 10 May 1784 Benjamin Carver of East Windsor sold his
homestead to Samuel Wolcott.

    On 21 Dec. 1784 Benjamin Carver and wife Elizabeth of
Castelton VT sold 16 acres that had been owned by her father
Hezekiah Porter to Thomas Starkweather.

    Benjamin Carver was 3-1-3 in the 1790 census of Castleton
VT.

    On 27 Aug. 1801 Benjamin Carver gave his son Benjamin Jr.
acres in Castleton and on the same day he gave his son Ralph part

of his home lot in Castleton. On 29 Feb. 1804 he gave his sons Ralph, Martin, and Benjamin all the land not specifically devised in his will.

On 27 Aug. 1801 he gave his dau. Olive Fisher, wife of Peter Fisher, land in Castleton.

The will of Benjamin Carver of Castleton, County of Rutland, VT, dated 2 Aug. 1803, proved 29 March 1804, names wife Elizabeth; sons Ralph Carver, Martin Carver, and Benjamin Carver; son Elizson(?) Carver; dau. Elizabeth Rice; dau. Olive Tinkham; and dau. Theodotia Carver. Probate mentions widow Elizabeth Carver. A 27 Feb. 1805 agreement bet. the widow and the heirs names Elizabeth Carver (widow) and Rolf Carver, Martin Carver, and Benjamin Carver, all of Castleton.

Children (CARVER) b. East Windsor CT; all but Chloe named in will:

i   OLIVE[6] b. 2 April 1760 (based on age at d.)
ii   CHLOE   bp. East Windsor CT 29 Sept. 1763; perhaps the child who d. East Windsor CT 24 Sept. 1775.
iii   RALPH b. ca. 1766 (age 84 in 1850 census of Ohio Township, Clermont Co. OH)
iv   MARTIN
v   BENJAMIN b. ca. 1774 (based on age on g.s.)
vi   ELIZABETH
vii   ELISON
viii THEODOTIA

References: Windsor CT LR 10:253, 254(Benjamin Carver). East Windsor CT LR 3:200(Hezekiah Porter); 4:21; 5:135 (Benjamin Carver). Hartford CT PR 18:24(div. of Hezekiah Porter est.). NEHGR 88:320-1. Castleton VT TR(d. Benj., Eliz.). Castleton VT LR 3:219(to Benj. Jr.), 220(to Ralph), 268(to Olive), 339(to sons); 4:288(agree.). Windsor CT VR 2:411(b. Elizabeth). CASTLETON CEMETERY INSCRIPTIONS, Margaret R. Jenks, Richardson TX, 1988, p. 7(deaths). Fair Haven Dist. VT PR 3:256(Benjamin Carver). East Windsor CT Church records(bp. Chloe; d. child).

261 ELIZABETH CARVER[5] (Elizabeth Snow[4], Benjamin[3], Rebecca[2] Brown, Peter[1]) b. Bridgewater 10 Sept. 1731; living 28 June 1773 (deed).

She m. Bridgewater 13 Dec. 1757 SAMUEL PACKARD, b. Bridgewater 21 Dec. 1734; living 19 Feb. 1777 (deed); son of Samuel and Susannah (Kinsley) Packard.

On 31 Oct. 1765 Samuel Packard 4th of Bridgewater and Elizabeth Packard and Susanna Packard sold to George Packard land bought from his father Samuel Packard and land held jointly with his brother Abijah.

On 28 June 1773, ack. 28 June 1773, Samuel Packard 3rd of Bridgewater, with wife Elizabeth participating, sold land to Abner Hayward of Bridgewater.

On 28 June 1776, ack. 19 Feb. 1777, Samuel Packard of Easton, yeoman, sold to Anne Packard, widow of Abijah Packard land including the homestead of Lt. Samuel Packard, dec.

No Bristol Co. PR or LR for Samuel Packard.

Children (PACKARD) b. Bridgewater:

    i   BETTIE[6] b. 4 Sept. 1758
   ii   SILVIA b. 16 Nov. 1760

References: VR BRIDGEWATER 1:239(b. Bettie), 248(b. Samuel), 249(b. Silvia); 2:282(m.). BRIDGEWATER BY MITCHELL pp. 130-1, 266, 270. Plymouth Co. LR 54:216; 57:50; 63:96 (Samuel Packard).

NOTE: BRIDGEWATER BY MITCHELL p. 270 surely errs when it says Elisabeth Carver married Samuel Packard, son of Samuel and Anne (_____) Packard.

262 SARAH CARVER[5] (Elizabeth Snow[4], Benjamin[3], Rebecca[2] Brown, Peter[1]) b. Bridgewater 14 Feb. 1736/7; d. East Windsor CT 1 March 1806 ae 68 yrs.

She m. Bridgewater 25 Sept. 1757 HEZEKIAH PORTER, b. Windsor CT 9 Sept. 1735; d. East Windsor CT 10 July 1807 ae 72; son of Hezekiah and Hannah (Ashley) Porter.

On 3 Jan. 1804, ack. 3 Feb. 1804, Hezekiah Porter of East Windsor sold his dwelling house and land in East Windsor to

Wareham Porter (his son).
No CT PR for Hezekiah Porter.

    Children (PORTER) b. Windsor CT:

      i   ABIAZER[6] b. 23 Dec. 1757; d. East Windsor 30 Oct.
           1776 in 19th yr.
      ii   ISRAEL b. 27 Sept. 1759
      iii ROXALENA b. Jan. 1762; d. 9 Dec. 1762 ae 11m
      iv TIMOTHY b. 5 Feb. 1764
      v   WARHAM b. 1 Oct. 1766
      vi RUHMA b. East Windsor CT 26 Feb. 1775 "dau. of
           Hezekiah and Sarah."

References: VR BRIDGEWATER 2:302(m.). BRIDGEWATER BY
              MITCHELL p. 131. THE HISTORY OF ANCIENT
WINDSOR, Henry R. Stiles, 1892, reprint Somersworth NH, 1976,
2:622. Windsor CT VR 2:410(b. Hezekiah), 418(b. Abiezer), 420(b.
Israel), 422 (b.&d. Roxalena; b. Tim.), 424(b. Wareham).   East
Windsor CT VR 1:22(b. Ruhma), 76(d. Abiezer). Hale Cem. Recs.,
South Windsor CT(d. Hezekiah, Sarah).   East Windsor CT LR
10:89(Hezekiah Porter).

NOTE: Stiles lists a dau. Naomi b. 13 Oct. 1761. She is not in VR
and the birth is too close to Roxalena.

263 EXPERIENCE CARVER[5] (Elizabeth Snow[4], Benjamin[3],
Rebecca[2] Brown, Peter[1]) b. Bridgewater 2 May 1739; d. East
Windsor CT 21 Feb. 1816.
    She m. ca. 1763 LUKE LOOMIS, b. Windsor CT 15 Oct. 1736;
d. East Windsor CT 8 March 1811; son of John and Abigail
(Elsworth) Loomis.
    The will of Luke Loomis of East Windsor dated 6 Oct. 1810,
sworn 15 March 1811, "considerable advanced in years" names
wife Experience, son Simeon Loomis, and son Russell Loomis.
    The will of Experience Loomis of East Windsor dated 17 Feb.
1815 "considerable advanced in years" names son Simeon; Corena
Loomis the present wife of Russel Loomis his son. Simeon Loomis
posted bond as exec. 6 Aug. 1816.

Children (LOOMIS) b. East Windsor CT:

    i   ANNE[6] b. 11 July 1764; d. 4 Aug. 1764
    ii   SIMEON b. 11 Sept. 1767
    iii   RUSSELL b. 5 Aug. 1769
    iv   ANNE b. 16 Jan. 1772

References: THE DESCENDANTS OF JOSEPH LOOMIS, Elias
Loomis, New Haven 1870, pp. 30, 45. East Windsor
CT PR #1815(Experience Loomis), #1833(Luke Loomis). Windsor
CT VR 2:378(b. Luke). East Windsor CT VR pp. 18(b. ch.), 72(d.
Anne).

264 ROBERT CARVER[5] (Elizabeth Snow[4], Benjamin[3], Rebecca[2]
Brown, Peter[1]) b. Bridgewater 2 June 1742; d. Providence RI 1784.
      He m. Providence RI 15 Nov. 1778 LYDIA GRAFTON; dau.
of William and Sarah (Glaser) Grafton.
      On 19 Dec. 1777 Robert Carver was chosen by the General
Assembly adjutant of the regiment of artillery and in Feb. 1779
he was chosen Captain-lieutenant of the 5th Company of the same
regiment.
      Letters of adm. were granted to his widow, Lydia Carver in
1784.
      In 1795 William Barton was appointed by the Court to be
guardian of Robert Carver's sons Isaac and John.

Children (CARVER) b. Providence RI:

    i   ISAAC[6] b. 22 Jan. 1782
    ii   JOHN b. ca. 1783

References: RIVR 14:574(m.). THE GRAFTON FAMILY OF
SALEM, Henry W. Belknap, Salem MA 1928, pp. 42,
53. NEHGR 96:304-5(1784 & 1795 recs.). Providence RI Town
Council Bk. No. 5, p. 291. Providence RI PR No. A 1519 &
1520(Robert Carver).

265 SETH PRATT[5] (Sarah Snow[4], Benjamin[3], Rebecca[2] Brown,
Peter[1]) b. Bridgewater 21 June 1729; d. there 30 Dec. 1795 in 66th
yr.

He m. Bridgewater 27 April 1753 HANNAH WASHBURN, b. Bridgewater 6 Sept. 1733; d. there 26 Aug. 1824 ae 90; dau. of Joseph and Deliverance (Orcutt) Washburn; a descendant of Pilgrim Francis Cooke.

Seth Pratt was a Deacon.

The will of Seth Pratt of Bridgewater, gentleman, dated 29 Nov. 1796, proved 6 Jan. 1796, names wife Hannah; sons Nathaniel, Simeon, Sylvanus, Asa, Joseph and Seth; dau. Cloe Conant wife of Jeremiah; dau. Joanna Bessee widow; and grandson Marshall Bessee under 21.

No Plymouth Co. PR for Hannah Pratt.

Children (PRATT) b. Bridgewater:

i	NATHANIEL[6] b. 1 Feb. 1754
ii	JOSEPH b. 1 April 1756
iii	NEHEMIAH b. 20 Nov. 1757; d. there 3 Aug. 1778 in 21st yr.
iv	SIMEON b. 16 Sept. 1759
v	SETH b. 8 Sept. 1761
vi	SARAH (or SALLY) b. 31 July 1763; d. there 12 Aug. 1778 in 16th yr.
vii	HANNAH b. 2 Feb. 1766; d. there 25 July 1778 in 13th yr.
viii	CHLOE b. 25 Feb. 1768
ix	SYLVANUS b. 20 May 1770
x	JOANNA b. 9 April 1772(see b. of Joanna Keith)
xi	ASA b. 22 April 1774
xii	NEHEMIAH b. 27 Jan. 1781; d. 18 Feb. 1784 in 4th yr.

References: VR BRIDGEWATER 1:266-71(b. ch.), 329(b. Hannah); 2:310(m.), 544-5(deaths).   BRIDGEWATER BY MITCHELL pp. 290, 343. Plymouth Co. PR 35:448(Seth Pratt).

266 SUSANNA BYRAM[5] (Hannah Rickard[4], Rebecca Snow[3], Rebecca[2] Brown, Peter[1]) b. Bridgewater 27 April 1721; d. there 1 Nov. 1781.

She m. Bridgewater 11 Nov. 1741 Capt. JONATHAN BASS, b. Braintree 19 July 1720; d. West Bridgewater 1800; son of

Jonathan and Susanna (Byram) Bass, a descendant of Pilgrim John Alden.

Jonathan Bass was a Capt. in the Rev. War.

No Plymouth Co. PR for Jonathan Bass and no Plymouth Co. deeds to children.

Children (BASS) b. Bridgewater:

i	BETHIAH[6] b. 27 Aug. 1742; d. 11 June 1747
ii	RUTH b. 15 April 1745; d. 20 June 1747
iii	MARY b. 1 Feb. 1747; d. 22 June 1747
iv	SUSANNA b. 13 Feb. 1749
v	OLIVE b. 20 Feb. 1751
vi	JONATHAN b. 2 April 1753
vii	RUTH b. 3 July 1755
viii	EUNICE b. 12 June 1758
ix	BATHSHEBA b. 24 Jan. 17- - (1760)
x	SARAH bp. East Bridgewater 11 Oct. 1761

References: VR BRIDGEWATER 1:41-2(b. ch); 2:42(m.), 434(d. Bethia, Mary, Ruth). VR EAST BRIDGEWATER pp. 21 (bp. all ch. exc. Bathsheba), 336(d. 1st 3 ch.). BRIDGEWATER BY MITCHELL pp. 110,128. BRAINTREE RECS p. 707(b. Jonathan). DAR PATRIOT INDEX p. 42. MD 32:159(d. Susanna).

267 THEOPHILUS BYRAM[5] (Hannah Rickard[4], Rebecca Snow[3], Rebecca[2] Brown, Peter[1]) b. Bridgewater 8 Aug. 1725; d. North Yarmouth ME 10 Oct. 1812 ae 87.

He m. East Bridgewater 27 April 1749 ELIZABETH (BLACKMAN) BEALE; b. Dorchester 2 Nov. 1723; living 14 April 1788 (ack. deed); dau. of Thomas and Mary (Horton) Blackman. The 11 Jan. 1760 division of the estate of Thomas Blackman of Stoughton names dau. Elizabeth Byram and others. She m. (1) East Bridgewater 17 Oct. 1745 Samuel Beale by whom she had David and Samuel.

Ebenezer Bacon of Dedham and wife Rebeckah sold to Theophilus Byram of Bridgewater rights in land in North Yarmouth of their father Thomas Blackman dec. being formerly a proprietor, signed 30 June 1760.

On 10 May 1774 Theophilus Byram of North Yarmouth, yeoman, and wife Elizabeth deeded land in North Yarmouth to son Oliver Byram of Cumberland.

On 12 April 1788, acknowledged 14 April 1788, Theophilus Byram, bloomer of North Yarmouth, and wife Elizabeth, deeded their homestead to Oliver Byram.

The probate records for Cumberland Co. for this time frame no longer exist.

Children (BYRAM) b. Bridgewater, except last 2 b. North Yarmouth ME:

i	JOSIAH[6]	b. 22 March 1750; d. 4 May 1750
ii	OLIVER	b. 14 May 1751
iii	DAVID	b. 23 Feb. 1753
iv	JAMES	b. 30 Aug. 1756
v	MELZAR	b. 1 Feb. 1759
vi	SYLVINIA	b. 22 March 1761
vii	JOSIAH	b. 26 March 1765

References: VR BRIDGEWATER 1:63-4(b. 1st 5 ch.); 2:443(d. Josiah). VR EAST BRIDGEWATER pp. 32-3(bp. ch.), 167(her 1st m.), 180(m.). NORTH YARMOUTH ME VR pp. 13(b. last 2 ch.), 311(d. Theo.). BRIDGEWATER BY MITCHELL pp. 113, 129. OLD TIMES, 8 vols., Yarmouth ME 1877-1884; reprinted 8 vols. in 1, Somersworth NH, 1977 pp. 714(bp. Sylvinia), 1175-6 (fam.). Suffolk Co. PR 56:40(Thomas Blackman). Cumberland Co. ME LR 1:331 (Ebenezer Bacon); 10:102; 18:201(Theophilus Byram). DORCHESTER VR 1:72(b. Elizabeth).

268 MEHETABEL BYRAM[5] (Hannah Rickard[4], Rebecca Snow[3], Rebecca[2] Brown, Peter[1]) b. Bridgewater 25 May 1730.

She m. Bridgewater 3 April 1750 DANIEL BEALE, b. Bridgewater 25 March 1729; son of Samuel and Mary (Bassett) Beale.

On 1 Jan. 1754, acknowledged 25 March 1754, Daniel Beale of Bridgewater, wheelwright, with wife Mehitabel releasing dower, sold land to Benjamin Johnson. On 7 June 1758, ack. same day, Daniel Beall of Bridgewater sold land in Bridgewater, with wife Mehitable releasing dower, to Joseph Wesley.

No Plymouth Co. PR for Daniel or Mehetabel Beale.

Children (BEALE) b. Bridgewater:

i	SAMUEL[6]	b. 8 Nov. 1750
ii	DANIEL	b. 19 March 1753
iii	JOSHUA	b. 26 May 1755
iv	MEHETABLE	b. 30 Jan. 1758

References: VR BRIDGEWATER 1:47(b. Daniel; b. ch.); 2:47(m.).
BRIDGEWATER BY MITCHELL pp. 113, 128.
Plymouth Co. LR 45:38, 51:237(Dan. Beale).

269 REBECCA BYRAM[5] (Hannah Rickard[4], Rebecca Snow[3], Rebecca[2] Brown, Peter[1]) b. Bridgewater 26 Aug. 1732; d. Wrentham 14 Oct. 1817 ae 86y.
   She m. East Bridgewater 18 March 1755 SAMUEL BOWDITCH, b. Braintree 25 Feb. 1728/9; d. Wrentham 11 March 1803 ae 74; son of William and Mary (Bass) Bowditch, a descendant of Pilgrim John Alden.
   Samuel and Rebecca Bowditch were received into the Milford Church from the Third Church, Bridgewater 28 Aug. 1763 and were dismissed to Wrentham in 1786.
   Samuel Bowdridge was 2-0-4 in the 1790 census of Wrentham.
   No Probate found in Norfolk Co. for Samuel Bowditch.

Children (BOWDITCH) first 3 b. East Bridgewater:

i	BETHIAH[6]	bp. 8 May 1757
ii	MOLLY	bp. 4 June 1758
iii	MARY	b. 16 Aug. 1760; bp. 24 Aug. 1760
iv	SUSANNA	b. Mendon 20 April 1763; bp. Milford 28 Aug. 1763
v	JONATHAN	bp. Milford 4 Aug. 1765
vi	RUTH	b. Mendon 28 July 1767; bp. Milford 6 Sept. 1767
vii	SAMUEL	b. Mendon 23 March 1770; bp. Milford 13 May 1770
viii	MATILDA	bp. Milford 11 Dec. 1774

References: VR   BRIDGEWATER   2:58(m.).   VR   EAST
                BRIDGEWATER pp. 28(bp. 1st 3 ch.), 173(m.). VR
MENDON p. 34(b. Mary, Susanna, Ruth, Samuel).   VR
WRENTHAM p. 416(d. Rebecca, Samuel).   HISTORY OF
MILFORD MA, Adin Ballou, Boston, 1882, p. 586(bp. last 5 ch.;
church records). BRIDGEWATER BY MITCHELL pp. 119, 128.
NEHGR 79:179-81. BRAINTREE RECS p. 763(b. Samuel). VR
MILFORD p. 25(bp. last 5 ch.).

270 LEMUEL RICKARD[5] (Samuel[4], Rebecca Snow[3], Rebecca[2]
Brown, Peter[1]) b. Plympton 6 Nov. 1722; d. there 21 Sept. 1756 in
34th yr.

He m. Plympton 8 Feb. 1749/50 PERSIS (HARLOW) SHAW,
b. Plympton 8 Feb. 1728/9; d. Carver 28 Aug. 1802 in 75th yr.; dau.
of James and Hannah (Shaw) Harlow. She m. (1) Plympton 18
Sept. 1746 Isaac Shaw, who d. Plympton 6 June 1747. She m. (3)
Plympton 6 Feb. 1786 Perez Churchill.

The will of Perez Churchill of Middleboro, gentleman, under
many infirmities, dated 18 March 1797, sworn 2 Nov. 1797, names
sons Perez and Isaac. They to maintain their honored mother
Persis Churchill, she to have furniture she brought with her and
it shall descend to her children or their heirs at her decease.

No Plymouth Co. PR for Lemuel Rickard or deed to
children. No Plymouth Co. PR for Persis Churchill.

Children (RICKARD) b. Plympton:

    i   CONTENT[6] b. 24 Feb. 1751/2
    ii   MEHITABEL b. 2 Nov. 1752
    iii ISAAC b. 25 July 1754
    iv ABIGAIL b. 13 April 1756

References: VR CARVER p. 149(d. Persis). VR PLYMPTON pp.
                113(b. Persis), 161-5(b. ch.), 372(m.), 506(d. Lemuel).
Plymouth Co. PR #4087(Perez Churchill). SHAW GEN pp. 14, 29-
30.

271 THEOPHILUS RICKARD[5] (Samuel[4], Rebecca Snow[3],
Rebecca[2] Brown, Peter[1]) b. Plympton 26 Jan. 1725; d. there 1
March 1779 ae 52y 25d.

He m. Plympton 18 April 1749 HANNAH HARLOW, b.

Plympton 27 Jan. 1723/4; d. there July 1792 ae 69y 5m; dau. of James and Hannah (Shaw) Harlow. The will of James Harlow of Plympton dated 3 Feb. 1759 names dau. Hannah Rickard.

On 5 Jan. 1782 Hannah Rickard widow and Jonathan and Lemuel Rickard agreed that Lt. Elijah Bisbe is to administer the estate of Theophilus Rickard late of Plympton dec. Undated list of heirs names eldest son Jonathan to have 2 shares; 9 other shares to Jonathan, Lemuel, Theophilus, Samuel, Simeon, Hannah, Betty, Rebecca, Sylvia, and Ruth, all Rickards.

No Plymouth Co. PR for Hannah Rickard.

   Children (RICKARD) b. Plympton:

   i   BENJAMIN⁶ b. 25 Jan. 1749/50; d. Cornish VT 8 June 1780; unm.
   ii   HANNAH b. 20 May 1751
   iii   JONATHAN b. 22 Jan. 1753/4; d. there 24 March 1785 in 33rd yr.; unm. The will of Jonathan Rickard of Plympton, yeoman, dated 25 Feb. 1785, proved 2 March 1785, names mother Hannah Rickard; brother Simeon Rickard; sister Hannah Rickard; and brother Lemuel Rickard.
   iv   BETTY b. 28 Sept. 1754 [sic]
   v   LEMUEL b. 29 May 1757
   vi   REBECCA b. 24 Feb. 1759
   vii   SYLVIA b. 13 April 1761
   viii SAMUEL b. 30 April 1764
   ix   SIMEON b. 9 Oct. 1766
   x   RUTH b. 25 March 1768; d. there 6 March 1813; unm. No PR.

References: VR PLYMPTON pp. 112(b. Hannah), 161-6(b. ch.), 374(m.), 506-7(deaths). Plymouth Co. PR #9225 (James Harlow); #16930(Theophilus Rickard); 29:287-8; 396 (Jonathan Rickard). HARLOW GEN pp. 225-6.

272 SAMUEL RICKARD⁵ (Samuel⁴, Rebecca Snow³, Rebecca² Brown, Peter¹) b. Plympton 12 Oct. 1727; d. Plympton 9 Nov. 1815 ae 87y 16d.

   He m. Kingston 18 Oct. 1757 RUTH CUSHMAN, b. Kingston 22 Dec. 1735; d. Plympton 2 Nov. 1826 ae 90y 10m; dau. of Robert and Mercy (Washburn) Cushman, a descendant of Pilgrims Isaac Allerton, John Billington, and John Howland.

The will of Samuel Ricard of Plympton, yeoman, dated 25 April 1800, presented 5 Feb. 1816, names wife Ruth; 3 kinsmen Isaac, Samuel, and Simeon Rickard to have all real estate; kinswoman Ruth Rickard single to have use of part of house; money to Content Atwood wife of Joseph; Mehitable Cobb wife of Nehemiah; Abigail Shaw wife of Ambrose; Hanah Cobb wife of Timothy; Bettey Rickard wife of Elijah; Lemuel Rickard; Rebecca Doten wife of Ebenezer; heirs of Silva Vaughn dec.; to Ruth Rickard; to Joseph Everson and Samuel Everson, sons of his sister Elizabeth Eaton; to Hannah Crandall, William Harlow and Samuel Harlow children of his sister Rachel Harlow dec.; friend Elijah Bisbe Jr. Exec.

The will of Ruth Rickard of Plympton, widow, dated 27 March 1821, presented 20 Nov. 1826, names brother Isaac Cushman of Hebron; Deborah Doty dau. of Ebenezer of Carver; 2 kinswomen Patience Atwood, wife of Samuel of Carver and Lydia Bradford, wife of Perez of Plympton; exec. Samuel Atwood.

No known children.

References: VR KINGSTON pp. 56(b. Ruth), 267(m.).   VR
              PLYMPTON p. 507(deaths).   CUSHMAN GEN pp.
131, 144-5.   Plymouth Co. PR #16925(Samuel Rickard);
#16922(Ruth Rickard).   MF 17:79.

273 LAZARUS RICKARD[5] (Samuel[4], Rebecca Snow[3], Rebecca[2] Brown, Peter[1]) b. Plympton 29 May 1730; d. there 19 Aug. 1756; ae 26y 2m 10d.

He m. Kingston 24 Oct. 1754 MARY EVERSON, b. Kingston 14 Aug. 1734; d. after 26 Feb. 1787; dau. of John and Silence (Staples) Everson.   She m. (2) Plympton 25 Feb. 1764 Ebenezer Doten by whom she had Sarah, Lydia, Edward, and Mercy.

Appraisers were appointed on Ebenezer Doten's estate 2 Dec. 1786.   Dower was set off to widow Mary Doten 26 Feb. 1787. Order to divide the dower of widow of Ebenezer Doten was dated 2 Oct. 1795, he late of Carver dec.; 2 of children: Ebenezer and Edward to take land paying Caleb; Amazariah; Elizabeth, wife of David Wood, Jr.; Phebe, wife of James Harlow; Sarah, wife of Jonathan Tilson; and Lydia, wife of John Sherman Jr. Division was made 26 Nov. 1795.

No Plymouth Co. PR for Lazarus Rickard.

Child (RICKARD) b. Plympton:

i   SAMUEL[6] b. 22 Oct. 1755 (as ch. Lazerus and Moley); d. Plympton 22 March 1756 ae 5m 20d

References: VR KINGSTON pp. 70(b. Mary), 267(m.). VR PLYMPTON pp. 164(b. Samuel), 308(her 2nd m.), 506(d. Lazarus), 507(d. Samuel). Plymouth Co. PR 30:123, 124(Ebenezer Doten); 35:356(Mary Doten). DOTY GEN p. 161.

274 ELIZABETH RICKARD[5] (Samuel[4], Rebecca Snow[3], Rebecca[2] Brown, Peter[1]) b. Plympton 2 March 1732/3; d. Kingston 26 Dec. 1803 in 72nd yr.

She m. (1) Plympton 24 Oct. 1754 JOHN EVERSON, b. Kingston 11 Sept. 1730; d. there bef. 21 Aug. 1763 (when bp. of ch. Samuel calls him dec.); son of John and Silence (Staples) Everson.

She m. (2) Kingston 23 July 1772 LOT EATON, b. Kingston 18 May 1744; d. there 1822 ae 78; son of David and Deborah (Fuller) Eaton, a descendant of Pilgrims Francis Eaton and Samuel Fuller. There were no children by this marriage.

On 8 Oct. 1766 Elizabeth Everson of Kingston, widow, was appointed administratrix of the estate of John Everson, late of Kingston, mariner, dec. On 7 March 1774 Lot Eaton and wife Elizabeth swore to her account as administratrix of John Everson.

A share of Samuel Rickard's estate was paid to Elizabeth Everson in 1771.

No Plymouth Co. PR for Lot or Elizabeth Eaton.

Children (EVERSON) b. Kingston:

i   JOHN[6] b. 9 June 1756 (not named in uncle Samuel's will.) (See #272)
ii   JOSEPH b. 3 Aug. 1759
iii SAMUEL bp. 21 Aug. 1763

References: VR KINGSTON pp. 68(b. Lot), 70(b. John; b. son John, Joseph), 71(b. Samuel), 215(2nd m.), 216(int.

1st m.), 344(d. Lot, Elizabeth). VR PLYMPTON p. 216(1st m.).
Plymouth Co. PR 19:391, 522; 21:336(John Everson). MF 9:121-2.

275 RACHEL RICKARD[5] (Samuel[4], Rebecca Snow[3], Rebecca[2]
Brown, Peter[1]) b. Plympton 17 May 1736; d. bef. 25 April 1800
(brother Samuel's will).
 She m. Plympton 2 June 1757 ABNER HARLOW, b.
Plympton 10 June 1733; son of James and Hannah (Shaw) Harlow.
 On 19 April 1762 Abner Harlow of Plympton, yeoman, sold
land in Plympton to Simeon Bonney; signed by Abner and Rachel.
On 28 Dec. 1763 Abner Harlow of Plympton, husbandman, sold
land in Plympton to Jonathan Parker Jr.; signed by Abner and
Rachel.
 Abner Harlow was in Plympton in the 1771 Tax list with
only 1 cow, no house or land.
 Abner Harlow served in the Revolution 1775-1778. He is
listed as a casualty in 1778.
 No Plymouth Co. PR or LR to children for Abner or Rachel
Harlow.

  Children (HARLOW) b. Plympton:

   i LAZARUS[6] b. 17 March 1758 (not named in
      uncle Samuel's will. See #272)
   ii HANNAH b. 29 Sept. 1760
   iii WILLIAM b. 4 May 1762
   iv SAMUEL (Named in the 25 April 1800 will of his
      uncle Samuel Rickard. See #272)

References: VR PLYMPTON pp. 111(b. Abner), 112-4(b. 1st 3 ch.),
     327(m.). (PLYMOUTH) ANC LANDMARKS 2:126.
THE MASS. TAX VALUATION LIST OF 1771, Bettye Hobbs
Pruitt, Ed., Boston, 1978, pp. 662-3. Plymouth Co. LR 48:251;
50:224(Abner Harlow). MSSR 7:288-9.

NOTE: HARLOW GEN p. 228 says Rachel m. (2) Windsor VT 19
Dec. 1782 Capt. John Packard (Congregational Church Record,
Windsor VT 2:2).

276 BENJAMIN HARRIS[5] (Mehitabel Rickard[4], Rebecca Snow[3], Rebecca[2] Brown, Peter[1]) b. Bridgewater 30 Sept. 1731; d. East Bridgewater 13 Jan. 1803 ae 71.

He m. Bridgewater 18 Dec. 1751 SARAH SNOW, b. Bridgewater 6 April 1732; d. East Bridgewater 6 Sept. 1807 ae 75; dau. of James and Ruth (Shaw) Snow (see #226).

Benjamin Harris was a Lt. in the Rev. War.

Benjamin Harris was 4-0-2 in the 1790 census of Bridgewater.

On 25 May 1801 Benjamin Harris sold his homestead to sons William Harris and John Harris. On 8 Nov. 1810 ten acres of Woodland near Robbins Pond in East Bridgewater was divided among Arther Harris, yeoman, William Harris, trader, Benjamin Harris Esq., all of Bridgewater, Samuel Harris of Boston, housewright, and John Harris of Bridgewater, yeoman.

No Plymouth Co. PR or LR for Benjamin or Sarah Harris.

Children (HARRIS) b. Bridgewater:

  i   ARTHUR[6] b. 18 Oct. 1752
  ii   SARAH b. 24 March 1755; d. 19 May 1782. No PR.
  iii BENJAMIN b. 7 April 1757; d. 23 July 1757
  iv   JAMES b. 11 July 1760; d. 3 Aug. 1778
  v   WILLIAM b. 11 Aug. 1762
  vi   BENJAMIN b. 25 Dec. 1764
  vii ISAAC b. 4 March 1767; d. 10 May 1767
  viii SAMUEL b. 2 July 1768
  ix   JOHN b. 15 Aug. 1770

References: VR BRIDGEWATER 1:132-3(b. ch.), 303(b. Sarah); 2:159(m.), 479(d. 4 ch.). VR EAST BRIDGEWATER pp. 355(d. Benjamin), 356(d. Sarah). BRIDGEWATER BY MITCHELL pp. 177, 316. DAR PATRIOT INDEX p. 306. Plymouth Co. LR 95:244(to sons); 116:150(division).

277 SILAS HARRIS[5] (Mehitabel Rickard[4], Rebecca Snow[3], Rebecca[2] Brown, Peter[1]) b. Bridgewater 8 Nov. 1734; d. 15 Jan. 1778 in the Rev. War.

He m. bef. 18 Sept. 1765 ABIGAIL SHAW, b. Bridgewater 25 Aug. 1740; d. prob. Cummington bef. 3 July 1788 (when Jonathan

Gannett remarried); dau. of Ebenezer and Mary (Read) Shaw. She m. (2) Cummington 15 Nov. 1785 Jonathan Gannett.

On 18 Sept. 1765 Silas Harris and wife Abigail sold land to John Young.

Silas Harris was a Pvt. in the Rev. War and fought at Valley Forge and may have died there.

Apparently no children.

No Plymouth Co. PR for Silas Harris.

References: VR BRIDGEWATER 1:287(b. Abigail). VR CUMMINGTON p. 118(her 2nd m.). VR EAST BRIDGEWATER p. 217(int. her 2nd m.). BRIDGEWATER BY MITCHELL p. 177. KNOWN MILITARY DEAD DURING THE AMERICAN REVOLUTIONARY WAR 1775-1783, Clarence S. Peterson, Baltimore 1959, p. 81. GANNETT DESCENDANTS OF MATTHEW AND HANNAH GANNETT OF SCITUATE, MASSACHUSETTS, Michael R. Gannett, Chevy Chase MD 1976, p. 50. Plymouth Co. LR 50:133(Silas Harris). MSSR 7:357-8.

278 LUCY HARRIS[5] (Mehitabel Rickard[4], Rebecca Snow[3], Rebecca[2] Brown, Peter[1]) b. Bridgewater 27 July 1739; d. there 1797 ae 53 [sic].

She m. Bridgewater 26 May 1757 NEHEMIAH LATHAM, b. Bridgewater 1 Nov. 1733; d. East Bridgewater 21 Nov. 1807 ae 74; son of Arthur and Alice (Allen) Latham, a descendant of Pilgrim James Chilton. He m. (2) Bridgewater 6 Oct. 1801 widow Hannah (Pratt) Allen.

In Sept. 1751 Nehemiah Latham and Jane Latham, minor children of Arthur Latham, late of Bridgewater, dec., named Nathan Haward as their guardian. On 1 April 1758 Jane Latham of Bridgewater sold to her brother Nehemiah Latham all rights in land which "our father Arthur Latham deceased had of our grandfather Chilton Latham."

Nehemiah Latham was a Lt. in the Rev. War.

Nehemiah Latham was 4-1-3 in the 1790 census of Bridgewater.

No Plymouth Co. PR for Nehemiah or Lucy Latham.

Children (LATHAM) b. Bridgewater & East Bridgewater:

i   ARTHUR[6]   b. 16 Feb. 1758

ii   ALICE   b. 5 April 1760

iii   MEHETABEL   b. 7 Jan. 1762; d. 9 May 1788 ae 26; unm. No PR.

iv   LUCY   bp. 11 March 1764

v   NEHEMIAH   bp. 19 April 1767

vi   child   d. bet. 23 Dec. 1767 and 3 Dec. 1769

vii   BETHIAH   bp. 8 Oct. 1769

viii   ALLEN   bp. 1 Sept. 1771

ix   ROBERT   b. 6 Sept. 1773; d. 1 Sept. 1782 ae 9

x   BELA   bp. 10 March 1776; d. 8 Sept. 1793 ae 18

xi   CONSIDER   bp. 18 June 1780; d. 8 Sept. 1782 ae 2

References: VR BRIDGEWATER 1:200(b. Arthur, Alice), 201(b. Nehemiah, Mehetabel); 2:228(m.). VR EAST BRIDGEWATER pp. 82-4(bp. ch.), 368-9(d. Nehemiah, children). BRIDGEWATER BY MITCHELL pp. 177, 231-2. DAR PATRIOT INDEX p. 403. MF 15:104. Plymouth Co. PR 12:392(gdn.). Plymouth Co. LR 45:91(Jane Latham).

279 MARCY RICKARD[5] (Eleazer[4], Rebecca Snow[3], Rebecca[2] Brown, Peter[1]) b. Plympton 6 July 1740; living 20 July 1799.

She m. Plympton 15 Dec. 1768 JAMES WRIGHT, JR., d. bef. 18 Sept. 1797; apparently the son of James and Elizabeth (Waterman) Wright, a descendant of Pilgrim Francis Cooke.

James Wright Jr. was 1-2-1 in 1790 census of Plymouth.

James Wright of Plymouth, yeoman, sold to James Wright Jr. of Plymouth, laborer, land in Plymouth, part of land given to Dr. Lazarus LeBaron late of Plymouth deceased's heirs which their father bought of Samuel Shaw at Long Pond bounded by John Blackmer and Perez Wright, signed 2 March 1791, ack. 13 May 1791.

Mercy Wright, widow, administratrix posted bond with Perez Wright and Caleb Wright all of Plymouth for the estate of James Wright late of Plymouth, yeoman, dec., dated 18 Sept. 1797; she made oath to inventory 9 April 1798; on 20 July 1799 she presented account noting the estate was insolvent.

On 7 March 1810 Caleb Wright and James Wright of Carver sold to Nathan Hayward of Plymouth land in Plymouth which was set off to their late mother Mercy Wright as her dower in the

estate of their father James Wright of Plymouth.
No Plymouth Co. PR for Marcy Wright.

Children (WRIGHT):

  i CALEB[6] b. ca. 1769 (based on age at d.)
  ii JAMES b. ca. 1774; (under 26 in 1800 census; over 45 in 1820 census)

References: VR CARVER p. 178(d. Caleb). VR PLYMPTON p. 432 (m.). Plymouth Co. PR #23519(James Wright). Plymouth Co. LR 75:33 (James Wright); 112:177(Caleb & James Wright).

280 ELEAZER RICKARD[5] (Eleazer[4], Rebecca Snow[3], Rebecca[2] Brown, Peter[1]) b. Plympton 22 July 1742; living 29 Oct. 1783(father's will).

  He m. Kingston 29 Nov. 1764 ELIZABETH CUSHMAN, b. Kingston 12 Feb. 1741/2; dau. of Jonathan and Susanna (Benson) Cushman; a descendant of Pilgrim Isaac Allerton. The will of Jonathan Cushman of Plymouth dated 4 Dec. 1775 names wife Susanna and dau. Elizabeth Rickard, wife of Eleazer Rickard.

  The 1771 Plympton Tax List shows both Eleazar Rickard and Eleazar Rickard Jr., so he was living in Plympton then.

  No Plymouth Co. PR for Eleazer Rickard.

  No known children.

References: VR KINGSTON pp. 54(b. Eliz.), 267(m.). VR PLYMPTON p. 37(m.). Plymouth Co. PR 24:61-3(Jonathan Cushman). THE MASS. TAX VALUATION LIST OF 1771, Bettye Hobbs Pruitt, Ed., Boston, 1978.

281 ABNER RICKARD[5] (Eleazer[4], Rebecca Snow[3], Rebecca[2] Brown, Peter[1]) b. Plympton 28 Sept. 1744; d. Cornish NH 2 July 1827 ae 84.

  He m. Plympton 23 March 1769 SUSANNA WRIGHT, b. Plympton 14 Nov. 1751; d. Cornish NH 1 Jan. 1833 ae 81; dau. of Joseph and Sarah (Brewster) Wright, a descendant of Pilgrims William Brewster, Francis Cooke, and George Soule. The will of

Joseph Wright dated Plymouth 27 Feb. 1788 names dau. Susanna, wife of Abner Rickard.

Abner Rickard was a Col. in the Rev. War.

Abner Rickard of Croyden NH, Perez Wright of Plymouth, husbandman, and Joseph Ransom of Plimpton sold to George Donham of Plymouth half a pew in Lakenham (in Carver) formerly of Eleazer Rickard signed and ack. 9 Oct. 1784.

On 20 Feb. 1833 Lemuel Rickard was appointed to administer the estate of Abner Rickard. An account of 25 Jan. 1837 names the heirs as Ezra, Sarah, Abner, Lemuel, Susanna, Elijah, and Deborah Rickard.

In the 1800 census of Croyden NH Abner Richards [sic] had 2 males 16 to 26; 1 male over 45; 2 females under 16 and 1 female over 45. Sons Abner Jr. and Elijah (both called Richards) are also listed in that census.

Children (RICKARD) b. Plympton:

i	EZRA[6] b. 21 Feb. 1770
ii	SARA b. 9 June 1772
iii	SUSANNA b. 25 Feb. 1775
iv	ABNER b. 8 April 1777
v	LEMUEL b. 15 Jan. 1780
vi	ELIJAH b. ca. 1784
vii	DEBORAH

References: VR PLYMPTON pp. 161-6(b. 1st 5 ch.), 240(b. Susanna), 371(m.). MF 3:146. Plymouth Co. PR 40:94(Joseph Wright). Plymouth Co. LR 63:110(Abner Rickard etc.). DAR PATRIOT INDEX p. 569. Sullivan Co. NH PR A:81; 1:332(Abner Rickard). Cem. at the Flat, Cornish NH(g.s. Abner & Susanna).

282 MARY (or MOLLY) RICKARD[5] (Eleazer[4], Rebecca Snow[3], Rebecca[2] Brown, Peter[1]) b. Plympton 29 Aug. 1747; d. Carver 27 Feb. 1824 ae 76.

She m. Plympton 14 Dec. 1780 CONSIDER CHASE, b. ca. 1732; d. Carver 29 Oct. 1801 in 69th yr. He m. (1) Plympton 7 June 1759 Eunice Tillson who d. Carver 14 July 1779 by whom he had Levi, Martha, Sarah, and Lucy.

Consider Chase was 2-1-1 in 1790 census of Carver.

The will of Consider Chase of Carver, yeoman, dated 25 June 1798, sworn 17 Nov. 1801, names wife Molly to have all moveable estate she brought when he married her; son Levi; son Lewis; daus. Martha Ransom, Sarah Dunham, Lucy Washburn; wife and son Levi executors.

No Plymouth Co. PR for Mary Chase.

Child (CHASE) b. Carver:

    i   LEWIS[6] b. 3 Sept. 1781

References: VR CARVER pp. 21(b. Lewis), 149(d. Consider). VR PLYMPTON pp. 276(his 1st m.), 279(m.). New Bedford Mercury Obits 1807-45. Plymouth Co. PR #3847(Consider Chase).

NOTE: Mary is called Molly in mar. rec., but see her father's will for proof.

283 SARAH RICKARD[5] (Eleazer[4], Rebecca Snow[3], Rebecca[2] Snow, Peter[1]) b. Plympton 9 Oct. 1749; d. bef. 30 June 1825.

She m. Plympton 23 Oct. 1778 **PEREZ WRIGHT** of Plymouth, b. Plympton 1751; d. Fletcher, Franklin Co. VT 29 July 1833 or Aug. 1832 ae 82; prob. son of James and Elizabeth (Waterman) Wright, a descendant of Pilgrim Francis Cooke. He m. (2) Croyden NH 30 June 1826 Lucy Dunbar.

Perez Wright was 1-2-2 in 1790 census of Plymouth.

On 7 April 1791 James Wright of Plymouth, yeoman, deeded land in Plymouth to Perez Wright, laborer of Plymouth.

Perez Wright of Plymouth, yeoman, mortgaged to James Clark of Plymouth all his real estate in Plymouth on south side of Long Pond he bought of his father James Wright late of Plymouth dec. signed and ack. 18 Oct. 1799.

Perez Wright of Plymouth, yeoman, sold to Thomas Caswell Jr. of Plymouth part of land Dr. Lazarus LeBaron bought in 1738 on south side of Long Pond, signed by Perez and Sarah 29 May 1799, ack. by Perez 17 Sept. 1801.

On 8 Jan. 1816 Oliver and Hosea Wright, both of Croydon, sold land in Cornish to Jonathan Wyman.

On 7 Jan. 1820 Perez Wright, Hosea Wright (his son) and Achsah Wright (wife of Hosea) sold land.

On 29 Aug. 1820 Perez Wright of Croyden was appointed administrator of the estate of his son Oliver Wright late of Croyden.

On 31 Aug. 1832 Perez Wright of Franklin Co. VT made a deposition that he was born in Plimpton in 1751.

Children (WRIGHT) b. prob. Plymouth:

prob. i   ELIZABETH[6] b. ca. 1781; d. Croyden NH in 1824 ae 43; unm.

ii   HOSEA b. MA ca. 1784 (age 76 in 1860 census of Cambridge VT)

iii   OLIVER

References: Plymouth Co. LR 75:33-4(James Wright); 86:248; 91:139(Perez Wright). VR PLYMPTON p. 434(m.). Croyden NH m. cert.(2nd m.). New Hampshire LR 80:485-6(Perez Wright, etc.). Boston Daily Advertiser, issue of 7 Aug. 1833, p. 2(d. & age of Perez). Keene NH PR #339(Oliver Wright). PLYMOUTH VR p. 266(int.). Cheshire Co. NH LR 75:123(Oliver and Hosea Wright). Croydon NH TR p. 150(d. Elizabeth). MD 43:10-1. Rev. War Pension #W11022(Perez Wright).

NOTE: No Perez Wright in 1800 census of Plymouth.

284 KEZIAH RICKARD[5] (Eleazer[4], Rebecca Snow[3], Rebecca[2] Brown, Peter[1]) b. Plympton 26 Aug. 1753; d. Carver 29 Sept. 1801 in 49th yr.

She m. Plympton 20 June 1781 JOSEPH RANSOM, living 1809.

Joseph Ranson was 1-2-3 in Carver in 1790 census.

Joseph Ransom of Carver, yeoman, sold to Samuel Barrows of Plymouth land bounded by land of Benjamin Ransom, wife Keziah releasing, signed 25 June 1798, ack. by Joseph 25 June 1798.

Joseph Ransom was taxed from 1805-1809 at Croydon, Cheshire Co. NH.

On 10 Feb. 1808 Joseph Ransom of Croyden sold Elijah

Rickard 20 acres in Croyden NH.

No death, cem., or probate record for Joseph Ransom were found in NH.

Children (RANSOM):

i   CONTENT[6] b. Plympton 8 Jan. 1782
ii   ELIJAH b. Plympton Aug. 1783 (based on age at d.)
iii   DAVID b. ca. 1785
iv   MARY b. 1787; d. Carver 5 Oct. 1801 ae 14

References: VR CARVER p. 165(d. Keziah, Mary). VR PLYMPTON p. 369(m.). Plymouth Co. LR 89:62(Joseph Ransom). TILSON GEN(4 ch.). Croyden NH TR 2:63, 86, 167, 173(tax rec.). Cheshire Co. NH LR 64:652(Joseph Ransom).

285 ELIJAH RICKARD[5] (Eleazer[4], Rebecca Snow[3], Rebecca[2] Brown, Peter[1]) b. Plympton 24 Jan. 1756; d. Grantham NH bef. 15 Feb. 1843.

He m. (1) Plympton 17 Nov. 1785 BETSY (or BETTY) RICKARD, b. Plympton 28 Sept. 1754; d. prob. Croyden NH 1804 or 1805; dau. of Theophilus and Hannah (Harlow) Rickard, a descendant of Pilgrim Peter Brown (see #271iii).

He m. (2) Croyden NH 16 April 1815 MARY (_____) CARPENTER; d. bef. 7 Feb. 1838. She m. (1) John Carpenter.

Elijah Rickard was a private in the Rev. War and served at Valley Forge and other campaigns.

Elijah Rickard of Carver, yeoman, sold to Nathaniel Sherman of Carver land in Carver he bought of his father Eleazer Rickard and his dwelling house, signed by Elijah and Betty 2 Feb. 1792; ack. next day by Elijah.

On 16 April 1792 Elijah Rickard of Croyden, Cheshire Co. NH bought 41 1/2 acres of land in Croyden from Ebenezer Wright.

Elijah Rickard was still living in Croyden in 1809 when he was taxed there. He apparently was living in that part of Croyden which was joined to Cornish NH on 24 June 1809.

In his pension application of 21 Jan. 1832 Elijah Rickard

gave his age as 76 yrs.

On 7 Feb. 1838 Elijah Rickard sold to John Carpenter, Jesse Carpenter, Helim Persons, and Ira Rickard the "Carpenter farm" in Croyden which belonged to Mary Rickard dec.

Elijah Rickard was living alone age 70-80 in the 1840 census of Claremont NH.

On 15 Feb. 1843 Ira Rickard of Grantham was appointed administrator of the estate of Elijah Rickard of Grantham.

Children (RICKARD) first 3 b. Plympton, 3 b. Croyden NH:

i	JONATHAN[6]	b. 31 March 1787
ii	DEBORAH	b. 10 July 1788
iii	ELEAZER	b. 19 Feb. 1790
iv	dau.	b. June 1793; d. 16 July 1793
v	HANNAH	b. 25 March 1795
vi	IRA	b. 17 Oct. 1797

References: VR PLYMPTON pp. 161(b. Betty), 162-3(b. 1st 3 ch.), 371(m.). Plymouth Co. LR 72:220(Elijah Rickard). HISTORY OF THE TOWN OF CORNISH NH, William H. Child, repr. 2 vols in 1, Spartanburg SC, 1975, p. 313. MSSR 13:198. Rev. War Pension S14298. Cheshire Co. NH LR 18:491(Elijah Rickard). Croyden NH TR 1:333(2nd m.); 2:173 (taxed 1809). Sullivan Co. NH PR A:232, 21:318(Elijah Rickard). NH Deaths Index, Concord NH(d. dau.). Cornish NH TR 1:336(b. ch. exc.dau.).

NOTE: Elijah Rickard was not in the 1790 census of MA, but he must be the Elijah "Richard" in the 1790 census of Carver 1-2-2.

ABBREVIATIONS

ae	aged	n.d.	no date
b.	born	n.f.r.	no further
bef.	before		record found
bet.	between	n.p.	no place
bp.	baptized	N./No.	north
bur.	buried	NS	Nova Scotia
ca.	circa, about	N.S.	new style date
Cem./cem.	cemetery	O.S.	old style date
ch.	children	p./pp.	page(s)
Ch.	church	pos./poss.	possibly
Co.	county	PR	probate record
Col.	colony	prob.	probably
Comm.	committee	pub.	published
d.	died	rec.	record(s)
dau(s).	daughter(s)	rem.	removed
dec.	deceased	repr.	reprinted
Dist.	district	res.	resided
d.s.p.	died without		
	issue	S./So.	south
d.y.	died young	sic	copy correct
E.	east	Soc.	Society
ed.	edition	TR	town record(s)
G.S.	gravestone	unm.	unmarried
gdn.	guardian	unpub.	unpublished
granddau.	granddaughter	vol(s).	volume(s)
LE	land evidence	VR	vital records
LR	land records	W.	west
m.	married	wid.	widow
m. int.	marriage		
	intention	-y -m -d	years, months, days
MS(S).	manuscript(s)		

When no state is indicated after a city or town, when first mentioned in a family, the reader should assume Massachusetts. The following two-letter abbreviations are used for states:

CT Connecticut   IA Iowa
MA Massachusetts   ME Maine
MI Michigan   NH New Hampshire
NJ New Jersey   NY New York
RI Rhode Island
          SC South Carolina

KEY TO ABBREVIATED TITLES

The following is an alphabetical list of abbreviated titles used in the references of the family genealogy in this volume. When the abbreviated title is in capital letters, the reference is in print - a book or periodical.

Other abbreviations used in the references and in the genealogies themselves, as well as in this Key to Abbreviated Titles, appear on the opposite page.

BANKS PLANTERS
Banks, Charles E. "The Planters of the Commonwealth." 1930; repr. Baltimore 1961, 1972, 1979

BARKER GEN
Barker, Elizabeth Frye. "Barker Genealogy." New York, 1927.

BOSTON NEWS OBITS
"Index of Obituaries in Boston Newspapers 1704-1800." 3 vols.; Boston, 1968.

BRAINTREE RECS
Bates, Samuel A. "Records of the Town of Braintree 1640- 1793." Randolph MA, 1886.

BRIDGEWATER BY MITCHELL
Mitchell, Nahum. "History of the Early Settlement of Bridgewater including an Extensive Family Register." Boston, 1840; repr. Bridgewater 1897; Baltimore 1970

BRIDGEWATER EPITAPHS
Latham, Williams. "Epitaphs in Old Bridgewater Mass...Report of the Committee on the Old Graveyard." Bridgewater 1882; re-print Middleboro 1976.

CARY (JOHN)
Cary, Seth C. "John Cary the Plymouth Pilgrim." Boston 1911.

CHURCHILL FAM
Churchill, Gardner & Nathaniel. "The Churchill Family in America." Boston, 1904.

COBB FAM
Cobb, Philip L. "A History of the Cobb Family." 3 vols.; Cleveland OH 1907-1923.

CONANT FAM
Conant, Frederick O. "A History and Genealogy of the Conant Family 1520-1887." Portland ME 1887.

CT MARR
Bailey, Frederick W. "Early Connecticut Marriages as Found on Ancient Church Records Prior to 1800." 7 vols, New Haven CT, 1896-1906; reprint 1 vol. Baltimore MD 1968, 1982.

CUSHMAN GEN
Cushman, Henry W. "A Historical and Biographical Genealogy of the Cushmans: The Descendants of Robert Cushman, The Puritan, 1617-1855." Boston 1855.

DAR PATRIOT INDEX
Published by the National Society of the Daughters of the American Revolution; Washington DC 1966; Supplements: 1, 1969; 2, 1973; 3, 1976.

DOTY GEN
Doty, Ethan A. "The Doty-Doten Family in America." Brooklyn NY, 1897.

DUNHAM GEN
Dunham, Isaac W. "Deacon John Dunham of Plymouth MA 1589-1669." Hartford CT, 1907.

EASTON HIST
Chaffin, William L. "History of the Town of Easton, Mass." Cambridge MA 1886; reprint 1975.

EDDY FAM
Eddy, Charles. "Genealogy of the Eddy Family." Brooklyn 1881.

GEN ADVERTISER
Greenlaw, Lucy H. "The Genealogical Advertiser" a Quarterly
Magazine of Family History; vols. 1-4, 1898-1901; reprint
Baltimore MD 1974.

GREAT MIGRATION BEGINS
Anderson, Robert C. "The Great Migration Begins." 3 vols. Boston
1995-6.

HANOVER FIRST CH
Briggs, L. Vernon. "History and Records of the First
Congregational Church, Hanover, Mass. 1727-1865." Vol. 1, Boston
1895.

HARLOW GEN
Williams, Alicia C. ed. "Harlow Family, Descendants of Sgt.
William Harlow of Plymouth, Massachusetts." Baltimore, 1997.

HINGHAM HIST
"History of the Town of Hingham, Mass." 3 vols.; Hingham MA
1893; reprint Somersworth NH 1982.

LO-LATHROP GEN
Huntington, E. B. "A Genealogical Memoir of the Lo-Lathrop
Family." Ridgefield CT 1884, reprint 1971.

MA MARR
Bailey, Frederick W. "Early Massachusetts Marriages Prior to
1800." 3 vols. in 1; 1897-1900; reprint Baltimore MD, 1968, 1979.

MD
"The Mayflower Descendant: a quarterly magazine of Pilgrim
history and genealogy." Vol. 1, 1899.

ME NH GEN DICT
Noyes, Sybil; Libby, C. T.; Davis, Walter G. "Genealogical Dictionary of Maine and New Hampshire." 1928-35; reprint Baltimore MD, 5 parts in 1, 1972, 1983.

MF
"Mayflower Families Through Five Generations." Published by the General Society of Mayflower Descendants; 15 vols.

MQ
"The Mayflower Quarterly." Vol. 1, 1935; a publication of the General Society of Mayflower Descendants.

MSSR
"Massachusetts Soldiers and Sailors of the Revolutionary War." 17 vols; Boston 1896-1908.

MIDDLEBORO BY WESTON
Weston, Thomas. "History of the Town of Middleboro" (Mass.). Boston 1906.

MIDDLEBORO DEATHS
Wood, Alfred. "Record of Deaths, Middleboro, Massachusetts." Boston 1947.

NEHGR
"New England Historical and Genealogical Register." Vol. 1, 1847; published at Boston by the New England Historic Genealogical Society.

NGSQ
"National Genealogical Society Quarterly." Vol. 1, 1912; published at Washington DC by the Society.

NJ ARCH
"Archives of the State of New Jersey." 47 vols.; Trenton NJ, 1880-1949.

(PLYMOUTH) ANC LANDMARKS
Davis, William T. "Ancient Landmarks of Plymouth." 2nd edition
1899; reprint of Part Two under title "Genealogical Register of
Plymouth Families"; Baltimore MD 1975.

(PLYMOUTH) BURIAL HILL
Kingman, Bradford. "Epitaphs from Burial Hill, Plymouth,
Massachusetts, from 1657 to 1892." With biographical and
historical notes; Brookline MA 1892; reprint Baltimore MD 1977.

PLYMOUTH CH RECS
"Plymouth Church Records, 1620-1859." 2 vols.; New York
1920-23; reprint Baltimore MD 1975.

PLYMOUTH COLONY RECS
Shurtleff, Nathaniel B. & Pulsifer, David. "Records of the Colony
of New Plymouth in New England." 12 vols.; Boston 1855-61;
reprint 12 vols. in 6; New York 1968.

PLYMOUTH CO CT RECS
Konig, David T., ed. "Plymouth County Court Records 1686-1859."
16 vols.; Wilmington DE 1978.

PLYMOUTH TOWN RECS
"Records of the Town of Plymouth." 3 vols.; Plymouth 1889, 1892,
1903.

PN&Q
Bowman, George E. "Pilgrim Notes and Queries." 5 vols.; Boston
1913-17.

RHODE IS 1774 CENSUS
Bartlett, John R. "Census of the Inhabitants of the Colony of
Rhode Island and Providence Plantations 1774." Providence RI,
1858; reprinted Baltimore 1969.

RI VR
Arnold, James N. "Vital Records of Rhode Island, 1636-1850." 21
vols.; Providence RI, 1891-1912.

SAVAGE
Savage, James. "A Genealogical Dictionary of the First Settlers of New England, showing three generations of those who came before May 1692..." 4 Vols; Boston 1860-62; reprint Baltimore MD 1965, 1981.

SEARS DESC
May, Samuel P. "The Descendants of Richard Sares (Sears) of Yarmouth, Mass. 1638-1888." Albany NY, 1890.

SHAW GEN
Shurtleff, Benjamin. "John Shaw of Plymouth, Massachusetts." Kenilworth IL 1973.

SHERMAN DESC
Sherman, Roy V. "Some of the Descendants of Philip Sherman, the First Secretary of Rhode Island." 1968.

SHURTLEFF DESC
Shurtleff, Benjamin. "Descendants of William Shurtleff of Plymouth and Marshfield Mass." 2 vols; Revere, 1912.

SPOONER DESC
Spooner, Thomas. "Records of William Spooner of Plymouth, Mass. and His Descendants." Vol. 1; Cincinnati OH 1883.

TABER DESC
Randall, George L. "Taber Genealogy." Descendants of Thomas, son of Philip Taber; New Bedford MA 1924.

TAG
"The American Genealogist." Vol. 1, 1922.

THOMAS GEN
Raymond, John M. "Thomas Families of Plymouth County, Massachusetts, Genealogies of the Families of David Thomas of Middleboro (1620-1689), John Thomas of Marshfield (1621-1691) and William Thomas of Marshfield (1573-1651)." Menlo Park CA 1980.

THOMSON (JOHN) DESC
Thompson, Charles H. "A Genealogy of Descendants of John Thomson of Plymouth, Mass., also sketches of families of Allen, Cooke and Hutchinson." Lansing MI 1890.

TILSON GEN
Tilson, Mercer V. "The Tilson Genealogy from Edmund Tilson at Plymouth, N.E., 1638-1911." Plymouth 1911.

TORREY'S MARRIAGES
Torrey, Clarence Almon. "New England Marriages Prior to 1700." Baltimore MD, 1985.

VR
Vital Records. The abbreviated titles VR DUXBURY, SCITUATE, etc. indicate alphabetized vital records; the abbreviated titles MARSHFIELD VR, MIDDLEBORO VR etc., followed by page numbers, indicate vital records published non-alphabetically.

WAREHAM CH RECS
Smith, Leonard H. Jr. "Records of the First Church of Wareham, Mass. 1739-1891." Clearwater FL, 1974.

WATERMAN GEN
Jacobus, Donald L. "Descendants of Robert Waterman of Marshfield, Mass." Vols. 1 & 2; New Haven CT, 1939-42. "Descendants of Richard Waterman of Providence RI." Vol. 3; New Haven CT, 1954.

WEYMOUTH BY CHAMBERLAIN
Chamberlain, G. W. "History of Weymouth" with genealogies. 4 vols.; Boston 1923.

WOOD OF MIDDLEBORO
Wood, Bethel & Wood, Elijah Francis. "Henry Wood of Middleboro MA." Sisseton SD, 1939.

YARMOUTH NS HERALD GEN
Genealogical columns in the Yarmouth, Nova Scotia Herald, Nov. 1896 to May 1902. Copies at NEHG Society, Boston MA and Mayflower Society, Plymouth MA.

INDEX OF NAMES

With a few exceptions, each name in the text and footnotes is indexed. The names of authors and titles of reference works are not indexed.

Each married woman is indexed under her maiden name, and also under her married name(s), showing her maiden name and any previous married name(s) in parentheses. For example, Hannah TINKHAM (page 84), who married thrice, appears also as Hannah (Tinkham) VAUGHAN, Hannah (Tinkham) (Vaughan) WESTON, and Hannah (Tinkham) (Vaughan) (Weston) SEARS. A married woman of unknown maiden name is shown as Content (---) ATWOOD.

When variant spellings of a surname occur, they are alphabetized under the more popular spelling, followed by one or more of the alternate spellings. Given names have been standardized in most cases.